New
Urban
Immigrants

ILLSOO KIM

New Urban Immigrants

The Korean Community in New York

Princeton University Press

Princeton, New Jersey

Copyright © 1981 by Princeton University Press
Published by Princeton University Press, Princeton, New Jersey
In the United Kingdom: Princeton University Press, Guildford, Surrey

All Rights Reserved
Library of Congress Cataloging in Publication Data will be
found on the last printed page of this book

Publication of this book has been aided by a grant from
the Paul Mellon Fund of Princeton University Press

This book has been composed in Linotype Caledonia

Clothbound editions of Princeton University Press books
are printed on acid-free paper, and binding materials are
chosen for strength and durability

Printed in the United States of America by Princeton
University Press, Princeton, New Jersey

To my wife, Munja

Contents

List of Tables   xi
Acknowledgments   xiii
The Transliteration of Korean Words   xiv
A Note on Sources   xv

Introduction   3

PART I
*The Korean Immigration
to the United States*

CHAPTER ONE: United States Immigration Law as It Affects
        Koreans   17
  The Older Immigrants   17
  The Immigration Act of 1965 and the New Immigrants   24
  The Connection between Immigration Policy and Labor Policy 28
  Social and Economic Characteristics of Korean Immigrants 30
    *Entry Mechanisms · Cultural and Political Push-Factors ·
    Selective Characteristics · Settlement Patterns · The Immigrant
    Family*
  Conclusion   46

CHAPTER TWO: The Formulation of South Korean Emigration
        Policy   48
  The Population Explosion as a Push Factor   48
  The Classification of Emigrants   53
  The South Korean Reaction to the Immigration Act of 1965 55
  The Role of Emigration Companies   60
  The Flight of Dollars from South Korea   64
  Conclusion   69

CHAPTER THREE: South Korean Urbanization and Economic
        Development as They Affect Emigration   71
  The Overurbanization of South Korea   72
    *The Agrarian Crisis · The Economic Push from "Rice Paddies to
    Factories" · The Magnetic Pull of Primary Cities · The Educational
    Migration*

President Park's Political Economy   79
The Export-Oriented Economy   81
  The Economic Basis of the Export-Oriented Economy
The Labor Policy of the South Korean Government   86
The Impact of Exporting on the South Korean Class Structure   88
  The Formation of the Upper Industrial Class
The Reaction to Rapid Economic Development   95
Conclusion   97

PART II
*Economic Bases of the Korean Community
in the New York Metropolitan Area*

CHAPTER FOUR: Small Business as an Entry Point for Korean
            Immigrants   101
The Shift to Commercial Enterprises   102
Classification of Korean Business Enterprises   105
  Running the Newest Businesses
The Fruit and Vegetable Business: A Case Study   112
  *The Emergence of Korean Greengrocers · The Three Causal
  Factors · Intraethnic Conflict · Interethnic Conflict · The Green-
  grocery Business as a Means of Capital Accumulation*
The Wig Industry in Both South Korea and the United States:
  A Case Study   121
  *The Impact of American Fashion · The Emergence of Korean Wig-
  Manufacturers · The "Putting-out" System · The Decline of the
  Wig Industry in Korea · The Entry of Korean Immigrants into
  the Wig Business · The Wig Industry in America · Intraethnic
  Conflict over the Wig Market · The Intervention of the South
  Korean Government · Wig Peddlers · The Ambivalence of
  Korean Wig-Merchants · Consequences of the Wig Business*
Conclusion   143

CHAPTER FIVE: The Mobility of South Korean Medical
            Professionals   147
The Influx of Korean Medical Professionals   147
Pull Factors in American Medical Institutions   149
The Marginal Role of Asian Medical Professionals   154
Adjustment Patterns of Korean Medical Professionals   156
The Development of South Korean Medicine as It Affects
  International Mobility and Migration   159
The Impact of the "Medical Exodus" on South Korean Medicine   162
Immigration Law and the Life Chances of Korean-American
  Physicians   169
Conclusion   176

PART III
The Emergence of a Korean Community

Introduction: The Korean Community in the New York
        Metropolitan Area   **181**
   The Phenomenological Base · The Founding Fathers · The New
   Wave of Immigrants · The Nonterritorial Basis of the Community

CHAPTER SIX: The Church as a Basis for the Community   187
  The Emergence of Korean Churches   187
  Christianity in Korea   188
  Churches as the Grass-Roots Community   191
   The Geographical Dispersion of Korean Churches · Changes in
   Church Membership · The Dominance of Professionals in Lay
   Life · Small Businesses and Church Life · The Age Distribution
   of Church Members · Church Affiliation in the Homeland and
   the United States · Nondenominational Protestant Churches
  Immigration Policy and the Proliferation of Churches   198
  The Church as a Pseudo Extended-Family   199
  The Church as a Broker   201
  The Emerging Lay Leadership and the Politics of Church
    Governance   203
  The Ambivalence of the Churches toward Material Success   205
  Conclusion   207

CHAPTER SEVEN: Secondary Associations of the Korean
        Community   **208**
  The Scope of Secondary Associations   209
  The Korean-American Pseudo Extended-Family   210
  The Origins and Focus of Secondary Associations: Homeland vs.
    New Land   213
   Alumni Associations · Medical Professionals' Associations · Or-
   ganizational Patterns Common to Korean-American Profession-
   als' Associations · Korean Associations Focused on Purely Intra-
   ethnic Activities · The Korean Scientists' and Engineers'
   Association—an Exception · Korean Associations Focused on
   American Issues
  Conclusion   225

CHAPTER EIGHT: The Politics of the Korean Community   227
  The South Korean Government as a Community Organization   228
  The Role of the KCIA in the Community   233
  The Korean Association as "Community Government"   237
  Schisms in the "Community Government"   240
   The Korean Cultural Center · The Korean Community Foundation
  The Korean Association of Greater New York as an Umbrella
    Organization   242

Homeland Politics and Community Leadership 245
Conflict and Cleavage in the Korean Association 248
The Effect of the "Koreagate" Scandal and of Rev. Moon of New
York's Koreans 252
The Rise of Indigenous Politics 255
  KAPA and Korean Participation in Domestic Politics · The Korean
  Response to Black Anti-Koreanism
Conclusion 259

CHAPTER NINE: Ethnic Media as a Mechanism of Community
          Integration 262
The Ethnic Media 263
The Two Daily Newspapers 264
The Roles of the Two Daily Newspapers 266
  Social Integration · Issue Definition · Relationship to the Home
  Government · Involvement in Community Politics
Conclusion 276

PART IV
The Basis of the New York
Korean Community in the Historical
Development of Korea

CHAPTER TEN: The Origin of the Character Structure of Korean
          Immigrants 281
The External Factors of Korean History 283
  The Korean State Bureaucracy · Class and Status in Yi Society ·
  Mobility Patterns of the Yi Classes · The Primitive Capitalism of
  Yi Society
The Impact of the State Bureaucracy on the Formation of the
  Korean Character 294
Confucianism as a Source of the Korean Character 298
Conclusion 303

Conclusion: The Future of the Korean Community in the New
          York Metropolitan Area 305

Selective Bibliography 321
Index 325

List of Tables

1.1 The Number of Koreans Admitted to the U.S. as
Permanent Residents, 1950-1976   26

1.2 Entry Mechanisms of Korean Immigrants, 1967-1975   32

1.3 The Number of Koreans Who Gained Permanent
Resident Status and Their Status at Entry, 1966-1975   36

1.4 Percentage of Korean Immigrants by Their Occupation
and Year of Entry   39

1.5 Occupational Distribution of Korean Householders (at
the Time of Their Departure from Korea) in the New
York Metropolitan Area   40

1.6 Occupational Distribution of Korean Householders in
the New York Metropolitan Area   40

1.7 Educational Level Attained before Leaving Korea by
Korean Householders in the New York Metropolitan Area   40

1.8 Age and Sex of Korean Immigrants, 1966-1975   41

1.9 Korean Immigrants' Intended Place of Residence,
1970-1975   43

1.10 Marital Status of Korean Householders in the New York
Metropolitan Area   45

1.11 Number of Working Family Members of Korean Householders in the New York Metropolitan Area   45

1.12 Distribution of Gross Family Incomes of Koreans in the
New York Metropolitan Area   45

4.1 Types of Korean Business Enterprises   105

5.1 Korean Medical Professionals Admitted to the U.S.,
1965-1973   148

5.2 Distribution of Korean Medical Doctors in the U.S., 1976   157

5.3 Specialization of Korean Medical Doctors in the U.S., 1976   158

5.4 Medical Schools from Which Korean Doctors in the U.S.
Graduated as of 1976   164

5.5 Distribution of Korean Medical Doctors in the U.S. Who
Graduated from Seoul National University College of
Medicine by Their Year of Graduation, as of 1976   169

6.1 Religious Populations in South Korea, 1977   190

6.2 Locations of Korean Christian Churches in the New York
Metropolitan Area, 1978   192

7.1 Types of Korean Voluntary Associations   213

Acknowledgments

I AM greatly indebted to the intellectual guidance and teaching craftsmanship of Professor Joseph Bensman, who has helped me shape the basic theoretical framework of this study. He has always been willing to make helpful suggestions and to give criticism and encouragement. He has also undertaken the tedious task of editing the initial drafts of this study.

I also wish to express gratitude to Professors Setsuko M. Nishi, William Kornblum, Sylvia F. Fava, and Arthur J. Vidich for their comments and suggestions on the first draft of this study.

Finally, Mrs. Gail Filion and Mr. William Hively, of Princeton University Press, have provided advice and comments and, especially in the case of Mr. Hively, invaluable editorial suggestions and corrections in preparing my original manuscript for publication.

I extend my special thanks to my wife, Munja, to whom this study is dedicated, for her patience and understanding throughout a long period of my "idle" pursuit of intellectual work.

The Transliteration of
Korean Words

In ORDER to transliterate Korean words consistently, I have followed
the transliteration system adopted by the Korean Ministry of Education. However, with regard to Korean names, especially the names of
authors mentioned in footnotes, I have not followed the rules set up by
the Ministry of Education, because I feel that I have no right to alter
the spelling of names transliterated originally by the authors themselves.

A Note on Sources

THE wide range of dimensions that come under analysis in this study has called for the use of an equally wide range of sources. The principal sources include:

(1) Historical treatments of Korean social and economic institutions.

(2) Economic and demographic statistics and data for South Korea.

(3) Similar data for the United States, especially immigration data based on the annual reports of the United States Immigration and Naturalization Service.

(4) Analyses of South Korean and American social policies concerning manpower, education, and immigration or emigration.

(5) Articles in English- and Korean-language newspapers, especially the latter, that report recent and current developments in South Korea and in the Korean community in the United States.

(6) Institutional leaders as informants. I have used especially some twenty "informal" informants representing six kinds of institutions—religious, political, and business institutions, the media, medical professions, and the home government. Most of these informants were institutional leaders, with whom I used long, unstructured interviews. These interviews necessarily reflected the unique social positions, experiences, and biases of the informants; but I have cross-checked the information gathered from each informant with that provided by other informants, and with other sources of similar data.

(7) Participant and nonparticipant observation. During the past four years I have attended, for research purposes, a countless number of community meetings, church meetings, cultural affairs, and other collective activities.

(8) Informal, unstructured interviews. I have also interviewed several hundred Korean immigrants mostly in the United States (but some in South Korea) about their careers, life histories, and particular problems. These interviews thus include informal conversations and gossip. In doing this I have tried to take an outsider's point of view as far as I could. These interviews have been collected and related to the specific analytic dimensions of this study. Because re-

spondents have only been able to speak in terms of their particular experience as immigrants and as members of the community, the interviews have not been standardized. And because the interviews have been conducted during the entire course of this study, the questions asked reflect continuously emerging perspectives and dimensions of analysis; the respondents consequently do not constitute a uniform sample.

In the organization of this book, economic and political data have been mixed, where appropriate, with informants' reports, my own observations, and interview data. Long or formal quotations from the last three categories of sources are cited as "field notes." Less formal quotations, paraphrases, folk sayings, and similar data are simply given without citing a source, for they are common knowledge among Korean immigrants living in the New York metropolitan area.

The result of this method of research and analysis is the book itself. For better or worse, what follows from its publication must be the justification of the methods employed.

New
Urban
Immigrants

Introduction

SINCE World War II, new urban ethnic communities have arisen within America's major metropolitan areas, reflecting new internal and international migrations. The new immigrants are substantially different from older immigrants to the United States. Especially since the passage of the Immigration Act of 1965, the traditional pattern of the immigrants' ethnic and racial origins as well as of their social characteristics has changed. New immigrants, reflecting recent changes in United States immigration policy, are largely made up of urban middle-class professionals and skilled blue-collar workers. In addition, the new immigrants come largely from Asia, Latin America, and the Caribbean Islands, with a concomitant decline in the proportion of immigrants from European nations, the historically dominant source.

These new patterns of immigration reflect social and economic changes in both the United States and the sending countries. New immigrants enter a contemporary American society that has undergone a tremendous change—a change toward an urban and suburban welfare state, a mature "postindustrial," service-oriented society. At the same time, most of the sending countries have experienced a violent process of urbanization, industrialization, and a "population explosion," all of which serve directly or indirectly as push factors causing certain elements of their population to emigrate. These groups possess a wide range of skills, education, values, languages, and motivational complexes, and their characteristics are thus quite different from those of older immigrant groups. Most of the new immigrants are well prepared psychologically and occupationally to enter a society in which the occupational structure is tilted toward white-collar, managerial, professional, and service work. This trend makes the sociological paradigms that were developed for the older immigrant communities obsolete and requires us to develop new paradigms for the study of the new immigration.

In the classic studies of the older immigrants, the continuum between gemeinschaft and gesellschaft, or folk and urban societies, served as the basic paradigm for analysis.[1] Such immigrant groups as

[1] William I. Thomas and Florian Znaniecki, *The Polish Peasant in Europe and America*, Boston, Gorham Press, 1918-1920; William I. Thomas et al., *Old World Traits Transplanted*, Montclair, New Jersey, Patterson Smith, 1971 (Originally

3

Italians, Russians, Jews, Poles, and the Irish—most of whom, except for Jews, were of peasant origin and provided a huge labor force for the rapid industrialization of America at the turn of the century—were viewed as being "uprooted," in Handlin's term, as they shifted from gemeinschaft (folk and rural life in their homeland) to gesellschaft and the urban society of the new land. In being "uprooted" and in the processes of acculturation, they experienced vast social disorganization, family dislocation, anomie, and other types of pathology. This was observed particularly by Chicago sociologists, whose familiar concepts such as "social disorganization," "social control," "marginality," and "natural areas" were evolved during the rapid urbanization of Chicago at the turn of the century.[2] (Chicago absorbed a huge influx of immigrants from abroad and migrants from rural areas in America.) In this urbanization process, some theorists, by leaning upon the continuum between folk and urban societies, or the theory of "old world traits transplanted," discovered communal institutions, habits, and social organizations even in urban ghettos.[3] The Chicago theorists tended to view the development of urban ghetto communities as a "natural" step toward acculturation and assimilation into the larger society. Even in the discovery of the idea of an "ordered segmentation" of urban communities,[4] there was a tendency to assume that the construction of urban ghetto communities was a reaction to the anomie, isolation, and demoralization of a foreign community that had migrated and relocated in an alien and hostile environment for which its culture and traditions did not prepare its members.

However, it appears that the problems of anomie, pathology, and social disorganization, which were the focal issues confronting older urban theorists, do not overwhelm new immigrants nearly as much in their attempts to construct new urban communities. The present immigration to the United States takes on the character of urban-to-urban migration involving immigrants who were already "uprooted" in their

---

published in 1921 by Harper & Brothers, New York, with authors Robert E. Park and Herbert A. Miller); Oscar Handlin, *The Uprooted*, New York, Grosset & Dunlap, 1951.

[2] Frederic M. Thrasher, *The Gang: A Study of 1,313 Gangs in Chicago*, Chicago, The University of Chicago Press, 1927; Clifford R. Shaw et al., *Delinquency Areas*, Chicago, The University of Chicago Press, 1929; Harvey Zorbaugh, *The Gold Coast and the Slum*, Chicago, The University of Chicago Press, 1929; Robert Faris and Warren H. Dunham, *Mental Disorders in Urban Areas*, Chicago, The University of Chicago Press, 1939.

[3] Thomas, *Old World Traits Transplanted*; Louis Wirth, *The Ghetto*, Chicago, The University of Chicago Press, 1928.

[4] Gerald D. Suttles, *The Social Order of the Slum: Ethnicity and Territory in the Inner City*, Chicago, The University of Chicago Press, 1968; see also William Foote Whyte, *Street Corner Society: The Social Structure of An Italian Slum*, Chicago, The University of Chicago Press, 1943.

homelands; therefore the kinds of "social problems" suggested by the traditional folk-to-urban paradigm are not paramount among most new immigrant groups. That is, the majority of new immigrants have either migrated from rural to urban societies in the homeland prior to emigration, or they are descendants of urbanites; in either case, they have all or many of the attributes of the so-called urban mentality. Thus the notion suggested by the older urban theorists, that the members of the new urban ethnic communities display the nonrational mentality or characteristics of peasants and primitives, is simply outdated.

It is increasingly clear that new immigrants attempt to construct urban ethnic communities by self-conscious, rational planning, that is, by ideological attempts to deal with macrocosmic "policy issues." This is so simply because new immigrants encounter an entirely different milieu from that faced by the older immigrants. They are entering the United States after the rise of the welfare state, state capitalism, and state intervention in almost every major area of contemporary American society. They are entering when civil rights and anti-discrimination policies have limited the most manifest discrimination against all ethnic and racial minorities, which encourages the new ethnic and racial minorities among them to gain access to the various resources of the welfare state. In response, older white ethnic groups are tending to heighten and revitalize their racial and ethnic consciousness as well, even though these groups are assumed to have gone far in the direction of acculturation and assimilation.[5] Furthermore, most of the new immigrants come from new nations that emerged after World War II, and thus they are imbued with nationalism and "third-world consciousness." They are deeply concerned with the national affairs of their home country and attempt to achieve ethnic solidarity in the United States by identifying themselves with their homeland even though they might have come from different racial, religious, cultural, or language groups in their home country.[6] The development of modern communication and transportation has made possible a new, close contact with the political, economic, and cultural activities of the homeland.[7] All these trends suggest that organization around "policy issues" in relation to macrocosmic changes has become a major factor in the

[5] Michael Novak, *The Rise of the Unmeltable Ethnics: Politics and Culture in the Seventies*, New York, Macmillan, 1971; Knight E. Hoover, "Organizational Networks and Ethnic Persistence: A Case Study of Norwegian-American Ethnicity in the New York Metropolitan Area," Ph.D. dissertation, The City University of New York, 1979.

[6] Maxine P. Fisher, "Ethnic Identities: Asian Indians in the New York Area," Ph.D. dissertation, The City University of New York, 1978.

[7] Monica H. Gordon, "Identification and Adaptation: A Study of Two Groups of Jamaican Immigrants in New York City," Ph.D. dissertation, The City University of New York, 1979.

emergence of new ethnic communities and of new social forms in old communities.[8]

Although the older patterns of spatial segregation have persisted for some immigrant groups, other groups have tended to create ethnic "communities" without territorial bases. The question as to how new immigrants create ethnic "communities" without such bases provides a radical point of departure from traditional studies of ethnic communities, which tended to focus on ethnic and social groups concentrated in specific urban localities or ghettos.[9] The question also suggests the need for a thorough revision of older ecological models in which territorial bases or "natural areas" are assumed to be a primary condition for the construction of urban communities.[10] Traditional urban theorists tended to ignore racial and ethnic minorities who dispersed themselves throughout a large metropolis, and they also neglected multiethnic communities within a large metropolis.

THIS is a study of the creation of a new ethnic community within the New York metropolitan area—the Korean community. It is a community that began to emerge in 1967. Since that year, about half a million Koreans have entered the United States, of which some eighty thousand have settled in the New York metropolitan region—the seven counties in New York, New Jersey, and Connecticut that comprise that area. Prior to 1967, the Korean community in the New York metropolitan area consisted only of some two thousand settlers, who had entered the United States between 1903 and 1965. They were concentrated in the Upper West Side of Manhattan near Columbia University. The sudden influx in 1967 was due specifically to the Immigration Act of 1965 and, more generally, to a wide variety of social, economic, and political factors that will be discussed in the following chapters. Yet we are not concerned with that emigration and immigration per se. We are concerned with the creation or the lack of creation of a Korean community in the New York metropolitan area. Our most general problem is: To what extent has the large-scale immigration of this new population to the United States resulted in the creation of the organizations, institutions, and sentiments that are conventionally subsumed under the concept of "community"?

[8] Joseph Bensman and Arthur J. Vidich, eds., *Metropolitan Communities: New Forms of Urban Sub-Communities*, New York, The New York Times Co., 1975.

[9] Caroline C. Ware, *Greenwich Village 1920-1930: A Comment on American Civilization in the Post-War Years*, New York, Houghton Mifflin Co., 1935; Whyte, *Street Corner Society*; Herbert J. Gans, *The Urban Villagers: Group and Class in the Life of Italian-Americans*, New York, The Free Press, 1962; Suttles, *The Social Order of the Slum*.

[10] Robert E. Park and Ernest W. Burgess, *The City*, Chicago, The University of Chicago Press, 1925.

In traditional sociological theory, a community is conceived of as a human group with so broad a range of institutions, culture, and activities that individuals can live their full lives within its confines. A community generates the deeply held common sentiments, identifications, and loyalties, and the culture and institutions, that make such a life possible. The concept of the community in traditional sociology implies the continuous existence of a "natural" community with the attendant sacredness and inviolability of its historic norms, values, and culture.

When such a natural community is transformed by migration, industrialization, urbanism, and the bureaucratization of society, and by the growth of the mass media and secondary and tertiary organizations, it is always assumed that an original community has existed since time immemorial but is in the process of being transformed by these "external" institutions and developments.[11]

The Korean migration to the New York metropolitan area provides us with an opportunity to study the creation of a community in vivo. That is, we are able to study that community at almost the same time that it is being constructed. We are also able to apply to a specific case the vast amount of insights and research provided by the authors of classic studies of the community. And we can use the revisions and corrections to these studies made by later students who have responded not only to the original theories of the community but also to studies of changes in particular communities caused by the external, modern society that forms their social framework.[12]

Given these advantages, we are not constrained to accept the romantic biases that may have underlain the classic conception of community. Thus the question as to whether the construction of a community necessarily involves a deep-seated emotional identification, that is, the gemeinschaft, is a problem we raise in this study. Nor are we constrained to accept the notion that in the modern world it is even possible for a community to exist in isolation from the larger urban, commercial world. Instead, we must be willing to consider the possibility that, despite the new immigrants' experience of modernization and urbanization in the homeland prior to their emigration, they may nonetheless be able to form some of the associations and cultural commitments that are the basis of an ethnic community. If such evidence

---

[11] Maurice Stein, *The Eclipse of Community: An Interpretation of American Studies*, Princeton, Princeton University Press, 1960.

[12] Robert S. Lynd and Helen Merrell Lynd, *Middletown in Transition: A Study in Cultural Conflicts*, New York, Harcourt, Brace & World, 1937; W. Lloyd Warner and J. O. Low, *The Social System of the Modern Factory*, New Haven, Yale University Press, 1947; Arthur J. Vidich and Joseph Bensman, *Small Town in Mass Society: Class, Power and Religion in a Rural Community*, Princeton, Princeton University Press, 1958.

emerges from our study, we may have to revise the traditional concept of community as developed in the classic literature. We can also regard as problematic the idea that migration and the construction of a new community necessarily involves one or more generations of social disorganization and psychological disorientation, again, of course, allowing the evidence to emerge from our study. We shall conclude, in chapter eleven, with a tentative answer to these problems. Until this answer is given, all uses of the term "community" in this study should be interpreted not as nostalgic references to this sociological and pragmatic ideal but as simple acknowledgments of the fact that Korean immigrants in the New York metropolitan area are attempting to build a community, whatever that may ultimately mean.

In relation to this general issue, we shall ask more specific questions about the formation of modern urban communities. The fact that South Korea is an industrial and bureaucratic society in which a strong, centralized government pursues authoritarian social policies allows us to pose questions as to how the political, social, and economic policies of the home government facilitate or inhibit both emigration from the homeland and the construction of new communities in the new land. At the same time we can ask how the political, social, and economic policies of the host country aid, impede, or alter the construction of a new community. In addition, we can raise questions as to how the development of international trade, markets, and economic organizations in the modern capitalist world affect not only immigration but also the construction of communities. Finally, we can raise questions as to how the culture, motivational structures, values, and traditions of an immigrant group, all embedded in the homeland social structure, affect the capacity of that group to respond both to changes in its own home society and to the new social environments it enters, in which it may or may not create a community.

Given these exigencies of modern "postindustrial" society, which all affect the construction of a community, we can ask our ultimate questions: In what sense can an urban ethnic community exist? Is the concept of community adequate to the understanding of new immigrants and their attempts to create favorable social environments? We will attempt to answer these questions in detail, of course, only with reference to the object of our study, the Korean community in the New York metropolitan area.

In attempting to understand the emergence of the new Korean community, we ask, in addition, a number of specific questions that arise from the theoretical dimensions of this study. These questions will be discussed briefly here, though the reader will understand that they are the very warp and woof of both the collection of data and of the organization and presentation of the findings.

In studying the emigration and immigration that has produced the new community, we first of all ask: What are the specific push and pull factors accounting for Korean migration to the United States? Push factors are factors that make emigration from Korea seem necessary; pull factors are those that make immigration to the United States seem desirable. The bald assertion of separate push and pull factors is an oversimplification, however. To discover and analyze specific push and pull factors, it was first necessary to study such demographic factors within South Korea as population growth, internal migration, and the occupational structure of the South Korean economy, along with urbanization and industrialization. Moreover, it became necessary to study the internal politics of South Korea as well as its international relations, especially the threat of another war with North Korea, which greatly reinforces the desire of South Koreans to emigrate.

The explicit domestic policies of the South Korean government are also major push factors. For example, population policies have been aimed at encouraging emigration in order to overcome the "population explosion" within South Korea. Yet these, it was discovered only in the course of the research, may have been less important than policies that had the effect of making the homeland so unattractive that emigration became desirable. Thus we must examine the policies that led to "overurbanization" and to the decline of traditional sources of income and well-being. This leads us to study the major economic, labor, and educational policies of the Park regime, which ruled South Korea from 1961 to 1979. But in addition, with respect to the push factors, we must study the major economic policies of outside powers, especially the United States, as working to push emigrants out of South Korea. Thus we shall also explore American economic policies during the early 1950s, especially with regard to the overproduction of grain in the United States. This led to the dumping of grain into South Korea and contributed to a drop in South Korean grain prices, depopulation of rural areas, overurbanization, and, ultimately, the desire to emigrate. Most of these push factors have not been the basic stuff out of which community studies are constructed; but our particular problem and, to some extent, the development of post-World-War-II community studies have led us to explore pre-migration factors in the construction of communities.[13]

If these push factors "external" to the Korean community in New York are important, then pull factors are even more important. What

[13] Warner and Low, *The Social System of the Modern Factory*; Vidich and Bensman, *Small Town in Mass Society*; Stein, *The Eclipse of Community*.

are the specific changes in the United States that have caused new waves of immigrants to want to enter? A complete analysis would include the whole course of international relations between South Korea and the United States; but we are forced here to focus on more immediate relationships. We shall examine American immigration policy, especially the United States Immigration Act of 1965 and its revisions in 1976, as providing entry points for immigration. We shall also consider, in less detail, the policies of Latin American nations and of West Germany. The policies of accepting or not accepting Korean migrants, and the specific terms under which they are implemented, leads to an analysis of larger issues and policies that initially seemed to have little direct bearing on South Korea and South Koreans themselves. Such general policies were aimed at all immigrants or at the internal problems of the United States; they especially include education and manpower policies and policies toward ethnic groups who had already immigrated, and toward their descendants. But Koreans used such policies as a basis for emigration, and to the extent that these policies affected the number and the demographic characteristics of Korean emigrants, and the emigration policy of the South Korean government, they have been included in this study. The impact of policies with respect to the American medical system has been especially significant. The growth of new forms of medical care within the United States resulted, for a time, in labor shortages and educational bottlenecks in the United States that Koreans who had been trained in Korean medical and nursing schools partly filled. This special emigration of medical professionals profoundly affected the main features of the Korean immigration.

The list of pull factors is inexhaustible. It was discovered, for instance, that the "Americanization" of South Korea contributed to the new emigration. This is to say that America "exported" its pull factors directly to South Korea in the form of cultural and economic dominance after World War II, especially during and after the Korean War. But specific pull factors have also included the development of South Korean export industries that rely heavily on the United States market. Thus we are again led to study the vagaries of the American market, which affected Koreans in America to the extent that Koreans in both the homeland and the United States were able to take advantage of new opportunities. The wig craze in the United States of the 1960s and the expansion of American medical delivery systems under Medicare, Medicaid, and other prepayment systems are two cases in point. We study these fashions and institutional developments insofar as they provided entry points and channels for Korean immigration.

In a negative sense, we also study certain areas of the developing American economy that have offered resistance to the entry or advancement of Koreans, given their special talents and their disabilities as immigrants. Closed as well as open doors have determined the economic bases and the character of the Korean community.

These factors are not usually considered to be directly related to the study of a community. Indeed, they lead us far beyond the scope of the traditional concept of the community by including international and national relations, issues of war and peace, the multinational corporation, the welfare and authoritarian state, and such "macro" systems as the medical system of the United States. Yet such issues, including even class and occupational changes within South Korea caused by its rapid economic development, affected the Korean migration to the United States, and hence the new community. Furthermore, this experience contributed to the formation of the evolving character structure of contemporary South Koreans. Our principle in raising these theoretical questions has been that everything is relevant insofar as it affects the amount and character of the Korean immigration and insofar as these in turn have affected the processes by which Koreans have attempted to construct a community in the New York metropolitan area.

In Part III, we explore the traditional dimensions of the community: its social and economic organization, "class" leadership, politics, and problems and prospects. We here raise issues of cultural contact, isolation, acculturation and assimilation, and the overall adjustment of Koreans to American society. We must be especially careful, however, to relate these aspects of a possible emerging community to the unique characteristics of American society and the Korean homeland society. Thus our historical focus is necessarily different from that of community studies done in earlier eras. The structure of the larger societies within which recent migration and community construction has occurred is substantially different from the structures that implicitly or explicitly framed earlier studies. We must be especially mindful of how these historical differences affect the process of community construction.

The relationship between the governments of the United States and South Korea takes on a new importance in Part III, for the South Korean government systematically intervenes in the construction of overseas Korean communities. We are thus forced by events and by the data to ask how Korean immigrants have responded to both the homeland government and to the "Koreagate" scandal. This leads us, finally, to examine indigenous community movements for cultural and political autonomy from the homeland and its government. In this connection, we shall pay special attention to the way that the economic independence of certain Korean immigrants from the homeland and especially from its government contributes to the political autonomy of the Korean community in New York.

Thus all the external analyses of "macro" systems in Part I of this study become the basic dimensions of the "micro" analysis of the community in Parts II and III. Our analysis in Part II of the economic adjustment of Korean immigrants in the United States, especially of their outstanding success despite unfavorable circumstances, leads us into issues not originally designed to be part of this study. But we have to account for the unusual economic aggressiveness, motility, and mobility that Koreans have exhibited both in the United States and in the process of emigration and, incidentally, in South Korea itself. This leads us to examine Korean history in order to discern the preindustrial emergence of a Korean economic and social character that has been fully liberated in the process of modernization and industrialization. In this context, we examine Confucianism in Part IV as a "religion" and as a work ethic, especially as it was modified in Korea. We also examine the peculiar history of Korea, which, like ancient Judea, was the victim of endless conquests that produced a "marginal" character and worked against the emergence of a feudal traditionalism. We are forced to inquire as well into the influence of Protestant Christianity at the turn of the twentieth century, especially Presbyterianism, on the Korean Christians who migrated to the United States. The sources of the current economic and social character of Korean immigrants are thus barely suggested in Part IV. More convincing proof of the hypothesis presented there must await a more detailed examination; Part IV represents only tentative gropings toward explaining the Korean "miracle."

The ultimate questions of this study are: Have Koreans been able to construct a viable permanent community in the New York metropolitan area? And is such an attempt even possible? The concluding chapter is an attempt to answer such questions. Definitive answers are, of course, the task of future historians of the American Korean community. Instead, we attempt to assess the factors that may or may not lead to the creation of a stable or permanent community. Because the dispersed pattern of Korean settlement in the New York metropolitan area is substantially different from the concentrated settlement of most traditional ghetto communities of the American past, we also attempt to analyze the factors in the Korean experience that might lead to the dispersion and assimilation of Korean immigrants and their culture into American society and culture.

Ultimately, Korean immigrants in the United States will, in response to their own background, their social structure, and the exigencies of their current situation, write their own history. We can only make an educated guess, on the basis of data currently available, as to the future of the Korean community in the United States. That educated guess is our conclusion.

PART I

*The Korean Immigration to
the United States*

CHAPTER ONE

United States Immigration Law as It Affects Koreans

Historically, Koreans have migrated to foreign countries largely out of their sense that Korea is an international pariah—a status that is a product of Korea's vulnerability to military intervention and to threats of domination by neighboring and distant superpowers. The Korean diaspora in the modern era began with the loss of Korean sovereignty to the Japanese empire at the turn of the twentieth century. During that time, some ten thousand laborers, political refugees, and students took steamships to American shores. But their attempt to construct a Korean community in the new land was severely hampered by white nativists, whose anti-Oriental movements eventually resulted in legislation against the entry of Asians.

When the United States Congress passed the Immigration Act of 1965, however, a "blessing from heaven" fell upon Asians in general and Koreans in particular; thanks to the act, Asians have become a dominant immigrant group. The passage of the act reflected the liberal, egalitarian, and civil rights movements of the 1960s and had nothing specifically to do with Koreans either in the United States or in South Korea. The immigration of Koreans was a serendipitous by-product of these larger and basically internal political pressures.

As we shall see, United States immigration policy, as embedded in the Immigration Act of 1965 and the 1976 amendment, has become the very warp and woof on which the Korean community has been constructed in the United States; it has determined both the number and the social characteristics of Korean immigrants—their sex, age, occupation, and education. At the same time, anxieties about the prospects of another Korean War have contributed to the exodus of upper-middle-class Koreans to the United States; the status of Korea as an international pariah continues to effect emigration.

The Older Immigrants

During World War II the Japanese government drafted forty-five thousand Koreans as slave laborers for the coal mines of Sakhalin. One of these men recently sent a letter to his wife in South Korea from Sakhalin (now part of the Soviet Union) that describes his plight.

> Why did you and I become husband and wife? Over 30 years have passed without my being able to see you. When I think of the life we could have had if I had not been forced to come to Sakhalin I almost go out of my mind. I have become an old man with white hair and live for the hope of being reunited with you.[1]

When the laborers were sent to Sakhalin, a cold and bleak island to the north of Hokkaido, the Korean peninsula and southern Sakhalin belonged to the Japanese empire. However, at the end of World War II the peninsula was liberated from Japanese rule and divided into North and South Korea; the Soviet Union annexed southern Sakhalin and recognized only North Korean citizenship. Since most of the Korean slave laborers had come from provinces in South Korea, they had refused to become North Korean citizens and thus to be repatriated to North Korea.

This is only one example of how Korean migrations have been interwoven with Korea's history of "national tragedies." As a result, Koreans have developed a number of ethnocentric defenses, and many Koreans today still express shame when they discuss the history of their emigrations. Out of self-defense and a sense of national pride, some Koreans today, especially historians, novelists, and journalists, prefer to use the terms *yumin* (drifting people) or *gimin* (abandoned people) rather than the formal term *yimin* (emigrants) when they refer to middle-class Koreans emigrating to the United States partly from fear of another Korean War. Korean intellectuals use the terms *yumin* or *gimin* in order to emphasize the hardships and sufferings of the Korean diaspora that began when Korea lost its sovereignty to imperial Japan. Despite their nation's hardships, Koreans are proud of their national identity and their "5,000-year-old history," the early part of which is derived from mythology; and they boast of their "single" race, although they are actually a hybrid of Mongols, Manchurians, Japanese, Chinese, and Polynesians. Yet they sometimes use disparaging nicknames when referring to the Chinese, Manchurians, or Japanese because throughout their recorded history they have been harassed by these neighboring peoples. Koreans have also expressed their ethnocentrism in a negative attitude toward their own emigrants. During the period of the Yi dynasty (1392-1910), Korean kings frequently ordered the Pyongyang governors in the northwestern province of the peninsula to stop Koreans who were migrating to Manchuria because of famine in their home villages. Their decrees called for the death penalty for

[1] *New York Times*, February 27, 1977.

subjects who attempted to cross either the Yalu or the Tumen rivers to enter the Manchurian virgin lands.[2]

In modern history, Korean emigration has been closely linked with struggles among China, Japan, Russia, and the United States over the domination of the Korean peninsula, a strategically vital region in the Far East. Broadly speaking, the more than 3 million Koreans now residing in the Soviet Union, China, Japan, and the United States are there directly or indirectly as the result of struggles among the four big powers that began at the turn of the century. The struggles still continue along the Korean demilitarized zone, which is manned by more than 1 million soldiers of North and South Korea.

The Sino-Japanese War in 1894 and the Russo-Japanese War in 1904-1905 broke out mainly as a result of conflicting claims for suzerainty over the Korean peninsula. Japan won both wars, and in 1910 Japan annexed Korea outright. As a part of its direct colonial rule, the Japanese government conducted a nationwide land inspection program during the years 1910 to 1918, by which the Japanese expropriated lands from Korean peasants as well as from the royal families of the Yi dynasty. By 1930 the Japanese government had taken about 40 percent of the arable land in Korea. This expropriation produced a mass of landless Korean peasants, most of whom became tenant farmers for Japanese landlords or for a Japanese reclamation company, the so-called Dongcheog.[3] These encroachments were added to the internal development of a "usury capitalism" in Korea, which in the nineteenth century had brought a heavy concentration of land into the hands of a small percentage of Korean landlords.[4]

These changes in land ownership, which favored a small number of Japanese and Korean landlords, forced a vast number of landless peasants to migrate to Manchuria and Siberia. During the Japanese colonial

[2] Sung-je Ko, Hangug iminsa yeongu [A study of the history of Korean emigration], Seoul, Jang Moon Gak, 1973, pp. 84-94.

[3] Gi-back Lee, Hangugsa sinron [A new approach to Korean history], Seoul, Il Jo Gak, 1967, p. 362; Ho-jin Choi, Geundae hangug gyeongjesa [The recent history of the Korean economy], Seoul, Dan Moon Moon Go, 1973, p. 72.

[4] The money economy was fully developed by the beginning of the nineteenth century in urban commercial centers, and it later spread through the rural areas. Consequently, at the end of the nineteenth century the Korean government began to collect taxes from peasants in cash rather than in local products, the traditional means of payment. This change in tax collection forced peasants to raise cash by selling their products in local markets. Partly because of the lack of local markets, however, peasants had to borrow money from usurers at high interest rates in order to pay taxes. In this Korean "usury" form of capitalism, if the debtors failed to pay their debts, their wives and children became serfs of the creditors. The usurers ranged from landlords and public officials to the government itself. See Gi-june Jo and Duck-young Oh, Hangug gyeongjesa [The history of the Korean economy], Seoul, Bum Moon Sa, 1962, pp. 325-333.

period (1910-1945), the Japanese governor general of Korea induced 1.2 million landless Korean peasants to resettle in southern Manchuria, some parts of which needed massive reclamation.[5] As of 1961, about 1.3 million Koreans were reported to be still living in Kirin, Manchuria.[6] It was also reported that 1.5 million live in mainland China and that 0.5 million are Soviet citizens in central Asia.[7] About 0.6 million Koreans in Japan constitute the second-largest Korean community overseas and are the largest ethnic group in Japan. They are the remnants and descendants of the 18.8 million Korean migrants to Japan during the Japanese colonial period.

The Korean emigration to the United States dates from the turn of the century, when the United States received massive waves of immigrants from eastern and southern European nations as well as from Japan and China. A small number of students, some political refugees, and a few ginseng peddlers were the first Koreans to land in the United States: several political refugees sought asylum in the United States after they led the abortive Gabsin coup in 1884, the object of which was an attempt to modernize Korea by fashioning it after Japan; and in 1881 North Korean ginseng peddlers came to the West Coast via China in order to sell their product to the Chinese immigrants, but their numbers were too small to be designated as an immigrant contingent.[8] Official Korean immigration to the United States and its territories began in 1903, when American sugar planters in the Hawaiian Islands imported Koreans as contract laborers for their labor-intensive sugar plantations. Between 1903 and 1905 a total of 7,226 Koreans arrived in the islands; then the Korean government, which was degraded by 1905 to a de facto Japanese protectorate, suddenly forbade emigration; the Japanese government wanted to protect Japanese immigrants in the Hawaiian Islands from the competition of Koreans. The Japanese ambassador to Korea at that time remarked that "the Korean emigration [into the Hawaiian Islands] was banned by the will of Japanese emigration companies. They do not want the Korean immigrants to be competitive with the Japanese immigrants."[9] This statement is understandable when we consider that the sugar planters imported Koreans as strikebreakers against Japanese workers, who initiated strikes and demanded wage increases after they had served their time as contract laborers.

[5] Tai-hwan Kwon et al., *The Population of Korea*, Seoul, The Population and Development Studies Center, Seoul National University, 1975, p. 28.

[6] *China News Analysis*, Hong Kong, no. 569, June 18, 1965.

[7] *Hankook Ilbo*, March 27, 1974.

[8] Sung-lak Kim, "Yeogsajeog euro bon bugmi hangug-in" [Koreans in the United States in historical perspective], *Shinhan Minbo*, April 29, 1976.

[9] Ko, *Hangug iminsa*, p. 211.

The Hawaiian Islands served as a stepping stone for Japanese and Korean laborers entering the United States mainland: from 1905 to 1910, 2,012 Koreans living in the islands, largely enticed by better economic opportunities, moved to the West Coast.[10] During the decade after 1910 some 541 Korean students entered the United States in order to study at American educational institutions.[11] In addition to these official Korean entries came the unofficial immigrants: during the period from 1910 to 1924, the year when the National Origins Act became effective, some 2,000 Koreans, most of them political refugees from Japanese domination, came to the United States without passports, usually through Shanghai.[12]

The experience of Koreans in the United States was similar to that of Japanese and Chinese immigrants: they all faced economic adjustments and exposure to the anti-Oriental movements on the West Coast. The Koreans engaged in rice and vegetable farming, railroad construction, and in the restaurant and hotel business. Like the Japanese and Chinese, their economic ventures were greatly limited by white nativistic racial discrimination.[13] And like the Japanese, the Koreans were successful in agriculture. Here is one aspect of their success story:

Korean settlers in California, Oregon, Colorado, Montana, Kansas, and Nebraska began vegetable farming as early as 1911. They followed with successful ventures in orchards, nurseries, and vineyards. In 1916, a group of sixty Koreans in the Manteca, California area pooled their resources to lease 1,300 acres for experimental sugar beet production. Business thrived, and a small cooperative village was organized nearby. A smaller group of Koreans in Logan, Utah, succeeded with a 292-acre melon farm. By far the most successful of all Korean enterprises before 1924 were the rice and fruit farming operations in the San Joaquin Valley. One California Korean, Kim Chong-nim, celebrated as the "Rice King" in 1917, was able to expand his operations to 2,085 acres in rice. Near Reedley, two brothers, Kim Ho and Kim Hyŏng-sun, began a truck farming business in 1921, eventually working 500 acres. Their business grew to

[10] Kim, "Yeogsajeog euro bon."
[11] Lee Houchins and Chang-su Houchins, "The Korean Experience in America, 1903-1924," *Pacific Historical Review* 43 (1974): 558.
[12] Kim, "Yeogsajeog euro bon."
[13] For instance, the Japanese and Korean Exclusion League was formed in 1905 in San Francisco, and membership expanded to more than 75,000 within a year. The Exclusion League, supported by foreign-born white laborers, declared as one of its aims that "the Chinese exclusion laws be extended so as to exclude all classes of Japanese and Koreans, exempted by the terms of the Chinese Act, from the United States and its insular territories." Raymond Leslie Buell, "Anti-Japanese Agitation in the United States," *Political Science Quarterly* 37 (1922): 614-623.

$400,000 annually, as they expanded into nectarine and other fruit production and wholesaling along with canning and large-scale nurseries.[14]

When the anti-Oriental movements in California were in full force at the turn of the century, the Koreans were lumped together with the Chinese and Japanese as Mongolians, and all were subject to the same discrimination. And yet they maintained their national pride and identity despite this victimization.

In late June 1913, at the height of the anti-Japanese labor movement in California, eleven Koreans were severely beaten as they attempted to work in an orchard near Riverside. When an official of the Japanese consulate in Los Angeles visited the victims and offered assistance, the Tae-Han Kungminhoe (THK) interfered. Refusing to accept any offer of help from Japanese officials, the THK's leadership dispatched a telegram to William Jennings Bryan, U.S. Secretary of State, making the following points: All Korean residents of the state of California arrived before 1910, when Korea was annexed by the Japanese; they were Koreans, who opposed Japanese domination of Korea; Japanese government assistance was refused, particularly because the acceptance of such aid would imply that Koreans were Japanese subjects; and all matters regarding Koreans in America should be taken up with the community organization, the Tae-Han Kungminhoe, or Korean National Association of North America. Bryan's prompt response, favoring the THK position, was widely published, and the THK gained recognition as a quasi-diplomatic organization representing the Korean immigrant community.[15]

Koreans preserved their ethnic identity and solidarity in the United States by politicizing their ethnic organizations in opposition to Japanese domination of their homeland. In this aspect, Korean immigrants were different from the Japanese and Chinese; and this difference was due to the international pariah status of Korea caused by the big powers' struggles for hegemony over the peninsula.[16] It is thus understandable that Korean anti-Japanese movements and a strong nationalism emerged wherever Korean emigrants settled. Koreans engaged in guerrilla warfare against Japanese colonial rule in Manchuria and in the Vladivostok area; North Korean President Kim Il-sung led one of

[14] Houchins and Houchins, "The Korean Experience," p. 563.
[15] Ibid., p. 561.
[16] The Korean government allowed its subjects to emigrate to the Hawaiian Islands in the hope that, by doing so, it would receive support from the United States in coping with the Japanese political and economic encroachment upon Korea. Ibid., p. 548.

these guerrilla groups. In Shanghai, a Korean provisional government was formed and a revolutionary army was manned by the Korean immigrants in China. Even the United States became a main political center for the Korean independence movement.

The political situation in Korea helps to explain why students or political refugees constituted a high proportion of the Korean immigrants into the United States; but there were religious motivations as well. Most were Protestants regardless of whether they were political refugees or laborers. American missionaries had encouraged and persuaded Korean Christians to depart from their homeland, which was deeply imbued with the Confucian culture of ancestor worship. Most of the Korean plantation workers in the Hawaiian Islands came from port cities and towns in northern provinces of the peninsula, where they had engaged in manual labor; less than 14 percent of them were peasants.[17] American missionaries thus played a decisive role in selecting Koreans for emigration, and this largely explains why Protestant churches became a major community organization in the Hawaiian Islands. Even non-Christian immigrants participated in church life, because churches provided the only opportunities for social interaction.[18] (As we shall see in chapter six, this church-centered community life continues among the new Korean immigrants in the New York metropolitan area.) These religious ties and the Korean national pariah status account for the heavy concentration of political refugees, students, and clergymen among the Korean immigrants at the turn of the century, and thus account for the unique character of the Korean community as compared with the Chinese and Japanese communities. As we shall see, the same factors still apply in the analysis of recent Korean immigration to the United States.

Mainly because of the long time interval that separates the first Korean immigration from the new one, there is at present little social interaction between the two groups. Furthermore, the older Korean immigrants were so few that they could not establish the kinds of ethnic institutions that might link the two contingents. In addition, most of the descendants of the older Korean immigrants have lost their sense of identity as Koreans because they have chosen wives from among other ethnic groups. For instance, from 1960 to 1964, 77 percent of the Korean males who belonged to the second or third generation of immigrants to the Hawaiian Islands chose their spouses from among

[17] Bernice Bong Hee Kim, "The Koreans in Hawaii," *Social Science* 9 (1934): 409.

[18] Nam Han, "Miju hanin imin gwa doglibsa" [Korean immigrants in the United States and the history of their national independence movement], *Hankook Shinmoon,* May 17, 1975.

other racial groups; for Korean females, the interracial marriage rate amounted to 80 percent.[19] This high rate of interracial marriage could be partially attributed to the fact that only about 10 percent of the original Korean immigrants were women; the shortage of Korean women was the most serious problem facing unmarried men. Many of the Korean males solved their problem by relying on the "picture marriage," a marriage arranged between unknown parties who selected each other between exchanges of photographs. During the period between 1910 and 1924 more than one thousand Korean women came to the islands as "picture" brides.[20] But the shortage of Korean women persisted.

Despite the absence of social interaction between the original immigrants and the newer ones, recent Korean immigrants have a strong tendency to idealize and romanticize the hardships of the *ilse*, the first generation of immigrants. For instance, Koreans in the Hawaiian Islands, under the auspices of their home government, have campaigned to organize and collect the cultural remnants of the *ilse*. Korean ethnic newspapers have frequently covered the success stories of the *ise*, the second generation, and the *samse*, the third generation, with the explicit intention of portraying individuals from these groups as model cases of the *hngug iminsa* (the history of the Korean immigration). They do so despite the fact that most of the heroes or heroines they present do not commit themselves, either psychologically or socially, to the affairs of the Korean immigrant community.

THE IMMIGRATION ACT OF 1965 AND THE NEW IMMIGRANTS

The United States Immigration Act of 1965 selects new kinds of Korean immigrants. The older immigrants landed on the Hawaiian shores after enduring the hardships of long steamship voyages; the new ones arrive three times a week on the Korean Airline, which virtually commutes from Seoul to New York City and Los Angeles. Unlike the older immigrants, most of whom were illiterate, poor, and low-skilled laborers intermingled with some few highly educated political refugees, a majority of new immigrants are well-educated, skilled, urban-middle-class Koreans. As they wait to board the jumbo jet at Kimpo International Airport, which is heavily guarded against possible attacks by North Korean infiltrators, they are neatly dressed, healthy, and sophisticated. While waiting for customs inspection, some attempt to hide, deep down in their bags, illegal American dollars. They attempt to mask

[19] *Jayoo Shinmoon*, June 14, 1974.
[20] Houchins and Houchins, "The Korean Experience," p. 559.

their anxiety, for discovery of the dollars could lead to a conviction for violating the South Korean currency law.

Many of these emigrants are highly skilled workers who have signed labor contracts with American employees, usually through Korean employment agencies. Almost all of them have contacted relatives or friends in the United States in order to find jobs and housing in the regions where they intend to reside. They have notified their relatives or friends of their arrival time at a major airport so that they will be quickly picked up upon landing.

As of 1980, the new Korean community in the United States is made up of some 500,000 Koreans, most of whom have entered the United States since the enactment of the Immigration Act of 1965.[21] The figure includes immigrant aliens "admitted for permanent residence" and nonimmigrant aliens "admitted in temporary status." As shown in table 1.1, from 1950 to 1976 a total of 186,128 Koreans entered the United States as immigrants; 81 percent of them entered during the years from 1970 to 1976. Another group of 32,028 Koreans, or 15 percent of the total, had previously entered the United States as nonimmigrants and managed to acquire permanent resident status during that period. Because a majority have begun to reside in the United States since 1970 and because some 100 Koreans enter the new land daily with the intention of settling, the Korean community has been undergoing a tremendous change. During the period of 1970 to 1976, a total of 42,135 Korean aliens became citizens after five years of permanent residence. These constitute 19 percent of the total Korean permanent residents. Since a majority of the recent Korean immigrants claim citizenship when they meet the residence requirements, the naturalized number has drastically increased since 1974: the number of naturalized Koreans increased from 3,562 in 1973 to 7,450 in 1976.

This new inflow of Koreans is a direct product of the Immigration Act of 1965. The act was not specifically aimed at Korean immigrants, but it opened the door for the creation of a new Korean community in the New York metropolitan area, as we shall see.

---

[21] No one knows the exact number of the total Korean population in the United States. Since the influx of Korean immigrants has mostly taken place since 1970, the 1970 United States Census data on the Korean population is outmoded. However, partly based upon the data of the *Annual Report(s) of the Immigration and Naturalization Service*, we might crudely estimate that the total Korean population in the United States exceeds, as of 1980, half a million. This estimate takes into account the unknown number of illegal aliens, temporary visitors, older immigrants, new immigrants' offspring born in the United States, and those Koreans admitted to the United States via third nations such as Latin American nations, Canada, and West Germany. Such demographic factors as the return-migration rate and the mortality rate of Koreans in the United States are negligible.

TABLE 1.1 THE NUMBER OF KOREANS ADMITTED TO THE U.S. AS PERMANENT
RESIDENTS, 1950-1976

Year of Entry[a]	Status at Entry		Total
	Immigrant	Nonimmigrant[b]	
1950-54	538	n.a.	538
1955-59	4,990	n.a.	4,990
1960-65	11,686	1,583	13,269
1966	2,492	598	3,090
1967	3,956	1,424	5,380
1968	3,811	1,098	4,909
1969	6,045	1,820	7,865
1970	9,314	2,079	11,393
1971	14,297	4,049	18,346
1972	18,876	5,513	24,389
1973	22,930	4,961	27,891
1974	28,028	4,658	32,686
1975	28,362	2,364	30,726
1976	30,803	1,881	32,684
Total	186,128	32,028	218,156
(percentage)	(85)	(15)	(100)

SOURCE: Adapted from *The Annual Report of the United States Immigration
and Naturalization Service* (1950-1976).

[a] The year ended on June 30. Hereafter, this fiscal year applies to all tables
based upon statistics compiled by the United States Immigration and Naturalization Service.

[b] The category of nonimmigrant applies to persons who had previously entered
the United States with nonimmigrant statuses like student, visitor, or businessman
and who changed their status to that of permanent resident.

In 1965, the *Congressional Quarterly Almanac* recorded a historical
moment: "A 40-year campaign by minority groups for reform of the
federal immigration laws ended October 3, when President Johnson
signed into law an Administration-backed bill (H.R. 2580) eliminating the national origins quota system as the basis of immigration to
the United States by persons born outside the Western Hemisphere.
The change had been sought by every President since Harry S. Tru-
man."[22] For Koreans, this change was an accident: it created opportunities for the entry of new Koreans, but neither the Korean government nor the older Korean immigrants in the United States had engaged in such a "40-year campaign." Because Koreans have constituted
the third-largest immigrant group since 1973, they are among the largest beneficiaries of this change. However, one cannot say that they

[22] *Congressional Quarterly Almanac*, 89th Congress, 1st session, 1965, 21:459.

have reaped these benefits for doing nothing; it would be more accurate to say that, because their admission into the United States was previously prohibited by the National Origins Act of 1924, they were deprived of the chance to participate in the campaign to change that law. The fundamental reason for the change can be found in the changing bases of ethnic politics in the United States.

First of all, it must be pointed out that the ethnic-racial components of the United States population had been undergoing dramatic changes: according to the census of 1960, 65 percent of the United States population had non-Anglo-Saxon origins; about 34 million were of foreign or mixed-parentage stock, and 83.6 percent of these lived in urban areas. This shift in the ethnic, social, and economic composition of the population in favor of new ethnic groups made up of foreign-born stock, second- or third-generation southeastern European immigrants, and blacks from the South created large urban voting blocs that elected a two-to-one Democratic majority in each congressional chamber; and that Congress carried out President Johnson's plan to reform the federal immigration law. This political atmosphere favorable to immigration reform was strengthened by the revolutionary tenor of the 1960s, during which time the civil rights movement was in full swing. Owing to this pluralistic and egalitarian political climate, the Johnson Administration repealed the national-origin quotas, which were designed in the 1920s to perpetuate the cultural and political dominance of northern and western European stocks and which had been reaffirmed during the Eisenhower administration by the Immigration Act of 1952.

In sharp contrast with the bigotry of the 1920s, in 1965 no nativistic groups undertook a systematic opposition to immigration reform. Senator Edward M. Kennedy, who chaired hearings of the Subcommittee on Immigration, recalled the social circumstances in which the Immigration Act of 1965 was passed:

> During the courses of the hearings I personally met with representatives from several of these organizations, including the American Coalition of Patriotic Societies, the American Legion, the Daughters of the American Revolution, and the National Association of Evangelicals. There was a candid exchange of views between myself and those who joined the discussion. While most of those with whom I met were skeptical regarding the various reform channels, and for reasons which varied among the organizations represented at the meetings, I believe it is fair to say that all recognized the unworkability of the national-origins quota system and at the close of the meeting expressed a willingness to cooperate in finding a new for-

mula for the selection of immigrants. No significant opposition to eliminating the national origins quota system was organized by any of their organizations. . . .[23]

President Johnson pointed out the essential element of the new Immigration Act in his speech at the Statue of Liberty on October 3, 1965: "This bill says simply that from this day forth those wishing to emigrate to America shall be admitted on the basis of their skills and their close relationship to those already here." As a result, almost all the immigrants admitted to the United States since the passage of the act can be divided, on the basis of their qualification for entry, into two groups: one group is made up of those who were able to enter by virtue of having close relatives in the United States; the other group consists of those who possess specific skills that are defined as contributing to the growth of the United States economy. The new legislation simply replaced racial discrimination, as embedded in the National Origins Act of 1924, with a new form of selection based upon skill and kinship. However, prospective immigrants, even though they are blessed with either close relatives in the United States or with specific skills needed in the economy, are not equally qualified for admission. The Immigration Act of 1965, which took effect in 1968, still operates under the legal framework of quota preferences.

THE CONNECTION BETWEEN IMMIGRATION POLICY AND LABOR POLICY

The influx of highly skilled immigrants into the United States varies from occupation to occupation as well as from year to year. This fact indicates that immigration policy has been geared to importing workers according to specific manpower needs in each occupation and period.

The Immigration Act of 1965 gave the Department of Labor the authority to select immigrants with specific skills and thus initiated a definite institutional linkage between national manpower policy and immigration policy. The authority stems from the following provision: aliens are not eligible for admission if they are "seeking to enter the United States, for the purpose of performing skilled or unskilled labor, unless the Secretary of Labor has determined and certified to the Secretary of State and to the Attorney General that (A) there are not sufficient workers in the United States who are able, willing, qualified, and available at the time of application for a visa and admission to

[23] Edward M. Kennedy, "The Immigration Act of 1965," *The Annals of the American Academy of Political and Social Science*, September 1966, p. 10.

the United States and at the place to which the alien is destined to perform such skilled or unskilled labor, and (B) the employment of such aliens will not adversely affect the wages and working conditions of the workers in the United States similarly employed."[24] Consequently, prospective immigrants with specific skills must find, before their entry to the United States, an employer willing to hire them; and they must obtain from him a document certifying their prospective employment in order to receive the secretary of labor's certificate of clearance establishing the provision as quoted above. The labor certificate is essential for prospective immigrants in applying for a visa at the United States consulate in their home country. However, "members of the professions, scientists, and artists of exceptional ability" had been exempted from this requirement until the end of 1976, when the act of 1965 was amended. This exemption applied largely to foreign medical professionals and facilitated their influx to American medical institutions, for which labor was definitely in short supply.

As the application for certification is being processed, the Bureau of Employment Security's United States Employment Service, which received from the secretary of labor the authority to select and administer immigrant workers, determines "the availability of United States workers" and "the adverse effects" of the influx of foreign workers "on wages and working conditions of United States workers." In doing this, the federal agency relies on such sources of information as public employment service offices, professional associations, labor unions, and employers. The number of labor certificates that it finally issues varies from region to region and from year to year. For instance, California and New York have been the two largest sources of requests for certification. Partly because of this, these two states have received the bulk of Korean immigrants; and, as we shall see, the two largest Korean communities have emerged there.

Facing deep economic problems like the energy shortage, high unemployment, and inflation, some segments of the native population have shown negative reactions to the new immigration. For instance, Zero Population Growth Society expounded in 1976 a restriction of immigration in order to protect American jobs from immigrants and conserve national resources.[25] In response to these economic problems and to complaints that illegal aliens were stealing "American" jobs, Congress in 1976 amended the Immigration Act of 1965. One of the amendments downgraded professional immigrants like nurses, physi-

[24] Quoted by Frank H. Cassell, "Immigration and the Department of Labor," *The Annals of the American Academy of Political and Social Science*, September 1966, p. 107.
[25] *New York Times*, August 4, 1976.

cians, and dentists from the "third preference" to the "sixth preference." This meant that they too would have to find, before entry, an American employer willing to hire them. This change in immigration policy has affected the life chances of thousands of Korean medical professionals; their situation will be described in detail in chapter five. New waves of refugees and "millions" of illegal aliens continued to flow into the United States, however; in 1978 Congress created the Select Commission on Immigration and Refugee Policy in order to develop a new immigration policy.

This reappraisal of immigration policy is taking place, however, within the general framework of the Immigration Act of 1965. Once the United States liberalized its immigration policy by selectively accepting immigrants regardless of race and nationality, there appears to be no going back. At least in the near future, there are not likely to be such Draconian restrictions against nonwhite races as were enacted in past legislation. This appears to be so partly because contemporary American society is still imbued with a liberal ideology and partly because its ethnic and racial structure is so much more diversified now than in times past. Furthermore, such discriminatory legislation would put a serious strain on international relations. In this larger context, contemporary American society faces the fundamental and agonizing problem of how to perpetuate the ideology of the American dream in the midst of the very social-economic scarcities that deny it.

SOCIAL AND ECONOMIC CHARACTERISTICS OF KOREAN IMMIGRANTS

Entry Mechanisms. Korean ethnic newspapers in the United States as well as the major newspapers in South Korea have carried as front-page stories all the United States legislative and administrative changes in the Immigration Act of 1965, whereas the American mass media have paid little attention to these events. Thus Koreans are much more aware of changes in United States immigration law than are Americans. Almost every Korean immigrant knows what each preference category stands for, and the Korean ethnic newspapers report biweekly or monthly on which "preferences" are currently open to prospective emigrants in South Korea. For example, *The Hankook Ilbo* (March 15, 1977) reported: "According to the report of the United States Department of State, all the 'preferences' except of the 'sixth preference and nonpreference' are now open, as of March 15, 1977. The opening of the 'fifth preference' is applicable only to those who finshed visa petition prior to May, 1976. . . ." This was good news for those Korean immigrants who claimed a "family reunion" by using "relative preferences"; but it was bad news to thousands of would-be emigrants who have waited for several years for the opening of the "sixth preference" or "nonpreference" quota.

Shifts of United States immigration policy also greatly affect Koreans already in the United States who "are troubled with green card problems." Here is an example of the anxiety of nonstatus Koreans:

> Three years have passed since I arrived at this strange land of America. Three years ago I set my foot on this unknown land, the land where I have difficulty in passing my words—with an enormous hope to lead a better life and thereby to raise my children well. Here I have felt an enormous difference from what I heard in my country, so that several times I wished to return home. Now, after a three-year experience of this hard American life, I feel some confidence in making a living here. But my longing for my old country is getting stronger and stronger day after day.
>
> I had to endure frequent belittlements and contempt—such a contempt that no human being can bear. Whenever I found myself surrounded with an inferiority complex, I almost burst into tears and began to indulge in self-pity, screaming and yelling like a lunatic.
>
> Sometimes I attempted to escape from reality by thinking of my family and my children whom I have left behind—how much my children are grown. I received education as much as man should have, but no one in America recognizes my learning in my country. This is America. . . .
>
> Green card! When shall I grasp a green card in my hand? I need it as urgently as a moment of breaking bones. Whenever I think of this problem, I feel as if I have become insane. . . .[26]

The importance of the United States immigration law to the Koreans concerned—to their hopes, aspirations, despair, and sorrows—can be more vividly understood when we look at the entry mechanisms of the recent Korean immigrants, as illustrated in table 1.2. The following are the distinctive features that can be extracted from the table. First, the percentage of Korean entries under the "occupational preferences" reached its peak of 45.1 percent in 1972; since then it began its drop, falling to 22 percent in 1975. This phenomenon generally reflects the condition of the United States economy, which has faced a deepening recession since 1972; the economic recession has been translated into immigration policy as a restriction of the influx of immigrants with specific skills into the American labor market. On the other hand, in contrast to the sharp percentage decline of "occupational preference" immigrants, there has been a steady percentage increase of "relative

[26] *Hankook Shinmoon*, September 11, 1976.

TABLE 1.2 ENTRY MECHANISMS OF KOREAN IMMIGRANTS, 1967-1975

Year of Entry	Immigrants under the Numerical Limitations (percentages)				Immigrants Exempt from the Numerical Limitations (percentages)						Numerical Totals
	2nd Pref.[a]	4th Pref.[b]	5th Pref.[c]	Occupa-tional Pref.[d]	Parents of U.S. Citizens	Wives of U.S. Citizens	Husbands of U.S. Citizens	Spouses of U.S. Citizens[e]	Children of U.S. Citizens	Other Special Immigrants[f]	
1967	5.7	0.3	4.3	32.7	1.6	35.3	2.0	—	16.4	1.2	3,956
1968	7.6	0.6	4.6	27.8	2.2	35.6	1.5	—	18.1	1.7	3,811
1969	8.6	0.1	8.8	30.1	1.9	32.3	1.5	—	15.7	0.6	6,045
1970	8.8	0.4	14.2	30.8	1.9	28.4	1.0	—	13.0	1.0	9,314
1971	7.7	0.2	13.5	41.9	1.5	21.2	0.7	1.3	11.0	0.8	14,297
1972	7.9	0.2	15.2	45.1	1.8	11.4	0.6	6.3	11.4	0.8	18,876
1973	14.0	0.2	22.0	32.2	2.6	9.3	0.4	6.6	11.6	1.1	22,930
1974	15.0	0.3	21.6	33.5	2.3	8.8	0.4	5.6	10.2	2.6	28,028
1975	16.7	0.3	30.0	22.2	3.1	7.6	0.4	2.7	11.7	4.8	28,362

SOURCE: Adapted from *The Annual Report of the United States Immigration and Naturalization Service* (1967-1975).

[a] The category applies to "spouses, unmarried sons and daughters of resident aliens and their children."

[b] The category applies to married sons and daughters of U.S. citizens and their spouses and children.

[c] The category applies to brothers and sisters of U.S. citizens and their spouses and children.

[d] The category applies to immigrants in professions and with special skills and their spouses and children. It includes the 3rd preference, 6th preference, and nonpreference categories.

[e] Category established after the act of April 7, 1970.

[f] The category applies to immigrants such as ministers of religion and employees of the U.S. government abroad and their spouses and children.

preference" immigrants, especially in the category of the "second" and "fifth preference." The percentage increase under the fifth preference can be explained by the fact that a large number of Koreans have become American citizens, as we noted before, and thus are entitled to a "family reunion." Second, during the early period of Korean immigration, a high percentage of immigrants entered the United States as wives of native American citizens. They were largely made up of Korean War brides, who married American soldiers serving in South Korea. This pattern of Korean immigration existed long before the Immigration Act of 1965. In this sense, Korean War brides are one of the Korean social groups that laid the foundation of a kinship-centered immigration.

Cultural and Political Push-Factors. Generally speaking, the political, economic, and military involvement of the United States with South Korea since the end of World War II has provided the foundation for the recent Korean immigration into the United States. One of the consequences of this continuing involvement is that the United States forces in South Korea (still maintained at an authorized strength of 39,000 troops as of May, 1980) have transmitted American mass culture into South Korea. South Koreans, although noted for their ethnocentrism, have been deeply impressed with American affluence and mass consumption. The Korean urban elite classes in particular have emulated, since the end of the Korean War, a hodgepodge of American life styles. For Korean urbanites, wearing American-made shoes, hats, gloves, sunglasses, and wristwatches, most of which flow illegally from the PX's of United States military compounds, has been a powerful means of enhancing status. American popular songs and movies have fascinated Korean urban youth, and many Korean urban intellectuals today tend to ignore Korean television and radio programs in favor of the American ones that are beamed by the United States army station, American Forces Korea Network (AFKN). Finally, learning English has become a major tool by which businessmen, white-collar workers, public officials, and military officers strive for upward social mobility. This cultural impact has been cumulative: Korean urbanites yearn more and more for American life styles and mass consumption. Thus, American soldiers and businessmen in South Korea have unknowingly taken the role of recruitment agents who, like the older immigrants at the turn of the century, advertised and exaggerated the prosperity and well-being that an emigrant could hope to find in America.

However, as a cause of the Korean exodus into the United States this cultural impact is somewhat less important than the unstable military and political situation of the Korean peninsula. On August 18,

1976, when two American officers were reportedly killed by North Korean soldiers during a minor dispute over trimming tree branches at Panmunjom, the *New York Times* correspondent reported:

> The immediate area around Panmunjom, where two American soldiers were killed yesterday, has been the scene of so many violent incidents since the armistice that ended the Korean War 23 years ago that it is the only part of the Korean peninsula still officially designated a combat zone by the United States. It is now the only site in Asia where American combat troops directly confront Communist forces. Incidents there range from obscene hand gestures and spitting to mine-laying and machine-gun ambushes.
>
> Forty-nine Americans have died in such skirmishes in the demilitarized zone, along with a total of more than 1,000 Koreans on both sides. Incidents usually occur without warning. They erupt so quickly and end so fast that there is little time for reaction. Generally both sides—the South Koreans and Americans under the United Nations Command, on the one hand, and the North Koreans on the other—blame their opponents.[27]

Immediately after the so-called "axe-murder incident," a deep anxiety over another Korean War swept through some segments of the population of Seoul, which is located so near the demilitarized zone that it could be bombarded by the Soviet-made long-range artillery on the North Korean side. In general, upper- or upper-middle-class residents like businessmen, high-ranking government officials, professionals, and independent proprietors are most sensitive to this unstable military situation. In the days following this incident, these classes were relieved to see that the prices of jewelry, gold, or small boats—the solid means by which some wealthy Koreans could escape to Japan if war breaks out—did not jump as high in the domestic market as they did after the Communist takeover of South Vietnam.

Some Korean immigrants in the United States, who have left their close relatives behind, were also deeply concerned over the military tension caused by the incident. In a sense, Korean immigrants in the United States are more sensitive to the "Korean problem" than their fellow countrymen in the homeland. A Korean woman mentioned the incident in a letter to her friend in America.

> J. [in New York City] wrote to me saying that she is looking for someone there who will visit Korea and who, when returning to America, can bring her three-year old daughter back to the United States. Here [in South Korea] people are not so fussy over the inci-

27 *New York Times*, August 19, 1976.

dent as in the United States. This time, the gold price did not jump. People here seem to be immune to that kind of thing. Things here seem very peaceful. . . .

The letter attests to the sense of having a pariah status, which still contributes to the exodus of Koreans. However, this is not to say that all Korean immigrants to the United States have been "pushed" by the fear of another Korean War. The fear varies from one segment of the population to another.

It is the North Korean refugees in South Korea who are most vulnerable to the aggravated political and military tension between North and South Korea. Thus, given the "abundance" of the economic opportunities in the United States, which has operated as a main pull factor for a majority of Korean immigrants, the North Korean refugees have been disproportionately "pushed" by the unstable political and military situation in the homeland. No direct statistical evidence can be presented for this, but North Koreans constituted 50.6 percent of the 423 Korean emigrant families who entered Latin American nations as immigrants from 1962 to 1968.[28] As we shall see, a great many of the Koreans in Latin American nations have migrated again to the United States.

North Korean refugees and their descendants in South Korea numbered in 1977 some 5.1 million and constituted 14 percent of the South Korean population.[29] Before taking refuge in South Korea during the Korean War, they predominantly belonged to business, professional, and landlord classes, and they were largely Christians. In South Korea more than half of them engage in commercial businesses.[30] Because of their bitter experience of being persecuted by the North Korean communist regime, many of them are single-minded supporters of the South Korean version of anticommunism. And they express a deep anxiety over another Korean War because they would be the first to suffer if North Korean communists gained control over the South. In addition, since they are refugees, they do not have strong kinship ties in South Korea, and this facilitates their emigration to the United States and other countries. As we shall see, this North Korean contingent dominates church-centered community activities as well as business activities in the Korean community of the New York metropolitan area.

Apart from this regional factor, which is strongest for North Korean refugees, political and military instability have generally been the

[28] Sung-je Ko, *Imin hyaengjeong josa yeongu* [A study of emigration administration], Seoul, The Manpower Development Institute, 1969, pp. 52-53.
[29] *Joong Ang Ilbo*, June 27, 1977.   [30] Ibid.

prime factors in the exodus of wealthy South Korean businesmen, high-ranking retired government officials, proprietors, and well-qualified professionals, whenever opportunities to enter the United States are available. Many of these have brought large sums of dollars, and, as shown in table 1.3, many of them have entered the United States under a nonimmigrant status like "businessman and investor" or "temporary visitor for pleasure" and have changed their status after entry to that of permanent resident. In acquiring permanent resident status they have heavily relied on the technique of investing capital in business enterprises like small shops (wig stores, liquor stores, garment shops, and so forth) in the United States, a technique by which both prospective immigrants and nonimmigrant aliens living in the United States are entitled to become permanent residents. On October 7, 1976, however, the minimum amount of capital necessary to qualify an investor for permanent resident status was raised from $10,000 to $40,000. The rationale for this increase was that "investment" immigration, which was originally set up to induce foreign capital into the United States in order to stimulate the economy, had become nothing more than a means by which aliens were receiving a green card in exchange for investing only a modest sum of money.

TABLE 1.3 THE NUMBER OF KOREANS WHO GAINED PERMANENT RESIDENT STATUS AND THEIR STATUS AT ENTRY, 1966-1975

| Year | Status at Entry | | | | |
	Temporary Visitor for Pleasure	Student	Businessman and Investor	Others[a]	Total
1966	105	360	13	120	598
1967	283	861	29	151	1,424
1968	289	595	31	183	1,098
1969	470	850	93	407	1,820
1970	614	907	141	417	2,079
1971	879	975	250	1,945	4,049
1972	1,071	1,011	448	2,983	5,513
1973	1,151	811	708	2,291	4,961
1974	924	775	624	2,335	4,658
1975	436	397	280	1,251	2,364
Total	6,222	7,542	2,617	12,183	28,564
(percentage)	(22)	(26)	(9)	(43)	(100)

SOURCE: Adapted from *The Annual Report of the United States Immigration and Naturalization Service* (1966-1975).

[a] The category of "others" includes government officials, exchange visitors, temporary workers and trainees, dependent housewives and children, etc.

For this sort of emigration, South Korean newspapers have coined a new term, "runaway emigration," which carries a connotation of immorality or irresponsibility. To a large extent, the term reflects the deep resentment of many South Koreans against such "lucky" people. Here is a South Korean newspaper article, entitled "Wealthy Runaway Emigrants Are National Traitors," dispatched by a South Korean correspondent stationed in New York City.

> A majority of ordinary [Korean] immigrants here are successfully overcoming the numerous barriers and hardships that they encounter in their adjustment to alien life styles and language, although they face an intractable problem of estrangement that is involved with immigrant life. In a contrast to these ordinary immigrants, there is another kind of Korean immigrant who should be dealt with from a different perspective. They are aristocratic immigrants who brought here several millions of dollars [from South Korea] in order to enjoy a luxurious and aristocratic life style. They can be found in any place where Korean immigrants settle and they are objects of a deep resentment by many Korean immigrants here. In the case of New York, these aristocrats bought in cash several acre houses in the Fort Lee area, where only rich Americans can reside. They drive Lincolns or Cadillacs, and frequently shop at Saks department store, where they used to surprise salesmen by purchasing several-thousand-dollars' worth of goods. They invest the dollars they smuggled in from our country into real estate such as land and apartment buildings. Their investments are conducted under pseudonyms. All these pompous life styles cause Korean immigrants to criticize their home government and thus contribute to the antigovernment [of South Korea] movements here.[31]

Since the end of the Korean War, in 1953, more than 10,000 Korean students have crossed the Pacific Ocean in order to receive a higher education at American universities.[32] Among them, as shown in table 1-3, a total of 7,542 changed their student status to permanent resident status from 1966 to 1975. Their eligibility for permanent resident status is largely derived from learning or professional skills acquired in America, and they want to settle in the United States mainly because of its economic opportunities, social stability, and political freedom. Furthermore, many of them cannot find a job in their home country that is compatible with their new educational training. As far

[31] *Dong-A Ilbo,* January 9, 1975.
[32] According to a report of the Korean Ministry of Education, a total of 10,789 Korean students entered the United States on student visas during the period of 1953-1973.

as the manpower needs of the South Korean economy are concerned, they are overqualified and overspecialized. Since most of them come from the upper-middle classes in South Korean society, they further accentuate the selective social character of Korean emigration by sending for their families in South Korea.

To sum up, all these "nonimmigrant" immigrants—businessmen, investors, tourists, students, and government officials—are drawn from the "elite" classes of South Korean society. They become a main source of the kinship-centered immigration as governed by the Immigration Act of 1965. However, this group of Korean emigrants is small compared with the number of Koreans who were admitted to the United States as immigrants.

Selective Characteristics. Given the push and pull factors—in this case, the political instability and other socioeconomic malaise of the South Korean society on the one hand, and the socioeconomic well-being of American society on the other—the United States immigration law generally governs the demographic, social, and economic characteristics of Korean immigrants.

In the first place, the Korean immigrants had undergone an urbanization experience prior to their entry into the United States; a majority of them were from the urban middle classes of South Korean society. This is clearly indicated in tables 1.4, 1.5, and 1.6. Table 1.4 shows us that a majority of Korean immigrants with a reported occupation were drawn from urban occupational classes, especially from professional classes; this fact is reinforced in table 1.5, in which more than half of the Korean householders in the New York metropolis were engaged in white-collar urban occupations at the time of their departure for the United States. The prevalence of "medical professionals" in table 1.5 draws our attention and indicates a selective demand by American medical institutions for foreign medical workers. We shall discuss in detail this aspect of Korean immigration in chapter five. What is interesting in table 1.6 is that 34 percent of the Korean male householders in the New York metropolis are engaged in commercial businesses, for which they showed but little propensity in their home country, as shown in table 1.5.[33]

In the second place, a majority of Korean immigrants were highly educated in their home country, as indicated in table 1.7, which shows that 67 percent of the Korean householders in the New York metropol-

[33] The two sample surveys contain a regional bias and cannot represent Korean immigrants in the United States. For instance, the high percentage of medical professionals is largely due to the concentration of leading medical institutions in New York's inner city, which attract a bulk of Korean immigrant medical workers.

TABLE 1.4 PERCENTAGE OF KOREAN IMMIGRANTS BY THEIR OCCUPATION AND YEAR OF ENTRY

Occupation	Year of Entry									
	1966	1967	1968	1969	1970	1971	1972	1973	1974	1975
Professional, technical, and kindred workers	14.0	20.9	18.7	17.8	17.3	21.5	18.6	12.7	10.8	10.9
Managers, officials, and proprietors	0.6	0.9	1.1	1.3	1.2	1.6	2.5	3.9	3.4	3.2
Clerical and kindred workers	1.5	1.8	1.6	2.0	1.6	1.3	1.5	1.6	1.7	3.0
Sales workers	0.2	0.2	0.2	0.2	0.2	0.2	0.2	0.3	0.4	0.7
Craftsmen, foremen, and kindred workers	0.2	0.3	0.8	0.8	2.1	2.0	3.0	3.3	5.0	4.4
Operatives and transport operatives	0.2	0.6	0.6	2.7	0.7	0.8	0.7	1.1	1.3	2.2
Private household workers	0.08	0.6	1.3	2.0	0.7	0.3	0.4	0.5	0.9	0.4
Service workers except private household workers	0.7	1.3	1.3	1.5	0.9	1.3	1.7	1.6	2.0	1.8
Farm laborers, foremen, and managers	—	0.12	0.02	0.10	0.05	0.04	0.04	0.4	0.33	0.38
Laborers except farm and mine	0.1	0.1	0.2	0.2	0.1	0.1	0.2	0.2	0.2	0.3
Housewives, children, and others with no occupation or occupation not reported	82.1	72.8	73.7	72.8	74.6	70.3	71.6	74.4	74.0	72.7

SOURCE: Adapted from *The Annual Report of the United States Immigration and Naturalization Service* (1966-1975).

itan area finished college in their home country.[34] This has enabled them to command, at the least, a simple conversational English upon arrival in the United States.

In the third place, Korean immigration is selective in terms of age and sex. A majority are young and thus economically active, and female immigrants outnumber males by two to one. As is shown in table 1.8, more than 90 percent of the Korean immigrants who entered from 1966 to 1975, were under the age of thirty-nine, and the percentage of

[34] The university enrollment of South Korea amounted to 223,600 in 1973, constituting about 8 percent of the college-age population. Nena Vreeland et al., *Area Handbook for South Korea*, Washington D.C., U.S. Government Printing Office, 1975, p. 131.

TABLE 1.5 Occupational Distribution of Korean Householders (at the Time of Their Departure from Korea) in the New York Metropolitan Area

White-collar office workers	31%
Students	6
Teachers	8
Medical professionals	24
Engineers and mechanics	5
Proprietors	5
Small business owners	6
Unemployed	6
Others	9
	100% (560)

Source: Sample survey conducted in 1975 by Jae T. Kim.

TABLE 1.6 Occupational Distribution of Korean Householders in the New York Metropolitan Area

	Male	Female
Retail and wholesale business	29%	3%
Catering business	5	1
Professionals[a]	19	24
Clerical, office workers	5	3
Engineers, mechanics, and operatives	19	2
Students	1	1
Housewives	—	60
Others	22	6
	100% (100)	100% (100)

Source: Sample survey conducted in 1976 by the Korean Consulate General in New York City on the basis of the registration of Korean nationals in the New York metropolitan area.

[a] Professionals mostly consist of medical professionals

TABLE 1.7 Educational Level Attained before Leaving Korea by Korean Householders in the New York Metropolitan Area

High school	12%
Junior college	16
College	67
Other	5
	100% (560)

Source: Sample survey conducted in 1975 by Jae T. Kim.

TABLE 1.8 AGE AND SEX OF KOREAN IMMIGRANTS, 1966-1975

Age	Sex	Years of Entry									
		1966	1967	1968	1969	1970	1971	1972	1973	1974	1975
Under 10	Male	6.4%	6.8%	6.9%	7.7%	7.9%	8.6%	9.4%	11.1%	11.7%	12.9%
	Female	14.2	10.9	12.5	11.6	11.7	12.2	13.7	14.7	14.1	15.9
10-19	Male	3.2	3.3	3.6	2.7	4.1	4.1	4.9	5.9	6.9	8.0
	Female	5.7	6.4	5.8	5.8	5.9	6.0	6.4	7.7	8.2	8.8
20-29	Male	4.2	4.9	5.8	5.9	7.4	6.8	7.5	7.1	6.6	7.4
	Female	39.6	33.5	35.5	35.2	33.1	29.2	25.1	22.3	21.3	18.2
30-39	Male	8.3	13.0	10.1	10.8	10.0	12.7	12.2	9.7	9.4	8.2
	Female	14.0	14.8	12.9	12.5	12.3	12.7	11.7	10.4	10.1	9.4
40-49	Male	1.1	2.0	1.7	1.9	2.0	1.9	2.8	3.0	3.6	3.4
	Female	0.8	1.6	1.6	1.7	2.1	2.1	2.5	2.8	3.2	3.0
50-59	Male	0.2	0.3	0.4	0.5	0.7	0.6	0.9	1.0	1.0	1.1
	Female	0.7	0.8	1.1	1.0	1.0	0.9	1.3	1.9	1.4	1.3
60 and over	Male	0.2	0.5	0.3	0.2	0.3	0.4	0.5	0.7	0.7	0.8
	Female	0.8	0.18	0.8	0.7	0.7	0.7	1.1	1.7	1.4	1.5
Total %	Male	24.0	31.0	29.0	31.0	33.0	36.0	38.0	39.0	40.0	42.0
	Female	76.0	69.0	71.0	69.0	67.0	64.0	62.0	61.0	60.0	58.0
Total number of immigrants		2,492	3,956	3,811	6,045	9,314	14,279	18,876	22,930	28,028	28,362

SOURCE: Adapted from *The Annual Report of the United States Immigration and Naturalization Service* (1966-1975).

immigrants between twenty and thirty-nine years old declined from 66.1 percent in 1966 to 43.2 percent in 1975. This decline was largely caused by the percentage decrease of female immigrants in this age group.

The peculiar numerical prevalence of female immigrants over their male counterparts needs a specific explanation for each age category. In the twenty to twenty-nine age group, a massive influx of Korean nurses and Korean war brides is largely responsible for the high proportion of female immigrants; during the period 1962-1970 a total of 14,554 Korean women came to the United States as wives of American citizens.[35] Most of the citizens, as we have noted, were American soldiers. In addition, the Korean Nurse Association in South Korea estimated that some 7,000 Korean nurses were admitted to the United States either directly from South Korea or by way of third nations, like West Germany and Canada, where they had been previously admitted as migrant workers. On the other hand, the emigration of Korean men

[35] *Chosa Wolbo*, The Korean Industrial Bank, November 1970, p. 27.

in the same age group is seriously limited by the Korean emigration law, which permits exit visas only to those men who honorably finished three years of compulsory military service. According to the law, draft evaders in South Korea are systematically excluded from overseas travel and emigration. This legal restriction partially explains why female immigrants outnumber males in all adult age categories, as shown in table 1.8.

The great number of females in the age groups of fifty years and over is mainly due to the tendency of Korean working couples in the United States to send for their mothers in order to use them as baby sitters or housekeepers. Of course, it cannot be denied that a genuine "filial piety" is also responsible for this phenomenon.

The discrepancy between female and male children under nine years old can be largely attributed to the fact that more girls than boys have been adopted from Korean orphanages by American citizens, who have adopted some 13,000 since 1955.[36] The early adoptions were largely of the abandoned or mixed-blood children produced by the Korean War; later, Americans adopted children abandoned by the urban poor, most of whom had migrated to cities from rural areas. As South Korea has undergone rapid industrialization, the number of abandoned children has increased annually: more than 6,000 children were found abandoned in 1976.[37] Some of them were lucky enough to be adopted, usually in pairs, predominantly by white middle-class Protestant families living in American rural areas or small towns. For reasons of cultural assimilation and aesthetic value, the American families prefer girls to boys; and Korean families under economic privation would rather abandon girls than boys.

Settlement Patterns. Korean immigrants have predominantly settled in the largest metropolitan areas of the United States. As shown in table 1.9, from 1970 to 1975 an average of 30 percent of the Korean immigrants settled in the metropolises of the eastern seaboard along Interstate Highway 95 in a series of adjoining suburbs surrounding major inner cities like Boston, New York, Newark, Philadelphia, Baltimore, and Washington D.C. During the same period an average of 21 percent of the Korean immigrants resided in the Los Angeles metropolitan area, where the 100,000 Korean immigrants constitute the largest single Korean community in the United States. In the New York metropolitan area is found the second-largest Korean community, with a population of some 80,000. In each of the major inner cities of the eastern seaboard exists a Korean ethnic association like the Korean

[36] *New York Times*, March 1, 1977.   [37] *Joogan Hankook*, April 11, 1976.

TABLE 1.9 KOREAN IMMIGRANTS' INTENDED PLACE OF RESIDENCE, 1970-1975

Area	Year of Entry					
	1970	1971	1972	1973	1974	1975
California	22%	19%	20%	21%	22%	23%
(Los Angeles)	(n.a.)	(8)	(8)	(8)	(9)	(9)
Hawaii	6	4	5	6	4	5
Illinois	6	7	7	6	6	6
(Chicago)	(n.a.)	(5)	(5)	(4)	(4)	(4)
Maryland	5	5	6	6	8	7
(Md.-Va. total)	(7)	(8)	(10)	(10)	(13)	(11)
Virginia	2	3	4	4	5	4
New Jersey	4	4	4	4	4	4
(N.J.-N.Y. total)	(15)	(17)	(19)	(15)	(13)	(12)
New York	11	13	15	11	9	8
(New York City)	(n.a.)	(9)	(10)	(7)	(6)	(5)
Pennsylvania	4	4	4	4	5	5
(Philadelphia)	(n.a.)	(2)	(1)	(1)	(2)	(2)
Other States	40	41	35	38	37	38
Total number of immigrants	8,314	14,297	18,876	22,930	28,028	28,362

SOURCE: Adapted from *The Annual Report of the United States and Naturalization Service* (1970-1975).

Association of Greater New York, the Korean Association of Greater Philadelphia, and the Korean Association of Washington D.C. During the same period about 6 percent of the Korean immigrants settled in the Chicago metropolitan area, where some 50,000 Koreans form the third-largest Korean community in the United States. Thus, the three largest urban areas of the United States have absorbed more than 55 percent of the total Korean immigrants. In this context, it should be recalled that these three areas have been the three largest sources of requests for labor certifications to import immigrant workers. During the same period about 5 percent of the Korean immigrants entered the Hawaiian Islands, and the remaining 40 percent scattered over the remaining major urban areas of the United States.

Many Korean immigrants tend to settle in the inner cities largely because of the economic opportunities and the low rents easily available to them. But this traditional tendency is not as strong as one might expect: the bulk of Korean immigrants have directly entered suburban and medium-sized cities wherever they did not encounter housing discrimination because of color and race.[38] Interestingly enough, the percentage of the Korean immigrants who settled in New York City has sharply declined—from 10 percent in 1972 to 5 percent in 1975. Meanwhile, a growing number of the Koreans are entering the Sun Belt, particularly at Houston and Dallas. This shift in the settlement pattern is generally attributed to the economic plight of New York City, which is aggravated by its budget crisis.

The Immigrant Family. Koreans have generally immigrated in their basic social unit, the nuclear family, although frequently a family is temporarily separated so that a pioneer member can establish an economic base, or because of a bureaucratic delay under the United States or South Korean emigration laws. The favorable conditions for either continuing the old family unit or creating a new family in the United States was laid by the humane nature of the Immigration Act of 1965, which permits reunion of immediate relatives. This is clearly indicated in table 1.10, which shows that 86 percent of the Korean householders in the New York metropolitan area are married. And, as shown in table 1.11, 40 percent of the Korean families in the New York metropolis are supported by two working family members, usually husband and wife. This contributes considerably to raising the overall distribution of family income, which is indicated in table 1.12.[39]

This family structure contrasts with that prevalent among the older Korean immigrants as well as the older Chinese immigrants, who encountered an immigration law hostile to the creation of their own families in the new land. As we noted before, a patchwork solution of "picture marriage" arrangements could not be a permanent answer for the extreme shortage of females among the older Korean immigrants. However, the opposite phenomenon, a female surplus in the marriage market, has occurred in the new Korean community largely due to the selective immigration demands of contemporary American society.

Since Korean women outnumber Korean men in the United States, marriageable women face a serious problem in finding husbands. To make matters worse, Korean men, still concerned with the traditional Korean virtue of female chastity, tend to distrust "Americanized" Korean women, who, they think, are too aggressive and disobedient. Thus there has been a strong tendency among eligible men to take a month-

[38] *The Annual Report(s) of the Immigration and Naturalization Service,* 1970-1975.
[39] Here again, the sample survey has a bias derived from the regional character of the New York metropolitan area. A heavy concentration of Korean medical workers and businessmen in New York City contributes to a much higher level of family income than that of Korean immigrants in other regions.

TABLE 1.10 MARITAL STATUS OF KOREAN HOUSEHOLDERS IN THE NEW YORK METROPOLITAN AREA

Single	10%
Married	86
Divorced	2
Separated	1
	99% (559)

SOURCE: Sample survey conducted in 1975 by Jae T. Kim.

TABLE 1.11 NUMBER OF WORKING FAMILY MEMBERS OF KOREAN HOUSEHOLDERS IN THE NEW YORK METROPOLITAN AREA

Number of Working Members	
0	13%
1	42
2	40
3	4
4	1
	100% (560)

SOURCE: Sample survey conducted in 1975 by Jae T. Kim.

TABLE 1.12 DISTRIBUTION OF GROSS FAMILY INCOMES OF KOREANS IN THE NEW YORK METROPOLITAN AREA

Under $10,000	15%
$10,000-15,500	33
$15,501-20,500	19
$20,501-30,000	21
Over $30,000	12
	100% (560)

SOURCE: Sample survey conducted in 1975 by Jae T. Kim.

long chartered plane trip to their home country in order "to pick out a brand-new bride"; and the immigrant women, if they do not find a husband in the United States, have resorted to the same technique. So far both groups have been successful in their marriage ventures because "homeland Koreans are crazy about the Korean-Americans." When negotiating for their marriage in South Korea, Korean-Americans tend to inflate their status in the United States; for instance, small shopkeepers in New York's ghetto areas refer to themselves as "New York businessmen." In an extreme case, a Korean-American converted his driving license into an ID card of the United States Central Intelligence Agency in order to swindle money from a Korean girl, under the pretext of marriage. All these marriage ventures have facilitated kinship-centered immigration because, after marrying in South Korea, Korean-Americans have filed for "family reunion" visas upon returning to the United States.

Returning to Korea to marry is, of course, just one channel of kinship-centered immigration. A high proportion of Korean immigrants send for their entire family once they have acquired citizenship. In this process, a kind of a chain reaction of kinship-centered immigration occurs. That is to say, under "family reunion" preferences, married family members can enter the United States with all their children, and they become eligible to send for their close relatives when they acquire American citizenship. Since immigration is becoming more difficult under the "skill" categories because of a deteriorating American economy, Koreans are now increasingly aware that kinship-centered immigration will become the main avenue for entering the United States. This partly explains why almost all Korean immigrants are looking forward to the day they receive citizenship.

CONCLUSION

The United States Immigration Act of 1965 has generally governed the economic, demographic, educational, and familial characteristics of recent Korean immigrants. But the extent to which their social characteristics have been determined by the selective nature of the act has depended upon their different entry mechanisms. We have seen that students, businessmen, tourists, and retired governmental officials often entered the new land with a nonimmigrant visa and then became permanent residents, which laid the foundation for kinship-centered immigration. Since they were from the "elite" classes of South Korean society, the families who followed them belonged to similar classes. Korean War brides and their families were an exception: most of them came from the lower classes of South Korean society. Needless to say, the selectivity of the immigration law has also been applicable to skilled and professional immigrants, especially medical professionals. The families they brought into the new land also came from the middle or upper-middle classes of South Korea. Thus, "skilled" immigration has produced a further "kinship" immigration within the framework of the immigration law. Perhaps a unique characteristic of the new Korean immigration lies in the easy formation of consanguineous families in the initial stage of socioeconomic adjustment to the new land. This would seem to be an unintended consequence of the Immigration Act of 1965; we shall see the importance of the Korean immigrant family as an economic unit.

The Immigration Act of 1965 resulted from the social and political changes of the 1960s, and so the recent Korean immigration is a serendipitous phenomenon. As far as the preferences for "skilled" immigration are concerned, the act reflects the professionalization, specialization, and centralization of the occupational structure of contemporary American society. Given these changes in the American occupational structure, some segments of the Korean population, especially medical professionals, became primary candidates for emigration to the United States and eagerly grasped this "serendipitous" economic opportunity, as we shall see in chapter five.

In general, a majority of prospective Korean immigrants must be, psychologically and economically, fit for survival in contemporary American society. As we shall see in detail, Korean immigrants experienced a rapid urbanization and industrialization in their homeland before entering the United States, and a high proportion brought with them the means for economic self-establishment in the form of either skills or dollars. This fact distinguishes recent Korean immigrants from the older immigrant groups at the turn of the century, most of which were made up of displaced peasants, the impoverished, and the low-skilled urban proletariat. In addition, mainly because of the selective nature of the Immigration Act of 1965, countries have varied in the number of emigrants each one has sent to the United States within its annual quota: some developing countries are well prepared to send part of their trained labor force into the United States labor market, while other countries are not. This leads us to the question of how occupational or manpower changes in South Korean society are conducive to the emigration of South Koreans to the United States.

We have presented the push factor involved in the Korean emigration mainly in terms of the peculiar political situation of the Korean peninsula—the historical pariah status of Korea as a nation, which is still manifest in the division of North and South Korea. In this context, we have pointed out that refugees from North Korea constitute a heavy portion of the South Korean exodus to the United States. Yet this political push provides us only with a partial explanation for the Korean immigration. We shall explore in the next chapter some basic changes of the South Korean political economy that explain the other aspects of the push factor.

CHAPTER TWO

The Formulation of South Korean Emigration Policy

$\mathbf{A}$s in most developing countries, a "population explosion" has emerged as the most urgent problem confronting South Korean society. The population increase is largely attributable to the adoption of Western preventive medical technology; but, as we shall see, it has other causes as well.

To mitigate this population pressure, the South Korean government in 1962 formulated a specific emigration policy designed to export its surplus people. But few nations have been willing to accept even a limited number of Koreans. Some Latin American nations have admitted Korean emigrants in order to settle their virgin lands; and West Germany, owing to labor shortages, has imported Korean miners and nurses as migrant workers. As we shall note, many of the Koreans in both Latin American nations and West Germany have again migrated to the United States and thus have formed an important part of the Korean-American population.

By the Immigration Act of 1965, South Korea, without exerting diplomatic pressure, was granted a substantial quota of emigrants to the United States. Since the South Korean government did not affect the way in which the United States immigration policy was formulated and carried out, South Koreans have responded to the new immigration law by taking individual initiatives to emigrate. As we shall see, such initiatives include gathering information about residential and job opportunities in the new land, acquiring specific skills that can be sold in the United States labor market, and amassing illegal dollars to be invested mostly in business enterprises in the inner cities of America.

The Population Explosion as a Push Factor

Korean immigrants after they have achieved economic "success" in the new land, feel a moral obligation, derived from their long cultural tradition of Confucianism, to return to their homeland to see their families and friends. The visit also gives them a chance to show off their new status or life style. To their families and friends in South

Korea as well as to their peers in the United States, the visit becomes a symbol of "making it." Consequently, 3,685 out of some 70,000 Koreans living in the Los Angeles metropolitan area visited their homeland during 1976.[1] When asked for their impressions, many noted the population explosion in South Korea simply by saying that "there are too many people. In the Myongdong downtown [district in Seoul] it takes five minutes to make one step forward," or that "there are no playgrounds for children except for roads."

Before entering the United States these emigrants had already experienced this population pressure, which was one of the main push factors for their emigration. But upon returning, they were able to perceive the "population explosion" more clearly because they could easily compare the crowdedness of their home country with the open space of the new land. In spite of the strong governmental attempts since 1962 to control population growth, the population of South Korea increased from 24.9 million in 1960 to 34.6 million in 1975, a 39 percent increase.[2] In 1974 population density in South Korea was 873.1 per square mile, as compared with 58.5 in the United States. The population density of South Korea is the second highest in the world, second only to Bangladesh. In all, about 35 million people compete with one another for the scarce resources of South Korea in an area that is only slightly larger than the state of Maine.

The adoption of Western preventive medical technology at the end of the nineteenth century is largely responsible for this recent population explosion. Antibiotics, insecticides, and immunization have combined to effect a drastic decline of the mortality rate far exceeding that of the fertility rate: the crude birthrate per 1,000 decreased from 35 in 1910 to 30 in 1970, while the crude death rate dropped from 34 to 9 during the same period.[3] The impact of this demographic revolution on the lives of South Koreans is one of the most significant effects of Korea's contact with the West.

The Korean population structure entered the first stage of its demographic transition in the 1920s.[4] The Japanese government, during its colonial occupation of Korea, formulated a comprehensive program of preventive medical services that effected a significant drop in the mortality rate among the Korean population. Immediately after the Korean War, which took a toll of 1.6 million lives, mortality rates drastically decreased again, largely owing to the adoption of preventive medical technology from the United States Army, as well as to massive grants

---

[1] *Hankook Ilbo,* January 23, 1977.

[2] *A Temporary Report on the 1975 Census,* Korean Economic Planning Board, 1976.

[3] Kwon, *The Population of Korea,* p. 46.　　　　　[4] Ibid., p. 18.

of surplus grains from the United States. At the same time, the birth-rate increased to 45 per 1,000 in 1955—a post-Korean War baby boom. Since international migration during that period was negligible, the increasing gap between birthrates and death rates set off a population explosion that continues to the present. This gap has not yet been narrowed enough to complete the last stage of a demographic transition, which is the achievement of a new population stability, largely because South Korea has accepted Western medical technologies without experiencing a comparable change in its traditional family and occupational structure, or its cultural bias against women.[5]

The Korean population structure has also been governed by a political factor that stems from the division of North and South Korea. At the end of World War II about 2.3 million overseas Koreans, most of them from Japan and Manchuria, returned to their homeland. About 80 percent of these entered South Korea, partly because they preferred its "democratic political system." In addition, during the years surrounding the Korean War about 1 million North Koreans took refuge in the South. This redistribution greatly increased the population density of South Korea, which had already been more densely populated than North Korea because its geography is more suited to agriculture. Furthermore, from the end of the Korean War (in 1953) until 1962 the Korean government, faced with a heavy toll of lives from the war, adopted a pronatalist population policy and discouraged emigration. A large population was viewed as a national asset in coping militarily and economically with North Korea. For the same reasons, North Korea adopted a similar pronatalist stance from 1953 to 1972.[6] But faced with population increases that strained its economic and geographic resources, the South Korean military government reversed its pronatalist stance and formulated a population control policy in 1962. This reversal was a part of the first five-year economic development plan.

Partly because of socioeconomic developments conducive to the dissemination of birth-control devices and partly because of the develop-

[5] Korean parents strongly prefer boys to girls. A kind of stigma is given to those families that "are rich with daughters." Thus there is a strong tendency for women "cursed with no son" to continually produce babies until one happens to be a boy. The discrimination against females is derived from Korea's traditional patriarchal family structure and the ideological support of Confucianism. For instance, during the Yi dynasty Korean women lost their names when they were married; only their family names were recorded in the *jogbo*, or family pedigree. This traditional discrimination against women is embedded in the Korean family laws, in which sons are given priority over sisters and even over their mother in the inheritance of property as well as in succession as head of the family.

[6] *Hankook Ilbo*, January 27, 1977.

ment of universal education, the mass media, and centralized bureaucracies,[7] the South Korean government has, since 1962, been able to
launch a successful planning program—so successful that it has been
construed as a model for other developing nations.[8] The annual rate
of population increase was reduced from 2.9 percent in 1961 to 1.64
percent in 1975. An optimistic view might arise from such an impressive accomplishment; however, past policies and tradition still govern
the population structure of the future. Females who were born during
the post-Korean War baby boom (1953 to 1958) are now entering the
reproductive age, and so it is estimated that the annual population
growth will continue to swing upward in the near future.

This prospect of further population increases in a country whose
population density is already the second highest in the world has provoked a sense of panic among South Korean economic planners. In
spite of the "green revolution" in the countryside, largely supported
by the development of new "miracle" hybrid strains of crops, South
Korean self-sufficiency in food dropped from 81 percent in 1970 to 73
percent in 1973. *Newsweek* magazine reported, "Even in Korea where
the HYV's [high yielding varieties] have helped to more than double
rice production, restaurants are forbidden to serve rice-based food for
two days each week and schoolmasters rummage through children's
lunch boxes to make sure that they do not contain more than the allotted measure of rice."[9] To make matters worse, South Koreans' consumption patterns have changed in response to both "a revolution of
rising expectations" and to a new dependence on international markets
and products. For instance, energy consumption per individual doubled between 1960 and 1973.[10] In South Korea, where "even one drop
of oil cannot be produced," this change of consumption patterns helps
explain why the portion of the national energy demand that is met by
foreign oil went up from 7.6 percent to 53.1 percent over the same
period. Thus the South Korean government faces the enormous problem of how to deal with an ever-increasing population that aspires to
a more affluent style of life with limited national resources.[11] Those

[7] Illiteracy in South Korea was at 6.8 percent in 1975. *The CBS News Almanac
1977*, Maplewood, New Jersey, Hammond Almanac, p. 561.

[8] For instance, "If the government continues to back the program as it is doing
now, there is a chance that Korea will be the first country in the world to reduce
its birth rate rapidly before major industrialization." S. M. Keeny, "Korea and
Taiwan: The Score for 1965," *Studies in Family Planning*, no. 19, May 1967, p. 4.

[9] *Newsweek*, Far East edition, May 17, 1976, p. 11.

[10] *The Population Problem of Korea*, a report on the seminar held in March
1976 in Seoul under the auspices of the Korean Development Institute.

[11] For instance, in 1973 South Korea imported basic raw materials whose total
value constituted 42 percent of the national gross product. Ibid.

Koreans who are most exposed to a revolution of rising expectations are most sensitive to the socioeconomic malaise caused by the "population explosion"; they think that "South Korea is not a proper place to live."

One way that the South Korean government could solve this problem is by reducing the sheer size of its population. Since the government cannot deliberately increase mortality rates, emigration and birth control are the two basic techniques available.[12] Consequently the military government, for the first time in the history of Korea, adopted a specific and deliberate emigration policy. The South Korean emigration law, which was amended in 1962, stated that "this amendment, by encouraging people to emigrate to foreign countries, is designed to be geared to a population control policy and thus to contribute to the stability of the national economy."[13] The amendment also aimed at enhancing the national prestige of Korea among the countries receiving its emigrants. This concern with national prestige, partly derived from the face-saving culture of Confucianism, influenced lawmakers to exclude from emigration such social outcasts as ex-convicts, alcoholics, psychotics, and those who cannot perform useful physical labor. Draft evaders or deserters were excluded from emigration because of South Korea's military situation.

In addition to relieving the population pressure, South Korean emigration policy also aimed at securing remittances sent home by Koreans abroad. This purpose, though not manifested in the emigration law, was clearly documented in a "White Paper on Overseas Contracts" published by the South Korean Manpower Administration.

> Overseas contracts and ordinary emigration provide us with the two ways by which we could earn foreign currencies and ameliorate the worsening unemployment problem. However, overseas contracts differ from ordinary emigration in the following points. First, because overseas contract laborers remit to their families the money they earn in foreign countries, they greatly contribute to the balance of payments as well as to the creation of national industrial capital.
>
> As we know, they will not spend their money in the foreign countries. Let us look at the Italian case. The Italian government does not allow its migrant workers to take their families with them, in order to make them send money to their families they left behind. Second, when they return home after finishing labor contracts, they

[12] The seriousness of the Korean population problem is well reflected in such slogans adopted by the Korean Wives Club as "1974 is the Year of Not-to-Become-Pregnant," and "Love Your Country by Engaging in Contraception."

[13] *Yimin baeg-gwa* [Emigration Encyclopedia], Seoul, Bak Moon Sa, 1964, p. 361.

greatly contribute to the development of national industry with the skills they learned in foreign countries.[14]

During the period from 1963 to 1974 the South Korean "overseas contract" workers and emigrants remitted about $720 million to their families in their home country.[15] The remittances from overseas Koreans totaled about $155 million during 1975.[16] Korean law requires that all foreign currencies sent from overseas be deposited in the Korean national bank, the Bank of Korea, in order to improve the Korean balance of payments. The families receive their remittances in the basic unit of Korean currency, the won.

THE CLASSIFICATION OF EMIGRANTS

Korean emigration law divides emigration into three categories. The first, called "group emigration," is made up of those emigrants whose entry into specific nations is arranged by negotiations between the South Korean government and the receiving nations. This group emigration is, at a practical level, identical with Korean emigration to Latin American nations since the amendment of the South Korean emigration law in 1962. The second category is called "contract emigration," in which each individual enters a contract with a prospective employer in the receiving nation. These are arranged largely by emigration companies in South Korea, and this group largely consists of "occupational" or "skilled" immigrants into the United States, as discussed in the previous chapter. The third category, called "special emigration," consists of those emigrants who have been invited by individuals or private or public organizations in the receiving nations. This group actually includes, with a few exceptions, immigrants into the United States like "relative preference" family members, Korean War brides, and orphans.

Overseas contract workers can be added to the previously defined "official" emigrant groups, although they are not defined as emigrants by the South Korean emigration law. Nevertheless, they constitute an unofficial emigrant contingent because a bulk of them have entered the United States via the nations into which they had previously migrated as contract workers between 1963 and 1974. For example, about 17,000 Korean nurses and miners (who were not miners but college-

<hr/>

[14] Haeoe chueob baegseo [White Paper on Overseas Contracts], The Korean Manpower Administration, 1966, p. 11.

[15] Of the total sum, $286.4 million was sent from Korean immigrants and contract workers in North American nations. Dong-A Almanac, Seoul, Dong-A Ilbo Co., 1975, p. 423.

[16] Hankook Shinmoon, Ootober 23, 1976.

educated and unemployed urban youth) migrated to West Germany and were employed in these two occupations.[17] Their legal status in West Germany was different from the status of Korean immigrants in the United States in that the United States has guaranteed citizenship to its immigrants, whereas West Germany has expelled its migrant workers when faced with economic recession. The more tolerant atmosphere of contemporary American society, plus its greater economic opportunities, has encouraged a heavy transfer of these Korean nurses and miners from West Germany to the United States since the passage of the Immigration Act of 1965. A majority of them have entered the United States as families in which the Korean miner is husband and the Korean nurse is wife; they were entitled to enter the United States by virtue of the nursing skills of the wife. South Korea had also sent some 25,000 contract workers to South Vietnam to work for American companies there during the Vietnamese War, and many of them have also entered the United States. Moreover, some 30,000 Koreans emigrated to such Latin American nations as Brazil, Argentina, Paraguay, and Bolivia since the amendment of the Korean emigration law in 1920.[18] Many of them have also entered the United States, usually with tourist status, and have managed to acquire permanent residency by investing a specified sum of money to set up small business enterprises in the United States.

In contrast with the United States, with which the South Korean government could not take the initiative in sending or resettling its emigrants, the four Latin American nations mentioned above have cooperated with the South Korean government and thus have allowed it a greater flexibility in fostering emigration. In fact, only these four Latin American nations and the United States have shown any willingness to accept Korean emigrants. With Latin American nations, the concept of "seed" emigration was evolved. These nations, especially Brazil and Argentina, have wanted to import Korean farmers to settle and develop their virgin lands, and the South Korean government has responded by emphasizing "group emigration," in which Korean emigrant families settle together in designated lands in order to develop vast agricultural colonies that serve as bases for inducing even more South Koreans to migrate. But this agricultural "group settlement" has not yet been successful. The crucial reason is that a majority of Korean immigrants had never been farmers, although farming experience was an official criterion for their selection. Most of them were well-educated urbanites, and, as we have noted in the first chapter, more than half were North Korean refugees possessing acumen for commer-

[17] *Dong-A Almanac*, p. 423.　　　　[18] *Hankook Ilbo*, May 5, 1977.

cial enterprises. Consequently, after arriving at the lands designated by Latin American nations, Korean immigrants began almost immediately to move to large cities in order to engage in commercial ventures.[19] They are now concentrated in a few large cities in Brazil and Argentina such as São Paulo, Buenos Aires, and Rio de Janeiro. In São Paulo, for instance, some 13,000 Koreans have established an ethnic territorial enclave by "invading" a slum area that was once a den of prostitutes.[20]

Many of these emigrants have remigrated to the United States. Like the contingent from West Germany, the Koreans in the New York metropolitan area who entered the United States via Latin American nations are noted for their business enterprises. Thus the United States has been the final gathering place for the Koreans abroad.

THE SOUTH KOREAN REACTION TO THE IMMIGRATION ACT OF 1965

The United States, after passing the Immigration Act of 1965, became the only nation willing to admit Korean immigrants in large numbers. For South Koreans, the word "emigration" is now almost synonymous with emigration into the United States. Since the change of South Korean emigration law in 1962, about 75 percent of all Korean emigrants have entered the United States; yet, unlike its effectiveness in Latin America, the South Korean government has not been able to affect the way in which United States immigration policy has been determined. Furthermore, the South Korean Ministry of Health and Social Affairs, which deals with the overall problem of emigration and overseas contracts, has had to take for granted the Korean emigration to the United States; it has not been able to formulate a national policy in this respect. Nevertheless, two phenomena have occurred in South Korea as a direct result of emigration to the United States. First, the South Korean government has formulated emigration policies to control the exodus of wealthy Koreans and their dollars and to influence the Korean immigrant community in the United States. Second, the Korean emigration to the United States has contributed to a change in the occupational structure of the homeland. Let us first focus on this second development.

As we have already discussed in the first chapter, Koreans have migrated to the United States by individual initiative, but within the basic framework of the United States Immigration Act of 1965. They have acted either from knowledge of specific skills needed in the labor

[19] "Nam-mi eui hangug-in" [Koreans in Latin America], Dong-A Ilbo, July 30-August 5, 1974.
[20] Hankook Ilbo, October 23, 1975.

market or from the advantage of having close relatives already living in the United States. In thus taking the initiative, prospective emigrants have contributed to a selective change in South Korean educational and economic institutions. As we shall see later in a case study, the selective demand for Korean medical professionals has caused a dramatic expansion of Korean medical schools, and this is but one of many examples showing a selective interaction of economic institutions in the form of labor exchanges and trade between the two nations. The processes of interaction, as determined by United States immigration and economic policies, have provided a high portion of Korean immigrants with major entry points into the American economy, but they have also produced an unequal distribution of these "emigration" or economic opportunities. A Korean newspaper in 1975 carried a front-page story on the bad fortune of more than 10,000 prospective Korean emigrants.

> In spite of the fact that "contract" emigration into the United States is no longer possible, because of the recent United States economic recession, the emigration companies [in South Korea], licensed by the Ministry of Health and Social Affairs, are still recruiting emigrants in order to receive a $1,200 commission for each contract. This will add more people to the long list of "emigration victims," numbering more than 10,000, who have finished all the necessary domestic procedures but who cannot receive visas from the United States Embassy [in South Korea]. . . . The number of the "emigration victims" has drastically increased since last April [1975], when the United States State Department decided that the embassy should not issue visas to the "contract" emigrants. The decision of the United States Department of State reflected the bad situation of the American economy, aggravated by the Arab oil embargo and by the influx of some 150,000 South Vietnamese refugees. . . .
>
> Unfortunately enough, most of these applicants for emigration have already sold their properties and quit their jobs. . . . And yet the B—— emigration company is still advertising the recruitment of "overseas" emigrants, saying that it has received new job offers from the United States for such workers as shoe repairmen, foundrymen, housemaids, mechanics, cooks, etc. . . .[21]

Except for highly trained and specialized workers like medical professionals and also excepting wealthy "runaway" emigrants, many Korean emigrants to the United States have prepared themselves in their homeland by acquiring the kinds of occupational skills useful for mak-

[21] *Hankook Ilbo*, October 24, 1975.

ing an initial adjustment to the United States economy. This is so regardless of whether they are "skilled" or "kinship" immigrants. Many "skilled" immigrants had learned, over a short period of time, the kinds of skills that could most easily get them labor contracts with American employers. Some of them acquired the specific skills only for the purpose of being entitled to the "occupational preferences" under the United States immigration law.

As a consequence of this demand for job training, all kinds of training schools, specifically geared to the needs of "overseas" contract workers or emigrants, have flourished in the urban areas of South Korea. Schools for operators of heavy construction equipment are now booming, since South Korea has sent more than 50,000 overseas construction workers to Arab nations.[22] They are currently working on more than $6 billion worth of construction projects run by South Korea construction companies. However, the schools that are most directly relevant to the economic adjustment of Korean immigrants are schools for auto repairmen, dressmakers, radio and television repairmen, welders, computer programmers, embroiderers, and hairdressers, to name a few. Thus, an advertisement in *Yeoseong Joong-Ang* (April 1976) for a dressmaking and embroidering school runs:

> Highly popular skills in the United States, Canada, and Latin American nations guarantee more than $2,000 a month. This school offers a special course for prospective overseas emigrants, and individualized and speedy instruction for those prospective emigrants who need the skills urgently. We are using designs that are currently popular in the United States.

Similar advertisements could be found for the other types of training. However, except for some labor-intensive skills like garment making, the skills learned over short periods of time in South Korea cannot be easily utilized in the United States. This is so mainly because of the different licensing systems in the United States, but the low level of skills acquired by Korean immigrants is also responsible. If the immigrants had a higher level of skill and more working experience, they would face much less difficulty in finding work.

On the whole, licensing systems in the United States have been a major barrier to all Korean immigrants wishing to use the skills they have brought with them, either in semiskilled or highly professional fields. Take Mr. Lee for example.

> Mr. Lee was able to immigrate to the United States about one year ago at the invitation of his brother, who came to the United States

[22] *New York Times*, June 19, 1978.

about fifteen years ago with a student visa and became a United States citizen. Mr. Lee's brother, Jin-ho, is a laboratory technician in the field of chemistry. Mr. Lee graduated from a teachers' college in South Korea with Korean literature as a major and was able to find a teaching job if he wished. But he did not want to make his career as a high school teacher belonging to the class of small "sarari" [salary] men. Thus he wrote to his brother in the United States, begging for his help: "I do not want to end up as a high school teacher. I do not want to inhale chalk powder until I die. Please, bring me to the United States."

In subsequent correspondence, Mr. Lee asked his brother for suggestions as to how he should prepare himself occupationally before his entry into the United States, because his academic knowledge of Korean literature is useless in the United States job market. Specifically, he wanted to know from his brother what skill that could be learned over a short period of time in South Korea would be most saleable in the United States labor market. His brother suggested that he might rather bring with him a small sum of capital than a skill, because his brother saw that many new Korean immigrants have successfully run small businesses in New York City. His brother also advised him to learn how to drive a car, and basic conversational English. However, Mr. Lee could not receive the desired sum of money from his father, who has made some money through land speculation at the outskirts of Seoul. Thus Mr. Lee decided to learn welding, after he read a Korean newspaper article on the "contract" immigrants to the United States. He enrolled himself at a small welding school in Seoul nine months before he came to the United States. At the welding school he met a Korean American from California who had temporarily visited South Korea in order to learn welding. Mr. Lee heard from him that there was a big shortage of welders in the United States in the construction of the Alaska pipeline and that many Korean welders in California earned more than seven dollars an hour, and that in the case of pipe welding they could make more than ten dollars an hour. Shortly before his departure for the United States, Mr. Lee finished welding school and received a diploma.

Mr. Lee entered Dallas, Texas, partly because his fiancee, who had arrived one year earlier, worked for a Korean-run wig store in a black neighborhood in Dallas, and partly because he thought that welding jobs were easily available there. When looking for a welding job in Dallas, Mr. Lee found that employers asked for an American welding license from the ASME and that the welding diploma he received in Korea was useless. Furthermore, he realized that his welding skill was extremely poor because of his lack of experience. He decided to attend welding school in Dallas in order to receive an American welding license, and he began to work as a welding helper during the day while going to school during evening hours (field notes).

During the summer of 1976 a daily newspaper in South Korea, the *Choson Ilbo*, carried a series of reports on the life of Korean immigrants in the United States. The reports, which were somewhat impressionistic but had some insight, became a national sensation. Although the author argued that he intended to check Korean fantasies about America by conveying the realities of Korean immigration—the hardships, estrangements, identity dilemmas, the whole tragicomedy— the reports acted instead as a boomerang: they intensified the "American fantasy" among many Korean urbanites. This is so because Koreans living in overurbanized cities with keen economic competition tend to romanticize the typical economic ventures of Korean immigrants in the United States.

The report aroused animated gossip and conversations. Some Koreans exclaimed, "they can save $3,000 a month in *yachaesang* (the vegetable business)" when they read the following account.

For Mr. L., counting money at night is the sole compensation for the hardship and estrangement he must endure as an immigrant. After taking out all the expenses [for a vegetable and fruit store], he makes a day's profit of $200. Korean vegetable and fruit stores have emerged as a famous ethnic business in New York City; the *New York Times* reported on them. Jews originally started this business, but Italians have replaced Jews; about four years ago Koreans began to take over the business from Italians. Blacks might have entered the business, but they wouldn't have been successful because of their lazy nature. On the other hand, Koreans work so hard that they can overcome competition. Furthermore, as far as the things that directly enter the mouth are concerned, customers like cleanliness. Koreans attract customers because they handle all kinds of vegetable stuffs cleanly.[23]

The series of reports was published as the book *Day and Night of Komericans: A Visit to Korea in the United States.* It became a national best seller not only because it dealt with the national issue of Korean emigration to the United States but also because it provided prospective emigrants with essential information as to how they might

[23] Yong-tae Kim, *Komerican eui naj gwa bam* [Day and night of Komericans], Seoul, Han Jin Sa, 1976, p. 90.

prepare themselves occupationally or psychologically for their future life in the new land. It has become a textbook for prospective emigrants by supplementing legal guidance on how to emigrate and secure overseas contracts. However, this episode is just one example of how prospective emigrants in South Korea are informed about possible economic opportunities in the United States. Similar reports sent by Korean newspaper correspondents in the United States and frequent visits from Korean-Americans returning to their homeland have also provided major communication channels to prospective emigrants. Nonetheless, Korean emigration companies and travel agencies have been the major organizations behind the emigration boom, for they are the chief means by which would-be Korean emigrants find their way into the economic institutions of the United States.

The Role of Emigration Companies

The United States Immigration Act of 1965 was enacted so suddenly and so unexpectedly that many Koreans, though well qualified to immigrate, did not know how to do so. In the absence of a government agency to prepare Koreans for dealing with various legal and economic problems, a number of emigration and overseas contract companies emerged in the United States to recruit workers from South Korea. By spreading among their potential Korean customers reports about the economic rewards available in the United States, they also contributed to the emigration boom in South Korea. And by engaging in extralegal or illegal activities, some companies reaped huge profits.

The Korean emigration companies were established and run by early immigrants, most of whom came to the United States with student visas and received their higher education in American universities. Here is an example of how a Korean emigration company was established and operated.

Mr. Nam came to the United States about twenty years ago in order to study at an American university, and he earned a master's degree. In the late 1960s, when Korean immigration into the United States had just started, he set up the New World emigration company in New York City with a branch office in Seoul staffed by close relatives. His main profit came from commissions he received for filling contracts between American employers and South Korean workers.

His branch office in Seoul also received commissions for executing domestic emigration procedures on behalf of Korean emigrants. Mr. Nam, usually operating out of his main office in New York City, tried to find American employers willing to hire Korean workers. One of his main focuses in recruitment was Korean nurses. In the late 1960s Korean nurses did not know how to find prospective American employers, although American medical institutions at that time faced a keen shortage of medical professionals and were eager to import foreign medical professionals. It is said that "he had brought in several hundred Korean nurses" to be employed at small county hospitals in New Jersey and Pennsylvania. He became a notorious figure among Korean nurses he had imported: he was accused of imposing an indenture system on the Korean nurses when he arranged contracts for them.

In order to import as many Korean nurses as possible, Mr. Nam sought out the hospitals that faced financial problems and thus were forced to hire cheap foreign-born nurses instead of expensive American ones. Since Korean nurses worked hard and rarely complained (mainly because of their language problem), hospitals tended to exploit Korean nurses through low wages and overwork. Thus when Korean nurses began to work at M. hospital in New Jersey, for instance, they found that a majority of nurses in the hospital were made up of foreign-born, Asian nurses, especially Filipinos. Unlike Filipino nurses, who occupied major positions on nursing staffs, the Koreans, being latecomers with poor English, had to endure great humiliation: only the Korean nurses did not receive sick pay; Korean nurses were told that they could not transfer to other hospitals and that, if they attempted to do so, they would be penalized for violating their original contractual obligations. However, as the Korean nurses became accustomed to America, they became aware that such treatment constituted a violation of American law. They knew that many hospitals in New York were willing to hire them under a temporary licensing system. But the hospital insisted that it could not write references for them. Thus some of the Korean nurses went to American lawyers and some to Korean community leaders in order to bring outside pressure to bear upon the hospital. The hospital was finally forced to release the Korean nurses who wished to work for other hospitals, and all the Korean nurses were ultimately able to escape the sweatshop hospital.

Although a majority of the Korean nurses could not have come to the United States without arrangements similar to Mr. Nam's contracts, they began to criticize Mr. Nam for his inhumane immigration business, in which he was presumed to sell the Korean nurses to exploitive American employers. Mr. Nam received a $400 commission for each nursing labor contract; he defended himself by saying that he had to hire American lawyers to work out the labor contracts. The Korean nurses paid the commission fee in installments out of their paychecks; they assumed that Mr. Nam had a direct deal with hospital personnel.

Mr. Nam's venture had become a community issue when Mr. Nam ran in 1971 for the presidency of the Korean Association of Greater New York. The opposition publicized his difficulties with the nurses as a means of attacking Mr. Nam (field notes).

This is just one of the unpleasant episodes that have stemmed from Korean labor contracts. In an extreme case, a Korean emigration company forged labor contracts; that is to say, the United States employers named in the contracts did not exist. This brought forth an investigation from the United States Immigration and Naturalization Service. Frauds have also taken place in South Korea through such devices as forged passports and labor certificates and bogus marriages with Korean-Americans. This sort of fraud has been so rampant that officials at the United States Embassy in South Korea reportedly joked with one another that "Koreans are such geniuses that they could receive the signature of God if we required it."

These kinds of emigration frauds have been stimulated by changes in United States immigration policy and practice, especially the sudden change in 1965, which has gradually caused an emigration boom among some segments of the Korean population. Those who were lucky could quickly sense the economic opportunities and other social benefits available in the United States, and thus they were able to immigrate much earlier than others. Most of them have achieved some degree of economic success in the United States. They are the *miguk gocham* (the old-timers). As we shall see, this term includes such professionals as medical doctors and nurses, and also wig merchants, garment importers, ethnic accountants, lawyers, and ministers, whose economic successes were largely made possible by their early arrival. Most of them have become suburban homeowners.

As the emigration boom enters full swing in South Korea—that is to say, while every qualified Korean is aware of all plausible rewards generated by "the crossing of the Pacific"—entry into the United States is becoming more and more difficult. This is so partly because of the United States restriction on skilled immigrants and partly because of the ever-increasing surplus of applications beyond the annual United States quota for Korean immigration. This discrepancy between the shrinking emigration quotas and the emigration boom in South Korea has generated the latest kinds of fraud. During the year 1975, the following headlines were spotted in major Korean newspapers; "Illegal Emigration Brokers Are Rampant As Emigration Becomes More Difficult," "Waves of Emigration Bankruptcies and Malpractices: Many

Victims Already Sold Properties and Stopped Children's Education," "International Marriage Emigration by Using False Birth Certificate," "A Major Government Crackdown on Camouflage Emigrants," "A Sudden Drop in Emigration Applicants: Reflection of Government Crackdown: A Special Measure Needed for Emigrants of Good Intention."

In order to prevent such frauds, especially in the arrangement of labor contracts with American employers, the South Korean government has imposed a licensing system on emigration activities, and it has recognized only two emigration companies. This decision dealt a serious blow to more than 100 emigration-related agencies both in South Korea and the United States, including emigration and overseas contract agencies, travel agencies, and overseas employment agencies. The government action is understandable in light of the fact that United States immigration policy is the decisive factor in Korean emigration; no matter how the agencies strive and compete with one another to establish labor contracts with American employers, they hardly affect the actual number of Koreans admitted to the United States. In this sense, some companies did not originally intend to commit "emigration bankruptcies," which means that they failed to establish labor contracts although they had received an advance on the emigration fee. They had to face emigration bankruptcies because they accepted emigration applications on the assumption that the United States would continue to admit skilled immigrants under their labor contracts.

In spite of the intended or unintended malpractice and fraud, emigration companies facilitated the Korean influx into the United States. Without their liaison role, a high proportion of the early immigrants, the skilled medical professionals and blue-collar workers, could not have entered the United States. However, many blue-collar workers were fired within a month of their employment in the new land, and many Korean nurses were not well placed, being almost illiterate in English. The following article in a Korean ethnic newspaper expressed this point of view:

Korean emigration brokers in Washington, D.C., and Baltimore met together July 2 [1975] at the office of the *Hankook Shinmoon* in response to the Korean government's recent adoption of a licensing system for emigration activities, which was followed by the government's investigation of the illegal practices of emigration companies [in South Korea]. They adopted a resolution stating that: (1) the Korean government should initiate an effective emigration policy; (2) the Korean government should provide an equal opportunity for all emigration companies to receive licenses; and (3) the Korean government should help establish "good" emigration companies. They also warned that, if their demands were not met by the Korean government, they would divert their business activities to other countries. . . . They reminded the Korean government of the fact that they had greatly contributed to making Korean immigrants the third-largest ethnic group to enter the United States during the last three years.[24]

THE FLIGHT OF DOLLARS FROM SOUTH KOREA

As has been noted, the seemingly endless confrontation between North and South Korea has stimulated the exodus of members of the South Korean urban elite. Their exodus has been accompanied by a flow of dollars into the United States, the safest place for Koreans to store their money. For many Korean immigrants, the dollars they have brought with them have been one of the main sources of capital for their small businesses in such inner cities as New York, Chicago, or Los Angeles. According to a *New York Times* report on this aspect of the immigration,

the second and more recent group includes many well-to-do Korean businessmen who do not necessarily oppose the current Government but are seeking a refuge for money because of fears that the Park regime might collapse or there might be a Communist takeover of South Korea. The exodus of such money has increased sharply, according to banking sources, since the fall of South Vietnam, which led to fears the United States might not act to block a North Korean invasion of South Korea.

According to banking officials and other people, hundreds of wealthy businessmen have smuggled in large amounts of cash out of South Korea during the last two years and invested in California real estate and small businesses, particularly liquor stores, bars, and small grocery stores.

It is not uncommon for real estate agents in some affluent communities here to tell stories of Korean wives who arrived here to buy homes costing more than $100,000 and paid for them in cash, sometimes out of paper bags.

A Korean-language newspaper reported that a former colonel in the South Korean Marine Corps, Kim Hae Young, who is said to have close ties to the Korean Central Intelligence Agency and who has organized a pro-government organization called the Korean-

[24] *Hankook Shinmoon,* July 15, 1975.

American Marine Association, had purchased a liquor store for $100,000 in $100 bills. He denied any improprieties. . . .

Many Korean business executives and, in some cases, Government officials have sent their wives and children here while they continue to work in South Korea. These executives regularly send large amounts of money to this country that are then invested in business or homes or other real estate, with the expectation that the head of the family will join the others here later, according to the sources. . . .[25]

From the South Korean government's point of view, it hurts the national interest to let wealthy Koreans escape freely to the United States with large amounts of dollars. Such an exodus is viewed as harmful because capital, which is largely amassed by commercial loans from advanced nations, especially from the United States, thus leaks back into the United States and because such "escape" emigration is thought to demoralize national solidarity in the confrontation with North Korea. Consequently South Korea formulated an emigration policy to curb the exodus of the urban elite and their dollars.

As noted in the *Times* article, the communists' victory in South Vietnam renewed the exodus of rich Koreans to the United States. In response, the South Korean government passed in 1975 a special immigration law exclusively dealing with "eligibility for overseas emigration." The following persons were excluded from emigration: (1) persons who own properties valued more than $100,000; (2) military officers and retired generals; and (3) high-ranking government officials, incumbent or retired, including national assemblymen, judges, presidents of national corporations, and others of similar status. In addition, an administrative censure was imposed on various Korean celebrities who were suspected of being "camouflaged emigrants," who had already taken some steps toward emigration such as acquiring large sums of dollars, moving wives and children to the United States, and taking out "multiple" passports issued by the South Korean Foreign Ministry.

When wealthy Koreans do manage to emigrate, they normally bring large amounts of dollars to the United States in spite of a strict South Korean foreign currency law designed to curb this outflow. A recent arrival said, "Anybody can bring in dollars if he has something to sell in Korea. If one makes up one's mind, there are many ways to bring in dollars." The amount of dollars that Korean immigrants carry in from their home country varies from person to person, reflecting a continuation in the new land of one's old economic status. But many Korean

[25] *New York Times*, October 30, 1975.

immigrant families were not well-to-do; they had to buy airplane tickets on credit, and they brought with them much less than the legal limit of $1,000 allowed for each member of an emigrant family. On the other hand, some middle-class families have been able to smuggle in fortunes of several hundred thousand dollars. These they usually produced by selling their Korean real estate. With the dollars thus amassed they usually start a small business in one of the United States' inner cities. And upper-class business families have sometimes brought in "several million" dollars apiece to invest in the United States real estate market.

There are several familiar ways by which dollars are smuggled from South Korea. The first is a primitive one in which prospective emigrants buy dollars from dollar merchants in black markets and come out of the Kimpo International Airport hiding dollars somewhere in their packages or on their bodies. The dollars, in the form of $100 bills, can be placed inside children's stockings or shoes, books, scrolls, or Korean hot-sauce (*gochujang*) pots. This method has been successful; few have been uncovered by custom officials at the Kimpo International Airport.

Dollar Alley is located in the westside section of the Myondong downtown [district] in Seoul, whose economic and cultural role is a combination of New York's Greenwich Village and Fifth Avenue. It has been called "Dollar Alley" since the end of the Korean War because woman "dollar merchants" squat at the corners of buildings and trade dollars. It is also a hustling and bustling place for black-marketing foreign goods. Those Seoul citizens who have just returned from overseas trips with dollars but have not reported their possession to custom officials come to Dollar Alley in order to change their dollars into Korean currency at a rate higher than the official exchange. In addition, foreign tourists, as well as those Koreans who have acquired some dollars by catering to American soldiers, come here for the same purpose.

The alley is also the place where prospective emigrants can exchange Korean currency for dollars with woman "dollar merchants," who have to risk frequent encounters with robbers who pretend to be customers and induce the women to go to nearby hotel rooms, where they sometimes kill them. These incidents have frequently occupied big headlines in major Seoul newspapers.

One undercover police agent from Namdaemoon Police Station hangs around in order to detect only big transactions. By taking regular payoffs from woman "dollar merchants," the authority concerned connives at small transactions. However, it is an informal obligation for "dollar merchants" to report to the undercover police agent when they engage in a transaction of more than 5,000 dollars. If prospective emigrants are involved in big transactions, the information could lead to their arrest. Thus it is a wise tactic for prospective emigrants to change dollars through a number of small transactions (field notes).

This is a typical, crude form of "dollar exodus" by which failure to some extent results simply from bad luck. As a modification of this method, some Korean emigrants have asked such Americans as missionaries, businessmen, or soldiers to carry their dollars to the United States for them, in return for commission or gifts. And some emigrants have asked American businessmen or those Koreans who open personal checking accounts at American banks to draw on them in return for Korean currency, since "personal checks are the easiest things to be smuggled out."

The second form of "dollar flight" evolves from the practice of most Korean immigrants in the United States of sending remittances to their families in South Korea. Prospective Korean emigrants pay Korean currency to the South Korean families of American immigrants in return for a pledge that they will be paid back in dollars by someone in America after they enter the United States. If a prospective emigrant cannot trust his or her "partner" in the United States, the transaction can be made almost simultaneously by using the international telephone system; that is to say, the prospective emigrant can ask the partner in the United States to deliver the corresponding amount of dollars to a third person in the United States, usually a relative or friend. Immediately after the third person confirms the delivery in code over the telephone, the prospective emigrant delivers the Korean currency to the partner's family. For Korean-American immigrants and their families in the homeland, this kind of transaction yields much more Korean currency than the official exchange rate allows. And since dollars do not physically come out of South Korea, this method does not evoke the agony of "being a national traitor."

The third form of "dollar exodus" is based upon the international trade between South Korea and the United States. Compared with the two aforementioned methods, the volume of transactions by this method is much larger: it involves millions of dollars. There are two mechanisms: the first derives from overvaluing imported raw materials; the second, from undervaluing exported goods. The first mechanism requires that, when Korean manufacturers import raw materials from foreign countries, especially from the United States (and thus convert Korean currency into dollars at the Bank of Korea, which regulates national inflows and outflows of dollars), the manufacturers falsify documents and inflate the prices of imported raw materials. They allocate the excess over actual costs to their branches in the United States, to brokers, or to American exporting firms, under the direction that the balance should be deposited in American banks or delivered to friendly Koreans in the United States.

The opposite technique can be applied when Korean manufacturers export their products to the United States: they undervalue their exported items. That is to say, they report lower prices to the Bank of Korea than they actually receive in payment from American importers and divert the balance to the United States. In addition to these two typical ways of exporting dollars, a majority of Korean exporting or importing companies, when reporting to the Bank of Korea, overestimate their expenses in the operation of overseas branches; and many Korean companies operating in foreign countries, such as construction and transportation companies, do not send back to South Korea some of the dollars they earn there.

In view of the South Korean government's centralized control over the flow of dollars, this sort of diversion of dollars by South Korean business firms is part of their normal operations. An immigrant who works for a South Korean business branch in New York City said, "All companies divert dollars into foreign countries. Without doing it they cannot run their businesses." This kind of dollar diversion, which is of course restricted to the South Korean upper business classes, is inherently linked with South Korean governmental corruption. A Korean economics student in New York City who once worked for the Bank of Korea said, "Without some protection from someone in a higher level, they cannot divert such big amounts of dollars into the United States. Governmental investigations have been focused upon small fish rather than big ones."

As we shall discuss in the next chapter, this exodus of dollars to the United States is clearly connected with the peculiar structure of the South Korean economy, which is heavily based upon commercial loans from advanced nations. It is also derived from the economic and ideological fragility of the new industrial and business classes of South Korea, whose emergence is largely made possible by the Korean government-guaranteed commercial loans from advanced nations. Some owners of "the foreign-country business-loan" firms have sent their wives and children to the United States, but they have to stay in South Korea in order to take care of their businesses, many of which are on the brink of bankruptcy.

"There is an amazing amount of money coming in," said a Korean-speaking attorney here [in Los Angeles] whose clients include some of these newcomers. "I know of one man who owns a big business in Korea. His son has bought a $150,000 home here, has a $400,000 business, and is now buying a $250,000 business; he is less than 30 years old."[26]

CONCLUSION

The South Korean population has rapidly increased, largely under the impact of Western preventive medicine. The widening gap between mortality and fertility rates due to the introduction of Western medical technology is a general cause of population increase in developing countries, but this does not sufficiently explain the rapid growth of the South Korean population; South Korean population dynamics also involve political and cultural factors. Mainly because of the government's view that a large population was a national asset in its continuing military and economic confrontation with North Korea, after the Korean War the South Korean government adopted a pronatalist population policy that remained in effect until 1962, when the military government formulated a population-control policy as part of the first five-year economic development plan. But the policy was adopted too late to prevent the post-Korean War baby boom, which is responsible for the vast number of women of child-bearing age in the 1970s.

Compared with other developing countries, South Korea has shown a modest rate of population growth since 1965. However, this modest growth has nonetheless provoked a sense of panic among the politically conscious South Koreans because South Korea is small, has few natural resources, and has a low level of domestic agricultural production, and because the population density of South Korea is the second highest in the world.

South Korean emigration policy was formulated in order to mitigate an increasing population pressure; it was an extension of the domestic population-control policy. In contrast to the nineteenth century, when European nations exported vast numbers of their surplus population also largely produced by an application of preventive medical technology, a worldwide demand for immigrants has not existed in the twentieth century. Only a few nations have been willing to accept South Korean emigrants: the United States Immigration Act of 1965 has allowed, as of 1980, the entry of some 350,000 South Koreans on the basis of skills and kinship; and a few Latin American nations accepted South Koreans who had experience in agriculture and who were willing to develop their virgin lands. But, since most Korean immigrants to Latin America were well-educated urban refugees from North Ko-

[26] Ibid.

rea, they settled predominantly in urban commercial centers rather than in the agricultural colonies designated by the receiving nations. A large proportion of these Koreans have remigrated to the United States. Similarly, many Korean contract workers in West Germany and South Vietnam have remigrated to the United States. Thus, the emerging Korean community in the United States has drawn its population from both Korea itself and from several way stations.

South Korean emigration to the United States has been especially sensitive to the selective interaction of the labor markets in the two countries: labor shortages in specific occupations in the United States have allowed the immigration of South Koreans with specific skills, who in turn have responded selectively to these specific manpower demands of the United States. A bulk of South Korean prospective emigrants, regardless of whether they are skilled or "kinship-centered," have prepared themselves by acquiring special skills or at least the appearance of having skills that could be utilized in the United States. In this process, South Korean emigration companies have been labor brokers between the two countries, thus facilitating Korean emigration to the United States.

In addition to their skills, many Korean immigrants have brought illegal dollars. We have specifically noted that the largest proportion of the "dollar exodus" is based upon the trade between South Korea and the United States. This inflow of dollars has been one of the main sources of capital for Korean businesses in the inner cities of the new land and has thus become one of the economic bases for the emerging Korean community in the United States. In coping with this "dollar exodus," the South Korean government in 1975 revised the emigration laws to make certain kinds of persons ineligible for emigration. These are persons whose skills, resources, and dollars are most valued in the homeland.

CHAPTER THREE

South Korean Urbanization
and Economic Development as They
Affect Emigration

As HAS been noted, population pressure is the general, objective factor pushing South Koreans into the United States. However, it does not sufficiently explain why a large number of South Korean urbanites feel a relative economic deprivation and presume that their opportunities would be greater in the United States. An analysis of the basic mechanisms of South Korean urbanization and industrialization may help us to understand these attitudes. Specifically, we need to analyze the extent to which urbanization in the homeland pushes South Koreans to migrate to the United States, and the extent to which this prior experience of urbanization helps the immigrants survive in contemporary American society. The analysis will also attempt to explain why South Korea is capable of sending more of its industrialized labor force to the United States and to other nations than are other developing countries.

Recent Korean immigrants differ substantially from the "uprooted" European and Asian immigrants who came to America prior to the enactment of the National Origins Act in 1924. Before that time the bulk of immigrants to America were drawn from preindustrial and rural areas; they had little experience of international trade, mass communications, modern transportation, and worldwide economic interdependence. Since World War II, however, South Korea has undergone an agrarian crisis that has pushed millions of peasants into a few primary cities. In addition, because of Korea's long tradition of rule by a centralized bureaucracy, primary cities like Seoul have been powerful magnets attracting rural emigrants. Thus South Korean cities are overurbanized in the sense that the urban infrastructure and economic opportunities in South Korea do not adequately accommodate the massive migration from rural areas. Overurbanization has resulted in such urban vices as overcrowdedness, unemployment, and underemployment; and these vices have directly and indirectly contributed to the recent emigration of urbanites to foreign countries.

71

Furthermore, after 1961, when President Park Chung-hee came to power, the South Korean government began to emphasize the development of an export economy, which created massive economic opportunities in urban centers and accelerated the rural-to-urban migration. As we shall see, the basic characteristic of this export economy is its dependence on markets, capital, and materials provided by advanced industrial nations, notably the United States. The development of an export economy has been accompanied by the emergence of new urban classes—a "new middle class," an upper-middle class, and an upper class of industrialists. Consequently, prior to emigrating, Koreans had already experienced these changes in social stratification and had thus acquired a heightened consciousness of the possibility of upward mobility. Korean immigrants had already been "uprooted" in their homeland.

THE OVERURBANIZATION OF SOUTH KOREA

South Korea underwent urbanization at an unprecedented rate after World War II, and this produced vast social changes throughout the entire country. During the period of 1960-1975 the proportion of the total population living in urban areas of 50,000 and larger increased from 28 percent to 51.7 percent largely owing to a massive influx from rural areas.[1] Perhaps no nation has ever experienced such rapid urbanization in such a short span of time. More than 20 percent of the nation's population is now concentrated in Seoul, the capital city, whose population increased from 1.6 million in 1955 to 7.4 million in 1977.[2] That city is nicknamed the "Republic of Seoul" to indicate its power as the capital. (Seoul is the source of most Korean emigration to the United States.) The three largest cities, Seoul, Pusan, and Taegu, embrace one-third of the nation's total population. In short, South Korea is an overurbanized developing country whose rural-to-urban migration does not correspond to its economic development or to the industrialization of its urban centers; the result is an urban crisis visible to any reporter.

[1] The following table indicates the percentage and total number of the South Korean population living in urban areas of 50,000 or over:

Year	Percent	Millions
1960	28.0	7.0
1966	33.6	9.8
1970	41.1	11.9
1975	51.7	16.8

SOURCE: Heung-yol Do, "Dosi sahoehagjeog yeongu" [A sociological study of the city], *Dosi Munje*, February 1976, p. 20; *A Temporary Report on the 1975 Census*, Korean Economic Planning Board, 1976.

[2] *Hankook Ilbo*, February 10, 1976.

Lee Yong Nam, an errand girl for a Seoul publishing company, still has not shed her soft southern accent. "I came to Seoul," said she, "for a job." Miss Lee comes from a small farming town called Chong-up, in Cholla Province. She is one of 400,000 rural emigrants who are crowding into this already overblown city each year, which is reeling under the impact of its 7.5 million inhabitants.

That is 20 percent of South Korea's population of 3.5 million, and Miss Lee's case is a dramatic challenge to the Government of President Park Chung Hee. At the beginning of the year, Mr. Park drove an urgency into the problem by saying that the only solution would be to relocate the capital elsewhere.

With so many people fighting for jobs and spaces, life in this 585-year-old city has become insufferable. Taxis are hard to obtain and are usually shared by four or five persons, each heading for a different direction.

People living in hillside shacks are suffering. With the summer coming, they are complaining about a water shortage. On top of pollution and congestion has been added a new shortage: electricity. . . .[3]

The Agrarian Crisis. The South Korean urban crisis has mainly been caused by a long-term agrarian crisis, which has pushed millions of Korean peasants into cities, especially Seoul.[4] Since Korean independence from Japanese rule in 1945, the urban economy has been maintained and developed at the expense of the rural economy and especially of the peasants.[5] The South Korean land reform of 1950 did not, as had been intended, solve the Korean agrarian crisis. The crisis had been caused by such factors as a rapid population increase, an exposure of the self-sufficient rural economy to the urban money economy, a lack of modern agricultural technology, and a concentration of land ownership within a landlord class.[6] The land reform redistributed

[3] *New York Times*, May 29, 1977.

[4] Rural-to-urban migration accounted for more than 80 percent of the total population increase of Seoul City during the years 1966 to 1970; during the same period, Seoul absorbed 60 percent of the total rural-to-urban migrants in South Korea. Eui-young Yu, "Components of Population Growth in Urban Areas of Korea: 1960-1970," unpublished paper.

[5] The Korean city dwellers' exploitation of peasants has long historical roots. During the Yi dynasty (1392-1910), for instance, such typical urban dwellers as royal families, government bureaucrats, literati, and soldiers made their livings on the basis of tax revenues collected from peasants. Since traditional times, rice has been a staple food and leading economic product as well as the medium of exchange in which the central government collected the bulk of its taxes. Since the end of World War II, when Korea was liberated from Japanese colonialism, rice prices have led the prices of other commodities.

[6] Lim An, *Hangug gyeongjeron* [Theory of the Korean economy], Seoul, Bom Moon Sa, 1961, pp. 245-266.

about one-third of all farmland by limiting the maximum holding to 7.5 acres, and it helped wipe out the economic exploitation of peasants by the landlord class; but by limiting the maximum landholding, the land reform also wiped out the very condition by which Western-type agrobusinesses might arise. Furthermore, rice production resists mechanization because it requires stoop labor.

Due to the lack of an effective urbanization or industrialization policy in urban sectors, containment of the rural population in labor-intensive rice production is socially desirable. However, for the reasons that will soon be apparent, millions of South Korean peasants have migrated since the 1950s to urban areas that cannot provide them with adequate jobs and housing. Yet in spite of this massive exodus, the average farmholding decreased from 3 acres in the 1920s to 2.2 in the 1970s, and about two-thirds of the South Korean farms in the 1970s are smaller than this 2.2-acre average.[7] An increasing population pressure on farmland, coupled with a government policy of keeping rice prices low, has produced a massive migration from farms to cities.

The Economic Push from "Rice Paddies to Factories." Since Korean independence from Japan, the South Korean government has controlled the price of rice and other grains in order to protect urban consumers and manufacturers. For instance, during the 1950s, when South Korea was troubled with the high inflation of a wartime economy, Korean farmers suffered from an acute price "lag" in which farm prices did not catch up with those of other industrial products such as fertilizer (which accounted for about 45 percent of their production costs in 1965). With this government policy of keeping rice prices low, Korean farmers have borne the major burden of an inflation that has been generated by other sectors of the economy.[8] The government's attempt to control inflation by cutting down rice prices has had the effect of an invisible tax on farmers, who were already heavily burdened with other forms of taxes. In addition, South Korean farmers have been vulnerable to the penetration of the urban money economy because of both the higher cost of urban consumer goods and the commercial practices of urban "rice middlemen," who have become their intermediaries in marketing. Only by taking over the monopolies in rice sales in the 1960s could the government have prevented rice middlemen from monopolizing rice and other grain commodities.

The South Korean government could not have succeeded in keeping grain prices low without a massive importation of surplus farm products from the United States. South Korea began importing surplus

[7] Vreeland et al., *Area Handbook*, p. 256.
[8] An, *Hangug*, p. 248.

grains in 1946, and in 1956 the two countries made an official agreement whereby the United States has sold millions of tons of surplus grains to South Korea at a loss.[9] The flow of surplus grains reached its peak during the 1950s and early 1960s, when the United States government took over and stored millions of bushels of wheat and corn under its domestic price-support program, at enormous cost to its taxpayers. By means of these massive imports and grants, the South Korean government has kept rice prices so low since World War II that Korean farmers have lost their economic incentive to grow rice and have migrated to the cities.

The government policy of fostering low rice prices has been geared since the early 1960s to creating an export-oriented South Korean economy. The policy has produced a huge labor force in urban centers and has kept its wages down because rice costs, a major element in the Korean worker's budget, were kept artificially low and because there are more persons driven from their farms to seek work than there are jobs available in the cities.

The migration to the cities has been accelerated by the lack of a coherent government policy for protecting farmers from the encroachment of urban land speculators. Even though the land reform of 1950 substantially standardized South Korean farms by limiting the maxiimum landholding to 7.5 acres, since the early 1960s South Korean rural lands have begun to be concentrated among rich farmers and absentee landlords residing in urban areas. According to the 1970 Korean Census, the number of farm households owning 7.5 acres or over increased by 90.3 percent during the 1960s and constituted about 1.5 percent of all farm households in 1970. During the same period, the number of households of tenant farmers increased by 31.8 percent and constituted 33.5 percent of the total farm households in 1970. Although no systematic study has been made of this fundamental change in land-ownership, one of the main reasons for it is that the urban business classes, ranging from big manufacturers to small businessmen, have invested heavily in rural lands and displaced a large number of farmers. Land speculation by urban land-hunters has boomed in rural areas adjacent to big cities like Seoul. The government once attempted to curb this land speculation by designating some rural areas surrounding the big cities as greenbelts, where construction is prohibited; but speculation has continued.

[9] Such sales constituted a major portion of South Korean agricultural imports: from 1961 to 1969 South Korea imported an annual average of 136,000 metric tons of rice, 111,000 of barley, 642,000 of wheat, and 40,000 of other grains. Willard D. Keim, "The South Korean Peasantry in the 1970s," *Asian Survey*, September 1974, p. 855.

Government policies such as importing grain or redistributing land have not affected all farmers in precisely the same way. South Korean farmers are conventionally divided into three groups—the *bunong* (rich farmers), the *jungnong* (middle farmers), and the *bin-nong* (poor farmers)—on the basis of the acreage they own for cultivation. Generally speaking, both the rich and middle-income farmers can produce surplus food for sale in the market. However, poor farmers are not self-sufficient even in producing their own food. Poor farming families eke out their livelihood by sending some of their members to work at menial jobs in cities or towns and by becoming sharecroppers. Since they have to buy grain for their own consumption, they oppose the raising of grain prices by the government. The youth of these families have responded to the agricultural crisis by migrating from rice paddies to factories; they have served as the huge and cheap labor force that is effectively exploited in the export-oriented urban economy. Since males are needed in labor-intensive rice production, females aged between fifteen to twenty-four have constituted the bulk of this urbanward migration.[10] They have largely been employed in labor-intensive jobs in the garment, wig, toy, and electronics manufacturing industries. They are called the *yeogong*. Others have become prostitutes, domestic servants, or barmaids.

The Magnetic Pull of Primary Cities. The South Korean rural population has not been immune to the revolution of rising expectations that has been generated by universal education, the mass media, and economic opportunities in urban areas. In addition, the revolution of rising expectations has evolved from South Korean historical traditions. Korean primary cities, especially Seoul, were dominant, powerful, and attractive to the entire population even in traditional Korean society because they were the places where the ruling bureaucrats of the central government lived and directed the political, economic, and cultural activities of the entire nation. Unlike most traditional societies, traditional Korean society lacked powerful and prestigious regional elites. The only path to success was to go to Hanyang (an old name for Seoul), pass a civil service examination, and become a bureaucrat.

The attracting power of Seoul, originally sustained by its centralized bureaucracy, still endures. At the administrative level, for instance, the military government passed in 1965 the Provisional Act for Local Self-Government, by which the military junta abolished local autonomy and provided for the central appointment of all public officials. This

[10] Rural girls in this age group accounted for 75 percent of the total "single" migrants to Seoul city during the period of 1966 to 1970. Jong-ju Yoon, "Population Concentration into Seoul—Its Problems and Solution," paper presented at the Korean Population Association's seminar in Seoul, April 2-3, 1976.

policy shift has enlarged the disparity between Seoul and the rest of the country. And under the authoritarian rule of President Park, national budgets and investments have been tilted even more in favor of Seoul. Consequently, Seoul embraces more than 20 percent of the national population in a land area that constitutes only 0.63 percent of South Korea. Seoul in 1975 had 87 percent of the nation's white-collar and managerial workers, 63.6 percent of its savings, 57.9 percent of its private cars, 44 percent of its telephones, 49 percent of its hospital beds, and 60 percent of its college students.[11] Seoul's magnetic attraction, which is political, bureaucratic, educational, and economic, has also bred the typical urban vices of developing countries. In 1975, 40 percent of Korea's urban unemployed roamed the streets of Seoul.

This concentration of cheap but industrious workers in a few primary cities has produced a chronic unemployment and underemployment and is a major reason why ordinary South Koreans migrate to foreign countries, especially to the United States, Latin American nations, Canada, and West Germany—if they are given the chance. Consider Mr. Hee-duck Lee, for example. A correspondent from South Korea interviewed Mr. Lee, who has become a millionaire from his Korean-food and restaurant business in California.

Why did you go to West Germany?
I was born in Gongju. I could not find a job after obtaining my B.S. in chemical engineering at Chungnam University; I was forced to come down to my rural village, where my parents and brothers lived. Nobody could understand my miserable status of living an unemployed life as a college graduate. In 1965 I applied for an overseas labor contract and mined for three years in West Germany. I remitted all the money I earned there to my family in the homeland.

Why did you enter the United States [from West Germany]?
I was afraid that I would become unemployed again if I returned to the home country. I wandered through some European nations for a while, but I could not find a proper place to settle. Upon arriving in the United States, I found a lot of jobs waiting for me.[12]

The Educational Migration. Traditionally, education has been the national road to economic success in Korea. And recently, the farmers' desire to educate their children has been one of the prime factors inducing them to migrate to South Korean cities, especially Seoul. This

[11] Choon-hi No, "Sudogwon eui ingujibjung yoin gwa bunsan bang-an" [Causal factors for population concentration into the capital city and proposals for population decentralization], *Dosi Munje*, September 1975, p. 17.
[12] Kim, *Komerican*, pp. 54-55.

desire was responsible for the urbanward migration of 51 percent of the total migrants to Seoul during the early 1970s. Just as rural youth during the Yi dynasty (1309-1910), if they were bright and had a family connection to the *yangban* (a ruling literati class of the dynasty), walked along dusty country roads toward Hanyang in order to take civil service examinations or to receive an education, so today the bulk of the rural youth has taken the "Seoul-bound night train" in order to study in Seoul. Since the end of the Korean War, a high proportion of South Korean farmers' income and capital has flowed to the cities in the form of educational expenses. An American Catholic missionary in South Korea described this hunger for education.

> With so much bloody horror in the world around us, how can I tell the simple tragedy of a 13-year old Korean girl?
>
> Veronica Park does not seem to be suffering. She is, in fact, perfectly healthy. . . .
>
> The tragedy lies in the fact that she can't go on to school—her father earns no more than $27 per month, and middle school fees in the Korean countryside amount to about $14 per month. And besides, Veronica has three younger brothers. That's important—because here boys come first.
>
> Veronica's is an all-too-common plight for children here. When I discussed it with her father, he was on the verge of tears because of his inability to pay her way to middle school for the coming year.
>
> In poor countries like Korea, education is a supreme must if one is ever going to escape living a life-time in a straw-roofed mud hovel infested by rats. No one realizes this more than the Korean parent. A family may mortgage a home, a farm, or a cow, or one of the older girls may even go into prostitution to raise the money to enroll a brother in a "good" school.[13]

The South Korean farmers' desire to educate their children even at the expense of land and cows has partly been caused by the dismal economic prospects of rural areas. In the absence of a better alternative, farmers prefer to invest their capital or income in the education of their children. Their investment is sure to pay off, because in the Korean family-centered success ethic a successful family member is obliged to take care of other family members. Having worked their way through the competitive and expensive educational system, urban youth of rural origin believe it is their duty to send for their rural family members. The Korean farmers' expenditure toward educating their children has thus siphoned off rural capital while greatly contributing

[13] Andrian Van Leest, "The Tragedy of Veronica Park," *Colomban Mission*, January 1974, p. 10.

to the creation of a new middle class of managerial, white-collar workers in urban centers. As has been noted in the first chapter, this new middle class, which had experienced one or two generations of urbanization, constitutes the majority of Korean immigrants to the United States.

As we shall see in the analysis of the character structure of Koreans (chapter ten), the national ideology of education is derived from the social structure of traditional Korean society: in the national culture of Confucianism, a kind of social stigma was imposed upon the uneducated; and in contemporary South Korean society, diplomas from urban schools have become a license for upward economic mobility. But the new middle class of wage earners has suffered from skyrocketing educational costs: the tuition fees of South Korean public universities increased by 710 percent from 1968 to 1978, while those of public high schools jumped by 920 percent.[14] Thus, given the economic and social malaise in overurbanized South Korea, "education for children" has become one of the prime motives for emigration to the United States. According to a recent survey, 44 percent of 2,715 Korean respondents in California cited "education for children" as their primary reason for migrating to the United States.[15] Related to this emigration is the migration from 1953 to 1973 of 10,789 Korean students to American educational institutions; most of these students, as we have noted, decided to settle in the United States mainly because of the lack of economic opportunities in South Korean urban centers.

PRESIDENT PARK'S POLITICAL ECONOMY

Taking advantage of the political upheavals and social chaos after the April 19 student revolution that overthrew the Syngman Rhee regime, Major General Park led the May 16 military revolution in 1961. Park, backed by young, ambitious colonels, toppled the Chang civilian government and seized power. After the coup, Park's power became ubiquitous and absolute. All limits on his presidential tenure were repealed under the so-called 1972 Yusin Honbeob (Constitution for Revitalizing Reforms), by which he revised the South Korean Constitution in favor of his lifelong dictatorship. His leadership was so powerful that he could constitutionally appoint one third of the national assemblymen. Since the coup, South Korean society has been transformed to embody Park's image of society.

The legitimation of Park's dictatorship was described by one of his followers: "It is obvious that President Park regards excessive enthusi-

[14] *Hankook Ilbo*, March 9, 1978.
[15] *Hankook Shinmoon*, October 22, 1977.

asm in politics as one of the greatest obstacles to economic development in underdeveloped countries."[16] Park once said that his aim was to transform Korea's "political democracy" into an "administrative democracy." South Korean supporters of Park's "strong leadership" argued that his monopolization of power was necessary because it pacified the volatile and sometimes violent elements of South Korean politics in order to create the social stability that is a prerequisite for economic development. According to one supporter, "A bulk of the gross national product was wasted in free elections to buy votes." Park's supporters believed that only he could save South Korea from the vicious cycle of military coups that characterizes the politics of most new nations. This ruling ideology, which puts economic prosperity ahead of political freedom, has been accepted by many South Koreans, especially by those who have "made it" by getting aboard "the 1970s express train" of rapid economic development. Moreover, largely under the impact of Western consumer culture, South Koreans suffer from a relative deprivation: it is painful for them to listen to the radio while the people of rich nations watch color television. By promising a greater supply of consumer goods, Park mustered substantial political support for his regime.

Historically, the initial steps of industrialization have required brutal repression, political as well as economic, to foster a primary accumulation of capital. In order to achieve political stability and economic discipline, Park established a pervasive, ruthless mechanism of repression —the Korean Central Intelligence Agency (KCIA). The agency is widely feared among South Koreans. Its function is to gather intelligence, survey economic and political activities, manipulate public opinion, engage in subversive activities against the regime's opponents, and control Korean communities in foreign countries.

The KCIA is but one manifestation, however, of the most important impact of Park's rule on South Korean society—that is, the deep penetration of military institutions into civilian life. This is the inevitable consequence of the United States government's massive support, since the Korean War, for the buildup of South Korean armed forces. The military has grown much faster than other forms of civilian institutions. The South Korean armed forces became the first coherent group to learn the intricacies of American technology, modern administrative skills and management, and organizational discipline. In the absence of other coherent, dedicated social groups or parties in South Korean

---

[16] Quoted by Sungjoo Han, "Power and Development in Contemporary South Korea," an unpublished paper delivered at the Conference on Power and Development in Contemporary Korea, the City University of New York, October 14-15, 1977, p. 27.

politics, it is no wonder that military leaders claimed power under the name of efficiency. Park himself demanded that his followers act like soldiers by emphasizing efficiency and discipline. At the same time, he introduced centralized military organization into civilian government.

Park could have been called a cool-minded pragmatist. His political ideology was nonideological in the sense that he accepted ideas from socialism, fascism, nationalism, and capitalism. If they were useful to his consolidation of power, he used them; for he thought that his personal tenure in power was essential to national economic development.

By thus putting economic development at the top of the nation's priorities, Park gave South Korea a controlled, managed national economy—"command industrialization" in the form of state capitalism. As in other developing countries, the South Korean ideology of modernization or industrialization derives from an invidious comparison with advanced industrial nations. In addition, the continuous confrontation between North and South Korea has forced Korea to perceive that a strong economy is indispensable as a means of coping with the North. Needless to say, the tug of war between North and South has strongly motivated South Koreans in their attempt to be first among the latercomers to industrialization.

THE EXPORT-ORIENTED ECONOMY

The development of an export-oriented economy is largely responsible for the well-publicized economic miracle of South Korea. Since 1961, the entire South Korean economic structure has been reshuffled toward this end. The first two five-year economic development plans, concluded in 1971, built up the industrial base for an export-oriented economy; exports rose spectacularly from $41 million in 1961 to $10 billion in 1977. "In 1974 foreign trade was the equivalent of 70 percent of the gross national product."[17] The bulk of South Korea's economic activities are directly or indirectly connected with exports, but in 1970 only about 0.6 million (or 8.8 percent) of the total labor force engaged in the export industry; by the end of 1976 the number had increased to 2.8 million, constituting 23.5 percent of the total labor force.[18]

Although South Korea was exporting its products to more than 130 nations by 1976, the United States and Japan have been the major markets for South Korean goods: in 1976, 30.9 percent of all South

[17] Vreeland et al., *Area Handbook*, p. 297.
[18] "Remarkable Increase in Exports Key to Korea's New Economic Status," an advertisement by the Korean Traders Association in the *New York Times*, January 30, 1977.

Korean exports went to the United States, while Japan imported 21.0 percent.[19] The United States and Japan have been not only the major importers of South Korean products but also the major suppliers of capital and technology to South Korean export industries. As we shall see, the economic activity of South Korea has been closely tied to the markets and financial situations of these two nations.

At the initial stage of South Korean economic development, exports were largely confined to labor-intensive consumer goods such as clothing, textiles, footwear, wigs, electronics, toys, and jewelry. However, since 1975 exports have become diversified by the addition of heavy manufactures—metal products, machinery, chemical products, and industrial equipment. The basic pattern has been to import raw materials, intermediate goods, and heavy capital goods and to produce finished products for overseas markets. In doing this, the abundant, well-educated, and highly motivated labor force is effectively employed and exploited. The following examples will suffice to show the essential character of the South Korean economy.

> Veteran executive M. Tezuka [in Japan] is trying to reconstruct a spinning company which went bankrupt two years ago owing close to $200 million: "A Japanese girl gets $10 a day for 270 days a year. A Korean girl gets $2.50 and works 365 days. We just can't compete with that," he explained. While the company's Japanese factory is narrowly breaking even, a joint venture in South Korea is reaping handsome profits.[20]

> The Hyundai Motor Co. [in South Korea] is likely to select the Middle East as the first target for the two to three thousand Ponies that will come off the Ulsan works before December. . . . Brazen or suicidal could be an apt description for this undertaking were it not for South Korea's known capacity for expanding its external sales even in years of shrinking world trade. . . .
> What Hyundai has produced is an interesting automotive hybrid with an Italian-designed body, a proven Japanese engine and British parts—all put together by the already legendary hard workers of this Northeast Asian peninsula.[21]

The Economic Basis of the Export-Oriented Economy. Broadly speaking, two causal factors can be identified to explain the rapid economic growth of South Korea during the late 1960s and early 1970s. The first factor is the existence of surplus labor in an industrious, well-educated labor force. This might be called an internal factor, the formation of

[19] Ibid.   [20] *Washington Post*, March 20, 1977.
[21] *Washington Star*, July 16, 1976.

which is largely determined by several long-range sociohistorical trends in Korean society; how the bulk of this labor force is susceptible to being pushed from rural areas to cities has already been discussed. The second factor lies in South Korean economic relations with advanced nations, whereby South Korea acquired not only foreign investments through multinational corporations, commercial loans, economic aid, and technology—but also overseas markets for its products. This might be called an external factor, since these relations involve a dependency on the economic institutions of advanced nations. Given the centralized authoritarian political system of South Korea, in which the government commands national economic activities, these two factors have jointly produced the South Korean export-oriented economy. Let us first discuss South Korea's economic relationship with advanced nations, especially with the United States and Japan.

The United States and Japan have been the major sources of capital for South Korea. Since the end of World War II, the United States has been politically and militarily involved in South Korea and has consequently spent an enormous amount of money that has flowed to South Korea in the form of military assistance, credit for the purchase of grain and weapons, economic assistance, and payments to South Korean troops in the Vietnam War. The total is estimated at about $14.8 billion during the period from 1946 to 1976.[22] In addition, by 1975 United States commercial banks had extended $2.3 billion in loans to South Korea, which constituted 83.5 percent of all commercial loans to South Korea.[23] Also, by 1975 South Korea had borrowed $155.5 million from Japanese commercial banks. Japan contributed additional foreign aid under the normalization treaty between the two countries, in which the Japanese government agreed to pay up to $300 million by 1975 for South Korean claims on property lost during the Japanese colonial period.

By extending loans to such developing countries as Brazil, South Korea, Mexico, and Taiwan, which are supposed to have a potential for economic growth, United States commercial banks have created financial opportunities in these countries similar to those made available in the United States during the mid nineteenth century. But the United States banking community and the United States Congress have shown a growing concern over the ability of these developing countries to meet their mounting foreign-debt payments.[24] South Korea, for instance, has shown uneven rates of economic growth because

[22] "Economic Crisis Looms for South Korea," International Policy Report, Washington D.C., Institute for International Policy, December 1975, p. 8.
[23] New York Times, November 21, 1975.
[24] New York Times, January 15, 1976.

the economy has been at the mercy of the vicissitudes of international trade, which is dominated by the United States, Japan, industrial Western nations, and OPEC. When this international system runs smoothly, the export-oriented economy of South Korea seems to work. However, when international trade deteriorates or when oil prices jump suddenly, the South Korean economy teeters on the brink of disaster. The basic problem is that, in a prolonged worldwide economic recession, the most succesful export-oriented developing economies, including that of South Korea, are dependent upon imported raw materials, foreign loans, and markets. These are most vulnerable to recession, and thus the whole development of the South Korean economy depends upon external markets that it cannot control.

> The continued progress of the Korean economy this year, the newspapers and other observers here said, depends on a number of "if's." Among them: If the price of oil does not go up and raise import costs, if the prices of other raw materials stay within reason, if exports (especially of textiles) keep going up, if economic recovery in the United States and Japan continues to provide expanding markets, if export prices can be firmed but kept competitive despite domestic inflation and if the loans and investments promised actually arrive.[25]

Largely owing to an expansion of exports immediately following the gradual economic recovery of the United States in 1976, South Korea's balance of payments has been substantially strengthened since 1976. Furthermore, Arab petrodollars have unexpectedly been added to the foreign-exchange earnings of South Korea, since more than 100,000 Korean construction workers have been sent to the Middle East by South Korean construction companies from 1972 to 1978. However, during the years from 1973 to 1976, South Korea had to borrow $5.4 billion from foreign countries in order to sustain its exports. Since the economic structure is geared to exports, and thus dependent upon foreign loans, markets, and materials, South Korea has no choice but to expand its economy even during situations unfavorable to international trade, just to maintain its credit worthiness.

South Korea has also borrowed technology from Japan and the United States in the form of either direct investments by multinational corporations or their joint ventures with South Korean corporations. Japanese corporate investments in South Korea are much larger than their American counterparts. During the period from 1962 to 1977, Japanese corporations invested $544 million, or 61 percent of

[25] *New York Times*, June 6, 1976.

their total foreign investment, in South Korean export industries, while American corporations invested $170 million.[26] By the end of 1975, a total of 152 Japanese corporations, most of which were affiliated with large industrial business concerns, the *zaibatsu*, had become involved in South Korean industries.[27]

A majority of the Japanese direct investments have gone to labor-intensive industries, for Japanese corporations are attracted by the low-cost labor force of South Korea. In addition, they have taken advantage of the South Korean government's benign neglect of pollution from such high-pollution sources as the chemical and petrochemical indus-tries, whose growth in both Japan and the United States has been seri-ously limited by environmentalists.[28] In sum, the South Korean gov-ernment has granted every possible favor to foreign multinational corporations in order to attract their investments; South Koreans have been exploited in wage rates and "raped" ecologically. Thus Koreans reenact the primitive capitalism of the nineteenth century. And by taking advantage of this favorable business climate, foreign multina-tional corporations have made handsome profits. During the years from 1962 to 1977, they garnered profits amounting to $170 million, or 24.3 percent of their total investment in South Korea.[29] While earning such high rates of return, however, foreign multinational corporations have created a favorable business climate for South Korea to acquire West-ern industrial technology. Overall, 58.7 percent of the technological input to South Korean industries originates from Japan; in small and medium enterprises, Japan's share of industrial technology is 75 per-cent.[30]

These two externally originated factors—foreign capital and tech-nology—have been successfully combined with internal factors—the industrious and cheap labor force—to make South Korea one of the first among the latecomers to industrialization. The cheap but hard-working labor force has been a bulwark of the fragile economic struc-ture of South Korea, and this labor force accounts for the resilience in the South Korean economy even during a worldwide economic reces-sion. However, even this reservoir of cheap labor has stemmed largely

---

[26] *Hankook Ilbo*, October 5, 1977.   [27] *Hankook Ilbo*, October 5, 1977.

[28] According to an estimate of a South Korean environmentalist group, 76 percent of the total foreign investments in South Korea from 1962 to 1974 were made in pollution-causing manufacturing industries. *Hankook Ilbo*, October 26, 1976. And yet the South Korean government has lent a deaf ear to this pollution problem. For instance, the *New York Times* reported, "United States Embassy officials said they had advised the Koreans to install antipollution devices in new plants, arguing that it would be cheaper now than later. 'They don't listen,' one said. 'They argue that antipollution measures are for rich countries.'" *New York Times*, November 29, 1975.

[29] *Hankook Ilbo*, October 5, 1977.   [30] *Korea Week*, April 15, 1976.

from Western technology. As we previously discussed, the South Korean borrowing of Western preventive medicine has drastically lowered mortality rates while increasing the proportion of the young, working-age population. In 1970, about 10 million South Koreans were economically active (employed or actively seeking employment) in the labor force.[31] Given the Confucian cultural tradition, with its emphasis on education, this young population is well-educated compared with that in other developing countries; it has become one of the most productive, industrious labor forces in Asia.

THE LABOR POLICY OF THE SOUTH KOREAN GOVERNMENT

Internally, the South Korean government's labor policy is designed to repress and exploit the working classes. Externally, it is directed toward the export of South Korean workers under overseas contracts. South Korean labor has been sacrificed in favor of the export industries. Organized labor has been prohibited from striking, whatever the grievances, in order to keep down wages and thus to keep export industries competitive in international markets. Furthermore, South Korean industrial workers have paid the costs of the high inflation that has been caused mainly by the rapid expansion of exports. During the period from 1970 to 1976—the period of an unprecedented growth of exports—the average annual wage increase of South Korean workers was 7.2 percent, while consumer prices went up annually by 15.4 percent.[32] In 1976 about 82 percent of a total of 5.6 million South Korean wage earners made less than sixty dollars a month and were therefore exempt from income taxes.[33]

The South Korean government is formally democratic, and the Constitution assures trade unions the right to organize and bargain collectively. In 1976 some 700,000 of the 5.6 million wage earners were unionized in seventeen national federations, which were affiliated with the central labor union (the Federation of Korean Trade Unions); but the federation has been a puppet organization controlled by the South Korean government in the interests of big industrialists. And yet, the government is portrayed, largely through a government-controlled press, as a benevolent patriarch defending the interests of industrial workers. According to the press, if private industries do not consider the workers' well-being, the government will intervene; the relationship between labor and industry should be managed like a family affair. Despite such assurances, the South Korean government, in order to accumulate more capital by relying on the expansion of export in-

[31] Kwon et al., *The Population of Korea*, p. 81.
[32] *Joong Ang Ilbo*, June 23, 1977.   [33] *Dong-A Ilbo*, May 4, 1976.

dustries, has ruthlessly repressed any genuine labor movement. Here is an example of how South Korean garment workers, the *yeogong*—whose cheap wages have forced some garment industries of the United States out of business—have been exploited in building up South Korean exports.

It is over 100 degrees in Shop 349 these summer days, and the 20 teenage girls who work in the crowded, airless loft in Seoul's Peace Market garment district get little relief from the one tiny fan.

The girls sew children's dresses, for export to the United States, and they work 11 hours a day, seven days a week, for $23 a month.

Under South Korea's labor law, the girls should not work more than eight hours a day, six days a week. But the uniformed police and the plainclothes members of the South Korean Central Intelligence Agency stationed in the corridors outside Shop 349 do not seem to notice.

There are also policemen and agents sitting regularly in the nearby office of the Urban Industrial Mission, a Protestant organization that has tried to improve conditions among South Korea's 1.5 million factory workers.

The mission's telephone is tapped—one day an officer picked up the phone only to hear an earlier conversation being played back—and 11 of the mission's staff, all Protestant ministers, are in jail, accused of roles in a Communist plot to overthrow the Government.

In this rapidly industrializing nation with no natural resources except its cheap work force, the cost of labor has become a critical issue to the government of President Park Chung Hee.

It has been Korea's plentiful supply of diligent and inexpensive workers that attracted American and Japanese investment and enabled the economy to grow 10 percent a year over the last decade.

Similar labor problems are faced by other developing nations in Asia—Taiwan, Hong Kong, Singapore, and even Japan—but South Korea's response has been one of the toughest.

In the view of some South Koreans and foreigners familiar with the labor situation here, President Park's effort to keep wages low and control the labor movement has resulted in even greater repression than the more publicized wave of arrests and trials of dissident students and intellectuals.[34]

The importation into the United States of such consumer goods as the dresses produced in this South Korean sweat shop lowers the prices paid by American consumers, but it may also reduce the number of

[34] *New York Times*, August 17, 1974.

jobs available to factory workers in the United States. On the other hand, as we shall see in chapter four, the importation of such consumer goods from South Korea has provided jobs for Korean immigrants in the United States. The new import businesses and the jobs they have created have become one of the major mechanisms by which Korean immigrants establish economic niches in the new land.

The Impact of Exporting on the South Korean Class Structure

South Korean society has been rapidly transformed under the impact of its "export boom." Entire cultural, occupational, educational, and familial institutions have undergone drastic changes under the influence of foreign trade. For example, Park's authoritarian rule legitimized and was legitimized by the export-oriented economy. Government propaganda stresses that the economic survival of South Korea depends on exports, and this is undoubtedly true; but it is true because the South Korean government's economic policy has, since the early 1960s, made the entire economy dependent upon exports. "The battle of exports" has become a total effort in which Korean national energy is mobilized. Ordinary South Koreans quickly respond to the leading economic indicator—the volume of letters of credit and of orders from foreign countries. And the South Korean government has coined the phrase "economic diplomacy" for the task of South Korean diplomats stationed in foreign countries; they are expected to take the role of salesman in exploring and expanding overseas markets for South Korean products.

The most important result of the export boom lies in the growth of urban middle class and the emergence of the nouveaux riches in the upper class of industrialists and businessmen. As we have noted previously, the majority of Korean immigrants in the United States are drawn from these newly emerging urban classes. And that is to say, further, that Korean immigrants have already experienced a violent change in their social positions prior to emigrating, for they have experienced the formation of these new urban classes.

The South Korean urban middle class can be divided into two groups. One group is made up of professionals, teachers, middle-level industrial managers, army officers, and skilled blue-collar workers. The other group consists of high-ranking government officials, top military officers, real estate speculators, proprietors, owners of medium or small business firms, and high-level managers of big businesses and industrial enterprises. The second group might be called upper-middle class, and many of its members "made it" without inherited wealth or higher education. The first group consists of salaried workers, most of whom are equipped with higher education. This group might be called a new middle class. These loosely defined urban middle classes —the upper-middle class and the new middle class—have one thing in common: they have been largely produced by the development of the export-oriented economy.

An American anthropologist observed of Seoul in the 1970s that

> rapid economic development is a reality, and a majority of city dwellers today are relatively well fed, clothed, and housed. In addition a rapidly growing elite of bureaucrats, politicians, and commercial, industrial, and educational entrepreneurs have been getting rich. Tens of thousands of new mansions, chauffeur driven cars, and fur and silk coated women decorate the city.
>
> The newly rich are energetically and competitively engaged in a flagrant and flamboyant display of wealth, while members of the growing middle class tend to invest whatever savings they are able to acquire in more elaborate consumption goods. Stores crammed with luxuries are crowded with buyers, while theatres, bars, cabarets, and restaurants provide a night life of great intensity and infinite variety. This dazzling display is an important factor in drawing migrants to Seoul, but once they are there, living in squatters slums, they are confronted daily with the discouraging contrast between the squalor of their own lives and the buoyant wealth around them.[35]

The development of the export-oriented economy has also effected a rapid change in Korea's occupational distribution. The white-collar occupations—professional, technical, managerial, clerical, and sales workers—have absorbed an increasing proportion of the work force. The proportion of white-collar workers increased from 17 percent in 1963 to almost one-fourth of the employed labor force in 1971.[36]

The Formation of the Upper Industrial Class. As the South Korean export-oriented economy has been constructed, an upper class of capitalists and industrialists has emerged as a formidable force in monopolistic control of the economy. As has been noted in chapter two, this new class is strongly inclined to funnel millions of dollars into the United States. The core group of the upper industrial class is called the *jaebeol*—the Korean version of the Japanese *zaibatsu*. An analysis of the growth of this class of tycoons will shed some light on the internal dynamics of the South Korean political economy.

[35] Vincent S. R. Brandt, "Problems of Social Integration under Conditions of Rapid Economic Development: Migrants and the Urban Slums in South Korea," quoted from Vreeland et al., *Area Handbook*, p. 96.

[36] Vreeland et al., *Area Handbook*, p. 59.

Hancho C. Kim, an influential Korean agent who allegedly participated in the Korean attempt to buy influence in the United States. Congress, wrote to the *New York Times* with the intention of slanting public opinion in favor of the Park regime. In doing so, he pointed out a crucial aspect of South Korean economic development—the alliance of the Park regime with small industrialists.

> In the early sixties, by a miracle of cooperative self-denial, a group of competing Korean small industrialists set their powerful competitive instincts resolutely aside for the well-being of their nation. They banded together with some of Korea's ablest industrial engineers, bankers, land-planners and technologists to wipe out Korea's bone-breaking poverty and to deliberately plan the most efficient use of Korea's literate, but mismanaged, manpower, its superb native skills and its inherent maritime and mineral resources.
>
> They were headed then and are led now by tough-minded, strong-willed, soft-spoken Park Chung Hee—who is president—a man sick and tired of violence, of the incredible waste of manpower and of the hunger and wretchedness that had appalled him as a native of rural Korea and as a young teacher in rural districts.[37]

The formation of the South Korean entrepreneurial elite described in this letter has been governed by specific political events. The new class has profited by taking advantage of new economic opportunities under such historical conditions as Korean independence from Japan in 1945, the Korean War, the May 16 military revolution, and the South Korean military involvement in the Vietnam War. The government has been a major dispenser of such new economic opportunities; South Korean business elites have gained special favors, *tughae*, in return for bribes.

When the Japanese lost colonial control of Korea after World War II, all Japanese properties and industrial assets were left to the Korean government as enemy assets. The government sold these assets to aggressive political entrepreneurs and to those Koreans who had previously worked for and been trained by the Japanese industrial firms. Massive bribery and special favors were involved. At the same time, a serious dislocation of the Korean economy occurred because few Koreans were adequately trained to operate or manage the Japanese enterprises.

With the outbreak of the Korean War, in 1950, economic aid from the United States flowed into South Korea and became the most important source of capital for the reconstruction of the economy. The

[37] Hancho C. Kim, "Park's Shining Korean Camelot," *New York Times*, March 12, 1975.

government distributed this aid to a select group of industrialists, most of whom had previously accumulated some capital by taking over the Japanese assets; they had become financially competent to buy special favors. Since the Korean War, buying powerful political officials has become a business norm, the central link between political and economic institutions. This interplay has resulted in a concentration of capital among a small number of industrialists, and it has been a basic part of the South Korean mixture of capitalism and political democracy. One example will suffice to illuminate this aspect of the South Korean political economy of the 1950s.

In the summer of 1952, when the war was still going on, the Syngman Rhee administration allocated over three million dollars of foreign exchange to 40 private firms. This fund earned through the export of tungsten was supposedly allocated for certain specific needs of the country. Instead, the Rhee government illegally distributed it to several entrepreneurs enabling them to import grains and fertilizers which were badly needed in a country still in the midst of a war.

By taking advantage of the discrepancy in foreign exchange rates and by monopolizing the price, these firms made enormous profits. The government was then offered a large contribution in return for the favor, which was allegedly used in Rhee's Liberal Party campaign for a constitutional amendment that permitted his election as president.[38]

The example is just a tip of the iceberg. Speculation, monopolization of commodities and markets, tax evasion, monopolization of contracts, illicit purchase of public properties and lands, and diversion of foreign loans were typical ways of getting rich. In these practices, entrepreneurs required protection from someone in the higher levels of government. However, compared with the period under President Park's rule, opportunities for reaping illegal profits in the South Korea of the 1950s were limited, because national economic development was in its initial stage and because foreign loans were small.

Opportunities for profiting through political connections have

[38] Kyong-dong Kim, "Political Factors in the Formation of the Entrepreneurial Elite in South Korea," Asian Survey, May 1974, p. 468.

Our analysis of the jaebeol is largely based on the following sources: Tong-jin Kang, "Hangug jaebeol eui hyeongseong gwa gyebo" [The formation and genealogy of Korean capitalists], Jeong-gyeong Yeongu, November 1967; Sung-du Kim, "Hangug dogjeom jaebeol hyeongseong eui teugiseong" [The characteristics of the formation of Korean monopolistic capitalists], Sasang Ke, September 1968; Hyong-son Moon, "Jaebeol ron" [On capitalists], Sasang Ke, May 1963; Myo-min Lim, "O-il-yug ihu eui jaegye gaepeon" [The change in the financial world after the May 16 military coup], Shin Dong-A, May 1968.

boomed during the last fifteen years, when the total South Korean foreign debt has climbed to more than $10 billion and annual exports have mounted to $10 billion as well. During this period of vast economic change, a group of South Korean industrial capitalists, the *jaebeol*, has emerged as a stable upper class. The unique character of this class consists in its combination of capitalistic monopoly with family-centered entrepreneurship and of the comprador with the plutocrat.

When the military junta took power in 1961, its leaders called for the eradication of political corruption and other old social vices. At the same time, they determined to achieve rapid economic development by relying on free enterprise. As a way of fostering social justice, they attempted to prosecute the *jaebeol*, who were a symbol of the old vices and an object of resentment among the Korean people; they investigated persons who had accumulated illegal wealth during the previous regime. At the outset, the young colonels of the military junta suggested that all the illicit profiteers be punished and that their illegally amassed fortunes be confiscated. However, in proceeding with the investigation they found themselves in a serious dilemma: they found that the *jaebeol's* illicitly accumulated capital and its business experience were essential to their ambitious plans for economic development. At the same time, they themselves became corrupt in their attempt to eradicate corruption. Since almost all the colonels in the military government were drawn from either poverty-stricken peasant or North Korean refugee backgrounds, they were longing for wealth.

> Within the hard-core junta circle, on the other hand, internal factionalism mostly rooted in regional loyalty began to undermine the solidarity of the regime. Disagreement was glaring on many issues including that of the handling of the illegal wealth. Having quickly noticed these political factors plaguing the junta leadership, the entrepreneurs under indictment wasted no time to take advantage of them. They moved to buy off various political bosses by promising or offering political kickbacks.
>
> And when the investigation committee handed down the decision, it was substantially toned down. Thirty elite entrepreneurs thus accused and convicted were asked to refund a designated amount of funds to the government by a given date.[39]

Since the May 16 military revolution of 1961, the massive flow of foreign loans has caused the already large capitalist firms to grow rapidly. In order to make them competitive in the world market, the gov-

---

[39] Kim, "Political Factors," pp. 468-469.

ernment earmarked a large portion of its foreign loans for accelerating the growth of these firms. The government also required domestic banks to make low-interest loans to favored industrial capitalists. In this process, the capitalists have continued to exert their political and financial influence to buy special favors. A South Korean poet, Chi-ha Kim, has portrayed the political corruption arising from this interlocking of business and politics in his famous poem, "Five Bandits."

Watch the tycoon demonstrate his skill!

Roasting the cabinet minister a beautiful brown, and boiling the vice minister red, sprinkling soy sauce, mustard, hot sauce, and MSG, together with red pepper, welsh onions, and garlic on them, he swallowed them up, together with banknotes collected from taxes, funds borrowed from foreign countries, and other privileges and benefits.

Pretty girls he lured, made his mistresses, and kept busy producing babies. A dozen daughters thus made were given as tribute to high officials as midnight snacks. Their tasks were to collect information on the pillow, thereby enabling him to win negotiated contracts, buy land cheaply, and make a fortune once a road was opened.[40]

As a result of these political and economic maneuvers, a major share of industrial capital has become concentrated among a small portion of big corporations. In 1976 the 100 largest corporations, among a total of 15,000, took 42 percent of the nation's gross sales receipts.[41] Thirty-seven of these 100 were subsidiaries of 13 of the 50 *jaebeol* groups that have emerged. Each *jaebeol* has spawned an average of 15.7 subsidiary corporations, and the entire South Korean economy is virtually controlled by these 50 *jaebeol* groups. These, in turn, are closely interlinked with the government. Along with the economic activities that have produced these results, the government has expounded an economic ideology of "guided capitalism," by which it has led and intervened in the South Korean version of a free enterprise system; but in fact the South Korean economic system is a mixture of capitalism and planned socialism.

The *jaebeol* groups made enormous profits during the 1960s by monopolizing the manufacture or processing of such goods as sugar, toothpaste, food, cement, fertilizer, clothing, and light machinery. They were also active in transportation and construction. Since 1970, as the South Korean economy has matured, they have competed in gaining dominance over profitable heavy industries such as petro-

[40] Chi-ha Kim, *Cry of the People and Other Poems*, Hayama, Japan, Autumn Press, 1974, pp. 27-28.
[41] *Hankook Ilbo*, August 12, 1977.

chemicals, machinery, oil refining, automobiles, airlines, electronics, factory construction, and the defense industry. They also have begun to control the hotel and tourist trades, insurance, mass media, the stock exchange, and educational institutions. In 1976 the ten largest *jaebeol* groups had total sales of $5.7 billion, constituting about 23 percent of the gross national product.[42]

Nine of the top ten *jaebeol* groups had their origins in the 1950s. Officials of three of them, the Lakee, Samsong, and Ssangyong, were convicted of illegal profiteering by the military junta. Except for these three, the *jaebeols* were small industries in the 1950s and became *jaebeols* in the 1960s and the early 1970s. The Hyundai and Hanjin, which were small contracting companies for the United States Army in South Korea in the 1950s, emerged as *jaebeols* in the late 1960s when they reaped enormous profits from construction and transportation work in South Vietnam.[43] The latest arrival, the Daewoo, became a *jaebeol* in the early 1970s by exporting clothing and wig products. The Kookjae entered into the ranks of the ten largest *jaebeol* groups in 1976 by exporting a record volume of footwear to the United States.

The *jaebeols'* rapid growth, largely supported by the government's low-wage policy and by politically favored access to foreign and domestic loans, has contributed to the formation of large-scale enterprises, which are essential to South Korean competition in international markets. However, one of the main problems facing the South Korean economy is how the *jaebeols* make use of the capital so accumulated.

The present data on the use of fraudulent subsidies indicates that a continued growth of South Korean capitalistic enterprises contains major dangers. First, the South Korean upper class of industrialists and businessmen has moved forward mainly under the direction, supervision, and instigation of the government. Most of the big enterprises have been family-centered, closed, and parochial organizations, so that they exclude participation by the public. Only the government could exert strong pressure to open stock ownership to the public. Second, most top business leaders have a strong inclination to reinvest their accumulated capital in nonproductive, speculative activities. They have purchased a vast acreage of agricultural lands, producing a large number of South Korean "Okies," and thus intensified the overurbanization

---

[42] *Hankook Ilbo*, April 3, 1977.

[43] The earnings of South Korea from the Vietnamese War were a major source of capital accumulation in the late 1960s and early 1970s. By sending military forces and civilian workers to South Vietnam, South Korea earned, for instance, about $2.3 billion during the three years from 1966 to 1968. David C. Cole and Princeton N. Lyman, *Korean Development: The Interplay of Politics and Economics*, Cambridge, Mass., Harvard University Press, 1971, p. 135.

of South Korea. They also want to make easy money by opening hotels and tourist businesses and operating ice cream, cookie, and golf concessions.[44] Third, the new South Korean upper class has wasted its acquired capital by indulging in vast amounts of conspicuous consumption. For instance, urban entrepreneurs have built up vast rural estates that are surrounded by landless peasants. Finally, as we have noted in chapter two, the new upper and upper-middle classes have shown a strong tendency to divert their acquired capital to the United States partly because of the fear of another Korean War and partly because of their lack of confidence in the future of the domestic economy.

THE REACTION TO RAPID ECONOMIC DEVELOPMENT

In their experience of rapid economic development, South Koreans' mental energies are dissipated through "invidious comparison." South Koreans compete intensely with one another to own and display consumer goods. In light of this competition, the unequal distribution of new economic opportunities has made the various South Korean urban classes more insecure, restless, and anxious than their counterparts in other developing countries. The following views of urban Koreans on recent socioeconomic changes reflect this insecurity.

"I cannot understand why my family cannot live by solely relying on my husband's salary. Nor do I understand why there are so many newly rich people around us," said Mrs. Chang-ock Kim. She has frequently told herself, "I will not envy the new life styles of my neighbors and alumni friends." But she cannot stop comparing herself with them. She further said, "I wish that the T.V. home dramas would not show us the life styles of rich people."[45]

I have made my career as a newspaper reporter since 1953—the year that the Korean War stopped. But now I realize that it is becoming difficult to stick to one's own vocation in this changing society in which money matches with "getting ahead." I sometimes feel that those who keep their vocations faithfully and honestly are now treated as fools.[46]

It is a tragedy that the Confucian gentleman's ideal of enjoying a pleasant life amid stable poverty has disappeared. In the old society we believed that there are things that we must not do. But now we seem to think that there are no things that we must not do.[47]

[44] Dong-A Ilbo, June 3-5, p. 135.
[46] Joong Ang Ilbo, August 1, 1978.
[45] Joong Ang Ilbo, November 11, 1977.
[47] Ibid.

In a booming economy, monetary value has quickly triumphed over other social values. The saying that "you cannot make money without breaking the law" is widely circulated among South Koreans. Bankruptcy is cited as one way of making money; many entrepreneurs have filed for bankruptcy after diverting funds borrowed from foreign or domestic banks into personal real estate speculation, on the pretext of building up export industries. Ordinary South Koreans have resented this kind of newly rich man, saying that "businessmen become rich even when their business firms go into bankruptcy."

Those who have "made it overnight" worry about how to spend it. By spending new earnings on consumer goods, they try to adopt an infinite variety of Western life styles. However, this intensive pursuit of conspicuous consumption is severely limited, partly because a vast number of South Korean have-nots frown upon the open display of new wealth, saying, for instance, that "golf fields should be converted into agricultural lands." Furthermore, these nouveaux riches are afraid that they might lose their money because of the uncertain economic, political, and military situation in South Korea. Specifically, they are afraid of another Korean War. Consequently some of them want to emigrate to the United States with the money they have so recently made.

Those middle-class urbanites (especially white-collar wage earners) who do not expect to "make it big," on the other hand, restlessly compare their economic status with the status of those who have "made it." Since most are college educated and have social pretensions, their status anxiety is severe. One of the psychological consequences of the booming economy is that consciousness of social mobility has been much intensified even among those unsuccessful in achieving a higher status. This mobility consciousness stimulates the inclinations of mobility-oriented Koreans to emigrate to the United States, where better economic opportunities are expected. Given their opportunities to emigrate, South Korean middle-class urbanites desire to start a second life in a new land, leaving behind in the old land all their shameful memories. The following example illustrates the results of this desire to start a new life.

In the Kent Village Apartments [near Washington, D.C.] about 90 percent of some 600 Korean residents are skilled workers; the remaining are salesmen. Even though they are doing blue-collar work, they had never touched machines in Korea. Tae-Kyong Kim, the president of the Korean Association of the Kent Village, is a graduate of the History Department of Y University [in Korea]. He had been a public official at the Korean Office of Monopoly for 15 years.

He also owned a small business, but he failed in that business. Thus he decided to migrate to the United States. After receiving five months of training in auto repair work, he could enter the United States as a skilled immigrant. About 50 percent of the Korean residents here are college graduates, most having studied social science. Most of the residents had led lower-middle-class lives in Korea. About 30 percent of them are from South Vietnam, where they worked as overseas contract laborers. It is really tearful to see how they adjust themselves to American society. . . . Because of their poor skills and language, they are subject to all kinds of contempt and discrimination.[48]

CONCLUSION

South Korea's rapid economic development and industrialization has occurred within the framework of the international economic systems of advanced capitalistic nations. South Korea has built up an export-oriented economy by relying on foreign capital, materials, technology, and markets. These external factors have been integrated with an indigenous domestic factor—cheap and industrious labor.

The formation of a huge, cheap labor force in a few urban centers has been the result of a rural-to-urban migration. A government policy of low grain prices, supported by subsidized, massive imports of United States surplus grain products, has caused a massive exodus of South Korean peasants from farms to cities. At the same time, the development of an export-oriented economy in the primary cities has produced economic opportunities that pull South Korean peasants into the cities In this process, the South Korean government has taken a crucial role, especially through its policy of keeping industrial wages low, which is designed to help export industries gain markets and accumulate capital.

The Korean tradition of a strong, centralized government has greatly contributed to the dominance of South Korea's primary cities, especially Seoul. Moreover, an ancient Korean tradition, by which centralized political bureaucracy has predominated over every sphere of life, has also contributed to urban growth. The emergence of the primary cities is thus a ramification of the power of a centralized bureaucracy in allocating and developing national resources. Consequently, South Korean urbanization has resulted in keen competition over scarce economic resources and in overurbanization. And the socioeconomic vices of overurbanization have directly or indirectly pushed

[48] Kim, *Komerican*, pp. 180-182.

South Korean immigration toward the United States and other nations that accept Korean immigrants or migrant workers.

Rapid economic development in the urban centers has produced new urban classes, from which the majority of Korean immigrants to the United States are drawn. These immigrants had to overcome the breakdown of traditional norms and values in their homeland. After living through "dog-eat-dog" competition in the South Korean urban economy, they acquired the urban personality traits of sophistication, smartness, and shrewdness. As we shall see in chapter ten, the development of this type of personality is also partly derived from the past —from the peculiar Korean class structure and the Confucian cultural tradition.

Finally, the impact of the United States economy on the South Korean economic structure has been decisive: among other things, the United States has been a main supplier, along with Japan, of capital and material; it has provided a vast market for South Korean consumer products; and, as we shall discuss in the next chapter, South Korean trade with the United States has provided the major economic entry points for Korean immigrants. The immigrants have been facilitators as well as beneficiaries of the trade between the two countries.

PART II

*Economic Bases of the
Korean Community in the New York
Metropolitan Area*

CHAPTER FOUR

Small Business as an Entry Point
for Korean Immigrants

IN SPITE of their good education, professional experience, and urban middle-class backgrounds in the old land, a large proportion of Korean immigrants to the New York metropolitan area have entered the American economy by starting small businesses. By opening small businesses in inner cities, they attempt to fulfill the American dream even while native Americans abandon that version of the dream.

The propensity of Korean immigrants to operate small businesses can be explained in structural terms. Korean immigrants are not immediately capable of entering the mainstream of the American occupational structure—professional, white-collar work—because such work requires proficiency in English and a long period of training in large-scale American businesses. In contemporary American society, the primary and secondary industrial sectors have given way to a service-oriented economy; lacking service skills, Koreans are handicapped. Yet, equipped with a strong drive for upward mobility, Korean immigrants are renewing the American dream via their small businesses.

Korean immigrants who open small businesses must take advantage of socioeconomic changes; in fact, several changes have become the very condition for their commercial activities. One of the relevant changes is the development of economic interdependence between the United States and South Korea. Korean immigrants have emerged as agents facilitating trade between the two countries; the Korean wig industry in both the United States and South Korea is a case in point. Another relevant change is the basic shift of American urban populations since World War II: middle-class whites have moved to suburbs or suburban cities, and new minorities such as blacks and Hispanics have "inundated" the inner cities, driving white merchants on the defensive. Capitalizing on this trend, Korean immigrants have opened shop in ghetto areas by taking over such businesses as fruit and vegetable stores from retiring white merchants.

The Shift to Commercial Enterprises

In the rapid economic development of their homeland, Korean emigrants acquired an intensified consciousness of the possibility of upward economic mobility. We have noted in chapter one that a negligible number of emigrants were industrial workers or farm laborers in Korea. In particular, 63 percent of the Korean male householders in the New York metropolitan area were engaged in urban white-collar occupations at the time of their departure for the United States. These immigrants showed little propensity for commercial activity in their homeland; yet 34 percent of them were running commercial businesses in 1976.[1] Except for medical professionals, most Korean immigrants could not continue to work in their old white-collar jobs after entering the United States. This strong tendency to shift from white-collar work in the homeland to commercial enterprises in the new land was dramatically expressed in a Korean ethnic newspaper, which carried a series of essays on the lives of Korean immigrants in New York. One of the essays starts thus:

> A Mr. Park, who was a college professor at a Korean university in Seoul, has grabbed a steering wheel and become a taxi driver in New York City. Shoe repairing is the first job for a Mr. Yang, who once aired his name as a radio announcer in Seoul. In a small shoe-repairing shop he stakes his future American life on the continuous sound of his nailing work. A Mr. Lee, an American Ph.D. in engineering, peddled, while driving from village to village, wigs and clothing. He has just set up a wholesale company and thus has entered the ranks of the big Korean businessmen in New York City. All these episodes reveal a naked facade of the economic struggle of our fellow countrymen. . . .[2]

Old-timers frequently tell newcomers that "running a *jangsa* (commercial business) is the fastest way to get ahead in America." The language barrier partly explains this inclination. In the present centralized and bureaucratic American occupational structure, occupational entry is standardized and regulated by one's facility in English, among other things. This is an insuperable barrier to most Korean immigrants; it deprives them of many opportunities glorified in the American dream and shuts the door to the economic bureaucracies that employ the bulk of the American labor force. This fact, combined

[1] According to a sample survey conducted in 1977 by Hyong-gi Jin, 32 percent of all Korean householders in Southern California are engaged in small business enterprises; another 28 percent are interested in running small businesses. *Hankook Shinmoon*, November 5, 1977.

[2] *Hankook Ilbo*, December 28, 1976.

with differences in both the skills demanded and the system of rewards in the United States, means that occupational status cannot be transferred from the homeland to the new land. A high proportion of Korean immigrants were thus forced to turn to small retail businesses, in which they could still determine their own fate and still find some opportunities.

In addition, a subtle racial discrimination against new minorities in large-scale business firms and public service jobs may force even those Koreans who received their higher education at American universities to engage in small businesses. For example,

> Mr. Sohn, who acquired an M.B.A. from a midwestern university, had a great deal of self-respect until he was suddenly discharged in 1977 from the General Motors Company's Manhattan office. As part of a reshuffling in its business organization, G.M. abolished the section to which Mr. Sohn belonged and transferred all eleven of its staff members, except Mr. Sohn, to other sections of the company. Mr. Sohn was not laid off but discharged, because his workplace no longer existed.
>
> According to Mr. Sohn, a definite racial discrimination was involved in his case. He recalled numerous subtle instances of discrimination that he had to endure at his workplace. He could not be eligible for unemployment benefits, because he was discharged. Nor could he find another job, because of "old age" or overqualification. He was thus forced to open a small grocery store on Long Island. He said, "Now I am very happy with this grocery business. No one will meddle in my affairs. I no longer worry about being laid off by an American company" (field notes).

Many college-educated Korean-Americans, if they are young and ambitious, shift their career objectives from large organizations to small businesses even without encountering overt discrimination. At the beginning of their work in large firms, they discover specific career limitations they will likely encounter because of their ethnic peculiarity, and this discovery prompts a search for greater economic rewards in small businesses. Here is the story of a Korean youth who quit an American business firm in New York City.

> Mr. Lee and his wife immigrated to the United States in 1970. His wife's nursing skill enabled them to enter, and she supported him while he was a full-time student at a university in New York City. Three years later he earned an M.B.A. and found an accounting job at the R Company in New York City with a starting salary of $13,500.

At his entry into the American white-collar job market, Mr. Lee was somewhat frustrated. He received only two job offers, while he saw native-born American students receiving "a lot of job offers from famous corporations." He chose the R Company because the other company offering him a job intended to send him to its overseas branch in South Korea. He rationalized this discrepancy in job opportunities, saying to himself that "I am an immigrant with poor English." But when he started to work for the company, he met a Chinese coworker who was born in the United States and had no foreign accent. The Chinese had worked in the same section for several years but received few promotions. "Many new American graduates bypassed him. One American guy, who started at the same time as the Chinese, reached the level of supervisor." The report of this experience caused Mr. Lee to strengthen his sense of the career limitations in the company, and so he decided to leave.

Meanwhile, Mr. Lee perceived that becoming a certified public accountant would provide him with better opportunities because many Korean businesses with branches in New York City were increasing their demand for ethnic accountants. Thus, even at the outset of his work for the American company, Mr. Lee had decided to quit when he had passed the C.P.A. examination.

While keeping his full-time job, he devoted himself to preparing for the examination. It took him three years to pass it. Meanwhile, with the additional steady income earned by his wife, Mr. Lee accumulated enough capital to set up a small business. In the summer of 1977 Mr. Lee resigned, and with a down payment of $40,000 on a total price of $80,000 he purchased a medium-sized stationery store in the Bronx from a retiring Jewish owner. He set up his accounting office in this store and tried to attract Korean customers. He now has three full-time Korean employees, two of whom are relatives (field notes).

This kind of shift from white-collar work, however, accounts for only a small portion of the business enterprises run by Koreans; the majority of them are run by new immigrants. Since 1970, their number has increased so rapidly that in almost every commercial section of New York City one can find Korean retail shops. It has not yet been precisely determined how many Korean enterprises exist in the New York metropolitan area, but some Korean business leaders estimate that the number, as of 1979, is somewhere between 2,500 and 3,000.[3]

[3] It was reported that, in Southern California, Korean small business enterprises numbered (as of 1977) about 4,500 and that 65 percent of the total of 110,000 Koreans in that area settled in the Los Angeles metropolitan area. *Joong Ang Ilbo*, September 15, 1977.

The enterprises include wholesale and retail operations, catering and other service businesses, and South Korean firms with overseas branches that employ Korean immigrants.

CLASSIFICATION OF KOREAN BUSINESS ENTERPRISES

Korean business enterprises in New York can be classified into four groups by interrelating the following two factors: (1) whether the customers they cater to are Koreans or other ethnic groups; (2) whether the goods or services are produced and sold within the United States market or depend on economic relations with South Korea. As shown in the matrix of table 4.1, each of the four groups has some distinctive characteristics.

TABLE 4.1 TYPES OF KOREAN BUSINESS ENTERPRISES

Supply-and-Demand Mechanism	*Ethic Origin of Customers*	
	Korean	*Other*
	I	III
Originating in the interaction between the U.S. and Korea	Korean food and gift stores; book stores; newspaper and television companies; travel agencies; emigration and employment agencies, etc.	Retailers or wholesalers of garments, wigs, handbags, and other miscellaneous goods; *taekwondo* gymnasiums, etc.
	II	IV
Originating within the U.S. market	Accounting and legal services; real estate and insurance brokers; restaurants and bars; beauty salons, barber shops, photographers; carpenters, etc.	Fruits and vegetable stores, fish stores, liquor and grocery stores; stationery stores, shoe stores, hardware and furniture stores; dry cleaning and laundry; gas stations; garment subcontractors, etc.

The businesses in the first cell deal with goods or services specifically geared to Korean ethnic tastes and cultural needs that can be satisfied by commercial interaction between the two countries. Korean food and gift stores and book stores sell South Korean products to Korean immigrants. Items such as books, gifts, magazines, cassette tapes, and records are directly imported from South Korea. The majority of Korean immigrants are unable or unwilling to accommodate themselves to American foods; they try to maintain old dietary habits that call for hot, salty sauces such as garlic, hot pepper, mashed-bean, and soy sauce, which are essential ingredients of Korean foods. In the refrigerators of the immigrants' homes one cannot miss the *gimchi*—hot, salty, and pickled oriental cabbage. Korean food and gift stores can be found in almost all the neighborhoods where Korean immigrants reside. About fifty retail food and gift stores and four Korean-food wholesalers have emerged in the New York metropolitan area since 1970. By taking advantage of the strong inclination of Korean immigrants to visit their homeland, about fifteen Korean travel agencies have emerged in the competition for ethnic customers. Also, more than ten emigration companies existed in the New York metropolitan area in the early 1970s when the United States accepted a large number of "skilled" immigrants from South Korea. Most of them are no longer in business, because the United States has restricted such immigration since 1974. In addition, three newspaper companies receive South Korean daily newspapers, which they photocopy and deliver to Korean immigrants.

The enterprises in the second cell do not have a commercial tie with the homeland, but they still cater to Korean immigrants. Businesses providing such services as accounting, legal counseling, and real estate and insurance brokerage help Koreans adjust to the institutions of the larger American society. These enterprises are run by early immigrants, most of whom entered the United States as students and have acquired higher education at American universities. And, in response to the immigrants' inclination to "stick together," Korean restaurants, bars, barber shops, and beauty salons have come into being. About twenty Korean restaurants and bars have emerged in New York City; some of them provide a *gisaeng* (a traditional household female entertainer) service to their customers. Koreans like to talk while eating or drinking; all the major community affairs, formal or informal, such as business luncheons and speeches, welcoming parties for South Korean celebrities, alumni meetings, meetings of ethnic associations, love affairs, match making, and singles' dances take place in Korean restaurants.

Since the enterprises in both the first and second cells cater mainly to Korean customers, their further growth depends as much upon an increase in the number of Koreans in the New York metropolitan area as it does upon their success in the new economic environment. Keen competition has arisen among these business enterprises as they try to attract ethnic customers from among a limited population. These businesses buy most of the commercial space and time in ethnic newspapers and on ethnic television programs. However, compared with the businesses in the third and fourth cells, the businesses catering only to Korean immigrants are few.

The enterprises in the third cell have been established and have expanded because of the international trade between the United States and South Korea. Except for the *taekwondo* (a Korean art of self-defense) gymnasiums, these businesses sell consumer goods largely aimed at non-Korean ethnic minorities living in American cities. As we shall see later, the majority of these shops are located in the vicinity of the ghetto areas of New York. Blacks and Hispanics are their typical customers, and the business enterprises presuppose a dominant trend of mass consumption among these minorities. Korean immigrants import such consumer goods as wigs, false eyelashes, clothing, handbags, gloves, and other similar goods from South Korea and "dump" them in the larger inner cities of the United States. These minority-oriented business enterprises constitute a large portion of Korean retail or wholesale businesses, and several millionaires have come out of such enterprises.

Stores dealing with cheap, miscellaneous goods are the fastest-growing businesses in the third cell. These stores are frequently called "discount stores"; the price of any one item rarely surpasses ten dollars. Some 250 Korean "discount" stores have emerged in the New York metropolitan area; moreover, a high proportion of the approximately 300 wig stores in the New York area, as we shall see later, have become "discount stores" by adding to their lines cheap accessory goods, most of which are imported from South Korea. Finally, some 200 clothing stores are run predominantly by Korean immigrants who have learned small-business skills in the United States. The clothing stores need competent Korean salesmen or salesgirls who speak English well and who are sensitive to the "salesmanship" required for American customers. Partly because Korean immigrants have not yet attained a high level of American cultural sophistication, and partly because most of the clothes they deal are imported from South Korea, clothing stores run by Koreans do not respond swiftly to changes in women's clothing styles. This explains why the Korean clothing-stores are mainly confined to men's wear. Indeed, except for wig wholesalers or importers, Korean importers dealing with consumer goods cannot react swiftly to sudden changes in American fashions, because consumer items are imported from South Korea, where styles change less suddenly. This has been one of the major problems for the Korean business enterprises. As one way of solving it, the South Korean government has simplified its procedures for exports. Another solution adopted by Korean businesmen in New York is to produce such labor-intensive consumer goods as clothing and jewelry right in the city. For instance, a Korean garment-importer has established a garment factory in downtown Manhattan. A Korean newspaper quoted him as saying, "By using current American designs we can supply fashionable items in good time. Furthermore, we no longer worry about the problem of quotas."[4]

Except for a very few of the largest garment stores, the retail businesses in the third cell were started with small amounts of capital: in 1978 initial investments ranged from $10,000 to $20,000. For this reason, new immigrants with little capital enter these retail businesses first. After they have succeeded as shopkeepers, many have shifted to business enterprises in the fourth cell, which generally require much larger investments. In addition to the advantage of a small capital requirement, which is often raised through ethnic ties, Korean retailers in the third cell can purchase their merchandise on credit from Korean wholesalers or importers, whereas the majority of them cannot gain access to credit from American wholesalers. This also explains why Korean clothing-retailers cannot handle expensive, fashionable clothing manufactured in the United States or imported by American wholesalers. The availability of credit from Korean wholesalers is an enormous advantage to the Korean retailers, who have little capital, but a big disadvantage to the wholesalers, who also have to run their businesses on limited capital. Because South Korean exporters are competing with one another, they sometimes overextend credit to the Korean importers in the United States, and the importers (or wholesalers) sometimes find it difficult to collect money from the retailers. Some Korean retailers have bought, on credit, as much as possible from Korean wholesalers—and have then sold out and simply disappeared. And some Korean wholesalers in America have done the same thing to South Korean exporters, after having established a credit line with them.

The Korean shopkeepers in the third cell maintain close commercial ties with various Korean wholesalers in New York's "Koreatown" on Broadway between Thirty-first and Twenty-third streets. One of the "discount store" retailers advised a newcomer: "If you want to run this business, you must keep close contact with the Broadway wholesalers. You must pick up things there almost every morning." The *New York Post* described the business climate of "Koreatown" in 1975.

> "This is probably the closest thing we have to a Koreatown," said Ben Q. Limb, a friendly 38-year-old Korean as he waved his hand around a smoky restaurant called Kalbi House, on Broadway between 30th and 31st Sts. "This reminds me of a teahouse in Korea, where people sit and talk for hours."
>
> At every table, conservatively-dressed Korean businessmen were busy exchanging business cards and eating their Kalbi (beef spare-

[4] *Hankook Shinmoon*, September 11, 1976.

ribs barbecued over charcoal) and Kimchi (the volcano-hot cabbage pickle found on most Korean tables). "No Koreans are living in this area," said Limb. "But on Broadway between 23rd and 31st Sts., there are 250 to 300 Korean import businesses and five Korean-owned restaurants."

Limb, who had agreed to introduce a reporter around, then beckoned the president of the Korean Hair Goods Dealers Assn. to the table. "Wigs," said Young Sam Song. "Korean-made wigs were a very big import item until recently. But now the wig business seems to be falling off, and people are importing everything from men's shirts to gift items. All the things that used to be Made in Japan," he laughed, "are now being made in Korea." And leaving his business card he went back to work.

Limb said both he and Song are typical of many Koreans, now in their late 30s, who came here as graduate students 10 years ago. "Neither of us had planned to stay," he said, "But as the political situation in South Korea grew more and more oppressive, I, for one, chose not to return."[5]

By 1978, "Koreatown" had greatly expanded, renovating the decaying business district. Its Korean character is emphasized by the Korean-language commercial signs that have been installed. During the three years from 1975 to 1978, the number of Korean restaurants in the area almost doubled, indicating a rapid increase of business transactions in "Koreatown." As the volume of trade between the United States and South Korea has increased recently, about 190 business branches of South Korean manufacturers have settled in and around the area.

By taking advantage of the commerce between the United States and South Korea, some Korean immigrants have begun to open business enterprises that are aimed at non-Korean customers but that are entirely new to the United States; Korean immigrants, for instance, have greatly contributed to the commercialization of wigs in the United States, and they have initiated the commercialization of *taekwondo*, the traditional Korean art of self-defense. Although they offer a service rather than goods, the *taekwondo* gymnasiums still depend upon commercial ties with the homeland; they are essentially businesses that import this art in a highly commercial fashion in response to the emergence of a youth-oriented culture in the United States since the 1960s. Some fifty *taekwondo* gymnasiums are now found in the New York metropolitan area. Korean *taekwondo* instructors have organized a World Taekwondo Association in the United States and have held annual *taekwondo* contests. Recently, the United States Army and the

[5] *New York Post*, August 8, 1975.

military academies have begun to recognize the military usefulness of *taekwondo* and to employ an increasing number of Korean *taekwondo* instructors.

Korean enterprises in the fourth cell are typical small American businesses. Both the supply of goods and services they provide and the demand for them are generated within the United States market. They cater to all racial and ethnic groups in the New York area, but a high proportion of them are located in "transitional areas" of the city. For Korean immigrants, operating such businesses as liquor stores, gas stations, stationery stores, or furniture and hardware stores is a manifest symbol of economic achievement in the United States because such businesses do not serve an exclusively ethnic market. With no Korean connection in their origin, style, or flavor, these businesses arc considered a "higher" level of enterprise; many successful shopkeepers in the third cell, especially wig retailers, have therefore switched to businesses in the fourth cell, the opening of which usually requires large amounts of capital. The shopkeepers who run these "capital-intensive" businesses tend to be old-timers with relatively long experience in American society, but many new Korean immigrants, who have smuggled in dollars from South Korea, have also entered these businesses. However, fruit and vegetable stores, fish stores, dry-cleaning establishments, laundries, and garment subcontractors are exceptions. As we shall see in a case study, fruit and vegetable stores in particular are usually run by new immigrants with little capital. It must be emphasized that, despite the differences within the fourth cell, Korean immigrants have succeeded older white ethnic groups in operating their small business enterprises in New York City.

In focusing their sales efforts on the new urban minorities, Korean immigrants have responded to changes in the structure of urban America. Most central cities have declined in population between the 1950s and mid-1970s; population growth has been concentrated in the suburbs, middle-sized cities, and exurbia. At the same time, there has been a heavy influx of blacks from the South and the West Indies, of Puerto Ricans, and of other minorities into the inner cities. This fundamental shift, although accidental to Korean immigration, is an important factor determining the way in which Korean immigrants have made occupational niches in the present economic structure of America. The majority of Korean retail shops in both the third and fourth cells cater to blacks and other minorities by being located in "transitional areas" where old Jewish, Irish, and Italian shopkeepers are moving or are dying out and being replaced by an increasing number of the new minorities. For instance, about thirty small Korean businesses such as furniture, liquor, toy, wig, hardware, gift, Korean food, fruit and vegetable, and "discount" stores have emerged since 1973 along the Fordham Road shopping areas in the Bronx.

> Gone, by the tens of thousands, are the middle-class Jews, Irish and Italians who used to come to Fordham Road to trade up to $200 suits and $1,000 bedroom suites.
>
> But in their place have come tens of thousands of generally poorer Spanish-speaking people and blacks who may have less to spend individually, but who collectively are spending heavily enough on moderately priced goods to keep Fordham Road the sixth biggest shopping center in the Metropolitan area.[6]

Korean immigrants are able to buy shops from white minority shopkeepers, especially Jews, because the second- or third-generation children of these older immigrants have already entered the mainstream of the American occupational structure, and so they are reluctant to take over their parents' businesses. In fact, established Korean shopkeepers have advised less experienced Korean businesssmen that "the prospect is very good if you buy a store in a good location from old Jewish people" (field notes). This sort of ethnic succession in business is typical of all the small businesses in the fourth cell; their total number runs to more than one thousand throughout the New York metropolitan area.

Korean shopkeepers who have acquired some capital out of either such labor-intensive businesses as fruit and vegetable stores and dry-cleaning stores (fourth cell) or the businesses selling cheap Korean products (third cell) tend to move toward "comfortable" and "clean" businesses in the fourth cell such as stationery, liquor, jewelry, shoe, and hardware stores. Or they tend to acquire chain franchises. Many of these higher-level (because "American") businesses are located in white neighborhoods or in suburban cities, and the Korean shopkeepers who locate there are proud of the fact that they are catering "only to whites." A typical example of such pride is, "In my shop the *New York Times* is sold in a greater number than the *Daily News*," or "No one touched my store during the last blackout."

Running the Newest Businesses. All of the newest Korean retail businesses have emerged during a fundamental decline among small businesses; American small businessmen are on the defensive because of competition from suburban shopping centers, big department stores, and franchised chain stores. By employing family labor and initiating aggressive commercial activities, however, Korean immigrants attempt to reverse this trend. One result, as Korean ethnic newspapers have

[6] *New York Times*, December 24, 1976.

frequently reported, is robberies of the Korean merchants who keep their stores in ghetto areas open until midnight. On the other hand, by utilizing their entire family, Korean shopkeepers can maintain long store hours without paying overtime wages. Furthermore, they rarely observe the various American holidays, and, since their employees are family members, they do not pay holiday wages. By thus cutting labor costs, Korean retail businesses reduce overall costs and are able to compete with supermarket and chain-store prices. The statement by a Korean businessman, "In this business you can earn only labor costs," means to Korean immigrants that, if they do not have any specific skills that are salable in the United States market, they might better employ themselves and their family members in labor-intensive businesses. Moreover, by employing family members or other close relatives, Korean retail businessmen hope to eradicate "inside enemies"—non-Korean employees who steal cash and goods or give away goods to their friends or relatives who visit the store as customers.

In addition to family members, Korean businesses as a whole predominately employ new Korean immigrants who lack capital or specific skills. Since greenhorns cannot find "American" jobs, they are easily exploited by Korean employers. Low wages, overwork, and unpaid overtime are the most common forms of exploitation. But, while being exploited, greenhorns learn how to run a business in the United States. Korean employers frequently complain about the absence of steady workers among the Korean immigrant population: "As soon as we have trained them how to manage a business, they quit to start their own."

These general statements need substantiation. By conducting a detailed study of the two predominant Korean businesses in the New York metropolitan area—the wig and the fruit and vegetable businesses—we will illustrate these generalizations. These two enterprises deserve special attention because they have provided Korean immigrants with major economic entry points into American society.

THE FRUIT AND VEGETABLE BUSINESS: A CASE STUDY

The Emergence of Korean Greengrocers. Korean immigrants began to enter the fruit and vegetable business in New York City in 1971. The number of Korean-run fruit and vegetable stores has increased rapidly since 1974, and by 1978 there were some 350 Korean stores in all, existing in almost every neighborhood—white, black, and Hispanic—of the New York metropolitan area; Korean greengrocers cater to all segments of the population. In entering the fruit and vegetable business, Koreans have revived an older immigrant pattern of striving for an ethnic takeover of certain ghetto business enterprises. A vivid illustration is provided by the *New York Times*.

"It's like this," said a veteran produce supplier in a raspy Brooklyn accent, as he unpacked a crate of extra fancy figs at a Bronx Hunts Point Market stall. "When I first came into this business—that was before the war—to do business here you had to know Jewish phrases. Then, some years later you had to pick up a few Italian words to make it. Now I'm trying for all the Korean words I can. There are that many Korean buyers now."[7]

If Ill Y. Chung were Chinese and he had immigrated here, he might well have gone into the laundry or restaurant business. If he were Greek, he might have gone into a coffee shop or delicatessen. But Mr. Chung is Korean and so he entered the newly popular Korean-American enterprise: he opened a fruit and vegetable store.

"What else can I do?" asked Mr. Chung, 35 years old and the holder of two masters degrees on city planning from a school in Korea and one in mechanical engineering from the University of Hawaii. "I need money but there are no good jobs for Koreans. . . ." In fruits and vegetables, traditionally an immigrant business, first it was Jews, when it centered in the Washington market area, then Italians. And now up in the Bronx, it's the Koreans.[8]

Korean immigrants who entered the United States via Latin American nations were the first to enter the fruit and vegetable business, in 1971. These immigrants had run various businesses in Latin America after having encountered severe difficulties in progressing from the designated agricultural colonies of their original settlements to the metropolitan areas of Latin America. From there they migrated again, to the inner cities of the United States. During the years of uncertain and hostile journeys in foreign countries, they acquired a remarkable business acumen and a special sensitivity to economic opportunities. Furthermore, as we might recall, they were heavily drawn from among the North Korean refugees in South Korea, who constitute a tough-minded, aggressive, and marginal group in South Korean society. It is no wonder that the members of this Latin American contingent first detected economic opportunity in the fruit and vegetable business when they settled in New York City. News of their success quickly spread throughout the Korean community in the area, and new immigrants from South Korea quickly followed them into the business. This

[7] *New York Times*, February 18, 1976.   [8] *New York Times*, June 25, 1977.

economic news also spread to Koreans in Philadelphia, resulting in the emergence of Korean fruit and vegetable enterprises in that city.

The Three Causal Factors. Three structural factors can be linked with the emergence of the Korean fruit and vegetable business. First, the business can be opened with little capital and can be operated and managed without much knowledge of English. Given the small amounts of capital available, Korean immigrants with high economic motivation have entered this business.

> Mr. Huh, who immigrated five years ago, started his immigrant life as a janitor; a few months later he became a T.V. repairman. During the first year in the United States he saved about $4,000; Mr. Huh found a Korean partner and invested his savings in the opening of a fruit and vegetable store in Manhattan. In four years he has earned more than $100,000. Mr. Huh now employs eight workers. . . .[9]

Second, Korean immigrants with an abundance of family labor but little capital have either pushed out or taken over the businesses of old Jewish and Italian shopkeepers, who are too old to compete with a new generation of relatively young and economically aggressive Koreans. A Japanese journalist observed the importance of family labor for Koreans running fruit and vegetable businesses in New York.

> Mr. Kim bought his store two years ago from a Jewish American for a total payment of $15,000—$10,000 for the store price and $5,000 in key money. He and his son daily purchase vegetables: at four o'clock every morning when the dawn is coming, they get up and drive to Hunts Point in the Bronx, where a city-run wholesale market is located. . . .
>
> In the market they run and run in order to buy at low prices as many as one hundred and seventy different kinds of vegetables and fruits. All the transactions are made in cash. At 7 o'clock they return to the store and mobilize the rest of the family members in order to wash and trim vegetables. Here we can find the Koreans' secret of economic success in the business. In American supermarkets they do not wash and trim. . . .[10]

Shopkeepers who do not have sufficient family labor employ new Korean immigrants who otherwise could not find jobs. They exploit these non-unionized immigrants. The president of the Korean Produce Retailers Association of New York wrote some revealing advice on this matter.

[9] *Hankook Ilbo,* December 28, 1976.   [10] *Jugan Hankook,* January 16, 1977.

Recently, officials from the Food Employee Union have frequently visited the Korean fruit and vegetable stores, asking for a collective mutual contract with the union. If we continue to turn down their offers, it may be possible for them to picket in front of our stores or to attach a protest statement to our store windows. Thus a ready-made answer should be prepared in advance to stave off their demands. We can make an excuse as follows: "This store is run by family members," or, "We, partners, run this store." It should be noted that American law allows three partners at a maximum. We should be especially cautious in employing Americans, because union officials may encourage them to become union members. Once they belong to the union, extra expenses such as overtime payments, the hourly minimum wage, and social security taxes follow. Small Korean fruit and vegetable stores cannot afford to pay all these extra costs. . . .[11]

Since new Korean immigrant workers are, as a whole, well educated, individualistic, and ambitious enough to start their own business or to find other, better economic opportunities, shopkeepers who cannot mobilize sufficient family labor face the problem of continually securing new laborers from among the latest arriving immigrants. Ethnic newspapers carry daily advertisements of jobs offered by owners of fruit and vegetable stores. One of the advertisements runs, "Urgently seek healthy young man who wants to work in a vegetable store." Nevertheless, there is a quick turnover of workers. One greengrocer complained, "To employ Koreans is really a headache. They work only two or three days and quit without giving notice. One guy started to work in the morning and disappeared in the evening without giving a word." Sophisticated and well-educated Korean immigrants are reluctant to work long hours at low wages; six Korean workers employed at a Korean fruit and vegetable store on Fourteenth Street in Manhattan petitioned the United States Labor Department because they felt that they were being exploited by being paid less than the minimum wage.[12] Mainly because of this difficulty in securing easily exploitable workers from among the Korean population, a Korean greengrocer suggested to a newcomer that "if you do not have sufficient family members willing to help you, you might be better not to start this business."

Third, Korean greengrocers who can employ sufficient family members are able to compete with supermarket chains because they can work the long hours it takes to do daily wholesale shopping at the Hunts Point Market. This shopping is necessary to provide a steady

[11] *Hankook Ilbo*, February 26, 1976.   [12] *Joong Ang Ilbo*, August 1, 1977.

supply of fresh fruit and vegetables to customers. In addition, family members are effectively employed in the clipping, sorting, and washing necessary to reduce spoilage and waste. Thus the existence of family workers gives Korean greengrocers a marginal advantage over their competitors, supermarkets and non-Korean fruit and vegetable storeowners, most of whom subscribe to a delivery service for their retail products.

Intraethnic Conflict. Partly because of these structural factors, many Korean immigrants have set up new fruit and vegetable stores without buying established businesses. Once a Korean immigrant opens a new store, nearby non-Korean stores face serious competition. Many of the older Jewish or Italian stores have been forced out of business, and this leads to a new form of competition among Korean shopkeepers themselves. Here is an example of how interethnic competition transforms itself into intraethnic competition:

> In 1975, Mr. Lee, his two brothers, and one sister set up a new fruit and vegetable store near the South Bronx. They invested their total savings, which they had earned through menial work. At the opening of their store, they were uncertain about their economic future partly because they had to compete with an established Italian shop located a few blocks away. But, Mr. Lee once boasted, "When we started our business, they (the Italian shop) operated with four cashiers. Six months later, the number of cashiers was reduced to two. About nine months later, the owner came to our shop and asked whether we were interested in buying his shop." Mr. Lee's family could not take over the shop, because of its lack of capital. The shop eventually went to another Korean, named Mr. Oh, who owned two fruit and vegetable stores when he purchased the shop. Since Mr. Oh's taking over the shop, a fierce intraethnic competition has taken place between the two Korean stores. Mr. Oh could purchase retail items from wholesalers at much lower prices than Mr. Lee because Mr. Oh, an owner of three retail stores, buys large amounts of retail items. Thus Mr. Oh's retail prices were generally lower than Mr. Lee's. Mr. Lee once grumbled that Mr. Oh's store was practicing "dumping" (field notes).

Intraethnic competition also takes place when Korean immigrants buy stores from native Americans. The "key money" necessary for buying fruit and vegetable stores in New York City has increased substantially because Korean immigrants have competed among themselves in purchasing stores from non-Koreans. In 1974 the amount of "key money" needed to purchase a fruit and vegetable store was approximately five or six times that of the total weekly sales of the store. By 1977, the ratio of "key money" to total weekly sales had increased to seven or eight to one. In face of this increased capital requirement, Korean immigrants have opened new stores by leasing stores that became vacant after their owners were forced out of business. These newly opened Korean stores have encroached upon the sales territory of nearby stores regardless of whether the latter are run by Americans or Koreans. If the new Korean greengrocers compete with small American-run stores, they can easily overcome the competition because of their lower costs. But, if they encounter other Korean greengrocers, chances are that "they will ruin each other." Korean ethnic newspapers frequently offer some standard advice to potential greengrocers: "Competition among our *gyopo* (fellow countrymen) should be avoided."

Thus, one of the major functions of the Korean Produce Retailers Association, which was established in 1974, is to defend the interests of established Korean stores against newer Korean greengrocers. The association has systematically discouraged new arrivals from opening fruit and vegetable stores in areas near established Korean stores. An example can be found in the following episode.

A Korean named Mr. Lee was in the process of setting up a new fruit and vegetable store in the vicinity of an established Korean store located in the South Bronx. The established Korean greengrocer, named Mr. Kim, reported this event to the association, saying that if Mr. Lee opened his business both of them would lose business because of the limited number of customers.

The association's officials came to Mr. Lee and tried to persuade him not to open the business, by promising to grant him all the expenses that he had spent in setting up his business out of the association's fund. But Mr. Lee turned down their offer. Thus, in order to set an example designed to curb new openings by other Koreans, as well as to rescue Mr. Kim's store, the association decided to open a new store in the same block where Mr. Lee was opening his store, and it planned to dump vegetables at wholesale prices (field notes).

Taking advantage of the widespread aspiration among Koreans for economic success, Korean business "hawks" emerged at the initial Korean entry into the greengrocery business. The hawks set up new stores and, after running them for awhile, sold them to Korean newcomers, reaping smart profits in the form of "key money." Or they purchased stores from older ethnic owners and resold them to recent arrivals at inflated prices. A gimmick frequently involved in this kind of resale was the fraudulent inflation of sales volume. A Korean ethnic newspaper reported one example.

A (Korean) couple in Flushing worked sixteen hours a day for two years and accumulated some savings: the husband had labored in menial jobs and the wife had toiled at a garment factory. Their dream was simple: they wanted to have their own business rather than work for someone else.

One day, a church member [in their Korean church] approached and asked them whether they wanted to buy a fruit and vegetable store, saying that the owner of the store was a conscientious Christian. He added that the business of the store was very good but that the store owner had to sell the store because of a lack of hands.

When the couple heard this offer, they were very excited. The couple loitered around the store for two weeks and watched the customers patronizing the store in order to determine the volume of transactions. Then they decided to buy the store for the payment of $20,000 in "key money" because the store had always been crowded with so many customers.

They finally took over the store. But two or three weeks later they realized that they had been swindled. The once-teeming block customers suddenly disappeared. The former owner had cut his retail prices in half while they watched his store.[13]

Interethnic Conflict. In entering the fruit and vegetable business, Koreans have encountered some discrimination from Jewish and Italian wholesalers at the Hunts Point Market. In response, Korean greengrocers, for the first time in the history of New York's Korean community, staged a mass demonstration in the spring of 1977 "to protest what they say is discrimination against them in pricing practices and even in the allocation of parking services."[14] A Korean ethnic newspaper covered this event as a front-page story with the headline: "The Demonstration Showed Our Solidarity for a Common Interest." About a hundred greengrocers participated in the demonstration, which was formally touched off by a "racist slur" by a Jewish salesman in the market. The salesman was interviewed by an *Eastside & Westside* reporter, and the reporter's interview, after being translated into Korean, attributed remarks to the salesman to the effect that all Koreans are "stupid" and that they are all controlled by Sun Myung Moon's Unification Church.[15] Confronted by the Korean greengrocers, the sales-

---

[13] *Joong Ang Ilbo*, August 4, 1977.   [14] *New York Times*, June 25, 1977.
[15] "Moonies," or followers of Reverend Sun Myung Moon, run fruit and vege-

man apologized and insisted that the newspaper report was quite different from what he had actually said. The Korean Produce Retailers Association used this episode as an excuse to flex its muscles, but basic structural conditions had led Koreans to undertake the demonstration.

American wholesalers have frequently taken advantage of the Korean retailers' inadequacy in English and their lack of business experience. Wholesalers have sometimes sold them rotten fruit or vegetables, and they have sold their products to Korean greengrocers at higher than market prices; some Koreans were beaten up when they tried to complain about such unfair business transactions. Koreans have been robbed at the market's parking lot in the South Bronx, and Korean retailers have frequently fought with white retailers over parking space. When fights broke out, Koreans became the victims because of their small size. In some cases, however, several Koreans ganged up and knocked out white Americans when they saw fellow Koreans fighting the Americans over parking space and other minor matters. However, all these attacks against Koreans have taken place on an individual basis. And there has been no systematic, conspiratorial discrimination by wholesalers against Korean greengrocers. But the Korean Produce Retailers Association, with an increasing membership, felt that the newspaper interview provided an appropriate opportunity for them to demonstrate Korean "clout" and thus to put psychological pressure on the Hunts Point establishment.

Most wholesalers at the Hunts Point Market welcome the entry of Koreans into the business. This is so because, as one wholesaler (whose family started their business three generations ago with a pushcart in lower Manhattan) said, "They're good businessmen, they buy good produce and they pay their bills in cash. . . . That's something we could use around here from everybody."[16] To show their good will, wholesalers contributed some $3,000 in 1977 to the Korean Produce Retailers Association. The association used part of this contribution to pay the cost of its 1977 (annual) picnic for its members and their families.

The Greengrocery Business as a Means of Capital Accumulation. For the majority of Korean greengrocers, the fruit and vegetable business is just a means to accumulate capital with which they can start "clean" and "comfortable" small businesses. Several Korean greengrocers own more than one store and have set up a "chain store" management to

---

table stores in New York City; but Korean greengrocers have nothing to do with the Unification Church.

[16] *New York Times*, February 18, 1976.

run them; but the majority do not enter this business permanently. Frequent changes in ownership characterize most of the Korean stores. Partly because of this, Korean greengrocers have not formed cooperatives through which (as some advocate) they could purchase as a group from the producers in California and Florida, at much lower prices. One of the basic reasons for the frequent turnover of Korean fruit and vegetable stores is that to run such a business requires painstaking work. Some Korean greengrocers said that, "no matter how much energy, health, and stamina one may have, one cannot stand more than two years of this daily toil." They use expressions such as "bloody urine," "drastic loss of weight," and "benumbed fingers like a leper's" when they describe the daily struggle of operating their businesses.

Many Korean greengrocers have "made it" by getting out of that business and reinvesting the capital they acquired from it in small businesses requiring less exploitation of themselves and their families. In doing so they have converted this self-exploited labor into capital and thus decreased the amount of primitive exploitation necessary for capital accumulation. Some of them, however, have sold their stores but have returned to the greengrocery business, saying that "no small businesses in America can beat the fruit and vegetable business." Some of them have become absentee owners by renting their stores to new Korean immigrants under agreements stipulating that a percentage of business profits be paid to them. Most of these absentee storeowners own and run other small businesses.

To sum up, the usefulness of the greengrocery business as an economic entry point for Korean immigrants depends upon several factors. First, we must recall that Korean immigrants could transfer their old family structure to the new land because the United States Immigration Act of 1965 made it possible for them to form a three-generation extended family in America. Consequently, some immigrants with an abundance of family labor but little capital have found economic opportunities in the labor-intensive fruit and vegetable business during the initial stage of their economic adjustment. Korean immigrants possess a family-centered success ethic that causes each family member to be willing to devote himself to the family business. This, together with the intense economic motivation of Koreans, establishes a "natural" affinity toward the greengrocery business, which requires intensive labor and a willingness to exploit oneself to gain economic mobility. Korean entry into the greengrocery business has revived and sustained a classic American immigration pattern of ethnic succession in economic activity. However, the economic opportunities for immigrants in the fruit and vegetable business are small compared with those in the wig business. Unlike the Korean fruit and vegetable business, whose economic boundary has largely confined it to a few big cities on the eastern seaboard, the Korean wig-business has established a national market. As the fruit and vegetable business is typical of Korean business enterprises in the fourth cell (table 4.1), so the wig business is typical of Korean enterprises in the third cell, in which the businesses in the United States maintain close commercial ties with South Korea.

THE WIG INDUSTRY IN BOTH SOUTH KOREA AND THE UNITED STATES: A CASE STUDY

The Impact of American Fashion. A sudden change in American life styles in the 1960s has largely affected the development of the wig industry in South Korea; and, in importing Korean-made wigs, many Korean immigrants found their occupational entry point in the United States economy.

The use of wigs, which had been abandoned since the rococo era—except by small circles in the theatrical and movie world and by aristocratically inclined upper classes in both America and Europe—resurfaced unexpectedly in the American fashion world of the early 1960s and spread over Europe, Japan, the Arab world, and Latin America. Wigs for both men and women came into fashion as part of the permissive, youth-oriented, antiestablishment social climate of the 1960s. The wig has appeared along with such ever-changing fashion items as boots, platform shoes, bell-bottom trousers, unisex clothes, mini-, midi-, and maxiskirts, pantsuits, and hotpants. All these styles reflect such attributes as "naturalness," "easiness," "carefreeness," and "chic." Coupled with these fashion modes, the "make-your-own-fashion" fashion constitutes an implicit ideology in contemporary America —the cultivation of an artificial sloppiness in the lifestyles of the urban masses. The masses accept and discard styles that seem to be natural, easy, and unrestrained; since they may choose every possible style, they can accept no particular style authentically—that is, with a natural, unselfconscious, taken-for-granted attitude.

The civil rights movement and black nationalism have greatly affected black dress and costume styles. One of the effects is a massive adoption of wigs by blacks as an expression of the idea of negritude itself, French-African in origin. The idea of negritude, with its emphasis on the glorification of an unknown African past, has been reflected in Afro-wig styles such as the so-called Numidian Lady and Nubian Queen. The term *Numidian* is derived from Numidia, which was an ancient kingdom of North Africa corresponding roughly to modern Algeria; *Nubian* means a member of a Negroid people of an ancient kingdom of northeastern Africa. However, wig styles for blacks have mainly been caricatures of traditional white styles. For instance, the classic Cleopatra style has emerged only slightly changed under names such as Skin Crown, Mushroom, and Skin-Top; the bouffant style has been imitated in Afro-wig styles such as Giant Afro Puff, Darling, and A Dome of Curls.[17] This kind of artificiality in blacks' life styles[18] has directly contributed to the development of the wig industry in South Korea as well as the emergence of the Korean wig-business in the United States.

The prevalent use of wigs among blacks since the middle of the 1960s cannot, however, sufficiently explain why the Korean wig-industry has prospered. Under the impact of a recent "cultural revolution," wigs have been worn by segments of the American population that include blacks and whites, males and females, poor and rich, young and old, and traditionalists and modernists. The psychological demand varies by segment of population and by timing in a fashion cycle. Middle-aged men, under the pressure of America's youth-oriented culture, are increasingly wearing toupees in order to retain an image of their vanishing masculinity.[19] Meanwhile, bank robbers, prostitutes, and stage entertainers use them for their deadly serious businesses. For middle-class white housewives, the use of a wig may be economical because it may cut down the cost of hairdressing at a beauty parlor. All these uses of wigs have made the hair-goods industry one of the fastest-growing industries in the United States. According to a trade journal, "Between 1965 and 1966, hair goods purchases by dealers from manufacturers and distributors increased by $4,200,000 or 44 percent.

---

[17] The labeling of wig styles for blacks takes place under the two categories of image making. One category depicts the image of casual naturalness by such names as "Windswept," "Cascade," "Freedom Puffs," "Sunny Flip," "Carefree," and "Sexama." The other category aims at a personification of styles in order to show a social characteristic of the wearer. It includes such styles as "Page Boy," "Private Secretary," "Boss Lady," "Baby Afro," and "Black Huntress"; in the case of male Afro-wigs, there are such styles as "The King," "The Sophisticate," "Score Man," and "Top Man."

[18] The use of wigs as a way of expressing life styles can be traced through the recorded history of the West. Originally, wigs were intended to protect the head from sun, heat, and cold. They were also intended to imitate nature in compensating for the loss of hair. Eventually, wigs became symbols of status and class, thereby losing their original functions of either protecting one from nature or imitating it. When wigs became an artificial symbol of life styles, their use in fashion might be seen, according to Huizinga's theories, as acting out a turgid playfulness in human culture. See Johan Huizinga, *Homo Ludens: A Study of the Play Element in Culture*, Boston, Beacon Press, 1955, pp. 183-186. For a detailed description of the history of wigs, see Richard Corson, *Fashion in Hair: The Five Thousand Years*, London, Peter Owen, 1965.

[19] *New York Times*, April 22, 1974.

This makes wigs, hairpieces, and accessories the industry's fastest growth item."[20]

When so many Americans suddenly adopted wigs, American wig-makers could not meet the demand by their domestic production. The basic reason was that they produced wigs in workshops as small handicrafts; they could not expand their enterprises into large factories, mainly because America lacks a cheap labor force. Furthermore, the wig industry, like the garment industry, cannot be completely mechanized or automated, because intensive manual labor is required in the process of planting individual hairs into wig pads.

In the early 1960s, before synthetic thread for wigs was invented, American wigmakers had to start importing human hair from South Korea, Hong Kong, Taiwan, Indochina, and India. Although they had previously shunned these ethnic hair types owing to their darkness, stiffness, and straightness, they had to import them because they could no longer meet the expanding demand for wigs by relying exclusively on European hair. A dyeing technique that was developed in the 1960s, however, could make the imported Asian hair look like European hair; in response to this technique and to the demand for human hair, Korean hair-exporters emerged in the early 1960s. Their immediate customers were American and Japanese wigmakers. As purchasing agents for these hair exporters, Korean peddlers made house-to-house visits in order to collect human hair from the heads of Korean women. At that time, they were frequently seen in every alley of Seoul yelling, "We buy human hair." It was also a common phenomenon in rural Korean villages to see these hair collectors inducing women to sell their center-parted long hair.

The Emergence of Korean Wig-Manufacturers. Meanwhile, Korean hair-exporters became aware of the economic opportunities in manufacturing wigs themselves. They could contemplate entering the wig business because they were already engaged in exporting such goods as clothes, gifts, and seafood products. Thus they were mentally equipped to move from exporting hair as a raw material to manufacturing and exporting finished hair-goods.

Most hair exporters also ran small brokerage companies facilitating foreign trade. In return for a commission, brokerage companies play an intermediary role linking foreign buyers to small domestic producers of labor-intensive goods. These brokerage companies are small and are staffed by business technicians who know how to transact foreign trade. In South Korea they are called *opa-sang* (*opa* is derived from

---

[20] *Modern's Market Guide*, Modern Beauty Shop Magazine, 1968, p. 79.

the English word "offer"; *sang* means "business" in Chinese characters). Mainly because of the emergence of big trade corporations—the South Korean industrial conglomerates, the *jaebeol* groups, which have encroached upon the traditional functions or interests of the *opa-sang* —the functional importance of the brokerage companies has been declining. Furthermore, with the great increase of foreign trade, the South Korean government instituted in the early 1970s a centralized brokerage company in order to facilitate exports by small and medium-sized producers. But the *opa-sang* played a crucial role in the initial growth of South Korean foreign trade, especially in the wig business.

At the initial stage of Korean wig-manufacturing, factories were small, and work was usually performed in the factoryowner's home. In most cases, hair exporters became wig manufacturers, and their production was confined to so-called handmade wigs. As the demand for wigs in the United States increased during the mid-1960s, the Korean producers of handmade wigs, who used human hair, could not meet the demand, because hair was becoming ever scarcer and rising in cost; but the Japanese invention of synthetic thread as a substitute for human hair revolutionized the wig business. A Japanese salesman for the manufacturer of the new product, called Kanekalon, came to South Korea in order to find Korean buyers. Only four Korean wig-producers appreciated the potential market value of the new thread; the majority of them could not anticipate a large demand for the synthetic product. The four manufacturers, however, acquired exclusive rights to the new product, and thus they outpaced their competitors, built larger factories, and became the leading wig exporters. A synthetic fiber called Venicelon, made in Italy, and Elura, made in the United States, followed the Japanese Kanekalon. These were supplied to selected Korean wigmakers; but those manufacturers who gained an early access to the synthetic materials expanded their businesses the most.

Many South Korean manufacturers of labor-intensive goods turned to the production of wigs in the following years. Partly owing to the production of wigs, the Daewoo industrial corporation, for instance, emerged as a leading South Korean *jaebeol*. During the late 1960s, about eighty Korean wig-manufacturers emerged, and at this time the South Korean government began to encourage and support them by providing special loans and exempting imported materials from taxes.

The "Putting-out" System. A "putting-out" system characterized the early stages of wig manufacturing in Korea. Later, as the demand for wigs in the United States increased, hair exporters expanded their factories and also began to put out work to smaller handicraft workshops run by subcontractors. Many hair exporters did not even own a factory; they pretended to be manufacturers when they contracted with foreign buyers, but when they received orders they put out the work to subcontractors. In one case, a big American wig-wholesaler provided a Korean wigmaker with capital, materials, and skills; the Korean wigmaker was a subcontractor, while the Korean subcontractors under the Korean wigmaker were sub-subcontractors. In the late 1960s, when the wig fashion in the United States began to boom, subcontractors increased substantially in number and spread from cities to rural areas. For example, the Dana wig-manufacturing company had more than a hundred subcontractors in the late 1960s. But the putting-out system was mainly located in urban areas.

Wigmaking in Korea was from its beginning tightly connected to the American market. Seventy-four percent of all Korean wig-products were sold to American consumers between 1966 and 1972;[21] the Korean wig-industry has been almost entirely governed by fluctuations in the demand for wigs in the United States. When Korean wig-manufacturers received orders from American or Korean importers in the United States, they did not have any difficulty in securing subcontractors, who either brought workers into their household workshops or sent out the job assignments to workers in their own households. Business was usually conducted on the basis of short-term orders. On rush days we can easily imagine a group of Korean girls, most of whom were rural-to-urban migrants, sitting around worktables continuously trimming, cutting, sewing, or planting synthetic threads or human hair on wig pads under sweatshop working conditions. Such workshops were usually a part of the subcontractors' households. When job assignments were sent to workers' households, subcontractors made house-to-house visits in order to direct and supervise the work. Some aggressive subcontractors became manufacturers by directly negotiating contracts with American or Korean buyers in the United States. Most of them, however, were technically incompetent and financially weak; consequently, they stayed under the control of wig manufacturers or exporters.

[21] The following table shows the annual amount of Korean-made wigs exported to the United States, in millions of dollars:

Year	Wig Exports
1966	$10.6
1967	19.9
1968	30.1
1969	51.6
1970	80.3
1971	57.1
1972	53.1

SOURCE: *Hae Oe Han-in Hoebo,* July 20, 1973.

Wig manufacturing in South Korea usually consists of four main operations, each performed by a special team: the first is the "roller" team, which cuts and screens synthetic threads; the second is the "cap" team, which makes wig pads; the third is the "post" team, which plants synthetic threads on the wig pads by means of sewing machines; the last is the "skin" team, which adds curling and other "artistic" touches to the products produced by the "post" team. Within each team there are also differentiated functional teams. Accordingly, subcontractors are highly differentiated by specific functions, and wig manufacturers assign them differentiated workloads.

Wig manufacturers own centralized factories that produce finished products by putting together the parts collected from subcontractors. This putting-out system was not efficient in meeting the increasing demand for wigs in the American market. For instance, many American buyers filed claims against Korean wig-manufacturers demanding compensation for poor-quality wigs. American buyers also complained that there were substantial differences in quality among wigs for which they had paid the same price. This lack of standardization can largely be attributed to the putting-out system, for producers cannot maintain a centralized and constant supervision over all phases of the work. Furthermore, when the number of subcontractors increased and when subcontracting spread to remote rural areas, wig manufacturers faced enormous difficulties in coordinating the work of their subcontractors. Although manufacturers sent their own men to the subcontractors to supervise and direct their work, subcontractors frequently bribed these supervisors with cash payments and by entertainment in local bars.

The putting-out system of wig manufacturing has been in rapid decline since the late 1960s and has been largely replaced by a centralized factory system. Manufacturers now directly recruit female workers for their new factories, and many have instituted dormitory systems in order to house young female migrant workers from rural areas. Big manufacturers employ thousands of female workers, who produce not only wigs but also other labor-intensive products such as false eyelashes and dolls. Thus, in less than ten years the Korean wig-industry has recapitulated as much as five hundred years of the history of the textile industry and related industries in the West.

The Decline of the Wig Industry in Korea. One of the main advantages of the wig industry in Korea is derived from the abundance of cheap but careful labor. This advantage neutralizes competition from advanced, industrial nations. As has been noted, wig production cannot be completely mechanized; it requires intensive manual labor for trimming, cutting, sewing, and curling. The Korean *yeogong*, female migrant workers between fifteen and twenty-five years old, are suitable for such jobs. In 1970 they received somewhere between twenty and twenty-five dollars per month for laboring under sweatshop conditions; at the initial stage of wig manufacturing, they were paid by the piece.

Taking advantage of this cheap labor force, Korean wig-manufacturers made substantial profits. In a reversal of earlier economic patterns, they make a finished product with materials imported from the developed nations, mainly from Japan. The prosperity of the industry has entirely depended on foreign nations both for its supply of materials and its final market. Japanese and American market conditions especially have had accelerating effects on fluctuations in the South Korean wig industry. For example, a hard blow struck the entire industry when the worldwide energy crisis of 1973 occurred during a gradual decline in the demand for wigs, especially in the United States; the number of Korean wig-manufacturers was reduced from eighty in 1970 to thirty-five in 1977.[22] The majority of the manufacturers who left the wig business turned to the production of toys, gloves, dolls, handbags, and similar items, which they could produce with little disruption to their established installations and methods of operation.

At a very early stage in wig manufacturing, the South Korean government, concerned with the Confucian idea of "saving face," prohibited Korean wigmakers from exporting their products, which at that time were all made of human hair, on the grounds that it would be a national disgrace to make money from such a frivolous product. This policy was immediately reversed. By 1970 the wig industry outpaced all other export industries in earning dollars and contributed about 10 percent, $94 million, to the total amount of national exports. In 1970 some leading wig manufacturers were awarded special citations by President Park Chung-hee for their outstanding accomplishments in the export trade, which Park's economic policy had encouraged in the effort to accumulate capital. The power and status of Korean wig-manufacturers was so enhanced during the period of their commercial expansion that they had held a series of conferences at leading hotels in Seoul, which were attended by high-ranking government officials along with Japanese, Italian, and American makers of synthetic fibers. In their business magazine, *Journal of Wig World*, they used as a slogan "the wig Korea," the advertisement of which supported the expansion of wig exports into Arab, Latin American, and European nations,

[22] *Joong Ang Ilbo*, August 30, 1977.

and into the United States. But this enhanced status of the Korean wig-industry has recently been tainted by massive dumping practices, which were largely caused by the decline of wig wearing in the United States. Still, in 1977 the Korean wig-industry supplied about 60 percent of all wigs manufactured in the world and about 90 percent of all wigs sold in the United States.[23]

The Entry of Korean Immigrants into the Wig Business. Korean emigration to the United States began during the same period that the Korean wig-industry emerged. This coincidence was crucial for the success of many immigrants, for wigs were used as a major entry point into the United States economy. The immigrants' business roles ranged from importers, wholesalers, and dealers to retailers and peddlers. Strictly speaking, there is no distinct line demarcating importers, wholesalers, and dealers; their market roles overlap. In 1974, Koreans ran 68 importing or wholesaling companies in New York City;[24] in the Washington D.C. area in the same year there were 30 such companies. Moreover, Korean immigrants owned and operated some 2,500 retail wig shops throughout the United States in 1974,[25] and in the New York metropolitan area they ran some 300 shops. But by 1977 the number of Korean wig-importers in New York City had been reduced by more than 50 percent from the peak years, as many turned to other importing businesses. Similarly, many of the Korean wig-shops have turned to other kinds of retailing. Korean wig-peddlers, who were once found in every ghetto shopping area of New York City, have almost all left; but during the early 1970s the comparatively small wig business had been the leading occupation that Korean immigrants entered in order to "make it" in the United States, despite the centralized character of the dominant business structure in contemporary American society.

The Wig Industry in America. Before the emergence of mass-produced synthetic wigs, American wig-men—wigmakers, dealers, and hairdressers—emphasized "scarcity" and "craftsmanship." A sense of scarcity was easily imposed on their clientele because human hair, especially European hair, is, as a commercial product, scarce; and its conversion into a wig calls for a great deal of skill. Thus wigmakers sustained an occupational image that they were artists and that their products were works of art. As a result, an "art" wig was not a thing to bargain about; the price charged depended upon what kind of client was buying.

[23] Ibid.
[24] The figure indicates the number of companies that were registered at the Korean Wig Union in New York City.
[25] *Hae Oe Han-in Hoebe*, July 20, 1973.

This occupational ideology of high craftsmanship has gone on the defensive since the mass production of machine-made wigs emerged. For instance, Joseph Fleischer, who as an immigrant brought wig craftsmanship from Austria to America and became a leading figure among American wigmakers during the 1940s, complained that "few care about skill to go through the tedious slow and complicated apprenticeship that was his as well as the master-craftsmen under his tutelage. . . . This is especially important in wigs since a machine-made foundation can never fit the head properly."[26] But the craft ideology still survives among French wigmakers as well as among traditional American wigmakers. In France, nevertheless, production is accomplished through an assembly line of female workers; individual craftsmanship has been replaced by a differentiation of functional skills in a factory system. And yet the advertising runs, "Delicately wefted for lightness and strength by master French craftsmen. The world's finest hand-made wig, created in France by master artists for the women accustomed to buying the very best."[27] These are the manufacturers who invented such sophisticated accessory items as wig cleaners, wig care kits, wig driers, wig color rings, wig sprays, wig pins, and wig perfume.

As the use of wigs increased among the American lower classes and among ethnic groups such as blacks and Puerto Ricans, conventional beauty shops could not satisfy the massive new demand for inexpensive, "wear-it-as-you-buy-it" wigs. A market researcher recommended to beauty-shop owners that

> wigs and hairpieces should never be regarded as strictly retail items. Many hairpieces today are sold as part of a professional styling service. A wig is also different from any other retail item as it gives the patron another "head" to have serviced and provides the dealer and shop owner with a whole new category of accessory products which of necessity must be sold in conjunction with the sale of hair goods.
>
> The wig business belongs in the beauty salon, for the salon is the one stop shopping unit for everything and anything connected with hairpieces. . . . Wigs are not only a commodity, they are a way of life. The sale of a wig is just as personal a matter as the sale of a personal beauty service. . . . The beauty salon staff has a close personal relationship with the patron, knows her needs, knows the way she wears her hair, and is capable of giving advice on her color shades, conditioning products, etc. Even if she knows all this and

[26] "The Saga of Joseph Fleischer," *Fashion-Right Hair Pieces* (New York: Joseph Fleischer Company, 1949), p. 143.
[27] *Modern's Market Guide*, Modern Beauty Shop Magazine, 1968, p. 88.

still goes ahead and buys the wig, the odds are she will be dissatisfied.[28]

In addition to not wanting to charge higher prices for furnishing individualized services, many beauty-shop owners were reluctant to offer new wig items and the accompanying shaping and cleaning services. This might explain the relatively slow acceptance of the new and profitable product by beauty-salon owners. In 1967, about 26 percent of the country's beauty salons retailed wigs and other hairpieces; in 1968, about 43 percent did some retailing of wigs and wiglets.[29] Thus, there was a discrepancy between the massive demand for wigs and the relative absence of retail centers to meet it. This opened the way for independent wig-shops or salons that exclusively sold wigs and provided service at reasonable prices to people with lower incomes. *Modern's Market Guide* for beauty shops reported,

> Some of the dealers who are more experienced and successful in handling wigs and hairpieces find that they have literally established a second business. They not only sell hair goods and accessories to their shop customers, in many instances, they actually service the wigs and hairpieces for those of their customers who are too timid to tackle the job themselves. These dealers frequently employ stylists to pre-style pieces and, as a consequence, expand their market.[30]

Under the circumstances, wide-open marketing conditions as well as the wig craze fostered the emergence of the Korean wig-industry in America. The industry emerged so suddenly and expanded so rapidly that Koreans did not enter into conflict with vested interests in catering to lower-class and nonwhite ethnic customers.

Intraethnic Conflict over the Wig Market. The segment of the wig business that Korean immigrants entered was a function of their time of arrival. Wholesalers or importers were the earliest Korean settlers, and they frequently boasted of their long experience in American society. Retailers and peddlers were, in comparison, newcomers. Most of the wholesalers played a crucial role in the development of the home wig industry in Korea by providing manufacturers with market information and criteria for styles when the wig craze began to emerge in the early 1960s. Some of them were able to accumulate large amounts of capital by building their own factories in South Korea, and some established retail chain systems throughout the United States and sent for their cousins and friends in Korea to manage and work in these stores. This also stimulated migration, of course.

[28] Ibid., pp. 88-115. [29] Ibid., p. 79. [30] Ibid., p. 90.

In ideal economic practice there are three phases in the delivery of goods from manufacturer to consumer: manufacturing, wholesaling, and retailing. In the Korean wig-community, however, these orderly phases disappeared. At one time, the ideal market channels existed, but Korean wig-manufacturers began to open their own branches in America, thus encroaching on the established importing and wholesaling domains of Korean immigrants, when the manufacturers became aware of the higher profits that could be made by selling directly to American customers. A black ethnic newspaper described a typical case.

> S. Z. Chuu came to the United States about a year ago. A few months later he opened a wig shop, Happy Chuu Inc., in the heart of the Black community in Bedford-Stuyvesant-Nostrand Avenue near Fulton Street. Chuu has one employee, a Black; the business he says is "doing well."
> Before coming here Chuu worked with the Korean Manufacturing Company in South Korea. Through the company he was able to obtain a four-year trade visa from the American Embassy in South Korea. Chuu says the company paid his air fare and provided the financing for his store.
> Chuu now imports his goods directly from the company. . . .[31]

The expansion into retailing and exporting by the Korean wig-manufacturers brought about a substantial lowering of wig prices. Whatever prices were charged, the large manufacturers still made some profit from mass sales in America because of the low labor costs in South Korea. During the wig boom, from approximately 1969 to 1972, sales agents of Korean manufacturers as well as immigrant Korean wholesalers and importers acted as if the American market for wig products was limitless and would continue to expand indefinitely. Partly because of the recession beginning in 1971 and partly because of the fact that potential wig users had already bought as many wigs as they wanted, however, the market began a gradual decline in 1971. Furthermore, since 1972 American fashion has been turning instead to hats and caps.

All these factors, which South Koreans could not control, caused the wig industry to pile up a huge inventory, which tied up capital and created a cash-flow problem. Moreover, in expanding and improving their factories in response to their expectations of an unlimited demand in America, many Korean manufacturers had received Korean-government-guaranteed commercial loans from American or Japanese banks.

[31] *New York Echo*, April 27, 1974.

In order to regain some liquidity, Korean wig-manufacturers had to re-sort to a mass dumping of their inventory into the American market; a drastic reduction in retail prices ensued. In the late 1960s Korean retailers sold wigs to American customers at a price somewhere between $15.00 and $30.00. At that time, production cost Korean manufacturers somewhere between $1.00 and $1.50 per wig. But, by 1977, the retail price of a wig fluctuated between $7.00 and $10.00, depending upon quality, despite the skyrocketing costs of synthetic fibers caused by a worldwide inflation and a steady rise in the price of oil, out of which the fibers are made.

During the high point of the wig boom, both the sales agents of South Korean manufacturers and the Korean importers (wholesalers) in the United States encouraged some Korean-American immigrants to become wig peddlers. In some cases sales agents or wholesalers organized their own peddling systems, independent of retailers, in which peddlers were hired at a base salary plus commission. Under these circumstances, a fierce conflict arose between peddlers, wholesalers, and sales agents on the one hand, and retailers on the other. When the market sagged, the conflict grew sharper. The agents of South Korean manufacturers and the wholesalers could still turn a profit when retail prices began to drop simply because of the large number of transactions they made; and the peddlers who worked for them could avoid fixed retailing expenses such as rent, taxes, and labor costs by selling in the streets or door-to-door. But the new dumping practices greatly upset Korean retailers as well as the American beauty-salon owners who ran their businesses under the aegis of "scarcity" and "craftsmanship."

The conflict between Korean retailers and peddlers became the shame of the entire Korean community in New York. Direct, violent encounters were occasionally touched off when Korean peddlers did their selling in the vicinity of Korean retail shops. Shopowners had to charge higher prices to cover rent and salaries paid to wig stylists. Since their customers were blacks and Puerto Ricans, the ecological niche of their businesses was limited to shopping centers in black and Puerto Rican communities. In such ethnic commercial centers, marketing space was so limited that the two groups of Korean wig-men could not coexist, and a Darwinian struggle ensued. For example, in the commercial section in Jamaica, Queens, a Korean peddler working for a wholesaler died in 1972 as a result of fighting with Korean retailers.

Except for cases in which a homicide was involved, Koreans tried to minimize police intervention in order to avoid publicity. They did not want to be accused by the wig community and by their fellow Koreans of creating unfavorable publicity for the whole ethnic community.

Korean ethnic newspapers frequently carried articles on this issue. For instance, an editorial in the *Koreapost* stated,

A series of violent incidents among Korean wig merchants in New York City provokes a sense of shame in our community and reminds us of the gangster warfare once rampant in the Myondong downtown district in Seoul. The fighting with knives among wig merchants in Jamaica and the recent fistfighting in the Bronx are among the incidents that have left a shameful spot on our community. Furthermore, on last June 18 our Koreans fought one another throwing dishes and chairs when they gathered in a Korean restaurant here to settle their dispute. It is our regret that the fighting eventually resulted in the arrival of three police cars. . . .[32]

The dumping practices by sales agents of Korean manufacturing have also provoked a keen conflict with American wig-dealers or wholesalers, who are of predominantly Jewish and Italian origin. While Koreans have mainly catered to blacks and Puerto Ricans through retailing and peddling, American wig-dealers have supplied imported wigs to beauty shops and department stores throughout the United States. Their economic practices and financial foundations are so secure that they have been able to keep prices for their "handmade" wigs stable despite the vicissitudes of supply and demand. The various advantages coming from their established status enabled them to control wholesale lines throughout the United States when the wig boom emerged in the early 1960s. Unlike Koreans, they developed sophisticated sales techniques through mail-order systems advertised in leading women's magazines. By relying on mail orders their market expanded into the Caribbean, to Mexico, and to Latin America and the new nations in Africa. They have also controlled "wig concessions" in leading department stores throughout the United States.

Korean sales agents soon encroached upon the markets of these American wholesalers. Immediately after arrival, Korean salesmen were equipped with new cars and sent to leading cities throughout the United States. They made direct contracts with beauty-shop owners and department stores by offering drastically reduced prices, and thus they "broke up" the established price patterns and sales lines of American wholesalers. As a result, in 1970, for instance, Korean-made wig and eyelash products constituted 44 percent of all such items imported by the United States from foreign countries.[33] The dumping practices

[32] *Koreapost*, July 6, 1974.
[33] In spite of the fact that the total value of Korean-made wigs exported to the United States declined from $80.3 million in 1971 to $25.6 million in 1974, Korean-

of Korean agents brought forth an immediate outcry not only from American wholesalers but also from independent Korean wholesalers or importers. Consequently, when Korean sales agents bid for contracts from American wig-wholesalers, they often received "the cold shoulder treatment" that said, in effect, "Your people have spoiled the wig business." Ironically, in the late 1960s, when American wholesalers or importers faced a keen shortage of wigs due to a growing United States demand, American wig-dealers went to South Korea and competed in bidding for wig goods from Korean manufacturers; by doing so they stimulated the whole industry. American purchasing agents frequently bribed Korean manufacturers and their employees to get larger allocations of wigs; at that time, Korean manufacturers did not send their sales agents to the United States market. In this context, Korean sales agents used to complain, "You know, at that time they knelt down before us and bid for more wigs. Now they even refuse to make an appointment with us."

The Intervention of the South Korean Government. Faced after 1971 with extremely unfavorable market conditions, in which wig prices were falling while the costs of raw materials were increasing, Korean wig-men ranging from manufacturers to wholesalers and retailers felt an urgent need to reform the market and rationalize the price system. In order to shelter their markets from new Korean manufacturers as well as from late-arriving small-scale Korean wholesalers or importers, in 1972 the established wholesalers in America formed the Korean Wig Union.

The Korean government intervened forcefully. Initially, it asked the Korean Wig Union to (1) establish a "check price," that is, a minimum retail price; (2) stop dumping practices; and (3) stop direct sales to street peddlers. The Korean government also warned, through the voice of the Manufacturers' Export Association in South Korea, that any violation of these regulations would result in the deprivation of the right to import wig products from South Korea. In return for the acceptance of these regulations, the Korean Wig Union asked for exclusive rights: only members of both the Korean Wig Union in America and the American Wig Union should be entitled to import Korean wigs, and all sales branches of Korean wig-manufacturers should either withdraw from the United States or become members of the Korean Wig Union and thus be subjected to the same regulations.

The two groups thus seemed to reach an agreement, at least at a formal level, through the intervention of the Korean government. But

made wigs constituted 86 percent of all the wigs that the United States imported in 1974. *Hankook Shinmoon*, June 15, 1975.

at a practical level the agreement could not be made effective. Manufacturers in South Korea could not accept the demands of the Korean Wig Union, simply because their economic position did not allow them to retreat from the American market. They could not withdraw partly because they had sold their products on credit and had a substantial outstanding debt. Moreover, there was no proper law-enforcement agency through which Koreans could regulate dumping activities in the United States, and the sales branches of homeland manufacturers were not responsive to American commercial law. On the other hand, many established wholesalers or importers in America had kept their own peddling system while urging the Korean government to prevent manufacturers from directly exporting wig products to retailers and other nonunion wholesalers. But those manufacturers who were able to receive favored treatment from the Korean government ignored the agreement with the union and exported their products to nonunion wholesalers and retailers who had not yet "made it" in America. In doing this they frequently used substandard raw materials and abused other makers' trademarks in labeling their products. Meanwhile, the established wholesalers' claim to an importing monopoly caused nonunion wholesalers and retailers to raise an outcry against the Korean Wig Union.

Seeing that the mutual agreement between the two groups had not become effective, the Korean government began to wield its legal authority. The basic decisions were made when the Korean Ministry of Commerce and Industry convened a series of meetings in February 1974. Staff members of both the Korean Wig Union in America and the Manufacturers' Export Association in South Korea participated in the meetings. The government decided (1) that Korean manufacturers should restrict the export of their wigs to members of both the Korean Wig Union and the American Wig Union; (2) that the manufacturers' sales branches should withdraw from the American market by the end of May 1974; and (3) that, if an established Korean wholesaler in the United States failed to import a minimum of $50,000 worth of wigs per year, he would be deprived of the right to import wigs from South Korea. Members of the Korean Wig Union were also granted permission by the government to import eyelashes, which Korean eyelash-makers had been selling exclusively to American wholesalers belonging to the American Wig Union. This was arranged in order to avoid dumping practices similar to those in wig exporting.

These arrangements by the Korean government violated the Sherman Antitrust Act; in August 1975, the United States federal court in New York City charged the Korean Wig Union, a de facto surrogate of the Korean government, with violation of the antitrust law. This resulted immediately in a great change in the Korean wig-community in the United States. The wig union held a series of meetings in which its members replaced its president and formed an ad hoc committee in an effort to deal with the lawsuit. The Korean Wig Union asked the Korean Consulate General in New York City for help. While the case was pending, the union decided to allow nonunion Korean wholesalers to become members, declaring that "the Korean Wig Union no longer claims the exclusive right to import wig products from the homeland." It took more than a year for the federal court to reach a verdict. The Korean Wig Union was somewhat relieved when the court fined the union only $2,500. But this decision also pleased nonunion wholesalers and retailers, who had accused the union leaders of misappropriating union funds: "They held union meetings in restaurants and on golf courses" (field notes).

In response to this event, the Korean government has, since 1976, reduced the export of wig products by imposing export quotas on Korean wig-manufacturers. Thus, large-scale wig manufacturers have survived, while small ones have been either forced out of business or absorbed by big manufacturers. Partly because of this, prices for Korean wigs have gone up slightly in the world market.

Wig Peddlers. Peddlers under the control of established wholesalers were few in number and had their own handicaps, either because of their visa status or their lack of money and skill. Instead, independent peddlers comprised the bulk of Korean wig-peddlers, and they increased in number as the wave of Korean immigrants began to surge in 1970. Contrary to the common public image, independent peddlers seemed to be the most tranquil group among Korean wig-men. Since they ran their business on the street on a day-to-day basis, with only a small investment, they were free from economic anxieties caused by long-term market fluctuations and from the chores of managing a regular shop. They also took advantage of a gradual awareness among wig consumers that there were few differences in quality between the wigs displayed at a regular beauty shop or wig salon and those on the street.

Independent peddlers can be subdivided into two groups: fixed and migratory. The fixed group was made up of those peddlers who made extralegal contracts with American shopkeepers—owners of bargain garment, shoe, and gift shops—for permission to do their peddling near the shop entrance. In return for receiving weekly payments from the peddlers, the shopowners were obliged not only to provide a proper space for them but also to protect them from police harassment as well as from intervention by Korean retailers. The sales of these fixed peddlers usually surpassed those of regular shopowners.

Like the shops of Korean wig-retailers, these peddling activities, with some exceptions, were limited to the business sections of black and Puerto Rican neighborhoods. The contract fee varied depending on the location of the store: it amounted to about $1,000 per month near the entrance to Gimbels' and Macy's department stores in Manhattan; at the business sections of Fourteenth Street in Manhattan, Eastern Parkway in Brooklyn, and Third Avenue in the Bronx, peddlers used to pay from $150 to $500 per month. However, they could not intrude into the black neighborhoods in Jamaica, Queens, where Korean wig-shops were so numerous and their owners so well organized that any attempts to do peddling there could be easily frustrated. As mentioned earlier, one Korean peddler committed hara-kiri there after he stabbed a Korean retailer in a dispute over commercial interests. When the wig boom was at its highest point, some aggressive Korean women dared to display wigs in the lounges of hospitals, nursing homes, and factories largely catering to black and Puerto Rican employees.

In addition to the fixed peddlers, whose economic activities were concentrated in the transitional areas of inner cities, there were migratory peddlers who moved from city to city and state to state seeking temporary sales opportunities. In doing so, they used station wagons to carry as many wigs as possible for the long periods of time they traveled before returning to their home bases in inner cities. There they rested and restocked their inventories from wholesalers. Some young Koreans formed peddling teams and used commercial airlines in order to respond more quickly to the demand for wigs in various parts of the country. During the summer vacation season, when the entire wig business was slow in the inner cities, these migratory peddlers rushed to national and regional resort areas such as Niagara Falls and Atlantic City. And during the winter season, when wig sales, especially street sales, slowed down in northern cities mainly owing to cold and windy weather, they took their businesses to the resort areas of Florida and the shantytowns of the Deep South. They had to be aggressive enough to endure frequent police harassment and attacks by local businessmen.

The Ambivalence of Korean Wig-Merchants. A sense of self-mockery, satire, and ironic self-defense characterized the mood of the Korean wig-community, but that attitude coexisted with the deadly seriousness of rational economic behavior. This ambivalence partly derived from a sense that the item being sold lacked authenticity and status. In the home country, wigs were rarely worn; until the 1960s, Koreans never thought that such a foolish item of adornment could become the means of making a living. Hence, Korean wig-men could not resist displaying their mockery and contempt for the business and for their clientele, especially when they saw how a slight change in wig styles could enormously affect their businesses. They laughed among themselves when they saw that wigs and eyelashes, which could not meet the Korean government's export standards, had suddenly become popular among American consumers because of their coarse (or natural) color combinations and wild shapes. But when interviewed by a black newspaper reporter, one of them said, ". . . besides the fact that Black women buy more wigs than white women, I think Black people are not as complicated as white people. They are easier to serve."[34] They were contemptuous of the extravagant life styles of blacks and Puerto Ricans, from whom they want to maintain a social distance. They also showed contempt for the foolishness of their typical customers when they said, for example, "Some of them have tried to buy wigs with food coupons," and, "On welfare day business is really good" (field notes). But Korean wig-men were serious in the pursuit of their economic goals. Korean peddlers doing business on the street by displaying conspicuous "wig trees" loaded with wigs often surprised bank tellers by making frequent deposits of large sums of money, and Korean peddlers were sometimes amused when tourists in New York City photographed them as poor new immigrants. Korean wig-men described contemporary American society as "stupid" or "loose," and America as a "dummy" country.

Yet, for the same reasons, Korean wig-men in the United States were psychologically on the defensive. Peddlers and retailers were reluctant to reveal their occupation to compatriots other than intimate friends, partly because the rest of the Korean community expressed an implicit contempt for the wig business. For Koreans, the phrase "wig business" automatically provoked such connotations as "peddling," "fighting," "quick fortunes," "vulgarity," and "swindling." A combination of shame and resentment lurked beneath such statements as "He has made big money out of the wig business"; "Elder X in that church is a wig merchant"; "With the money earned from the wig business he has opened up a liquor store"; and "He quit his good American job to set up a wig store in Newark." When forced to reveal their occupation, peddlers and retailers called themselves small independent businessmen without describing the commodity they sold. A sensitive listener

[34] *New York Echo*, April 27, 1974.

understood this as referring to the wig business. On such informal occasions as an alumni picnic or a party for a baby born in America, they revealed in self-derisive tones their work in America. In translating the English word "hair" into Korean, two Korean words can be used. In an ironic sense they frequently use the Korean word *tol*, which refers to the hairs on sexual organs, breasts, and animals rather than the word *mobal*, which originated from Chinese characters and means the hairs of the human head. The latter term is used in formal conversation and literature; wig merchants giggled when they said, "I am in the *tol* business."

This sense of self-mockery is partially derived from the Koreans' sense of having suddenly declined in prestige after immigrating to the United States. Since most Korean wig-men received a college education and, in many cases, enjoyed some degree of prestige in white-collar jobs in their home country, their joking reveals a bitterness arising from the comparison between their current occupational status and the social status they had in Korea. But they defend their current status because of the opportunity to make money: "What else can I do in this country if I want to make money?" This defense was more pronounced among owners of small wig-shops and peddlers who had not yet "made it" economically.

Korean wholesalers, on their part, reacted with self-righteous indignation when the Korean government made its alliance with homeland wig-manufacturers. They pointed out the manufacturers' greedy exploitation of the female workers of Korea by saying that "they are sapping the blood of the *yeogong*." They had not made such complaints before homeland manufacturers attempted to enter the wholesale market directly.

The ironical attitude was also due to the fact that most customers were blacks and Puerto Ricans, from whom the wig sellers wanted to maintain a social distance. Koreans in New York City derisively called their countrymen's wig business a "black" business. But among recent immigrants, this contempt has easily turned into envy when the newcomers learn that many of their predecessors have made a great deal of money in the "black" business. When discussing the limited opportunities for making money during the present economic recession, recent Korean immigrants recall the boom times of the wig business, saying that "I should have come over here at that time."

In New York City, Korean wig-men penetrated every nook and cranny of black and Puerto Rican communities, central Harlem excepted, for several reasons. First, wigs had become a social desideratum for a large part of the black and Puerto Rican population. According to a market survey on the use of wigs in America, 89 percent of black adult females in 1974 wore wigs, while only 43 percent of white adult females wore them.[35] Only black Muslims, largely under the influence of Elijah Muhammad, opposed wig wearing among blacks. Second, store rent in these ethnic neighborhoods is reasonably cheap, so that Korean immigrants were able to open stores with a relatively small amount of capital. Third, black- and Puerto-Rican-owned stores were few in number, and the owners could not compete with Koreans, who had the advantages of commercial ties among their own countrymen. In response to the invasion by Korean wig-men, a black newspaper carried the following item: "With the natural hair-style gradually losing its hold on the fancy of Black women, the return to hairpieces and wigs may be inevitable. . . . Capitalizing on this trend in many Black communities—including Brooklyn's Bedford-Stuyvesant and Crown Heights section—are a growing number of South Korean wholesale and retail wig merchants. So rapidly are their numbers growing that many Black-owned stores may soon be forced out of business."[36] Strictly speaking, the places where Korean wig-men flourished best were not the predominantly black ethnic communities but the racially balanced business sections where old Jewish, Irish, and Italian shopkeepers were abandoning their business enterprises. For example, Koreans did not invade the commercial sections of Harlem. They were often denied rentals by black landlords, who are afraid of economic pressure from their own ethnic group. However, some Koreans managed to open wig stores in Harlem, but only to be forced out by harassment and theft. One exception was a chain store on 125th Street that, although owned by a Korean, was managed by black employees.

In the competition for commercial space, Korean wig-men have encountered another barrier in their lack of a necessary combination of American business sophistication and capital. With some exceptions, they have not yet invaded the commercial sections of Fifth Avenue, where the luxurious beauty shops and wig salons are located, nor have they moved into the suburbs. In middle-class wig and beauty salons, an owner's relationship with his clients is direct, personal, and intimate. The "American" owners still assert the virtue of traditional craftsmanship and disparage the vulgar mass consumption of "wear-it-as-you-buy-it" wigs. These stores bear such titles as wig studios, coiffeurs, hair-weaving salons, and hair-replacement centers. They are predominantly run by Jews and Italians who deal with the finest wigs, including Korean human-hair wigs, Sicilian tresses, and French wigs and hair-

---

[35] Sok-man Yoon, "Gabal sijang eui jeongsanghwa e gwanhayeo" [On the normalization of the wig market], *Hankook Shinmoon*, July 26, 1975.
[36] *New York Echo*, April 27, 1974.

pieces. In contrast, Korean shopkeepers play down, to some extent, the deliberately arty and shiny decoration of such stores in order to evoke a "cheap smell." To attract customers, Korean peddlers deliberately avoid long, complicated, and sophisticated statements on style and quality in order to take advantage of Americans' image of Asians as naive and primitive. All they need are ten fingers to show the proper price and a few compliments such as "beautiful" or "*muy bonita.*" Korean wig-men ironically call themselves "saviors" of blacks and Puerto Ricans: "Without the cheap Korean wigs, how could they afford to wear wigs?"

Korean wig-men have also participated in designing wig styles that express black ethnic pride. Wholesalers and sales agents of homeland manufacturers sensitively read such leading black magazines as *Ebony, Essence,* and *Sepia* as well as such fashion magazines as *Vogue, American Hair Dresser,* and *Journal of Beauty* in order to keep up with trends in American hair-fashions. In response to new life styles among blacks, who have become increasingly self-conscious in making a stylized and idealized culture since the civil rights movement of the 1960s, Korean wig-men are aware that the only way to perpetuate the wig-wearing fashion among blacks lies in a continual renovation of styles. At the same time, they frequently complain that a fashionable style will not last more than two months.

Since the gradual decline of the wig boom, a major area of competition among Korean wig-manufacturers has become the invention of new styles. Manufacturers have now become aware of the fact that blacks' taste for wigs has become so sophisticated that cheap and coarse products such as the "Afro-Freedom" wigs are no longer bought. For instance, a Korean manufacturer recently advertised in *Ebony* and *Essence,* as well as in Korean ethnic newspapers, its "revolutionary styles and fibers for blacks. . . . Z wigs provide you with a new opportunity for making money. . . . Unlike traditional Afro-wigs made of cheap fibers, Z wigs will arouse new admiration from millions of black women throughout the United States." A Korean was reported as saying, "The Z wigs have satisfied the desire of blacks to return to natural human hairs. Without the invention of this new fiber style last year [1976], the Korean wig-industry would have been completely ruined."[37] Some Korean manufacturers have begun to recruit black hairdressers and fashion designers in order to create new black styles. In some cases Korean shopowners have taken on the role of fashion designer by exploring a new idea with black customers and black hairstylists. They report the idea to their wholesalers, who in turn send it to manu-

[37] *Joong Ang Ilbo,* August 24, 1977.

facturers in South Korea. However, Korean wig-men rarely create a new style; instead, in the process of making wigs, they generally carica-ture, exaggerate, and imitate the "natural" hair styles that have already been invented by black hairdressers and that have become popular among some segments of the black population. Only then do the Kore-ans advertise their wig products through leading black magazines and newspapers under the general title "Afro-Wigs," which, as they insist, are made of a synthetic thread especially designed for blacks under the trade name Afrilon, a name created specifically for such adver-tising.

When the demand for wigs suddenly increased among ethnic Amer-icans, some Korean wig-men, like the greengrocers, began seeking out commercial space in transitional areas and setting up stores with an eye to selling the stores to Koreans. Most buyers were recent arrivals with little or no experience of American society. The sellers pretended that they had set up the store as a permanent business, but for some unavoidable reason, such as having to return to the home country, they were forced to sell. They also enticed Koreans with visa problems to buy stores by claiming that "you can acquire a green card by showing this store as a capital investment in the United States."

When the wig business slowed down, some Korean shopkeepers laid off their wig stylists and turned their shops into "discount" stores by adding such items as cheap jewelry, eyelashes, "artistic" pictures and photographs, handbags, and so on. By selling wigs at so-called sale prices, others filled available demand in a neighborhood and then moved out to seek another place where they could set up either a wig store or another retail store. As the wig fashion in the United States gradually declined, an increasing number of advertisements for the sale of wig stores appeared in Korean ethnic newspapers. On the whole, Koreans do not now think that the wig business is stable enough to afford a lifelong livelihood.

Consequences of the Wig Business. The wig business has provided Korean immigrants with temporary economic opportunities through which they could accumulate enough capital and experience to enter other kinds of businesses such as gift shops, men's-wear stores, station-ery stores, grocery stores, small supermarkets, restaurants, dry-cleaning establishments, or candy and liquor stores. Some wig shopkeepers did not know how to reinvest their capital in other businesses, however; they bought suburban homes and paid the entire price in cash, pro-voking laughter among Korean shopkeepers who were more aggressive economically and more sophisticated. This phenomenon was more pro-nounced among the fixed-space peddlers, who were generally older than other Korean wig-men, their age averaging in the forties. They drove daily from suburban houses to transitional areas of the inner city in order to peddle on the street—a job they held for several years. Even those retailers and peddlers without a private house did their business in black and Puerto Rican communities while living in the white lower-middle-class neighborhoods of New York City. Thus, for Korean wig-men, racial and economic desegregation did not extend as far as housing. This reluctance to actually live among blacks is not merely confined to Korean wig-men but is extended to other Koreans doing small businesses in the inner cities of the eastern seaboard. As we shall discuss in chapter eight, it contributes to the animosity many blacks have felt against Korean ghetto-merchants.

Since wig sales have begun to decline, many Korean wig-wholesalers have started to import other labor-intensive goods from South Korea such as garments, handbags, jewelry, and gift items. A Korean wig-wholesaler who became a multimillionaire in the wig business and who has emerged as one of the leading Korean leaders in New York City has shifted to the garment business by importing clothes from South Korea. As has been noted, many retail wig shops have turned to a "discount" store or a store of miscellaneous goods by adding cheap consumer goods mainly imported from South Korea. In face of the declining trend of the wig business, Korean wig-wholesalers are on the defensive: "Now the wig business has become normalized. The windfall profits that we made in the past out of the wig business were abnormal. In a society like the United States, we cannot sustain such abnormal businesses on a long-term basis."[38]

As the American market began to decline, the Korean wig-manufacturing industry began to merge with other large industrial corporations. A similar merging has occurred in the United States; for example, Korean wig-wholesalers have explored and opened concessions in major department stores. Some one hundred Korean-run wig concessions have recently emerged on the eastern seaboard.[39] The owners of such concessions are obliged to pay somewhere between 20 and 25 percent of their total sales to the department stores in return for the space.[40] Under these circumstances, Korean wig-merchants emphasize their sophisticated styles and sales techniques rather than "cheap prices" and Asian "naivité."

CONCLUSION

The creation of ethnic businesses by Korean immigrants has depended upon broad structural changes in contemporary American society.

[38] *Joong Ang Ilbo*, August 25, 1977.   [39] Ibid.   [40] Ibid.

When they arrived in their new land, Koreans faced a centralized business and occupational structure that prevented them from acquiring the "boundless" economic opportunities embedded in the "American dream." Korean immigrants could not enter the mainstream of the new American middle-class occupations mainly because they did not possess the skills demanded in the United States labor market and also because their command of English was weak. This economic centralization, coupled with the discrimination against new minorities that is inherent in larger business firms, has forced a large number of recent Korean immigrants to operate small businesses, an activity in which some economic opportunities still exist.

In addition to the centralization and bureaucratization of the economic structure, Korean immigrants have encountered a new trend in American urbanism—the massive migration of the white middle-class population from central cities to the suburbs or suburban cities, leaving the central cities to be dominated by new minorities. Taking advantage of this transition, the majority of Korean immigrants have settled in inner cities, and a high proportion of them engage in small businesses. In this process, as we have seen in the case study of the Korean fruit and vegetable business, Korean immigrants have typically succeeded in the small business enterprises previously run by white minority shopkeepers such as Italians and Jews, most of whom are old and somewhat on the defensive in the face of the massive influx of new minorities. We have also noted that a Korean ethnic succession in business occurs only when Koreans sell non-Korean customers the kinds of goods that are produced in the United States.

In addition to these broad social changes—occupational centralization and suburbanization—Korean immigrants have entered the United States at a time when America has been inundated by waves of mass consumption. Even new American ethnic minorities or urban lower classes are not immune to the dominant trend of America's mass-consumption culture. South Korea stepped up its exports of labor-intensive consumer goods to meet the new demands of the American urban masses, and these exports have coincided with the entry of Korean immigrants to the United States. The market basis of Korean immigrant businesses such as wig, gift, garment, and handbag stores has thus been established. By taking advantage of the "cultural revolution" since the 1960s, in which a series of chic styles and fashions were quickly accepted and discarded, and by capitalizing on these two factors—mass consumption among urban lower classes and the South Korean exports of cheap consumer goods to the United States—Korean immigrants have established economic entry points in American inner cities. In facilitating South Korean exports to the United

States, Korean immigrants have become both agents and beneficiaries of the trade between the two countries. In this context, it is not coincidental that Korean immigrants have found a chief occupational entry point in the wig business. Wigs have become a necessary part of the new life styles sought by some segments of the American population; in particular, Korean immigrants arrived in the United States when blacks were attempting to develop a new ethnic identity by creating their own life style. Korean wig-manufacturers profited from the demand so created.

The case study of the Korean wig-industry shows us how a minor change in American consumption habits conditioned the whole pattern of supply and demand by which the Korean wig-industry emerged and then began to decline in both South Korea and the United States; and further, it illustrates how the economic institutions of advanced capitalistic nations have effected, through the nexus of international trade, a great change in South Korean industrialization and economic development. It also demonstrates how the selective interactions of economic institutions between the two countries have provided some Korean immigrants with serendipitous business opportunities.

Since large-scale wig use was a novelty in the United States, Korean immigrants encountered little resistance from established interests in their attempts to create and expand the Korean wig-industry in America. In contrast, the immigrants who have entered the fruit and vegetable business have taken the classic path of ethnic succession in that business and have consequently come into minor conflicts with established businesses. The Korean immigrants' massive entry into the fruit and vegetable business suggests that they have an elective affinity to certain economic opportunities in the new land. We shall discuss this later, in chapter ten, where these motivations will be shown to have a base in the historic character structure of Koreans as it has been developed in their home country.

The social structure of Korean immigration, the family and personality structure of the immigrants, the degree of their previous urbanization, and their educational experiences in the old land—all have been supportive of their economic ventures in the new land. We have focused, among other things, on how the transfer of the old family structure, which was made possible by the United States Immigration Act of 1965, has become one of their most important factors in the success of the immigrants' labor-intensive small business enterprises. We have also noted a "puritanical," urban personality among them. In pursuit of the American dream, Korean wig-men have exhibited among themselves a contempt for the artificiality of black life styles, but this attitude is normally concealed beneath the facade of their rational economic ventures. Korean wig-men are ironical, self-mocking, and defensive, not only because their black and Hispanic clients display a wasteful life style by adopting what Koreans consider to be unnecessary adornment, but also because they cannot maintain either an authentic self-respect or a confidence in the wig business, which, in addition to its low social status, has been at the mercy of sudden changes in American fashion and of fluctuations in the economic cycle.

CHAPTER FIVE

The Mobility of South Korean
Medical Professionals

THE massive influx of Korean medical professionals into the United States reflects the emphasis placed on skilled immigrants under the Immigration Act of 1965 and demonstrates the selective characteristics of Korean immigration. As a result of this selectivity, Korean medical professionals constitute the core of the emerging Korean community in the New York metropolitan area. They are a primary source of community leadership, and they help substantially in financing community activities and organizations, including churches.

The occupational mobility from Korean to American medical institutions has occurred in response to both specific pull factors in the United States and push factors in South Korea. First, the demand in the American medical industry during the 1950s and 1960s for "cheap" foreign medical professionals in general and for Koreans in particular has reflected the rise of a sort of mass consumption of American medical services. The demand was and is largely supported by federal and state-financed health-insurance plans. In spite of this massive demand, the American medical establishment until recently limited the number of American medical graduates in order to maintain its professional interests, income, and status. And yet this explanation does not exhaust the specific pull factors that cause foreign medical workers to migrate to America. The inclination to specialization by American physicians and their exodus from inner-city hospitals to suburban medical institutions have also created vacancies and provided "marginal" opportunities to immigrant medical professionals.

As we shall see, all these changes in American medical institutions have affected the way in which South Korean medical institutions, especially medical schools, have developed. This selective interaction of economic institutions between the two countries has occurred within the framework of the manpower policies of both nations.

THE INFLUX OF KOREAN MEDICAL PROFESSIONALS

More than 13,000 Korean physicians, nurses, pharmacists, and dentists have entered the United States since the passage of the Immigration

Act of 1965. According to the statistics of the United States Immigration and Naturalization Service, a total of 6,185 Korean medical professionals immigrated from 1965-1973. Among them are some 7,000 Korean nurses, currently employed at American medical institutions, who are one of the main sources of capital for their husbands' retail businesses. In addition, medical professionals constitute a large proportion of Korean suburban single-family houseowners.

TABLE 5.1 KOREAN MEDICAL PROFESSIONALS ADMITTED TO THE U.S., 1965-1973

	Doctors	Nurses	Pharmacists	Dentists
1965	11	2	0	0
1966	35	19	0	0
1967	70	26	4	5
1968	63	60	10	4
1969	128	102	17	7
1970	228	254	38	3
1971	965	526	81	20
1972	768	738	257	26
1973	598	744	346	30
Totals (6,185)	2,866	2,471	753	95

SOURCE: Based on the statistics of the Immigration and Naturalization Service.

Many Korean medical workers have entered via third nations. As has been discussed, the bulk of Korean migrant nurses in West Germany, who numbered 6,124 as of December 1973,[1] migrated again to the United States. Korean doctors who previously migrated to other foreign countries such as African nations through the arrangement of overseas labor contracts have also remigrated to the United States. Taking account of the Korean medical workers who have entered either via third nations or since 1974, we might estimate that by 1977 Korean medical professionals in the United States numbered at least 13,000.[2]

Koreans, however, constitute only a small portion of all foreign med-

[1] Jo-ja Kim, "Seodog jujae hangug ganhowon eui baljon eul wihan chieop siltae josa yeongu" [A study for the enhancement of Korean nurses in West Germany: Employment Status], *Daehan Ganho*, Korean Nurses Association, March-April 1975, p. 27.

[2] According to the *INS Reporter*, the total number of Korean doctors in the United States reached 3,888 in 1977 (*INS Reporter*, spring 1979); Korean Nurses Association in South Korea estimated that the number of Korean nurses in the United States totaled about 7,000 in 1976; the Korean Ministry of Health and Social Welfare estimated that Korean pharmacists in the United States totaled, as of December 1977, some 2,500 (*Joong Ang Ilbo*, April 17, 1978).

ical professionals admitted to the United States since the end of World War II. During the period from 1950 to 1975, a total of 68,305 immigrant doctors entered the United States.[3] And from 1966 to 1975 a total of 56,949 foreign nurses immigrated.[4] The entry of Asian doctors began at approximately the same time as the enactment of the Immigration Act of 1965. Non-Asian doctors, especially European doctors, were immigrating long before 1965. The inflow of Asian doctors, however, increased suddenly after 1966: in 1973, for instance, Asian doctors constituted 70.6 percent of the total of 7,119 immigrant doctors entering during that period;[5] Korean doctors alone comprised about 12 percent of the total.

PULL FACTORS IN AMERICAN MEDICAL INSTITUTIONS

The influx of foreign medical professionals has resulted from broad institutional changes in health care in the United States. Before World War II, health care was mainly based on the fee-for-service private practitioner. This system has diminished in importance and size as prepaid and group health-care plans have increasingly centralized the vertical professions. Big hospitals have become the new centers for the delivery of medical service as well the power base of American medical institutions; they are now teaching, research, and service complexes. Before World War II, physicians, dentists, and other private practitioners received more than half of the nation's total expenditures for health care. In 1974, however, only 26.8 percent of the total medical expenditures went to private practitioners of all types; 39 percent were spent for hospitals.[6] This centralization of the health-care delivery system has favored specialists and worked against general practitioners: "The old-style generalist, with less training than the specialist and with a wide field of practice, was with some justification withering away. Those who remained were fighting an uphill, ultimately a losing, battle to retain their professional standing in comparison with the specialist."[7]

This trend toward specialization has partly contributed to the immigration of foreign medical professionals. That is to say, at the bureaucratic organizational level, foreign medical professionals can be employed by big hospitals, and can adjust to them, without encountering the kinds of resistances and difficulties they might have faced in pri-

[3] *The Annual Report(s) of the United States Immigration and Naturalization Service.*
[4] Ibid.   [5] *Statistical Abstract of the United States,* 1976.
[6] Ibid.
[7] Rosemary Stevens, *American Medicine and the Public Interest,* New Haven, Yale University Press, 1971, pp. 293-294.

vate practice. One bit of evidence supporting this statement is that the largest employers of immigrant doctors are the Veterans Administration Hospitals, which constitute the largest single centrally directed medical complex in the United States. The Veterans Administration, operating 171 hospitals and employing about 200,000 persons, filled 52 percent of its residencies with foreign graduates in 1974. On the other hand, specialization has skewed the distribution of physicians with respect to some specialties: huge vacancies in "unpopular" specialties have been filled by "marginal," that is, foreign, doctors. Barry Stimmel pointed out the concentration of American-born doctors in the most popular specialties.

> Available evidence indicates that without intervention maldistribution in the United States is likely to continue. Before 1972, the number of sub-specialty certificates awarded by the American Board of Internal Medicine and those available in four subspecialty areas represented 11 percent of general certificates awarded. In 1972 this figure increased to 37 percent of general certificates awarded. In cardiology, candidates seeking certification from the Sub-Specialty Board in Cardiovascular Disease increased from 84 in 1969 to 543 in 1972. . . . Redirection of physician training to the field of primary care is therefore a distinct need.[8]

The centralization of health care is also associated with changes in health-care financing and improvements in medical technology. Before World War II, the American Medical Association successfully prevented government or private insurance agencies from initiating any kind of comprehensive health-insurance plan. Thus, those in need of medical service had to go to the offices of private practitioners and meet their medical expenses out of their own pockets. Now, insurance companies and other health plans, including Medicaid and Medicare, cover a large portion of individual medical expenses. This change in payment and in the whole organization of health-care benefits occurred at the same time that the mass consumption of medical service was emerging, and it has played a major role in the development of a service-oriented economy in the United States since the end of World War II.

The mass consumption of medical services reflects an increased emphasis on health and longevity in the United States. In 1950, 4.5 percent of the gross national product was spent for health care. In 1976, 8.6 percent, or $139 billion, was so spent.[9] Despite a massive infusion

[8] Barry Stimmel, "The Congress and Health Manpower: A Legislative Morass," *The New England Journal of Medicine* (July, 1975), p. 72.
[9] *Statistical Abstract of the United States*, 1976.

of federal and state funds for Medicaid and Medicare, New York City's municipal taxes for health care amounted to $1.2 billion in 1975, or 17 percent of all city tax revenues.[10] Robert P. Whalen has aptly described this mass consumption of medical services.

> We Americans are health worshipers. We have invested, and continue to invest, billions in our temples of health: our hospitals, medical schools and nursing homes. As no other society, we indulge physicians and surgeons, not only monetarily but technologically.
>
> Last year, we spent over $139 billion on health care—8.6 percent of the gross national product, or about $638 for every man, woman and child in the United States. Government at all levels contributed 42 percent of this money. In New York State, government's share was 49 percent and per capita spending for health exceeded $800 last year. Almost 25 percent of the nation's entire Medicaid outlay is spent in one state, New York.
>
> Can we really buy better health by spending ever-increasing sums on acute health care? There is a growing body of evidence that we cannot, that despite our faith in hospitals and curative medicine we may be worshipping in the wrong church.
>
> Since 1900, our average life expectancy has increased dramatically —from 47 to 72 years. But there has been a relatively small gain in longevity over the last decade, when health spending more than doubled and government spending for health quintupled. Most experts agree that further gains in life span seem unlikely in the near future.[11]

The development of a service-oriented economy in the United States grew in part from an awareness of an increasing number of people who were considered "deficient" in certain health-care services. The service-oriented economy produced a massive demand for medical professionals; however, the American Medical Association (AMA), among other medical groups, had successfully controlled medical policies and was relatively effective in limiting the number of students admitted to medical schools. The AMA was attempting to defend and perpetuate the professional interests, status, and power of medical doctors. According to Rosemary Stevens,

> The question of standards and content of medical education was one side of the coin. That of the number of physicians was the other. At a time of declining professional incomes it had been natural to at-

---

[10] *New York Times*, October 17, 1976.
[11] Robert P. Whalen, "Health Care Begins with the I's," *New York Times*, April 17, 1976.

tempt to restrict physician supply in the cause of raising educational standards, as the AMA did during the 1930's, and these attitudes survived World War II. The old arguments in relation to the "over supply" of physicians, the accelerated three-year medical curricula and increased production of physicians during the war (as a result of which some 7,000 additional medical students had been graduated), and the reappearance into civilian life of thousands of physician veterans seemed to indicate a need for continuing caution. As the medical schools relaxed back into their four-year peacetime curricula, the AMA established its policy of no major expansion in the number of medical students.[12]

This AMA policy greatly limited the supply of American physicians in proportion to population, and the population was increasing at a faster rate than the number of medical school graduates. Between 1950 and 1960, for instance, the physician-population ratio actually declined: in 1950 there were 149 physicians for every 100,000 people, but in 1960 there were 148 physicians per 100,000. This occurred despite the fact that 15,883 foreign medical doctors entered the United States during that decade. In fact, the total number of foreign medical doctors practicing in the United States is enormous when compared with the annual number of American medical-school graduates. In 1950, for instance, American medical schools produced only about 5,900 graduates. Stevens has discussed the social circumstances under which the United States has had to import foreign physicians.

> Nowhere was the cumbersome structure and lack of centralized responsibility for graduate medical education more evident than in consideration of the increasing flow of foreign medical graduates into internship and residency positions. . . .
>   Foreign physicians, ostensibly as students, were actively wooed·by many hospitals, at least in part to meet their staffing needs. Indeed, without substantial aid from abroad many hospitals would have had to function without house staffs, thus developing a very different staffing system. With the deliberate recruitment of foreign physicians for accredited educational programs, there was a real danger of the residency changing from its old education function to a form of cheap hospital labor; nor could this be controlled under the existing professional accrediting procedures.[13]

In order to increase the supply of domestically trained physicians, the federal government has, since 1963, financially supported American

[12] Stevens, *American Medicine*, p. 353.
[13] Ibid., pp. 396-398.

medical schools and encouraged their expansion. As a result, the number of medical schools increased from 91 in 1960 to 121 in 1974, and during the period from 1968 to 1974 the number of students enrolled in American medical schools increased from 35,833 to 53,554.[14] And yet the United States has been far from self-sufficient in providing medical doctors, and this deficiency is magnified by an unequal geographic distribution of physicians and their overspecialization.[15] Consequently, 44.5 percent of all doctors in the United States who were licensed to practice during 1973 to 1974 were graduates of foreign medical schools.[16] Such graduates or immigrant doctors constituted about 30 percent of all interns and residents in the United States in 1977, and in New York State they made up, in 1977, 52 percent of the total, with the heaviest concentration being in state, city, and municipal hospitals.[17]

In 1974, graduates of foreign schools filled 58 percent of the residencies in city-run hospitals throughout the United States.[18] This heavy concentration of graduates from foreign medical schools in city-run hospitals is an indicator of how immigrant doctors are distributed. New trends in urban residential patterns have partly contributed to this influx of immigrant doctors to the inner cities of the United States. With the movement to the suburbs, well-qualified white medical doctors have concentrated in more profitable private and group practice in suburban cities and exurbs, resulting in a substantial shortage of medical doctors in rural areas as well as in the ghettos of inner cities. For instance, the number of office-based medical practitioners in New York City has actually declined from 13,275 in 1966 to 10,453 in 1974.[19] The *New York Times* reported,

> In a city that has nearly twice as many physicians per capita as the national average, the New York City Department of Health has found a number of neighborhoods in poverty-stricken areas with grinding health problems that have virtually no physicians to deal with them. . . .
>
> Dr. Imperato also is expected to ask the Federal officials to consider sending in public-health physicians who would serve poverty-stricken areas or Indian reservations, seeing patients in an office and

[14] Stimmel, "The Congress and Health Manpower," p. 73.

[15] Ibid., pp. 70-71.

[16] *Statistical Abstract of the United States*, 1976.

[17] *New York Times*, January 5, 1977.

[18] American Medical Association, *Directory of Approved Internships and Residencies*, 1975-1976.

[19] Nora Piore et al., *Health Expenditures in New York City: A Decade of Change*, Center for Community Health Systems, Columbia University, 1976, p. 11.

dispensing medication. A similar request was recently made by city health officials in Newark.

The city department cited Health Planning Area 18 in the Tremont section of the South Bronx. It has a population of about 10,000 and not one practicing private physician except for a Medicaid clinic. A few blocks to the Southeast in the Morrisania section, Health Planning Area 59, within sight of where President Carter visited recently, has no physicians either and only one Medicaid Clinic. . . .[20]

In response to this unequal distribution of medical care, the federal government, in order to fill a shortage of 20,000 medical doctors in rural America, has recently formulated a policy in which priority is given to the training of general practitioners rather than specialized physicians. In addition, President Ford signed into law in October 1976 a $2.1 billion health-manpower bill that "for the first time ties Federal support to medical schools to the redistribution of doctors by location and choice of practice."[21] This law is designed to address two major problems: (1) the insufficient number of doctors in rural and inner-city areas; and (2) the decline in the number of doctors practicing "primary medicine"—general and family practice and pediatrics. Furthermore, native American doctors have also been reluctant to enter the military services since the draft ended in 1972; foreign medical graduates have filled this shortage. For instance, of the 190 physicians recruited by the navy in 1977, 106 were trained outside the United States, and 72 of these were aliens.[22]

The Marginal Role of Asian Medical Professionals

It is the Korean, Philippine, Indian, and Pakistani immigrants who have filled the shortage of medical workers in inner cities of the United States. In New York City, for instance, immigrant doctors, most of them Asians, make up more than half of the 2,700 interns and residents in the municipal hospitals; they constitute more than 80 percent of the house staff at some voluntary institutions such as the Brooklyn Hospital.[23] In New York City, these Asian immigrant medical professionals provide medical services to poor blacks, Hispanics, and other urban minorities who lack their own ethnic doctors and nurses. (In 1973 there were about 7,000 Philippine physicians in the United States as

20 New York Times, December 13, 1977.
21 New York Times, October 14, 1976.
22 New York Times, November 21, 1977.
23 New York Times, February 2, 1977.

compared with 6,000 American black physicians.)[24] Furthermore, non-white minority doctors, too, are reluctant to practice in their own ghetto neighborhoods.

One of the attempted justifications of the preferential procedure under attack in Bakke is based on the alleged willingness of nonwhite medical graduates to practice in their own ghetto. It should be emphasized that experience has failed to uphold this thesis.

In 1972, the highest concentration of black physicians was found in California, whereas the Southern states of Georgia and North Carolina did not even rank in the top 10 of black physician distribution. It was concluded that these doctors "are likely to shun ghettos of our large metropolitan centers." What scant evidence there is reveals a similar trend in the career plans of Hispanic medical students. . . . Large numbers of medical students of Asian extraction have chosen to practice here, where the rewards are noticeably higher than in their native lands.[25]

American medical schools have increased in number and have produced an increasing number of graduates since 1965, and so "the Congress further finds and declares [in October 1976] that there is no longer an insufficient number of physicians and surgeons in the United States such that there is no further need for affording preference to alien physicians and surgeons in admission to the United States under the Immigration and Nationality Act."[26] The United States now restricts the entry of such professionals as scientists, nurses, and pharmacists by degrading them to the sixth or nonpreference category with respect to priority for immigration visas. In chapter one, we have already discussed this new development in the immigration law. This new federal law has drawn protests from municipal and voluntary hospitals in New York City, however, which need a continuous supply of "cheap labor" in the form of immigrant medical professionals. The *New York Times* reported.

A new federal law that will drastically limit the recruiting of graduates of foreign medical schools by hospitals was assailed yesterday as posing a serious threat to effective health care. The criticism of the law, which goes into effect Monday, came in interviews with officials of New York City municipal and voluntary hospitals.

The new limitation is part of a comprehensive law approved by

[24] *U.S. News and World Report*, November 26, 1973.
[25] Sidney Schindler, "Of Doctors and Ghettos," *New York Times*, October 23, 1977.
[26] *New York Times*, January 14, 1977.

Congress last October that is designed to enable American medical schools to produce enough physicians to meet national needs by 1980. . . .

According to an official of the New York City Health and Hospitals Corporation, the hiring of licensed doctors to the work now being done by doctors in training—namely, interns and residents—would at least double the cost of such work at a time when hospitals faced major deficits.

While the new law would not affect the 15,000 alien physicians on hospital staffs, it would effectively prevent hospitals from recruiting any others for new intern and residency programs beginning next July.

As a result, hospital officials are attempting to persuade the United States Department of Health, Education, and Welfare to adopt a four-year phasing-in of the new limitations so that hospital staffs will not be precipitously cut off from an important source of interns and residents.[27]

ADJUSTMENT PATTERNS OF KOREAN MEDICAL PROFESSIONALS

We have indicated how broad changes in the delivery of medical service in contemporary American society have stimulated the influx of a large number of foreign medical workers into American medical institutions. Now we shall see how peculiar developments in these institutions have governed the way in which Korean medical professionals have been recruited by, employed at, and have adjusted to the American medical establishment. In spite of the danger of repetition, the following points must be emphasized.

First, the New York metropolitan area is the largest locus of concentration of Korean medical workers. This tri-state area in New York, New Jersey, and Connecticut has absorbed about 1,300 Korean immigrant physicians, or 35.3 percent of the total Korean doctors admitted to the United States. As shown in table 5.2, medical institutions in New York City itself have attracted 20.3 percent of the total number of Korean immigrant doctors. About 55 percent of Korean immigrant doctors have settled on the eastern seaboard in or near the inner cities of this area. Another 25 percent are found in the Midwest, especially in Ohio, Michigan, and Illinois.

A similar geographical distribution can be found for Korean nurses and pharmacists. In the New York metropolitan area there were in 1978 about 600 Korean pharmacists, some 190 of whom were licensed

[27] *New York Times*, January 5, 1977.

TABLE 5.2 DISTRIBUTION OF KOREAN MEDICAL DOCTORS IN THE U.S., 1976

State	Percentage
Massachusetts	2.2
Connecticut	1.7
New York	26.2
(N.Y.C.)	(20.3)
New Jersey	7.4
Pennsylvania	7.5
Maryland	7.6
Virginia	2.2
Ohio	8.4
Michigan	7.7
Indiana	1.2
Illinois	7.6
Texas	1.6
California	3.4
Other states	15.3
	100.0 (3,640)

SOURCE: Based on the directories of Korean medical school alumni associations in the United States.

by the New York State government.[28] The 600 Korean pharmacists represent about 24 percent of some 2,500 Korean pharmacists admitted to the United States. Korean nurses show a similar concentration in the New York metropolitan area.

Second, the concentration of Korean doctors in New York State is explained by the fact that large hospitals in New York's inner cities employ a large number of Korean medical workers. New York City, a medical capital of the world, boasts many excellent medical centers. But the majority of Korean medical professionals work for second- or third-rate public hospitals such as city, state, or federal hospitals that have recruited "cheap" foreign medical workers. For instance, in 1977 the Montefiore Hospital in North Bronx, one of the finest hospitals in New York City, hired about 10 Korean medical workers, whereas the Willowbrook State Hospital for mentally retarded children employed about 120 Korean medical workers including doctors, nurses, and nurses' aides in the same year. The patients served by Korean medical professionals are largely made up of blacks, Puerto Ricans, the elderly, and other marginal peoples whom American-born white doctors are reluctant to treat. Many Korean doctors in New York either work for

[28] The figures are based on the estimate of the Korean-American Pharmaceutical Association of New York.

small clinics in ghetto neighborhoods or engage in private practice in racially mixed neighborhoods.

Third, Korean medical doctors are heavily concentrated in several specialties that American-born doctors usually avoid. As shown in table 5.3, 62 percent of Korean immigrant doctors have been forced to choose such nine "fringe" specialties as anesthesiology, psychiatry, obstetrics and gynecology, pediatrics, radiology, pathology, physical medicine and rehabilitation, and general practice. Ambitious American-born graduates have avoided making a professional career out of these relatively low-paying specialties. In contrast, only about 15 percent of Korean doctors have managed to acquire positions in the eighteen "core" specialties that are included under the general titles of "medicine" and "surgery." Korean physicians have functioned as a backstop to American-born doctors in staffing hospitals. At the same time, American medical institutions have been reluctant to offer residencies in "core" specialties to Korean immigrant doctors, who have a different educational and cultural background.

TABLE 5.3   SPECIALIZATION OF KOREAN MEDICAL DOCTORS IN THE U.S., 1976

Specialty	Percentages
Medicine (including nine specialties)	6.6
Surgery (including nine specialties)	8.7
Anesthesiology	16.0
Psychiatry	12.6
Obstetrics and gynecology	8.3
Pediatrics	6.6
Radiology	7.7
Pathology	7.8
Physical medicine and rehabilitation	3.0
General practice	3.4
Other specialties and unidentified	19.3
	100.0 (3,640)

SOURCE: Based on directories; see table 5.2.

In South Korea the "fringe" specialties, which absorb the bulk of Korean immigrant doctors, were largely filled by either "dull" male doctors or female doctors. But in the new land a majority of Korean doctors, most of whom were either "bright" students or "promising" doctors in South Korea, have been forced, according to their own standards, to degrade themselves when entering the marginal sectors of the American medical industry because opportunities exist only in these sectors. They have also become marginal doctors in the United States in terms of geographical and organizational distribution. As we shall see, Korean immigrant doctors who have entered the United States most recently have not even been able to find jobs in inner-city hospitals and thus have been predominantly recruited by rural medical institutions. The high concentration of Korean nurses in the New York metropolitan area can be explained by their similar marginal status.

The Koreans' entry into the marginal sectors of the American medical system holds true in other fields of medicine. The heavy concentration of Koreans in pharmaceutical work is due to the short supply of American-born pharmacists in New York State, particularly in New York City. Enrollment in New York's pharmaceutical colleges has diminished partly because, given almost the same amount of investment and training, American students can enter medical schools rather than pharmaceutical schools. The pharmacology program of Columbia University, for instance, was recently shut down mainly because of a lack of students. Thus, New York is the only state in the United States that has granted, through a specific examination system, licenses to immigrant pharmacists without requiring specified training at American pharmaceutical schools. Registered Korean pharmacists are largely employed by inner-city medical institutions.

Korean immigrants are also active in such marginal positions as dental, laboratory, and X-ray technicians. In addition, many Korean nurses who cannot pass a licensing examination in the United States have become nurses' aides. Another marginal medical job in which Korean immigrants are very active is in dental laboratory work, that is, making dental ceramics. In New York City more than a hundred Korean dental technicians have emerged since 1973; they have largely succeeded Jews in that field. Americans have shied away from this profession because it takes a self-disciplined, tedious, and patient apprenticeship to become a skilled worker. In order to do dental, laboratory, and X-ray work, Korean immigrants have either learned the necessary skills in their homeland or have acquired them after arriving in the new land; but in either case the acquisition of these skills has been motivated solely by their utility for mobility or migration.

THE DEVELOPMENT OF SOUTH KOREAN MEDICINE AS IT AFFECTS INTERNATIONAL MOBILITY AND MIGRATION

The massive immigration of Korean medical workers to the United States presupposes a special kind of development in Korean medical institutions, for they must qualify their graduates for American internships, residencies, and certification in response to the demand for certain types of medical workers. The following analysis of the development of Korean medical institutions indicates how South Korea has contributed, since the United States Immigration Act of 1965, the second largest group of foreign medical professionals to the United States. During that period the emigration of Korean medical workers has effected a tremendous change in Korean medical institutions, especially in medical education.

Largely under the influence of American and Japanese medical practices, Korean medical institutions have become as well developed as those of other developed countries.[29] The impact of the United States on the development of Korean medical institutions was far greater than that of Japan; Koreans have adopted Western medicine and its institutions even as they have experienced political and cultural domination by these two countries.

American Protestant missionaries, especially those sent from Presbyterian and Methodist foundations in the late nineteenth century, introduced Western medical institutions in Korea. Horace Newton Allen, a physician-preacher from the American Presbyterian church, came to Korea in 1881 and demonstrated the effectiveness of Western medicine by providing medical service to the nobility and to royal families. In 1885, Allen persuaded King Kojong to set up a royal hospital, Gwang Hae Won, which became the first Western-type hospital in Korea.[30] Partly as a result of its success, Christian missionaries including Catholic priests were allowed to enter Korea. The missionaries, funded largely by philanthropic organizations in the United States, built modern medical schools and hospitals and instituted a modern medical system in Korea as part of their mission. In doing so, they imposed an indelible stamp on Korean medical institutions: the ideology of the American medical profession, the American hospital and medical education system, and Western medical knowledge were among the things that traditional Koreans learned from American missionaries. Allen, for instance, founded the Severance Hospital and the Severance Union Medical College, which has become one of the largest medical complexes in South Korea, the Yonsei Medical Center. About 800 graduates from the medical college, which was renamed the Yonsei University Medical College, have entered the United States. The college has also sent several hundred nurses to the United States.

The Japanese annexation of Korea in 1910 further facilitated the in-

[29] Young-bok Lee, *Ganhosa* [History of nursing], Seoul, Soo Moon Sa, 1975, pp. 166-169.

[30] Doo-jong Kim, *Hangug euihagsa* [The history of Korean medicine], Seoul, The Korean Research Center, 1960, pp. 97-98.

troduction of Western medical institutions. The Japanese derived their medical practices from the Germans. Thus American and Japanese-German medicine formed the two sources of Korean medical development; but Western medicine nevertheless took a somewhat different course in Korea during the period of Japanese colonialism. The Japanese focused on the institutionalization of public health programs in Korea; they imposed new immunization programs and public licensing systems.[31] They also built public hospitals and public (or national) medical or nursing schools, in which "Japanese textbooks were forced upon Korean students."[32] One of the medical schools was Kyongsung Medical College, which became Seoul National University Medical College after Korea was liberated from Japanese rule. This college has been the preeminent one in South Korea and has sent about 1,200 doctors, or about 50 percent of its total graduates, to the United States. After Korean independence, the two different forms of Western medical institutions began to fuse, and together they became the basic foundation upon which the present structure of Korean medical institutions has evolved.

The Korean War greatly accelerated the development of Korean medical institutions. One of the effects of the war was a massive flow of American medical technology into South Korea, which continued after the war. Thanks to the war, Koreans first encountered antibiotics. The United States Army, the United Nations Civil Assistance Command, and the United Nations Korean Reconstruction Agency were the specific agencies that introduced advanced American medical technology into South Korea.[33] These organizations initiated various programs under which hospitals and nursing schools were built. American Protestant and Catholic foundations also created nursing schools and helped existing medical or nursing schools to expand and streamline their educational programs. During and after the Korean War, Korean medical professionals, especially nurses, were being produced in large numbers in order to meet wartime manpower needs. Many of these doctors and nurses were chosen by various American foundations to continue their study at American medical schools or hospitals. They came home with a new knowledge of American medical technology that was adapted to Korean institutions. One of the American educational programs was the Exchange-Visitor Program, which the United States government promoted during the Cold War "on the assumption that bringing foreign visitors to the United States would give the world an introduction to freedom and democracy."[34] But American hospitals, facing a short supply of American doctors, used the program as a

[31] Lee, *Ganhosa*, pp. 175-176.　　[32] Ibid., p. 174.
[33] Ibid., pp. 194-204.　　[34] Stevens, *American Medicine*, p. 397.

means of recruiting "cheap" foreign medical workers. The program was designed so that the participant would come to the United States for medical training and then return to his or her homeland to utilize that training. But, as we shall see later, the majority of Korean participants did not return; they settled in the United States in order to reap greater economic rewards.

All these events governed the way Koreans borrowed Western medical technology, and they also shaped Korean medical institutions. It is a commonly accepted view in South Korea, but not in American hospitals, that Korean medical science can be competitive with that of Western nations. Moreover, Koreans, who are highly motivated in educational endeavors, can quickly borrow new medical technology from the United States. And the fact that medicine is an applied practical science has made the borrowing easier. Thus, once the United States Immigration Act of 1965 opened the door to the immigration of professional, skilled workers, South Korea was ready to send a large number of medical workers to the United States.

THE IMPACT OF THE "MEDICAL EXODUS" ON SOUTH KOREAN MEDICINE

In addition to influencing Korea's medical institutions, the massive emigration of Korean medical professionals has effected a tremendous change in the manpower resources of the South Korean medical professions. A South Korean newspaper expressed the overall impact of the emigration.

It costs more than $20,000 [in South Korea] to produce a physician through the process of a 6-year medical education and a 5-year training in internship and residency. A substantial portion of the doctors, produced at such an expensive cost, have emigrated to foreign countries, resulting in a serious loss in national manpower resources. This brain drain of medical professionals has caused a setback to our national health program. According to recent statistics compiled by the Ministry of Health and Social Affairs, a total of 3,800 doctors including dentists and "Oriental medicine" doctors have migrated to foreign countries. The figure constitutes 22 percent of the total 16,800 registered doctors in 1975. An annual average of 300 doctors flowed to foreign countries during the period from 1969 to 1975. The number represents about a fourth of the total annual graduates from 14 [Korean] medical schools. Consequently, the physician-population ratio, which decreased through the 1960s to 1,851 in 1973, has increased to 2,064 in 1976. This reversal is also applicable to nurses, dentists, and "Oriental medicine" doctors. This massive outflow of medical professionals has created a dislocation in the present government's attempt to formulate a comprehensive national medical insurance program. Government is now trying to solve the so-called problem of "the rural villages without doctors." Fortunately, the manpower shortage in medical fields is likely to be improved because the United States, which has accepted the majority of Korean medical professionals, is planning to restrict the entry of foreign medical workers. In addition, the two new medical schools [in South Korea] will produce new graduates next year.[35]

This statement needs some clarification. A geographical maldistribution of Korean medical professionals, as in the United States, has posed a serious threat to the balanced delivery of medical services. In 1970, for instance, about 50 percent of all medical institutions were concentrated in the two largest cities in South Korea, Seoul and Pusan.[36] Twenty percent were spread among the other major cities. Thus rural Koreans, who in 1970 constituted about 60 percent of national population, had access to only 30 percent of the total medical institutions, and these were poorly staffed and equipped. This maldistribution is a ramification of the rapid post-World-War-II urbanization of South Korea. As we have discussed, a few primary cities, especially Seoul, have been so powerful that they have attracted all major political, economic, and cultural institutions. Consequently, in the absence of a strong government policy on the regional distribution of medical facilities and personnel, South Korean medical institutions have become concentrated in a few metropolitan areas where the well-to-do settle. Of the 278 general hospitals in South Korea in 1972, the majority were private hospitals located in a few big cities. However, the big hospitals in urban areas, just as in the United States, cannot provide a sufficient number of well-paying jobs to ambitious medical graduates.

South Korean medical students have largely been recruited from the members of the middle- or upper-middle classes. They undergo keen competition to enter prestigious medical schools and incur large expenses while completing their education. When they graduate, they are reluctant to settle in poverty-stricken rural areas even though they could find ample job opportunities in the countryside. For college-educated urban youth, to move to a rural area is "to go into exile." South Korean medical graduates, deeply imbued with an urban culture and urban life styles, try instead to find lucrative economic opportunities either in South Korean cities or in foreign countries, especially the United States. As shown in table 5.4, 75.1 percent of the

[35] *Hankook Ilbo*, November 1, 1976.   [36] *Hankook Ilbo*, December 19, 1973.

TABLE 5.4 MEDICAL SCHOOLS FROM WHICH KOREAN DOCTORS IN THE U.S.
GRADUATED AS OF 1976

School	Percentages (N)	
Seoul National U.*	30.8	(1,120)
Yonsei U.*	21.2	(770)
Korea U.*	11.3	(410)
Catholic U.*	8.0	(290)
Yihwa U.*	3.8	(140)
Kyongbuk U.	12.6	(460)
Chonnam U.	7.7	(280)
Pusan U.	4.7	(170)
	100.1	(3,640)

SOURCE: Based on directories; see table 5.2.
* Located in the city of Seoul.

Korean physicians in the United States graduated from the five most
eminent medical schools in Seoul.

When South Korean medical graduates pass the National Medical
Board Examination, they are entitled to become private practitioners
without undertaking an internship and residency. Thus, upon graduation, they are roughly divided into two groups. One group is made up
of those whose family is affluent enough to subsidize their entry into
practice. The other, a majority, consists of those who cannot afford to
set up an office and thus must find jobs or internships in hospitals.
But entry into internship training has become competitive mainly because the Korean Medical Association has restricted the number of
hospitals that can grant training opportunities to medical graduates.
In 1975, for instance, only sixty-five general hospitals with sixty-five
beds or more were available for training new graduates. Furthermore,
the salary scale for South Korean interns has been low. As a result,
graduates who are financially incapable of opening their own offices
have shown a strong tendency to seek employment in the United States
and other foreign countries. The higher salary scale in American hospitals has been a major force pulling Korean medical professionals
from South Korea. In 1977 Korean immigrant doctors, during their internship and residency in the United States, were paid somewhere between $16,000 and $20,000 a year. If they were in South Korea, they
would have received about $3,000 during the same period. Thus, a
United States congressional report found a medical "brain drain" from
developing countries. "Between 1962-68, 1,914 Korean doctors came to
the United States, but only 49 had returned by early 1969. Between
45-60 percent of the graduates of Korea's 11 medical schools find em-

ployment abroad. . . . Meanwhile, only 1,000 doctors are practicing in rural areas where about half (some 15 million) of the South Korean population lives. . . ."[37]

In spite of the insufficient number of general hospitals that could provide apprenticeship to new graduates, the Korean medical profession could be proud of its "100-percent" full employment as long as United States medical institutions absorbed a bulk of the new medical graduates from South Korean schools. A heavy blow was inflicted upon Korean medicine, however, when the United States Congress approved in October 1976, upon the assumption that the shortage of medical professionals in the United States was coming to an end, the 1976 Health Manpower Act, which ended, effective January 10, 1977, the preferential treatment granted to professional and skilled workers wishing to immigrate. A South Korean newspaper presented a detailed description of this change in the United States immigration law.

According to the new regulations, such professionals as scientists, medical doctors, pharmacists, and nurses, who were classified as third-preference applicants under the former law, will belong to the sixth preference or non-preference categories.

They will also be required to have specific jobs awaiting them in the United States before they can qualify.

The regulation also states medical doctors must pass a new oral test in English and a professional examination more stringent than was required under the old regulations.[38]

This shift in immigration policy has caused a serious disruption in the South Korean government's manpower policy for medical professionals. Assuming that the emigration and overseas contracts of Korean medical professionals, especially nurses and doctors, would continue over a long period of time, the South Korean government had, since 1966, stimulated the mass production of Korean medical professionals. In addition, as South Korea has achieved rapid and extensive economic development, the government has attempted to raise the quality of national health care to the level of advanced Western nations by increasing the number of medical workers in Korea itself. The ratio of medical workers to the total population has actually decreased, however, mainly because of the massive exodus of medical professionals into foreign countries.

[37] Gregory Henderson, "Emigration of Highly Skilled Manpower from the Developing Countries," in A Study of the Persistent Issue of International Scientific Mobility, U.S. House of Representatives, Congressional Report by the Committee on Foreign Affairs, September 1974, p. 33.
[38] Korea Herald, January 7, 1977.

Under the government's stimulation, South Korea's medical establishment grew rapidly. From 1966 to 1969, the number of Korean medical schools increased from eight to thirteen. By 1977 there were fifteen medical schools in South Korea, which produced annually some 1,200 doctors. In 1966, when the United States, West Germany, and other advanced nations began to admit a large number of Korean nurses, the South Korean Ministry of Health and Social Affairs formulated a five-year plan to mass produce nurses. According to the plan, the number of nursing students in existing nursing schools was doubled, and twenty nursing schools were newly established.[39] In 1973 there were thirty-seven junior nursing colleges in South Korea, which would yield 2,546 graduates annually by 1976. In 1973 there were also two four-year nursing colleges and ten nursing departments, all of which were affiliated with medical schools. By 1976, a total of 648 graduates would come out of these four-year nursing schools annually. Finally, during the period from 1966 to 1973 some 20,000 nursing assistants (or aides) were produced by a special government training program.

The impact of the medical institutions of advanced nations on the labor situation among Korean nurses was much greater than on that among Korean doctors because a huge number of nurses have migrated to foreign countries. In this context, we may repeat, some 7,800 Korean nurses and nursing assistants were employed, as of September 1975, in the medical industry in West Germany. A high proportion of these nurses, and also those who initially migrated to Canada, have entered the United States. Consequently the Korean Nurses Association in South Korea claimed in 1976 that some 7,000 Korean nurses have settled in the United States.

Since 1975, as the demand for Korean medical workers by the United States and West Germany has shrunk, the Korean medical industry has been plagued by internal troubles. Urban medical institutions in South Korea do not have the capacity to employ, by themselves, a large number of graduates, but graduates continue to pour from domestic medical and nursing schools. The appearance of a vast number of unemployed graduates in recent years has undermined the prestige of the South Korean medical profession, which had previously claimed the highest occupational status in the country. A Korean newspaper reported on the decline.

The medical profession, which once boasted of "100-percent" full employment, has lost its popularity because employment through

[39] The statistics on Korean nursing education come from Ae-shil Kim, "Ganho gyoyug siltae" [The situation of nursing education], *Daehan Ganho*, Korean Nurses Association, November-December 1973, pp. 68-73.

overseas contracts has become virtually impossible for new graduates, whose number has almost doubled over the last 5 or 6 years. In order to seek internship positions, new graduates have recently stampeded a few general hospitals in Seoul, which are not affiliated with medical schools. According to one source, some of them have paid some $2,000 in commissions in return for a position. The officials concerned worry that the unemployment among new medical graduates will continue and be out of control unless the government makes a substantial investment in the expansion of medical facilities. In contrast with this fuss over job hunting, many villages in rural areas still have no doctors and nurses. . . .[40]

Korean nurses faced a similar situation much earlier. Their employment problem was much harsher than the one facing doctors because there was a much greater oversupply of nurses than of doctors. Fifty-nine percent of the 2,670 nursing graduates in 1973 were jobless.[41] A dean of a missionary school in South Korea observed that

in the past ten years there has been a tremendous increase in the number of young women seeking careers in nursing. Although modern medical centers have absorbed many of these graduates, many have been unable to find work in Korea and so have sought employment overseas. Many of these will not return because they find greater satisfaction and remuneration overseas, and because they have nothing similar to return to in their own country. The lack of development of health care facilities in rural and provincial areas in Korea has caused a migration to Seoul, a surplus of nurses in the capital and thus facilitates the movement out of Korea. Meanwhile the health level of the people in the rural and provincial areas has improved little. A large segment of the Korean people are still unable to meet their basic health needs. . . .[42]

In 1975, thirteen Korean medical schools produced 970 graduates, of whom some 580 acquired internship positions.[43] Some of the remaining 390 were self-employed, having opened their own offices. The rest were either jobless or became army doctors. New graduates jammed the traditionally unpopular specialties such as anesthesiology and radiology, and hospitals began to reject female graduates. Some young doctors in South Korea, in order to save new graduates from unemployment as well as to enhance their professional skills, have called for a reform in the training system. They have demanded that even

[40] *Hankook Ilbo*, November 1, 1975.   [41] Kim, "Ganho gyoyug," p. 72.
[42] Patricia A. Conroy, "Social Change and Nursing Perspective," *Daehan Ganho*, Korean Nurses Association, March-April 1974, p. 41.
[43] *Hankook Ilbo*, November 1, 1975.

small hospitals or private offices should be allowed to provide intern-ship training to new graduates. The government has recently encour-aged university hospitals to adopt the so-called all-specialty training system, in which new graduates would be assigned to general hospi-tals in order to receive training in all specialties over a two-year period. After training, they would be granted an "all-specialty" license. The proponents of this training system have argued that, since emigration is no longer possible, new graduates should be given training opportu-nities to improve their professional skills. The system is also designed to increase public confidence in private practitioners. Urban Koreans have increasingly been reluctant to seek treatment from private prac-titioners and have flocked to general hospitals because many private practitioners have not undergone internship training.[44]

The all-specialty training system would bring about a mass produc-tion of specialists, thus making the private practitioners competitive with the general hospitals. The Korean Hospital Association was op-posed to this new system, for it wishes to regulate the production of newly trained specialists. Similarly, the Korean nursing establishment has protested the government policy of mass producing nurses, arguing that "the increase in the number of nursing schools and students has resulted in a serious deterioration of the quality of Korean nurses."[45]

In sum, the life chances of a bulk of Korean doctors, nurses, and pharmacists both in the United States and in South Korea have been linked to peculiar changes in the manpower situation of American medical institutions. Korean professionals who graduated during the 1960s and early 1970s were able to enter the United States in rela-tively favored emigration categories, and the majority of them have reaped ample economic rewards by being absorbed into the expanding American medical industry. They were lucky simply because they happened to finish their education in South Korea at a time when United States hospitals were wooing foreign medical workers. For in-stance, as shown in table 5.5, about 83 percent of the Korean immi-grant doctors educated at the Seoul National University College of Medicine graduated during the period from 1957 to 1972. Doctors who graduated after 1972 constitute only 1 percent of the fifteen-year total. New graduates after 1973, many of whom chose the medical profession in the hope of emigrating to the United States, have missed these economic opportunities. With some exceptions, it is highly prob-able that none of the new graduates from the seven medical schools established after 1966 will enter the United States. Korean doctors in

[44] Dong-A Ilbo, February 6, 1975.
[45] Soo-bok Yoon, "Ganhowon eui sugub gyehoeg" [Manpower planning for nurses], Daehan Ganho, Korean Nurses Association, July-August 1973, p. 42.

TABLE 5.5 DISTRIBUTION OF KOREAN MEDICAL DOCTORS IN THE U.S. WHO GRADUATED FROM SEOUL NATIONAL UNIVERSITY COLLEGE OF MEDICINE BY THEIR YEAR OF GRADUATION, AS OF 1976

Year of Graduation	
1941-47	1.8%
1948-52	5.8
1953-57	8.9
1958-62	26.9
1963-67	33.0
1968-72	22.7
1973-75	1.0
	100.1%　(1,120)

SOURCE: Directory of Seoul National University College of Medicine Alumni Association of North America, Inc., 1976-1977.

the United States are entirely made up of the graduates from the eight medical schools that were producing doctors before the enactment of the Immigration Act of 1965.

IMMIGRATION LAW AND THE LIFE CHANCES OF KOREAN-AMERICAN PHYSICIANS

Korean doctors in New York are the most "successful" of Korean immigrants. They represent the largest group of Korean suburban house-owners; most of the Korean residents of Scarsdale are immigrant doctors. With MD plates on their cars, the Korean doctors in New York can display their highly esteemed status in white suburban neighborhoods. Since their professional skills have been badly needed in the United States market, they also enjoy the highest status among Korean immigrants. As we shall later see, they are deeply committed to church centered community affairs and exert a strong influence on the Korean community in New York. When well-established immigrant Korean doctors visit their homeland, they are frequently approached by Korean medical students who inquire whether there is any easy way for them to enter the United States. A Korean American doctor suggested that, if the students could enter the United States by whatever means, they would still easily find medical positions in rural America. But a dean of a Korean medical school recently told a Korean doctor from America about Korean medical students' academic morale: "Nowadays, senior medical students do not study at all. They'd rather play billiards all day long."

Differences in economic opportunity have existed even for Korean medical professionals, however, depending upon their time of entry into the United States. Early immigrants could easily and profitably accommodate themselves to the expanding economic opportunities simply because the market demand for them was greater than it was for the latecomers. Among Korean medical professionals, the discrepancy in economic opportunities between early immigrants and latecomers can be translated into the status difference between licensees and nonlicensees. This is so because Korean medical professionals have had an easy or difficult time in securing a license depending upon the varying "need" for practitioners as defined by the profession and by the licensing authorities who respond to such definitions of "need." A. H. Raskin reports,

> The list of professions and occupations in the region that need state or municipal licenses takes up at least one-third of the Yellow Pages in many telephone directories.
> The roster stretches past such quick-to-mind groups as physicians, dentists, lawyers, and accountants to scores of more plebeian occupations, from amusement-arcade operators to undertakers, pawnbrokers to manure haulers. . . .
> The danger that wolves will watch the sheep, under the guise of civic guardians against monopoly-gouging or other abuses, is as old as the market place. Medieval guilds, which were essentially devices for enforcing a closed shop, developed in this country into organizations that use government to insure restricted entry into crafts and professions. . . . In much the same way, medical societies and other professional groups, which determine the membership of boards that, in turn, decide who practices, can use the power of the state to sustain exclusionary practices and self-protective rules.[46]

A discrepancy exists between the inability of recently arriving Asian medical professionals to secure state medical licenses and the demand for their services, especially by hospitals. This has resulted in the prevalence of unlicensed medical practice by late-arriving Asian medical professionals. The following two reports address this problem, but from different perspectives. The first one reflects a nativist's point of view, while the second one represents an immigrant's outlook.

> A growing "medical underground" of thousands of foreign-trained doctors is practicing medicine without licenses and often without supervision in many American hospitals, according to a report published today in the New England Journal of Medicine. . . .

[46] A. H. Raskin, "Do Special Interests Control the Licensing?" *New York Times*, February 20, 1977.

The study raises basic questions about how well the quality of medical care in this country is regulated, particularly since the number of graduates of Asian medical schools practicing in the United States has soared after a change in immigration law in 1965. . . .

The report also rekindles the controversy about this country's growing reliance on graduates of foreign schools to treat patients. Last year the number of foreign medical graduates licensed in the United States almost equaled the number of doctors who graduated from American medical schools.

The report comes at a time when a record number of Americans— about 6,000—are studying medicine in foreign schools. . . .

American Medical Association records cited by the study's authors show at least 10,000 unlicensed physicians working in the health field in 1971. Dr. Henry Mason of the A. M. A., characterizing these people as "not quite physicians," has attributed the problem to "loopholes in our immigration laws" and to the practice whereby some states grant temporary licenses to uncertified doctors who work in state hospitals. . . .[47]

The viewpoint of Asian immigrants follows.

Some spokespersons for the foreign medical doctors alleged that those who had obtained employment as medical assistants were often exploited by private hospitals and clinics who assigned them duties usually given to a practicing physician. . . . At a meeting on November 7, 1974, . . . Dr. Cadag pointed out that foreign-trained medical doctors were working in paramedical jobs, such as laboratory technicians and medical assistants to licensed doctors. His presentation at the meeting included examples where unlicensed medical doctors were expected to handle duties and responsibilities normally and legally assigned to licensed medical doctors in private hospitals and medical clinics.[48]

The United States government regulation of foreign-trained doctors through a licensing system dates back to the 1950s. The influx of a large number of foreign-trained doctors through the Exchange-Visitor Program induced the American medical establishment to adopt some regulatory measures concerning the quality of foreign doctors. At first the AMA Council on Medical Education and the Association of American Medical Colleges attempted to screen foreign medical graduates by publishing a list of recognized foreign medical schools. But this

[47] *New York Times,* June 20, 1974.
[48] *A Dream Unfulfilled: Korean and Philipino Health Professionals in California,* report prepared by the California Advisory Committee to the U.S. Commission on Civil Rights, 1975, p. 27.

attempt proved to be impractical and ineffective. Another approach was made in 1957; the aim was shifted to testing foreign medical graduates before their entry into the United States. For this purpose, the Educational Council for Foreign Medical Graduates (ECFMG) was created in 1957 and sponsored by the Council on Medical Education, the Association of American Colleges, the Federation of State Medical Boards, the American Hospitals Association, and government agencies. From 1958 until 1976, when the United States immigration law was amended, the ECFMG test was an essential requirement for foreign medical graduates seeking jobs in the United States. Almost all foreign-educated medical doctors had to acquire ECFMG certification if they were to intern in a hospital. Another examination, the so-called FLEX test, was required for them to receive a state medical license. But with the amendment of the immigration law in 1976, the United States Congress declared in the Health Profession Educational Assistance Act of 1976 that "immigrant physicians should henceforth be required to pass the same professional examinations as the American-trained."[49] In previous legislation in 1975, federal aid to medical schools became based on "capitation," which means that a fixed amount of money was to be paid to the school per matriculated student. Capitation was linked to the regulation of foreign-trained doctors: ". . . previous legislation has mandated that as a requirement for American medical-student capitation, the positions of foreign medical graduates in residency programs in institutions affiliated with medical schools be decreased markedly from 40 to 35 to 25 percent of total house-staff positions over the next three years."[50] In addition, the federal government has recently shifted its policy to encourage the training of general practitioners rather than specialized physicians as a way of delivering sufficient primary health care to patients in inner cities and rural areas.

All these recent changes in the United States manpower policy for medical workers have worked against Korean doctors, whether they are in South Korea as prospective emigrants or latecomers to the United States. First, the ECFMG test was replaced in 1977 with the Visa Qualifying Examination (VQE). Since then, only "a few" Korean doctors in South Korea have passed the VQE test, which consists of a language test in English and a test on medical subjects. Korean doctors complained that the English test is much more difficult than the test of medical knowledge. Second, latecomers in the United States have encountered a tremendous difficulty in finding apprenticeship positions in hospitals because they arrived at a time when a "sufficient" supply of doctors had finally become a reality. Thus the American

---

[49] *New York Times*, January 14, 1977.
[50] Stimmel, "The Congress and Health Manpower," p. 73.

medical establishment could successfully launch its campaign that deprives foreign-trained graduates of job opportunities. Time has worked against the latecomers, and a structural underemployment has plagued many Korean doctors: "They have had to accept low-income jobs in fields totally unrelated to their knowledge and expertise in order to support themselves and their families."[51]

This underemployment problem is especially pronounced for the older generation of Korean doctors, most of whom received a Japanese medical education and somehow could not update their medical knowledge. Their old age and extremely limited command of English become a disadvantage when they seek jobs in.hospitals and attempt to acquire state licenses. Despite ample clinical experience in the homeland, some members of this older generation of Korean doctors work in New York City as hospital orderlies and as nurses' assistants. But Korean doctors who are young and "competent" can still find ample opportunities in rural medical institutions, and in fact one Korean employment agency in New York City is recruiting Korean doctors for rural areas. Its recruiting targets are those doctors who either have acquired ECFMG certification but have not yet received "AMA approved training," or have finished internship or residency training in American hospitals but have not passed the FLEX test. A majority of the latecoming Korean doctors have been sent to rural areas, but some of them have returned to New York City, saying that "life over there is very monotonous. There are no Koreans."

It is fair to say that foreign medical graduates could not have posed a threat to American physicians in private practice before the enactment of the Immigration Act of 1965. Before 1965, most foreign medical graduates entered the United States with nonimmigrant visas and were not eligible for certification by the specialty boards, because the boards required citizenship. The foreign graduates instead filled the labor shortage in internships and residencies; after this training they were expected to return to their home country. However, owing to the Immigration Act of 1965, these nonimmigrant foreign graduates could easily change their status to that of a permanent resident; after the five-year residency requirement, they could become United States citizens. This liberalization of immigration and naturalization law coincided with new requirements for the acceptance of foreign medical graduates. "In the meanwhile the dominant professional attitudes toward physician supply have changed firmly to acceptance that there is an acute physician shortage. The foreign medical graduate is finally being brought into the certification system on equal terms."[52] These

[51] *A Dream Unfulfilled*, p. 26.
[52] Stevens, *American Medicine*, p. 403.

two changes created golden economic opportunities for foreign graduates who entered the United States during the 1960s. Among Korean medical graduates, the changes produced a group of "golden" doctors, called the Kim Plan Group.

South Korean Defense Minister Kim contrived in 1964 a plan designed to facilitate the flow of Korean graduates into the United States under the Exchange-Visitor Program. The majority of Korean graduates at that time were eager to go to the United States under the program; but they were not eligible for the exit visas issued by the Korean government, because they had not met the requirement of compulsory military service. According to the Kim Plan, Korean medical graduates were temporarily exempted from the requirement of military service while they were receiving training in the United States. Upon returning to South Korea, they would be obliged to serve in the Korean military forces for five years using the skills they learned in the United States. The plan had two purposes: one was to expand training or economic opportunities for Korean medical graduates who otherwise would be unemployed or underemployed because of the limited training facilities in Korean hospitals; the other was to improve the quality of medical service in the Korean military forces by recruiting American-trained doctors. When graduates under the Kim Plan left for the United States, they took a solemn oath to abide by their agreement with the government. Thus some 200 Korean graduates entered the United States from 1964 to 1968 without being hampered by the Korean emigration requirement. But only a handful of graduates returned to South Korea. Thanks to the United States Immigration Act of 1965, the rest changed their status to that of permanent resident, and by the early 1970s almost all had become United States citizens. They were able to take advantage of the expanding economic opportunities in American medicine simply because they were in the United States when the American medical establishment, faced with an acute shortage of physicians, began to liberalize its licensing system in favor of foreign medical graduates. Furthermore, they had avoided "the three-year waste" in their career development by not serving in the Korean armed services. The Kim Plan doctors have "made it": many of them are suburban private practitioners, faculty members in American medical schools, and staff members in American hospitals. These doctors are the objects of resentment among late-arriving Korean doctors, who could not benefit from the plan. "They [the Kim Plan doctors] could not visit Korea. A KCIA-made blacklist awaits them at the Kimpo Airport and would pull them off the line" (field notes). They would be forced to fulfill their military obligation.

Korean nurses have had to overcome the same licensing problems as have Korean doctors. But nurses have not had as much difficulty in acquiring a license. Unlike Korean doctors, they were not required to take a test before entering the United States. But the "license problem" is nonetheless the problem that puts their whole life in the new land at stake. Once unmarried Korean nurses receive R.N. licenses, their value in the Korean marriage market is substantially increased. A Korean nurse wrote a letter to the journal of the Korean Nurses Association in order to give some advice to prospective emigrants.

> One year and a half have passed since I began a new life in New Jersey. Last July I took a licensing test both in New York and New Jersey State and passed both. Thus, my new life here has begun to take a stabilized form. My mental torment, mainly caused by the language barrier, is now much alleviated. I'd like to use this space in order to provide some information to those who wish to come to the United States.
>
> New Jersey State issues a temporary work permit to the [foreign] nurses who scored more than 447 points in TOEFL [Test of English as a Foreign Language] test. Once they receive the state work permit, they are treated on equal terms with registered nurses. Fortunately, I had taken the TOEFL test at USIS in Taegu [in South Korea]. Thus, when I arrived here, I could receive a work permit. . . . The Korean nursing licensing is not useful here. I have frequently seen Korean nurses who were officially licensed in Korea not trying to get a license here. An urgent economic problem forces them to work as nurses' aides.[53]

As in the case of Korean doctors, time of entry has determined the ability of Korean nurses to acquire a state license. Korean nurses who entered the United States before 1971 did not need to take the TOEFL test in order to qualify for a work permit in New York or New Jersey. Because of the demand for the "cheap" labor of foreign-educated nurses, New York was the most liberal state in granting licenses to foreign-educated nurses, especially Asian ones. Until 1971, New York State operated a special licensing system for foreign-educated nurses in which records of transcripts and clinical experience in the home country were evaluated and credited in the qualifications for state R.N. licenses. According to the system, foreign-educated nurses were required to take examinations in only those subjects in which they showed poor performance both in school and in practical experience. Thus, the early-arriving Korean nurses could acquire New York State's nursing licenses without too great an effort. But, since the early 1970s,

---

[53] Soon-dug Kwon, "Haeoe eseo on pyeongi" [A letter from overseas], *Daehan Ganho*, Korean Nurses Association, November-December 1973, p. 45.

New York State has imposed an identical examination on both foreign and domestically educated nurses seeking R.N. licenses. Foreign-educated nurses must take the National League for Nursing State Board Test Pool Examinations, which cover all the subjects of nursing education. This raising of examination standards for foreign-educated nurses has created an "examination hell" for unlicensed Korean nurses. They have reacted by organizing group study sessions, seminars, and special lectures on examination subjects, usually at Korean churches. Such programs have given a vital content to the community organization activities of Korean churches in America.

CONCLUSION

The emergence of a large number of Korean medical professionals in the United States is a byproduct of the expansion of the American medical economy. During the 1960s and the early 1970s, the demand for medical personnel rose as a result of the emergence of a service-oriented economy, which has increasingly characterized contemporary American society. But the United States was not self-sufficient in the supply of medical workers, partly because the demand for them was very large and had increased suddenly and partly because the American medical establishment had been unwilling or unable to produce enough medical workers to deliver proper medical service to the growing number of medically "deficient" Americans. This peculiar development in the American medical industry worked as the main pull factor that generated the selective emigration of Korean medical workers to the United States. Thus, vast economic opportunities were sudden and serendipitous for Korean medical workers.

The entry of Korean immigrants by way of the medical service occupations is in sharp contrast to the occupational entry of earlier immigrant groups. The latter entered into the primary or secondary sectors of American industry and were not highly educated.

Given the broad, expanding structure of the American medical industry, we have identified some specific pull factors in the United States that facilitated a massive exodus of Korean medical professionals into American medical institutions. First, there was a maldistribution of American-born doctors in terms of both geographical areas and specialty fields. Under the impact of suburbanization, well-qualified white medical doctors and nurses have concentrated their practices in suburban medical institutions while inner-city hospitals and rural medical centers have suffered from a shortage of medical professionals, especially physicians. This skewed distribution created many vacancies for foreign-educated medical workers in America's inner cities. The

New York area, with the largest inner city in the United States and many large hospitals, has attracted more Korean medical professionals than any other metropolitan area. They provide medical services to poor whites, the elderly, and blacks and Hispanics, who lack their own ethnic doctors and nurses. American-born and trained physicians tend to concentrate instead on more lucrative clientele. In addition, the concentration of American-born physicians in several "core" specialties at the expense of the "fringe" specialties produced vacancies in the "fringe" areas of medicine, which were eventually filled by foreign doctors in general and Korean doctors in particular. Thus, Korean doctors entered the marginal sectors of American medicine.

The selective demand for Korean medical professionals in the United States greatly contributed to changes in the South Korean medical system. In response to the importation of Korean medical workers by the United States and other countries, the South Korean government permitted and encouraged an increase in the number of medical and nursing schools. Since the United States changed its immigration policy to discourage the entry of foreign-educated medical professionals, however, the South Korean medical professions in both the homeland and abroad have been troubled with a "surplus" generation of doctors and nurses. In addition, the South Korean medical system has undergone an internal change: in order to save surplus medical graduates from unemployment, a reform movement has emerged in the intern-training system.

When the United States allowed the immigration of Asian medical professionals in 1965, South Korea was able to send a large number of medical workers to the United States mainly because it had already developed Western-style medical institutions. Specifically, American missionaries, Japanese colonialists, and the American military presence in South Korea during and after the Korean War contributed to the growth of medical institutions in a much more substantial way than it did to any other scientific institutions or professions in South Korea. We have also noted that a maldistribution of South Korean medical institutions was one of the prime push factors for the emigration of medical workers. The concentration of South Korean medical centers in a few primary cities is a product of the larger direction taken by South Korean urbanization: the nation's hospitals have located in a few primary cities with the highest concentrations of people and money. Meanwhile, most South Korean rural villages are a medical wasteland devoid of doctors and nurses. Given this skewed development, South Korean medical graduates, most of whom have been drawn from the urban middle or upper-middle classes, had to compete for a limited number of job opportunities provided by a limited number of urban medical institutions. Furthermore, South Korean medical graduates, being imbued with urban life styles and an urban culture, pursued a higher economic reward either by staying in South Korean cities or by emigrating to the inner cities of the United States.

United States government regulations such as those in the immigration laws and in state and federal licensing systems have governed the life chances of Korean medical workers. As long as United States immigration law was formulated in such a way as to accept Korean medical workers, they could seek to maximize their life chances in either the South Korean or the United States medical markets. And as long as the United States faced a keen shortage in medical workers, a liberal licensing system prevailed for Korean medical workers. But when the "shortage" of medical workers appeared to have ended, licensing and immigration opportunities dried up, and Korean medical professionals in both South Korea and the United States (especially recent arrivals) began to suffer from restrictions that were not of their own making. Impersonal, external forces shaped the destiny of each individual and the community in which he or she lived.

PART III

The Emergence of a Korean
Community

Introduction: The Korean Community in the New York Metropolitan Area

The Phenomenological Base. By separating themselves both socially and psychologically from the larger American society, Korean immigrants have attempted to achieve a sense of community among themselves. Since they are recent arrivals in a new land, they identify themselves primarily as Koreans and treat the institutions of the larger society as an alien force that is strange, unmanageable, and frequently hostile. Thus, the psychological basis of the Korean community in New York is built upon a widespread acceptance of a dichotomy that Koreans express by the terms "we" versus "they," or *gyoposahoe* (our countrymen's society) versus *migugsahoe* (American society). Almost all the major articles and essays in Korean ethnic newspapers that deal with "Korean problems" evoke this dichotomy, and Korean immigrants frequently use the terms that express the dichotomy in their daily conversations. By thinking of themselves as separate from the larger society, they can identify and evaluate their common situation, which, they think, is imposed upon them by the larger society. They can thus defend and to some extent strengthen themselves. For Korean immigrants, the "we" values, life styles, and customs are the basic means for sustaining a new life in a new social environment. "Korean-ness" functions as a castle into which Koreans can easily retreat whenever they feel assaulted by the overwhelmingly "hostile" institutions of the larger society.

This does not mean, however, that Korean immigrants do not endeavor to learn the "rules of game" in the new land. In fact, the kinds of conflicts, psychological as well as material, that Koreans experience with the larger society occur because Korean immigrants try, perhaps too quickly, to assimilate and adjust to the dominant culture, customs, and institutions of contemporary American society. Largely because of a character structure derived from the old land, Korean immigrants on the whole overreact to contemporary American culture and attempt to "master" it. They are predominantly preoccupied with the "education problem" facing their children, but many Korean women have undergone eyelid surgical operations or face lifting in order to acquire a facial structure resembling that of white old-stock Americans. In spite of these self-conscious efforts, and indeed perhaps because of them, Korean immigrants have not yet liberated themselves from the "un-American" attitudes and behavior that mark them as Koreans and separate them from native Americans. This situation, common to all Korean immigrants, has become the basis for constituting a Korean ethnic community in the New York metropolitan area.

The Founding Fathers. The historical development of New York's Korean community corresponded to the different phases by which Korean immigrants entered the United States. As has been noted in chapter one, a large proportion of the older Korean immigrants, the first phase, entered the United States before the enactment of the National Origins Act of 1924. These were students, political refugees, and Christians. Until the end of the Korean War, a small group of these immigrants and their descendants formed the nucleus of the Korean ethnic community in New York City. In 1920 some seventy Koreans lived in New York, and about thirty Christians from among them established the first Korean church in the city, which still exists, near Columbia University.[1] From that time until 1970, when a large number of Korean immigrants began to enter the city, the church was central to the community life of New York's Koreans. A small Korean ghetto formed around the church at 633 West 115th Street, and Korean students and political refugees, including some who later became prominent political leaders after Korean independence, were associated with it. An elderly Korean recalled the church-centered community life of 1929.

As the Great Depression deepened in the fall of 1929, a throng of paupers emerged and loitered on the street near Columbia University. They begged for penny after penny. I saw for the first time a white beggar. . . .

The Depression also hit our Korean students, forcing them to drop out of school. An increasing number of Korean students had become drifters.

At that time, the New York Korean Church, the only Korean church in New York City, provided an effective force of integrating our community life. Regular church membership numbered some 20, most of whom, if my memory is correct, were students. . . . In addition to being a house of God, the church was a center of the overseas Korean independence movement. All other community activities were merged into church life. The church provided various services to those Korean immigrants who visited New York City. The dormitory of the church, which occupied the third and fourth floors of the

[1] *Joong Ang Ilbo*, November 30, 1977.

church building, was always crowded with students and immigrants.
. . . There we Koreans used to spend a whole night talking about our
national independence and our bitter or sweet experiences with
American jobs and school life, etc. . . .[2]

As the first-generation immigrants aged, producing a negligible number of descendants, New York's Korean community was on the verge of
extinction. But with the influx of Korean students after the end of the
Korean War, New York's Korean community received fresh members.

The New Wave of Immigrants. The new group of Korean students included many physicians (classified as students) who entered the
United States for internship or residency training on the Exchange-
Visitor Program. This generation resuscitated New York's Korean community and later emerged as a dominant component as it grew in
number during the 1960s; for the majority of the students did not
return to Korea as officially expected after finishing their education
at American universities, mainly due to the bleak job situation in the
home country. A Korean scholar visited New York City from South
Korea in 1957 and reported on the Korean students in America.

In 1955 there were 288 Korean students including 75 medical doctors in New York City, 60 in Philadelphia, and 187 in Boston. . . .
The enrollment of so many Korean students in these prestigious
American universities was the result of the endless efforts of our
students who had arrived in the United States after the Korean War
with a proper life goal and a correct outlook on life. . . . Korean
students worked so hard in the hope that someday they would contribute themselves to our fatherland. But what bothered them was
the bad job prospects in our country. Many students had asked me
whether they would get a job if they were to return to our country.[3]

Korean students in New York City formed the Korean Students Association, through which they initiated a number of major community
activities. They became members in the New York Korean Church and
strongly influenced church-centered community activities. A substantial number of students, especially those specializing in the social sciences, switched after graduation (if they did not drop out of school)
to such commercial activities as importing from South Korea. Many
former students became well-established businessmen in the 1970s and
have achieved strong leadership roles in major ethnic organizations.

[2] Seung-in Han, "Migug yuhag sidae eui hantomag iyagi" [A story on American
school life], *Sem Mool*, The Korean Church and Institute, November 1973, p. 26.
[3] Hong-yol Yoo, "Miguge in-neun han-indeul" [Koreans in the United States],
Sasang Ke, April 1958, pp. 45-46.

Thus the leadership of the present Korean community in New York is largely derived from businessmen, medical doctors, and ministers who entered the United States with student status during the 1950s and early 1960s. These early arrivals were the pioneers of all major ethnic institutions. Korean students of theology established many Christian churches, which by 1978 totaled seventy-two. In so doing, students-turned-ministers have made a profound impact on the basic structure of the Korean community. Students-turned-businessmen initiated the major ethnic businesses, such as the wig business and Korean Karate institutes. Korean medical students who entered the United States under the Exchange-Visitor Program have become well established in American medicine and have played a vital role in the Korean Medical Association of America as well as in community activities. In addition, influential Korean professionals such as lawyers, accountants, social workers, and college teachers have emerged from the student population of the 1950s and early 1960s. With the rapid increase of Korean immigrants in the New York metropolitan area since 1970, these early arrivals became issuemakers and opinion makers, mediators with the larger society, therapists, labor exploiters, philanthropists, and preachers. All these activities, functions, and roles have their base in ethnicity. Korean leaders represent and "lead" Korean citizens, and they formulate Korean opinion on "ethnic" issues with respect to the outside world.

The Nonterritorial Basis of the Community. Except for some pocket areas, Korean immigrants in the New York area have not yet formed territorial enclaves; instead, they have scattered over the whole metropolitan area. Their residential areas range from poverty-stricken and crime-ridden South Bronx to affluent Scarsdale, from hustling and bustling lower Manhattan to remote suburbs on Long Island. But, in New York Ctiy itself, Korean immigrants have heavily concentrated in the white lower-middle-class neighborhoods of Queens such as Flushing, Jackson Heights, Woodside, and Sunnyside, in which they mingle with a second or third generation of old immigrants as well as with such new immigrants as Cubans, Greeks, and other Asians. Even in these neighborhoods Korean immigrants have not yet established a single-block ethnic residential enclave.

When Korean immigrants made their first substantial economic gains in the inner city, they followed the dominant trend, since World War II, of suburbanward migration. For the immigrants, to become a suburban homeowner is a manifest symbol of economic success in the new land; an increasing number of Korean immigrants have become suburbanites. This following of the typical but recent American pattern of upward mobility is one of the main reasons why Korean immigrants have not yet created residential, territorial enclaves in New York's inner city. However, this decentralized residential pattern does not mean that ethnic solidarity or ethnic community activities do not exist among Korean immigrants. In the absence of an ethnic territorial base, Korean immigrants have achieved an ethnic solidarity by intensifying organization-centered community activities. The basic characteristics of Korean community activities in the New York metropolitan area are as follows.

(1) As was the case for the older Korean immigrants, Korean churches have become a center of "grass roots" community activities. In addition to providing religious services, Korean churches respond to the direct needs of Korean immigrants by performing all kinds of secular functions.

(2) A large number of secondary groups such as professional, occupational, artistic, recreational, and alumni associations have emerged since 1973 and have become the basic mechanism for differentiated, segregated community activities. Membership in these associations is selective. Korean restaurants and churches are the main providers of space for the organizational activities of these secondary group associations.

(3) By informing geographically scattered Korean immigrants of community meetings and events, ethnic newspapers have emerged as a powerful means of provoking, leading, integrating, expanding, and enlightening some selective community values or opinions. Ethnic newspapers seek a community consensus by reinforcing Korean nationalism and culture.

(4) No centralized ethnic organization or leadership has emerged to integrate, coordinate, and direct the various community activities. Community activities and leaders are segregated mainly along occupational lines or among different walks of life. One of the main functions of each organizational leader is to link his or her group's activities to the corresponding set of institutions in the larger society, or to those of the homeland, or to both. Decentralization thus characterizes the Korean community structure.

(5) By supporting or inhibiting major community activities, the Korean Consulate General, a surrogate of the home government, has exerted a strong influence on the way in which some basic patterns of community organizations have formed. Almost all the major community organizations except for churches are ideologically or materi-

ally associated with the Korean Consulate General in New York City; one of the functions of community leadership is to link one's particular organization with the Korean Consulate General and thereby with the home government.

These five dimensions of the Korean community in the New York metropolitan area will be explored in detail in the following chapters.

CHAPTER SIX

The Church as a Basis
for the Community

As we have noted in chapter one, most Korean immigrants are drawn from the urban middle classes of their homeland, especially from among professionals and white-collar workers. The fact that many of them were Christians, mostly Protestants, plus the influx of Korean ministers as spiritual leaders, largely explains why Korean Protestant churches have flourished in the new land and have become a dominant institution organizing, leading, and "spiritualizing" the activities of Korean immigrants.

Korean churches are much more than simple sites for religious services. As we shall see, the churches, by assuming multiple, secular roles, are strong focal points for many social activities. Thus community church activities constitute the most important facet of day-to-day community life.

By opening membership to all segments of the population, the churches provide a grass-roots base for common action. At least for members, the churches provide some degree of integration and coordination for divergent life activities, an integration that does not exist in nonreligious organizations. In the absence of a territorial base for a "natural" community, church activities are all the more self-consciously organized. Indeed, the church community has become the substitute for a territorial ethnic community, and thus the interplay between the minister and devoted professionals produces a leadership crucial to the carrying out of both religious and secular activities. In addition, most community churches are ideologically and financially independent of the Korean Consulate General in New York City (which, as we shall discuss, exerts a powerful influence upon the remainder of the Korean community in the New York metropolitan area).

THE EMERGENCE OF KOREAN CHURCHES

The *Sunday News* described some activities common to all Korean churches in presenting a picture of one Korean church in Queens.

From the hills and cities of South Korea they come, their hearts filled with hope, their minds eager and alert, their backbones braced for a struggle.

They are the new immigrants, and for most of these hardy, intelligent, hard-working orientals, their first foothold in this new world is Flushing.

Flushing is the first stop, for here help awaits them in the presence of the Rev. Jim-Kwan Han, co-pastor of the Korean Church of Queens, and director of the Korean Community Action Center.

The Community Action Center sponsors numerous programs aimed at easing the adjustments the immigrants must make in a land far from home. They include instruction in English, employment counseling, vocational, legal and medical counseling, a housing service, and a nursery school. . . .

"They are very proud people," the Rev. Han said, "They will not accept anything they did not earn. It is beneath their dignity to take something without earning it. Every able-bodied person must work and contribute no matter how menial the work might be. . . ." Last year the center found employment for 110 people and 170 families. The center charges no fees for the services it provides. . . .[1]

Korean churches in the New York metropolitan area have increased in number from six in 1971 to seventy-four in 1978, reflecting the dramatic influx of Korean immigrants since 1970. Of the seventy-four churches, sixty-eight are Protestant, four Roman Catholic, and only two Buddhist.

CHRISTIANITY IN KOREA

The prevalence of Protestant denominations among Korean immigrants reflects the selective characteristics of Korean immigration. As has been pointed out in chapter one, the majority of Korean immigrants are drawn from the urban middle classes in South Korea. As Christianity in its early Western history was an urban, civic religion, so too the Christianity of Korea has mostly appealed to the urban classes since its introduction by Western missionaries at the end of the nineteenth century.

Because Christianity was accompanied by Western scientific knowledge and thought, Koreans called it the *seohag* (Western learning) movement. A number of Korean literati who were alienated from the inner circle of the centralized state bureaucracy were the first to accept Christianity. They turned to it in their attempt to solve the social and

[1] *New York Sunday News*, November 4, 1973.

political problems of the day, which were largely attributed to the international pariah status of Korea.[2] It was the inhabitants of what we now call North Korea who first received Christianity as an alternative to the established elite and the ruling Confucian ideology of Seoul. During the reign of the Yi dynasty, the government discriminated against North Koreans when appointing the literati to preferred positions in the state bureaucracy. This contributed to the emergence of a discontented merchant class—a despised class in the Yi dynasty—most heavily concentrated in the northwestern part of the Korean peninsula. It is here that Christianity flourished almost until the establishment of the North Korean communist regime. "Confucian principles were less respected at Pyongyang, and explanations of the strong favorable response to Christianity in that area rests in part on the fact that they did not have a solid vested interest in the *status quo*."[3]

As has been discussed in chapter one, up to and during the Korean War most of the Christians and clergymen in North Korea took refuge in the south and became a leading force in expanding the South Korean Protestant churches. They migrated south as refugees because their religion and their commitment to a free-enterprise system—that is, their merchant or professional class status—made them vulnerable to reprisals from the communist regime in North Korea. Thus the North Korean refugees in South Korea are the most sensitive to the military tension between North and South Korea. In addition, these migrants within Korea do not have strongly rooted multigenerational kinship or

---

[2] Spencer J. Palmer, for instance, described the impact of the Korean crisis at the turn of the century on the Korean acceptance of Christianity as follows.

> During these years surrounding the turn of the century, Korea was beset with an almost incredible sequence of tragic events. The queen was murdered. Japan announced its intention of exercising paramount control in Korean affairs. The Korean king's frantic efforts to gain American governmental support for his shaky kingdom failed. Two wars were fought between Japan and China and Japan and Russia, with Korea as the focal point of conflict. Korean domestic political strife remained at a bewilderingly high pitch. Famine and epidemics were everpresent threats to human life. The people were caught up in a spirit of despondency and decline (what Buddhists called *kali yuga* of the "last days"). Feelings of loss and shame pervaded the country. Finally, the fate of the people seemed forever sealed in 1910 when Japan, after having earlier coerced the king into abdicating his throne, politically annexed Korea into the Japanese empire.
>
> Each of these crises in turn had a profound effect upon Korean attitudes toward Christian religion, although there was not always an exact correspondence between specific crises and periods of increases in membership. Sustained social and intellectual pressures also had their longer-range historical ramifications in Korea, as well as in China. One response was a search for Utopia and a desire for messianic deliverance. . . . ("Western Religion and Korean Culture," in *Korea's Response to the West*, ed. Yung-hwan Jo, Ann Arbor, University of Michigan Press, 1968, p. 99.)

[3] Ibid., p. 102.

village ties in the south. This marginal status—political, religious, and familial—has mainly caused them to migrate again to foreign countries.

These structural and historical factors help explain why the majority of Korean ministers in America are of North Korean origin and why Protestant churches are a dominant religion among Korean immigrants despite the fact that Christianity is a minority religion in South Korea, as shown in table 6.1. As we shall see, the ministers of North Korean origin, most of whom came to the United States in order to study theology, were instrumental in founding and promoting the Korean immigrant churches in New York.

TABLE 6.1   RELIGIOUS POPULATIONS IN SOUTH KOREA, 1977

Religion	Number (millions)	Percentage
Buddhist	12.9	46
Confucianist	4.7	17
Protestant	5.0	18
Catholic	1.1	4
Cheondogyo[a]	0.8	3
Others	3.5	12
Totals[b]	27.0	100

SOURCE: *Annual Report on the Religious Population*, Ministry of Culture and Information of the South Korean government.

[a] A nationalist religion.

[b] The total religious population comprised 77 percent of the total South Korean population in 1977.

Since the turn of the century, and even during the Japanese colonial period, Korean Protestant churches have played a leading role in introducing and disseminating Western culture, science, and democratic ideas. As has been indicated in chapter five, the development of Korean medicine can largely be attributed to Western missionaries. In addition, Western missionaries, especially from the United States, founded a great many educational institutions through which Koreans acquired their knowledge of Western political ideas and institutions. The most prominent political leaders and opponents of Japanese domination were graduates of the Christian schools or students in them. Because Western democratic ideals were deeply planted in the minds of Korean Christians, today they constitute the only coherent group of believers in democracy, just as previously they engaged in serious opposition to President Park's authoritarian rule. This background has shaped, as we shall see, the ministerial leadership in the new land; Korean ministers in New York are relatively free from the influence of South Korean government agencies located in New York City.

CHURCHES AS THE GRASS-ROOTS COMMUNITY

Even though less than 40 percent of the Korean immigrants in the New York metropolitan area participate in church life, almost all routine community activities are centered in churches. This is because they are the only places where Korean immigrants can meet regularly. In the absence of effective community organizations that might meet the secular needs of all segments of the Korean population, Christian churches have emerged as a basic grass-roots community organization. Churches have become a focus for strengthening the immigrants' psychological defenses against the dominant institutions of the larger society. And for Korean immigrants, who have not formed any territorial enclaves, churches are the surrogates of ethnic neighborhoods. In their nonreligious roles, churches act as brokers between Korean immigrants and the dominant institutions of the larger society. They also serve as a surrogate for the extended family in a situation where immigration often severs the generational and local ties that constitute the basis of the extended family. But even more than this, the churches, in this nonreligious role, reinforce the secular culture of the homeland among Korean immigrants and keep alive, even strengthen, Korean nationalism.

The Geographical Dispersion of Korean Churches. With the exception of the two Buddhist churches in Manhattan, the geographical distribution of Korean churches indicates the loose settlement pattern of Korean immigrants in the New York metropolitan area: Korean churches have emerged wherever Korean immigrants have settled. As shown in table 6.2, the concentration of twenty-seven Protestant Korean churches and one Catholic church in Queens reflects a concentration of Korean immigrants in Flushing, Elmhurst, and Woodside, which are white lower-middle-class neighborhoods in Queens. The smaller number of Korean immigrants in Brooklyn and the Bronx reflects their attempt to avoid living in the black and Puerto Rican belts in these boroughs. As a result, there are only two Protestant Korean churches in the Bronx and three in Brooklyn. Only two Protestant Korean churches and one Catholic church exist on Staten Island, where Korean immigrants have difficulty in finding suitable residence mainly because of high rents.

Changes in Church Membership. All but four of these Korean churches were founded after 1970, and three-quarters of them have emerged

TABLE 6.2 LOCATIONS OF KOREAN CHRISTIAN CHURCHES IN THE NEW YORK
METROPOLITAN AREA, 1978

Location	Number
Manhattan	7
Brooklyn	3
Bronx	2
Staten Island	3
Queens:	
Flushing	10
Elmhurst	4
Woodside	4
Other Queens	10
SUBTOTAL FOR NEW YORK CITY	43
Other New York metro. area	8
New Jersey	19
Connecticut	2
GRAND TOTAL	72

SOURCE: Survey by author.

since 1974. The four churches founded prior to 1970 are the New York
Korean Church in Manhattan, the Brooklyn Korean Church, the
Korean Church of Queens, and the Korean Central Church in Manhattan. As has been noted, the New York Korean Church, which is located
on West 115th Street in Manhattan, was founded in 1921 by Korean
immigrants who entered the United States prior to the National Origins
Act of 1924. Its location near Columbia University and the Union Theological Seminary reflects the fact that many Korean politicians, intellectuals, and clergymen attended the church while they were students
at the two schools. Until the late 1960s the New York Korean Church
held a virtual monopoly over religious ministry to Koreans in New
York, and all Korean community activities took place there. Its membership was mainly composed of students before the influx of new
immigrants in 1967. As in the Korean community as a whole, new immigrants have replaced students and intellectuals in the membership
of the New York Korean Church. Partly because of its location in Manhattan and partly because of its reputation as the leading Korean
church in New York, many visitors from the homeland—businessmen,
artists, and tourists—attend the church. But new immigrant members
are continually moving to the suburbs, as do most Koreans in inner

cities. Thus the congregation is "always turning over." One church member said, "There are always new faces."

The Korean Central Church split from the Brooklyn Korean Church in 1968 and moved to East Forty-Second Street in Manhattan in order to become a rival religious center for Koreans living in New York City. Partly because of the ability of its minister, the turnover of its membership is less pronounced than that of the New York Korean Church. The Brooklyn Korean Church was founded in the early 1960s, and its congregation has recently declined in size partly because the medical professionals who constituted a bulk of its membership moved to the suburbs. A high membership turnover characterizes all the Protestant churches in the inner city because Koreans who have achieved some economic success generally move to the suburbs. This does not necessarily lead to a decline of the church population in the inner city, for new immigrants become new members or establish new churches. Thus several big churches, including the old churches mentioned above, maintain a size ranging from 200 to 400 members.

The upward mobility of Korean immigrants is clearly indicated by the emergence of Korean suburban churches since 1974. During the period from 1974 to 1978, twelve Protestant Korean churches and one Catholic church emerged in the New Jersey suburbs contiguous to New York City. During the same period, six Protestant churches came into existence in the New York suburbs. The suburban churches do not show any one pattern of concentration. They are scattered over the whole suburban area, from Long Island to White Plains, Englewood, and Montclair. This reflects the fact that Korean suburbanites have not yet concentrated in any one residential area. Unlike the churches in the inner city, the suburban churches have stable congregations. Their size, however, is small: membership ranges from 30 to 100. However, suburban congregations do not necessarily consist exclusively of Koreans who first established themselves in the inner city and then became successful. As has been noted in chapter one, there is a strong indication that many new and wealthy Korean immigrants have settled directly in the suburban areas of New York City.

The Dominance of Professionals in Lay Life. Not all types of Korean immigrants participate equally in church life. Church membership varies to a large extent with occupation. In every Korean church, without exception, medical professionals and other white-collar workers constitute the largest part of the congregation and dominate the lay leadership. Medical professionals—immigrant doctors, nurses, and pharmacists—have "made it" faster than the other groups of Korean immigrants. White-collar workers who belong to churches mainly consist of Koreans who came to the United States as students and received their education in American universities. They can afford to participate in church events mainly because they have the leisure in which to attend church services and related activities.

Medical professionals have played a leading role in the creation of some Korean churches. In fact, some ministers set up their churches by recruiting medical professionals for their congregations. The conspicuous participation of medical professionals in church life is partly due to the fact that in the homeland they were exposed to Christianity through their years of training in medical or nursing schools, many of which, as we have noted, were founded by Western, especially American, missionaries. This does not mean that all Korean medical professionals participate in church life, but rather that in the absence of ethnic gathering places they are the most prone to attend church. For example, graduates of the Yonsei University School of Medicine, founded by a North American Presbyterian missionary at the turn of the century, once constituted the largest part of the Brooklyn Korean Church's congregation. However, its members tended to move out of the city to suburbs. Another example can be found in the Korean Seventh-Day Adventist Church in Woodside: some 90 percent of its 70 members once consisted of Koreans who had either graduated from the nursing school founded by the American Seventh-Day Adventist missionary or who were affiliated with the hospital or schools run by the missionary. In fact, in every Korean church at least one-fifth of the congregation is made up of medical professionals and their families. In the New Jersey Central Korean Church in Orange County, physicians and their family members once constituted some 60 percent of the more than 100 members; in the Korean Church of the Bronx, physicians, nurses, and pharmacists once comprised about 30 percent of the 250 members.

Small Businesses and Church Life. With the exception of established businessmen who assume lay leadership positions after achieving success, Korean small businessmen are not committed to church life, simply because they are too busy or tired to participate in the leisure activities centered in the church: "If I had time to go to church on Sunday, I would rather sleep." Self-employed small businessmen work six or seven days a week and have little time to participate in church activities even on their day off. Even devoted Christians with a long history of churchgoing in the homeland tend to dissociate themselves from church life when they set up their own businesses. As has been noted, Korean small businessmen predominantly engage in "labor-intensive" enterprises in which they also employ their family members in order to save labor costs. They maintain long store hours and exploit themselves and their families, and this effectively prevents them from devoting themselves to church life.

Korean-food storeowners are an exception. They tend to participate in church life because their clientele comes from their own ethnic group. Similarly, businessmen catering to ethnic customers, such as insurance brokers, travel and employment agents, real estate brokers, and accountants, are strongly committed to church life. Some of them attend several churches in rotation in order to "make contacts."

The Age Distribution of Church Members. The composition of church membership also has special age-group characteristics. In every church, without exception, elderly women constitute the core, the most loyal membership. These women attend church every Sunday all year round, if they can secure a means of transportation. Most of them have been brought from the homeland by their sons or daughters for the purpose of baby-sitting. A language barrier confines them to their houses or apartments, and they do not even watch television. Thus the church has become their sole source of outside activities. In every Korean church there is a club for the elderly called the Gyeongnohoe, or the Association of the Respectable Elderly. In contrast, unmarried youth such as college students are the least committed to church life, because they are able to express themselves and find companions in the recreational facilities of the larger society.

In every church there is a large group of children ranging in age from four to twelve. While their parents are participating in the main religious service, the children are attending Sunday school classes, where they receive language lessons and learn Korean folk dancing, folk singing, and *taekwondo*. A high proportion of these children belong to the families of medical professionals and white-collar workers. Unlike small shopkeepers and blue-collar workers, medical professionals and white-collar workers have enough leisure time and interest in education to pay special attention to the education of their children. Many shopkeepers and blue-collar workers, however, send their children to Sunday school classes without ever presenting themselves to church activities. This provokes an almost instant negative reaction on the part of the minister: "Those children's parents send them to the Sunday school and sometimes even to church picnics. I have checked who they are. . . ."

Church Affiliation in the Homeland and the United States. In addition to occupational class and age variables, the religious experience of Koreans in the homeland also determines the degree of participation in the churches of the new land. This cuts across every other characteristic of Korean immigrants to determine membership in the four Catholic churches, the two Seventh-Day Adventist churches, the Baptist church, the two Full Gospel churches, the Episcopal church, and other informal meetings of Mormons and Jehovah's Witnesses. The memberships of these churches are almost all made up of immigrants who were affiliated with the same denomination in the homeland.

The activities of the two Korean Seventh-Day Adventist churches are linked with the American organization as well as with the denominational church in the homeland. Similarly, Korean Catholics in America, unlike the Protestant majority, had experience in Catholic churches in the homeland. In New York, the Queens Korean Catholic Meeting was promoted in 1974 to the official status of the Korean Catholic Church of Queens by a higher American Catholic institution. The Korean Catholic Meeting in Manhattan, which began in 1968 to hold services at Saint Andrew's Cathedral, was similarly promoted in 1978 to the Korean Catholic Apostolate of the Archdiocese of New York. The memberships of two Full Gospel churches, which are "branches" of a Korean evangelical church in the homeland, are mostly made up of immigrants who previously attended that denomination in the homeland. Before bringing their own minister from their headquarters in Seoul, they held services by listening to the tape-recorded sermons of a founding minister of their church, the so-called Sunbogeum Gyohoe, which means, ideographically, the Pure Gospel church. Its organizational and ideological structure is similar to that of the Unification Church. In addition there are the meetings of Korean Mormons and Jehovah's Witnesses, neither of whom have yet established their own ethnic churches at an official level. The membership of these two are so few that their existence is almost unknown to the Korean community at large.

Churches in which membership is mainly derived from the homeland have not been expanding as rapidly as other Protestant churches. This is mainly because the majority of Korean immigrants do not necessarily regard going to church as an attempt to gain religious salvation. Since they consider the church as a gatheringplace to maintain ethnic solidarity or as a place to escape the isolation they feel from the larger society, they frown upon rituals such as the Catholic catechism and the strict observance of the Sabbath in the Seventh-Day Adventist church. They also ridicule the Jehovah's Witnesses for their taboo of refusing blood transfusions and for making uninvited proseletyzing visits to poor Korean immigrants.

Nondenominational Protestant Churches. In the other Protestant or nondenominational churches, which constitute the majority, there has existed an implicit agreement not to ask newcomers whether they ever attended church in the homeland, and, if so, what denominations they belonged to, unless the newcomers volunteer the information. The minister does not want to embarrass newcomers, most of whom attend church because of secular needs rather than deep religious needs. The minister's desire to expand his church membership as much as possible is reflected in the slogan "a superdenominational church." The meaning of this slogan unwittingly coincides with the idea of ecumenicalism. The minister as well as the lay leaders know that if they expound the theology of any one denomination they will lose a significant number of their members who belonged to different denominations in the homeland.

The other reason for the prevalence of nondenominational churches is that Korean immigrant churches, especially the churches administered by Presbyterian ministers, have been denied admission to the American headquarters of the various denominations, which construe the numerical increase of Korean churches as a menace to their internal power. Moreover, many Presbyterian ministers, even though they have been admitted into the Presbytery of New York City, are extremely reluctant to call their churches Presbyterian. For instance, the four leading Korean churches in New York City—the Korean Church of the Bronx, the Korean Church of Queens, the Brooklyn Korean Church, and the Korean Central Church of New York—omit the word "Presbyterian" from the title of their churches in spite of the fact that they have acquired membership in the Presbytery of New York City. Privately, however, some ministers boast of the official recognition by the presbytery, especially when they compare their churches with the small new "masterless" churches lacking any affiliation with American denominational organizations.

On the whole, church attendance at most Protestant nondenominational churches fluctuates according to the weather. On sunny Sundays through the summer months attendance reaches its lowest point partly because the "cliff-dwelling" church members prefer to go to a beach rather than endure the absence of centralized air conditioning in their churches. On cloudy Sundays when outdoor recreation seems to be impossible, the size of the congregation increases dramatically. Attendance is also conditioned by the schedule of specific recreational programs as advertised in a weekly pamphlet: "After today's service there will be a show of a homeland film in the basement auditorium." The biggest turnout occurs when the church holds an "outdoor service day," which takes place twice a year, on the arrival of spring and fall, when a picnic is held.

IMMIGRATION POLICY AND THE PROLIFERATION OF CHURCHES

Simply because a church provides its minister with his means of livelihood and the same high prestige his profession enjoys in the home country, the minister's personal ambition plays a dominant role in the emergence as well as the functioning of churches. Most ministers intend to reside permanently in the United States. For most, their professional training, generally acquired in the homeland, could not be transferred to any other occupation in the labor market of the larger society. Thus the meaning of each minister's existence in both an idealistic and a materialistic sense is directed toward creating and leading his own ethnic church. This is one of the most important causes of the rapid increase in the number of Korean churches, and it may be the underlying reason why ministers have dominated the grass-roots community leadership, whose content and form is quite different from the leadership centered in the Korean Association of Greater New York (an umbrella organization) and other major community organizations.

Ministers can be divided into the three groups according to their visa status at their time of entry. The first group is made up of those who entered the United States as theology students and received their higher education in American seminaries. Most of the leading Korean churches with a relatively long history have been founded and administered by these American-trained ministers. Mainly because of their American higher education, these ministers dominate the leadership of interchurch activities and tend to espouse radical or "liberation" theology. The second group consists of visitors to the higher denominational institutions in the United States, or of ministers sent on official business from a Korean denominational church to its American counterpart. The third group is made up of ministers who immigrated at the invitation of the Korean churches in the United States. They were invited to administer a Korean church without a trained full-time minister or to assist the chief minister of the larger churches, and they came to the United States with immigrant status. Their number is small.

Except for the ministers belonging to the third group, most ministers have become permanent residents in the United States by taking advantage of the immigration law, under which any alien minister serving at least thirty church members is eligible for permanent residence. In the early 1970s, when Korean churches began to emerge in mass, there was keen competition in recruiting church members. Ministers who did not have enough members in their church to meet the permanent residence qualification frequently took church members from larger churches. In these struggles for membership, offering important lay leadership positions to new influential members was an implicit means of proselytizing. This partly explains the fact that most of the large churches have undergone an internal split, resulting in the emergence of a new church. In most cases the split was instigated by the assistant minister, who revolted against the chief minister. The assistant minister formed his own clique by gathering together the alienated lay leaders and church members. For instance, in the early 1970s a total of seven Korean Protestant churches were formed by secession from their main churches. In four of them, assistant ministers led the dissenters to form their own churches.

In an effort to prevent any more ministers from creating new churches, some established Korean ministers of large churches have asked white Protestant churches located in their vicinity not to rent their buildings to any additional Korean congregations. But their demand has been largely unheeded. On the whole, white Protestant churches in New York City have welcomed renting to Korean congregations as a means of solving their own financial problems. Most white Protestant churches in the inner city suffer from declining membership. Elderly women constitute the main body of the landlord churches' congregation, and no religious services are provided during the summer vacation season. Consequently, many Korean churches act like hosts to the internally fragile American Protestant churches from which they rent space. Koreans have said that "someday we will take over this church."

THE CHURCH AS A PSEUDO EXTENDED-FAMILY

One of the main functions of Korean churches is to provide church members with a "family atmosphere," which presupposes a small congregation in which everyone knows everyone else and everyone else's business. Through church-centered activities Korean immigrants attempt to cope with their overwhelming sense of alienation from the larger society. The search for a pseudo extended-family through church communities has also caused an increase in the number of small churches. Koreans who belong to a large church, with a membership of 200 or more, frequently complain about feeling crowded. They sometimes recall the good old days when the church had a small membership, which is a precondition for the creation of a "family atmosphere." Because of this longing of Korean immigrants for direct, personal interaction, the ministers of newly established small churches can easily draw a significant portion of their congregations from large churches. And for this same reason the assistant ministers can easily establish their own churches by assembling alienated members and lay leaders. To create a "family atmosphere" in the church is the most important task that a minister must carry out.

The congregation, like the community as a whole, uses the minister's nonreligious activity as the main criterion for judging him. Negligible weight is given to the minister's religious conviction and religiosity. The minister's extrachurch activities include all the mundane duties essential to the formation of a "family atmosphere": matchmaking, presiding over marriage ceremonies, visiting hospitalized members, assisting moving families, making congratulatory visits to families having a new baby, making airport pick-ups of newly arrived family members, interpreting for "no-English" members, administering job referral and housing services, and performing other similar personal services. In order to deliver these kinds of humane services, the minister is expected to know a great deal about American society. Thus the minister is judged by his degree of erudition as manifested by degrees received from American seminaries. Highly educated audiences admire the minister's encyclopedic knowledge, which he expresses through numerous quotations contained in his sermon. But the minister's ultimate competence is displayed in his ability to link his congregation with the dominant secular institutions of the larger society. Thus organizational and executive ability in operating church programs constitute the highest quality in a minister.

To conduct their many activities, all Korean churches, except for the two Buddhist churches, have in common the following auxiliary organizations: a Sunday school, a youth association, a women's association, a fathers' association, an elderly women's association, a high school students' association, a junior high school students' association, and a choir. All these associations have their own rules, goals, and budgets. Each association is subdivided into various sections; for instance, the youth association is made up of missionary, athletic, service, and arts-and-literature sections. After the main religious service, all major informal or formal church activities take place through the associations. But the activities of the Sunday school, in which the Korean language and dances and songs are taught to children, proceed while the main religious service is being held. (The Sunday school is also subdivided according to age groups.)

All these associations are designed to continue and expand church activities after the main religious service. However, they are only one dimension of the church community. Church members are also grouped according to the residential area in which they live; in every church at least ten "district service" areas are artificially created in order to extend group activities beyond the location of the church itself. The purpose of the district service area is to promote mutual assistance among nearby members and enhance their faith by holding a religious service at a member's residence on a rotational basis. Food is served, and informal social interchange follows these unofficial religious services.

By means of their intrachurch associations and district service areas, Korean churchgoers attempt to create a substitute for the extended family. This is their way of coping with feelings of estrangement from the larger society, and this is one of their mechanisms for achieving ethnic solidarity.

THE CHURCH AS A BROKER

In addition to these inner-oriented activities, the church acts as a broker to connect church members with the bureaucratic institutions of the larger society. In every church there exists a group of professional experts who assume positions of lay leadership. They provide church members with counseling on immigration and naturalization, employment, housing, health care, social security, and education. All these services are essential for Korean immigrants who are adjusting to the larger society. If the minister wants to earn a good reputation, he must be willing and able to organize these counseling services. Most of the large churches operate "life counseling centers," which are exclusively addressed to the adjustment problems of Korean immigrants.

Some large churches have provided unique programs directed toward specific segments of the Korean population. For example,

The Korean Church of Queens once provided for special lectures designed to help Korean pharmacists and nurses pass the New York State licensing examination. Although the lectures were given irregularly, they appealed greatly to unlicensed nurses and pharmacists throughout the community. Rev. Han of the church, a graduate of the Union Theological Seminary, is well known in the community for his active involvement in church-centered community activities (field notes).

The Korean Central Church in Manhattan conducted a series of lectures in order to help Korean immigrant doctors pass their medical board examination. The church sponsored the Korean Acupuncturist Association when the latter gave seminars to Korean acupuncturists. These special programs were entirely due to the work of a devoted elder whose name is well publicized in the community for his active participation in major community organizations such as the Korean Association of Greater New York, the Lions Club, the Korean Cultural Center, and the Korean Guidance Center.

In addition, the church has put on mini-operas since 1974 (field notes).

The Korean Church of the Bronx has, since 1973, held a series of seminars aimed at helping unlicensed pharmacists to prepare for the New York State licensing examination. The seminars have been initiated and organized by a leading lay leader of the church who has served as president of the Korean Pharmaceutical Association. Many unlicensed Korean pharmacists attend the church simply because of the existence of the seminars. In addition, the church set up in 1977 the Korean Language School of the Bronx, which became the fifth Korean language school in New York. The foundation of the school was initiated by a leading elder of the church, who received a doctoral degree in education from an Ivy League school (field notes).

The above examples illustrate only a small portion of the church programs that are addressed to the community as a whole. Two more examples should suffice: the Brooklyn Korean Church has provided Korean immigrants with a free counseling service on income tax returns, and the Korean Catholic Church of Queens set up a community health center in 1977 by mobilizing Korean Catholic doctors and nurses.

The kinds of church programs mentioned above have become a source of interchurch competition for membership and prestige. On the basis of such programs each large church claims to represent the Korean community. The claim is usually made in the form of advertisements in community newspapers.

A Guide to Summer School
for English and Mathematics

The Bronx Korean Language School of the Korean Church of the Bronx has received some financial support from the outside and has decided to open a summer school to provide a good opportunity for Korean children to improve their English and mathematics. . . .

*A Guide to Applying
for the Scholarship for New York's
Korean Students (The Scholarship
Fund of the Korean Methodist Church)*

Thanks to God's grace, your support, and this church's continuous service to our community, this church has grown and developed since the last 6 years, and has become the church for our countrymen. This year, as one of our series of programs, this church set up a scholarship fund for Korean students in New York. . . .

THE EMERGING LAY LEADERSHIP AND THE POLITICS OF CHURCH GOVERNANCE

The way in which church programs are initiated and executed is largely governed by the minister's capacity to organize and coordinate the professional skills of devoted lay leaders. Because Presbyterianism is the predominant denomination in the homeland and because most Korean ministers in the United States belong to that denomination, the organizational structure of the lay leadership in the majority of the Korean Protestant churches in New York is derived from the American Presbyterian church. Trustees, deacons or deaconesses, and elders constitute the lay leadership. Some old and large churches have relatively autonomous boards of trustees, which are responsible for the overall operation of the church. In these churches the deacons and elders are selected by popular vote. But only the New York Korean Church, which was founded in 1921, has an absolutely autonomous board of trustees that can hire and fire the minister.

In most new Protestant churches the founding minister controls most church affairs. Active church members, many of whom are founding members, become elders or deacons regardless of their religious faith; they can obtain these lay leadership positions after contributing money and professional skills needed to run the church. Big businessmen such as importers or wholesalers tend to become elders owing to their big cash contributions to the church. A former music professor in South Korea or an American conservatory student typically becomes the choir conductor. An accountant becomes the church treasurer; a television repairman runs the church movie projector. A former athlete becomes a leader of the youth association and organizes the church team for annual interchurch or community sports contests. Thanks to their economic and professional status, medical professionals, especially physicians, occupy the largest portion of lay leadership positions in almost all Korean churches. A church member said, "Whenever a new doctor first attends the church, the minister goes crazy over him and follows him to the entrance to see him off."

If the lay leaders who are capable of contributing skills and dollars to church activities have faith in God and a background of church life in the homeland, they try to lead a "perfect" Christian life in the new land. However, a high proportion of lay leaders started their church-going only in the new land, and this is frequently resented by believers: "He does not know how to pray for the congregation"; "He would have become a deacon even if he was not baptized." Sometimes believers play down the professional skills that "nonbelievers" contribute to the operation of the church: "Even if he is a well-known musician, he cannot really understand the tone and feeling of church music." This kind of resentment appears to have little impact on the management of church life, because it is expressed in private. But in many Korean churches a serious dislocation of church life has occurred when the "nonbelievers" in positions of lay leadership have attempted, out of their overzealousness, to control the entire spectrum of church activities; this has turned the believers' private resentment into overt hostility. The deep involvement of "nonbelievers" in church activities appears to be related to their status anxiety in the new land. They appear to find a home, a family atmosphere, in the church, and they give their all to their church; but their all does not include a fundamental religious conversion.

As has been indicated, church lay leaders are heavily drawn from among well-established and successful professionals and businessmen, most of whom are proud of their long experience in the United States. Far fewer businessmen than professionals are church members, all successful Koreans in these occupational classes have deeper status anxiety than do new arrivals struggling for everyday economic gains, because economic success allows more time for leisure activities and hence for status building. Even successful professionals cannot get along with their American colleagues in pursuing American lifestyles, for money alone does not guarantee successful businessmen and professionals a commensurate status recognition in the larger society. This sense of status alienation causes many successful professionals and businessmen to commit themselves deeply to church affairs as well as to other community activities. In these activities they can enjoy the prestige, granted by their fellow countrymen, that is denied them by their occupational or professional peers.

Intrachurch conflicts frequently occur when nonreligious lay leaders challenge the authority of the minister and bypass the due processes of decisionmaking in church government. They sometimes initiate am-

bitious programs that cannot be carried out with the available resources. In some cases they form their own cliques by recruiting new
members and attempt to fire the minister. Whatever form their challenge to the minister's authority takes, it poses a serious problem partly
because their professional skills and money are indispensable to the
development of the church and partly because many of them were
probably founding members when the minister established his own
church. Frequently, other believers in lay leadership positions emerge
to rescue the minister from the active "nonbelievers" on the lay boards.
They accuse the ambitious lay leaders of destroying the order and
harmony of church life, and they openly attack the overzealous lay
leaders' vulgarity or the secular manners they inject into church life.
For instance, a group of believers were upset when they heard that an
ambitious lay leader, an accountant who became church treasurer, said
to the minister: "Hey, minister, you want a pay increase?" In most
cases, the minister tries to minimize the internal conflict caused by the
intrusion of ambitious persons into the lay leadership.

The Ambivalence of the Churches toward Material Success

In response to the secular needs of Korean immigrants and because of
the peculiar life chances of the minister, an expansionary pragmatic
spirit characterizes Korean immigrant churches. In spite of this, church
life is organized to put forward an evangelical commitment to religious
ideals. The theme of the minister's sermon, which is conducted in
Korean, frequently lies in the condemnation of American materialism
as an evil that should be eschewed. The following sermon is typical.

> Since the middle of the 20th century American society has suffered
> from its highest development of materialistic civilization, which on
> the other hand has brought forth the corruption of religious and
> moral life. . . .
> The materialistic progress of American society has not produced a
> paradise. On the contrary, it has caused wholesale social problems—
> labor unrest, racial conflicts, the busing issue, prostitution, traffic
> congestion, and juvenile delinquency, and drug addiction. . . . The
> fundamental reason for all these social problems derives from the
> degradation of moral life among Americans. Is it right that the
> fetishism of material progress give rise to a belief that moral life is
> an individual matter? Is it right that moral education should be ex-
> cluded from the curriculum of elementary schools? . . . Materialistic
> civilization bases its existence on the premise that the human brain
> can solve all problems. This kind of civilization means idolatry. Mira-

cles will happen at the moment we liberate ourselves from idolatry and return to God. . . .

The above sermon is quoted from a monthly church pamphlet published by a Korean Protestant church in Queens. The same pamphlet shows the other facet of church life: it contains advertisements of annual church bazaars in which all kinds of Korean products including food, gifts, furniture, and ginseng are sold to the general public at discount prices. The profits yielded by the bazaar will be added to the church fund for purchasing its own building. The pamphlet also lists the names of newlyweds, new babies, donors to the fund for buying the church's building, and announcements by medical doctors and businessmen who have opened new offices or shops.

In order to help Korean immigrants cope with the larger society, the churches unknowingly revive and promulgate their version of the Protestant ethic of nineteenth-century America. The ideological coherence of the churches lie in their emphasis on endless self-abnegation, endurance, hardship, and frugality. These puritan virtues are compatible with Confucian values, which Korean immigrants, regardless of their religious affiliation, have already internalized in their homeland. As we shall see, the congruity between the values of the Protestant ethic and Korean cultural ethics based upon Confucianism partly explains why Korean immigrants have the Protestant discipline necessary for their socioeconomic adjustment to American society. Thus it is natural that the churches reinforce the traditional Korean values of self-control and self-abnegation in a Protestant context. The church makes Korean immigrants vigilant and ready to sustain the kind of combat discipline necessary for survival in the larger society.

In reviving the Protestant ethic, Korean immigrants juxtapose their common existence in a strange land against the hostile, alien, dominant forces of the larger society. "Special attention to our hardships in this strange land" is a commonly used phrase in their prayers. By pointing out the materialistic corruption of the larger society, Korean immigrants feel a moral superiority even though they have advanced their material status to a higher level in less time than has any other recent immigrant group. Mentioning the decline of the white Protestant churches in New York City (without knowing of the ascendance of black and Hispanic churches), one minister said, "We Koreans will rekindle religious faith among Americans."

This revival of Protestantism is meant to be thoroughly Korean, however, for the church is a bulwark protecting and reinforcing Korean nationalism and culture. Major South Korean national holidays such as August 15 (National Independence Day), March 1 (Anti-Japanese

Day), and Children's Day are strictly observed in the church; the traditional respect for the elderly is systematically enhanced by offering them special programs; and the use of the Korean language is systematically promoted, while the use of English in conversation is frowned upon. For children there is a Korean-language contest in which competition involves reciting Korean folk stories and writing short essays or poems. In reinforcing Korean nationalism and culture, the church provides Korean immigrants with an important psychological mechanism for defending themselves against the larger society.

CONCLUSION

In spite of but also because of the absence of a territorial base, the church has emerged as a basic grass-roots community organization around which Korean immigrants band together. Although Christianity is a minority religion in South Korea, Christian churches, especially Protestant churches, are dominant in organizing and leading community activities. This dominance reflects the selective operation of the Immigration Act of 1965. The entry of Korean ministers of North Korean origin especially contributes to the predominance of Protestant churches and points to the marginal status of Korean migrants within the homeland and of Korean immigrants to foreign shores.

In order to make a community life possible, the church accentuates nonreligious, secular functions. The church creates a family atmosphere in its intrachurch activities and becomes a substitute for the extended family. By linking its congregation to the bureaucratic institutions of the larger society, the church assumes the role of a broker; by sustaining and enhancing Korean culture and tradition, the church becomes a center of Korean nationalism. Thus, in participating in church-sponsored activities, Korean immigrants achieve some degree of integration in their life activities. In providing these multiple secular activities, the interplay between ministers and lay leaders is crucial. Korean lay leaders are often professionals whose skills are essential to the creation as well as the maintenance of church life.

And yet, the church has limitations in organizing and sponsoring activities for Korean immigrants. Simply because it is a religious institution it cannot absorb very many "active" nonbelievers, who constitute more than a half of the Korean population in the New York metropolitan area. Under these circumstances, Korean immigrants have created secular "secondary" associations. These will be discussed in the following chapter.

CHAPTER SEVEN

Secondary Associations of the Korean Community

COMMUNITY secondary associations have emerged as a basic mechanism by which Korean immigrants carry out their normal activities. By secondary associations we mean associations that are primarily oriented toward specific, limited tasks, usually professional and business activities. They are "secondary" in the sense that they are self-consciously organized and rationally operated. Within the precinct of secondary associations Korean immigrants also conduct their social and leisure activities and thus attempt to pursue communal needs. An uncountable number of routine, subcommunity activities take place through secondary associations. Most of these activities are unnoticed and unpublicized in community media; yet they are an underlying fabric that interweaves, supports, and influences the individual lives of ordinary community members. An analysis of secondary associations can thus tell us how Korean immigrants build up their ethnic solidarity and how they cope with their new social environment. Moreover, it can show us how they sustain a nonterritorial community. Largely by means of modern transportation and communication devices including the automobile, the telephone, and ethnic media, Koreans self-consciously organize complex but separate interpersonal networks throughout the New York metropolitan area and thus maintain an "associational community."

The secondary associations of the post-1965 immigrants act in sharp contrast with those of the older immigrants. The older immigrants achieved ethnic solidarity largely through primary-group togetherness, kinship associations, and rotating credit associations. All of these were forms of social or territorial segmentation based upon local and regional ties and loyalties originating in the homeland. In contrast, no kinship or territorial associations deriving from family or regional ties in the old land have emerged in New York's Korean community. This is so in spite of the fact that, as we shall see, a regional tie to one's homeland province once operated informally in community politics and that *gye* associations, traditional Korean cooperatives, are informally prevalent among Korean immigrants.

The achievement of solidarity on the basis of secondary associations reflects to a large extent the selective features of Korean immigration to the United States; that is, the associations reflect the character of an urban-to-urban migration consisting of highly professional, well-educated, and well-to-do people from the metropolitan areas of South Korea. As has been noted, the majority of Korean immigrants have been drawn from the urban middle or upper-middle classes, which have experienced one or two generations of urbanization. In addition, the immigrants' high educational accomplishments, their urban occupational experience, and their socialization in the old land have largely determined the way that the new forms of Korean ethnic solidarity in the United States have emerged.

As we shall see, the secondary associations that derive their membership from common institutional experiences in the homeland maintain close organizational connections with their corresponding institutions in South Korea. Their organizational activities tend to concentrate on the intraethnic aspects of their professional activities. In contrast, secondary associations in which membership is based upon economic interests that have emerged in the United States tend to break their ethnic shell and focus upon "American" issues. Finally, the majority of secondary associations, with the notable exception of the church communities, are ideologically affiliated with the Korean Consulate General in New York City.

THE SCOPE OF SECONDARY ASSOCIATIONS

Secondary associations emerge within every sphere of life. The following list is only an outline of some important types of secondary associations that have been created by Korean immigrants in the New York metropolitan area in the last ten years.

(1) RELIGIOUS ASSOCIATIONS Sixty-eight Protestant churches, four Catholic churches, and two Buddhist churches.

(2) POLITICAL ASSOCIATIONS Two anti-Park (South Korean President Park Chung-hee) associations and the Korean-American Political Association.

(3) BUSINESS ASSOCIATIONS The Korean-American Chamber of Commerce; associations of greengrocers, grocerymen (Korean food), dry cleaners, garment retailers, garment subcontractors, fish retailers, wig men, taxicab drivers, travel agents, taekwondo instructors, (Korean) restaurant owners, and (Korean) restaurant cooks.

(4) PROFESSIONAL ASSOCIATIONS Associations of painters, musicians, opera singers, stage entertainers, ministers, radio announcers,

medical doctors, dentists, nurses, pharmacists, X-ray technicians, computer technicians, dental laboratory technicians, athletes, political scientists, engineers and scientists, and Sunday school teachers.

(5) RECREATIONAL ASSOCIATIONS Associations of golfers, tennis players, hunters, baseball players, and mountaineers.

(6) VETERANS' ASSOCIATIONS Associations of anti-Park veterans, pro- (Korean) government veterans, (Korean) navy veterans, (Korean) air force veterans, and Korean veterans of the Vietnam War.

(7) SOCIAL AND CIVIC ASSOCIATIONS AND ORGANIZATIONS Associations of women, the elderly, youth, alumni, and students; the Korean Y.M.C.A. and Y.W.C.A., Jaycees, and Lions Club.

All these associations are formal organizations that have official goals, leaders, and financial resources. Their most notable activities are advertised and publicized through community news media. These formal groups, however, do not exhaust the catalog of Korean community organizations. Informal group activities also constitute an important part of community life.

THE KOREAN-AMERICAN PSEUDO EXTENDED-FAMILY

A practically infinite number of family groups are the basic molecular units supporting ethnic subgroup solidarity. Almost all Korean immigrant families belong to at least one family group. This group includes several nuclear families and is based on the husbands' or wives' common schooling or work experiences in the new or old land; it is not based on actual kinship. Nevertheless, members of a number of these family groups act as if they were related by blood or marriage. The groups also emerge from living in the same neighborhood or from having identical hobbies. These family associations are entirely different from an extended family. They are informal, composed from nuclear families, and have few traditions and rituals. At most, they are substitutes for the extended family, designed for the exchange of material and emotional support. During special occasions such as Christmas, New Year's Eve, and Chinese New Year's Day, they usually meet to enjoy Korean food, dancing, and talk. In many cases, family groups or associations also function as a *gye*, a Korean equivalent of the rotating credit association.

The *gye* association is one type of the traditional Korean cooperatives that were designed to promote mutual assistance, friendship, and good will. During the Yi dynasty, the cooperatives called *gye* were a dominant civic and economic institution, as opposed to the state economic bureaucracies. They were highly differentiated along the lines of major life activities: such cooperatives as cattle *gye*, horse *gye*, fishnet *gye*, forest *gye*, and shroud *gye* are a few examples. All these cooperatives served as de facto insurance companies and mutual benefit associations.[1] The shroud *gye*, for instance, provided funeral expenses to any member who had a death in his family; the cattle *gye* compensated a member who lost cattle. There were also *gye* associations for gambling and political activities. Loan *gye* associations were organized to serve as a bank: members pooled capital and loaned it to merchants and other qualified persons as well as to fellow members.

In contemporary Korean society, these traditional *gye* associations have almost disappeared; but the loan *gye* still continues in the form of the housewives' *gye*, which is equivalent to a rotating credit association. The housewives' *gye* has become widespread since the end of World War II in South Korea as a way of accumulating capital. In the face of chronic double-digit inflation, South Koreans feel that they cannot rely on bank savings.[2] Through the housewives' *gye* associations, ordinary South Koreans in groups of ten to twenty can acquire relatively small amounts of capital to be quickly invested in tangible commodities ranging from durable consumer goods to homes. In many cases, as providers of loans these associations become linked with a larger economic organization such as a business firm, a real estate company, or other small enterprises. They also serve as financiers of local electoral campaigns. In addition, they assume the function of a recreational and social club whereby regular parties or meetings are held.

In the United States, Korean immigrants continuously rely on these informal, clublike rotating credit associations as a means of accumulating capital for expanding common business activities and services as well as for financing recreational activities. But in the new land their focus has primarily shifted toward recreational and social activities and away from the original function of accumulating investment capital. An ethnic newspaper described this recreational aspect of one clublike activity as follows.

On the afternoon of May 22, twenty-six Korean housewives gathered at the colonial-style house of Mr. S. They heard a lecture on the subject of flower arrangement, which was given by Mrs. K at Old Tappan, Bergen County. After the lecture they enjoyed foods prepared by Mrs. S, who hosted the day's meeting; they exchanged

---

[1] Hei-chu Kim, "The Role of Religious Belief and Social Structure in Korea's Breakthrough into Modernity," Ph.D. diss., New School For Social Research, 1973, pp. 39-42.

[2] Sam-soo Kim, *Hangug sahoegyeongjesa yeongu* [A study of the history of the Korean social economy], Seoul, Pak Young Sa, 1964, pp. 17-30.

views on cosmetics and children's education. . . . This is one of the *gye* meetings of Korean housewives in North Bergen County. . . .[3]

Gye meetings such as the one described above are unusually well organized and planned; they have a larger number of members than the more normal small and unsystematic *gye* associations. Since most *gye* associations involve not only housewives but also husbands, they form the core of the family-group network and are its best example. One characteristic of the family groups is that they are short-lived, subject to constant grouping and regrouping. Economic status is a major factor determining their continuation or discontinuation. For instance, some families within a group have "made it" faster than their peer-group families; they have moved to suburbs and have acquired new life styles and new Korean friends. On the other hand, economic status can contribute to the formation of family groups. Nurses', doctors', and small businessmen's family groups are a few examples. In many cases, these kinds of family groups have become subgroups within a larger occupational association. For instance, the Korean Produce Retailers Association embraces several family groups. Another example is the getting together of several hundred ex-miners who entered the United States after working in West German mines. These ex-miners maintain an intense fraternal solidarity. They are also active in small business enterprises. In Chicago, for example, ex-miners have organized a powerful association in order to influence community business and politics. But the ex-miners in New York's Korean community have not yet transformed their informal meetings into an official association, and their organizational activities have never been made public. Korean War brides of non-Korean GI's have tended to segregate themselves from other Koreans and hence from Korean community life, but they have formed groups of their own on Long Island. On the other hand, a group of Korean immigrants from Latin American nations once occupied a small residential enclave in Queens and banded together in a cement-like solidarity and brotherhood. But their tiny ghetto also disappeared when they achieved enough economic success to move to the suburbs or to other residential areas. (As has been noted, Latin American Koreans were pioneers in the fruit and vegetable industry.)

The informal associations of ex-miners, Korean War brides, and Koreans from Latin American nations constitute typical examples of informal group associations. It is beyond our ability to identify and describe the many other types of informal groups, which exist in superabundance; most of their activities are clannish and intensely private.

[3] *Hankook Ilbo*, June 1, 1979.

We can only focus on the formal secondary associations whose activities have been publicized by community newsmedia as well as by community members.

THE ORIGINS AND FOCUS OF SECONDARY ASSOCIATIONS: HOMELAND VS. NEW LAND

We can classify Korean secondary associations into four categories by combining two factors: (1) whether the qualifications of membership are derived from the United States or from South Korea, and (2) the degree to which each association interacts with the larger society. As has been noted, Korean churches do not fit into any cell in this matrix. Both the scope and importance of church-related community activities are much greater than the community activities generated by secondary associations; yet secondary associations reach the areas that churches cannot cover—they cut across the total life activities of Korean immigrants.

TABLE 7.1 TYPES OF KOREAN VOLUNTARY ASSOCIATIONS

Origin of Membership	Interaction with the Larger Society	
	None or Low	Medium or High
Korea	I Sports, medical professionals', and ministers' associations; Y.M.C.A., Y.W.C.A., Jaycees, Lions Club; alumni and veterans' associations	II Pharmacists', artists' and performing artists', and *taekwondo* instructors' associations
United States	III Recreational associations; The Korean Scientists' and Engineers' Association in America; associations for the elderly, for women, for students	IV Associations for small businessmen; the Korean-American Chamber of Commerce (KACC); anti-Park associations; the Korean-American Political Association (KAPA)

Membership in the associations in the first cell is largely derived from common experiences in certain walks of life or organizations in the homeland. With membership originating in the homeland, the associations continue to act out and to some extent reinforce the old-country institutional ties. Since the associations are mainly concerned with intraethnic community affairs ranging from mutual assistance to social, recreational, and educational services, they have little or no interaction with the larger society.

Alumni Associations. Alumni associations are the most populous and active organizations in the first cell. Alumni associations of all the major universities and high schools in South Korea that are well known but not necessarily prestigious have been formed since 1972 and have attracted great numbers of Korean immigrants. The size of each association varies, depending upon both the school's prestige and the number of graduates who later migrated to the United States. The largest associations contain graduates of the big, prestigious universities and high schools of South Korea. These graduates have been the most inclined to enter, and have been the most capable of entering, the United States. About two-thirds of the Korean alumni associations in the New York metropolitan area have been created by graduates from schools in Seoul. Immigrants who have graduated from Seoul National University are so numerous that the alumni activities of its members have been organized for its individual colleges: the College of Liberal Arts and Sciences, the Medical College, the Pharmaceutical College, and so forth. The alumni associations of Yonsei and Korea universities, the two "Ivy League" schools in Seoul, are both made up of several hundred members. These two associations have maintained and held the Yeongojeon, which, in Seoul, is the annual festival of sports contests between the two rival schools.

Alumni activities differ from school to school in both nature and intensity, but the prevalence of recreational activities is common to all alumni associations. The focus on recreation provides Korean immigrants with a systematic means of escaping from their social isolation and their estrangement from the larger society. Almost all the alumni associations in New York hold parties or picnics for members and their families, usually at the turn of the seasons. At the advent of spring or autumn they have picnics in New York state parks. These include games, Korean food, and long, leisurely conversation. During the month of December they hold Christmas or New Year's Eve parties at Korean restaurants, and in doing so they usually engage Korean bands. When these alumni meetings take place, Korean ethnic newspapers carry advertisements announcing the meetings and articles describing past events. For example,

> December, with such big holidays as Christmas and New Year's Eve, has become the month for holding the parties or meetings of alumni associations. As December approaches, our countrymen, who are daily struggling in the "life front" far away from the motherland,

have begun to announce alumni association parties in order to renew the old friendship created by their school. . . .

In the face of this rush season of alumni association parties, our countryman Mr. Y. grumbled: "Even if I had ten different bodies, I couldn't participate in all those parties—the high school alumni party, the university alumni party, the business association's party, and other kinds of Korean parties. It would cost me several hundred dollars in admission fees to present myself at all those parties."[4]

In addition to these recreational activities, big alumni associations have published newsletters and journals, set up job counseling and finding services for their members, and raised scholarship funds for their schools in South Korea. In fact, a large number of alumni activities have been directed toward making financial contributions to the parent schools in South Korea. The *Journal of the Alumni Association of Chonnan National University Medical School*, for instance, summarized the main activities and plans that the association has initiated since 1973: (1) the incorporation of the association; (2) the plan to raise a $3,000 scholarship fund for the parent school; (3) the contribution of a library fund, medical books, and an X-ray film duplicating printer to the school; (4) the plan to grant financial help to the bereaved family when a member dies; and (5) the arrangement to have faculty members (of the parent school) invited to American hospitals.

The alumni association as a whole is generally too big to provide the face-to-face, carefree, and warm interpersonal relationships that Korean immigrants desire. (We have seen how their penchant for small gatherings affects church membership and pseudo family-groups.) Since in Korean culture age is an important variable in establishing and maintaining social relationships, the alumni association is subdivided by the year of graduation. Another way Korean immigrants create family groups is through meetings of old classmates, who tend to form congenial peer groups in the new land even though they may not have maintained close relationships in South Korea. At alumni parties or picnics small groups of former classmates usually eat, drink, and talk together; thus they maintain and intensify a solidarity among themselves beyond the formal level of the alumni association. Their solidarity evolves through such activities as making matches for unmarried persons, giving picnics or birthday or Christmas parties, forming a *gye* (a Korean rotating credit activity), and other kinds of mutual assistance.

In spite of the alumni associations' widespread popularity and functional importance in organizing Korean immigrants, they have made

[4] *Joong Ang Ilbo*, December 19, 1977.

no organizational contacts with the larger society. Instead, their activities are largely directed toward intraethnic mutual assistance and recreation. Moreover, the big alumni associations of famous universities and high schools are concerned with raising financial contributions for their homeland schools. This kind of concern or relationship with the homeland is the common characteristic of associations in the first cell simply because membership is based on common ties or experiences in the homeland.

Medical Professionals' Associations. Associations of Korean medical professionals in the New York metropolitan area include those for doctors, nurses, pharmacists, dental technicians, and X-ray technicians. Membership is based on common occupational or craft experiences in the homeland. The associations of doctors, pharmacists, and nurses were originally established by assembling each field among the various alumni associations, but since alumni associations are the basic units around which doctors, pharmacists, and nurses gather, the professional associations have lost their major functions to the alumni associations. That is, the alumni associations of prestigious medical, nursing, and pharmaceutical colleges have overpowered each corresponding professional association by the intensity and volume of their organizational activities. Yet the existence of the three professional associations has been justified because Korean medical professionals need an ethnic organization to represent them in the larger society when they deal with broad issues that affect their collective standing.

In this respect, the Korean Pharmaceutical Association in New York has been the most active of all the professional associations. As has been noted, only New York State has given foreign-trained pharmacists the opportunity to take its state licensing examination without requiring a previous period of training at an American pharmaceutical college. For this reason, Korean pharmacists throughout the United States have made long trips to New York City whenever a licensing examination takes place, and many Korean pharmacists have decided to settle in New York State. Consequently, the Korean Pharmaceutical Association in New York represents all Korean pharmacists in the United States. The association has established branches in Washington D.C., California, and Chicago. Compared with other associations of medical professionals, the pharmaceutical association's encounter with the larger society has been intense. A group of sixty Korean pharmacists in the Washington D.C. area took to the street with their families on August 8, 1976, demanding "No Discrimination, Equal Opportunity"; "Help K.P.A.! Why Don't the D.C. and State Boards Give Korean Pharmacists a Chance to Practice?" The New York association has become an ethnic branch of the American Pharmaceutical Association of New York as well as a branch of the Korean Pharmaceutical Association in South Korea, with which it has kept close ties. Korean pharmacists practicing in America annually submit to the Korean association in New York their application forms for renewing their Korean licenses; the presidents of both the Korean association and the American Pharmaceutical Association of New York participated in the 1977 Korean Pharmaceutical Conference in Seoul at the invitation of the South Koreans. By holding a series of seminars to enable unlicensed Korean pharmacists to prepare for the state license examination, the Korean association in New York has gained a coherent body of members.

In contrast, the Korean Nurses Association of New York has been inactive partly because some of the larger alumni associations of prestigious nursing colleges in Seoul have not recognized its legitimacy. To state it differently, the founding members of the nursing association have not been able to gain the participation of the alumni associations of major nursing schools in Seoul. For this reason, the association represents only a small portion of the Korean nurses in the New York metropolitan area. But in other areas, such as Chicago and Los Angeles, effective and strong Korean nursing associations have been founded by representatives of major nursing school alumni associations. The Chicago association was formed after the president of the Korean Nurses Association in South Korea, on a visit to Chicago, encouraged Korean nurses in the area to form their own association. All the Korean nursing associations in the United States have maintained organizational ties with the corresponding organizations in South Korea.

For the reason mentioned above, the major activities of the Korean nurses in the New York metropolitan area have been confined to the alumni associations of nursing schools. In the absence of an effective central organization, some Korean churches have provided unlicensed nurses with seminars or special lectures on the state licensing examination, and some churches have helped prepare them for the examination.

The Korean Medical Association of America was established in 1975 in New York City on the basis of existing medical alumni associations in that area. The association represents all Korean doctors in the United States and is planning to have its main office in Washington D.C. Under the association there are also regional associations in California, Chicago, the Washington D.C. area, and the New York metropolitan area.

Since Korean doctors are heavily concentrated in the New York metropolitan area, the national association has drawn most of its members from this area, which of course predominates as well in the leadership. The association aims to (1) pursue and consolidate the common interests of Korean-American doctors; (2) contribute to the well-being of the Korean community in the United States; (3) create organizational links with the American Medical Association; and (4) devote itself to the improvement of medicine in South Korea.

Since Korean doctors tend to organize and satisfy their community needs through medical alumni associations, which are powerful but separate units, the national association as well as the regional associations have so far focused almost exclusively on external affairs that bear on the common medical interests and concerns of Koreans. The Korean Medical Association of Greater New York, for instance, has delivered free medical checkups to Korean immigrants. It has also held annual parties at large hotels in New York City. The Korean Medical Association of America, the national association, has focused upon annual medical seminars in Seoul. These are cosponsored with the Korean Medical Association in South Korea. The national association has encouraged its members to participate in the seminars, through which Korean-American doctors are expected to contribute American medical knowledge and technology to South Korean medicine.

In addition to this purely academic purpose, group visits by Korean-American doctors to the homeland have been facilitated by the South Korean government as a part of its broad policy to create favorable opinion among Korean immigrants toward the South Korean government, or "to implant in overseas countrymen the right view of their fatherland." When a group of some 400 Korean doctors and their families visited South Korea on a reduced air fare during the summer of 1977, they were lavishly received by the South Korean government. An ethnic newspaper reported:

> During their stay for three weeks in Seoul, the academic seminar will be held from June 17 to 18, alternately, at the Seoul National University and the Yonsei University. In addition, they will make domestic tours to a major industrial complex, to Panmunjom, and to other famous historical sites. . . .
>
> They will stay for three weeks at the Plaza Hotel in Seoul. The Korean government is scheduled to provide a special touring service to children in order to lead them to recognize correctly [the features of] their fatherland.[5]

Organizational Patterns Common to Korean-American Professionals' Associations. We have so far described two kinds of influential com-

---

[5] *Hankook Shinmoon*, April 28, 1977.

munity organizations—alumni associations and the three major medical professionals' associations—in order to ascertain some basic organizational characteristics of secondary community associations. Several of their characteristics are found as well in other associations in the first cell (table 7.1), which have two factors in common: their organizational activities have little or no interaction with the larger society, and membership is based on common institutional experiences in the old land.

One major characteristic of the three medical professionals' associations is that alumni associations are the basic units that establish and support them. Alumni associations have played a uniquely important role in establishing and running the medical professionals' associations, but alumni members have also formed informal and diffusive subgroups within many other associations, such as ministers', *tae-kwondo* instructors', artists', and performing artists' associations.

Second, each professional asssociation has maintained organizational connections with the corresponding institution in the homeland. This organizational nexus between the two nations runs through all the associations in both the first and second cells simply because membership has originated in common institutional experiences in the homeland. Furthermore, as in the case of the Korean Medical Association of America, the homeland government has influenced the organizational activities of Korean immigrants. As we shall see, this kind of domination by the homeland government is a dominant pattern that governs community activities of Korean immigrants in the New York metropolitan area.

Third, of the three medical professionals' associations, only the Korean Pharmaceutical Association has broken its ethnic shell and succeeded in forming an ethnic branch in the larger American Pharmaceutical Association of New York. As has been noted, only New York State has granted foreign-educated pharmacists an opportunity to take a state licensing examination, mainly because of the great shortage of pharmacists in New York. In addition, a group of Korean pharmacists staged a mass demonstration in Washington D.C. to protest against the other states' discrimination against their taking licensing examinations. This kind of hardship largely explains why Korean pharmacists have concentrated in New York City and have organized such intense group activities directed toward the larger society. Thus the Korean Pharmaceutical Association differs from all other professionals' associations including nurses', doctors', dentists', X-ray technicians', dental laboratory workers', and veterinarians' associations; and therefore the Korean Pharmaceutical Association belongs instead to the associations in the second cell, whose membership derives from the homeland but whose organizational activities are directed toward the larger society.

The major activities of some organizations in both the first and second cells substantiate these generalizations. Specifically, the Korean Amateurs Sports Association and the Korean Veterans' Association are typical of organizations in the first cell.

The Korean Amateurs Sports Association in the East was founded in 1974 by former athletes including those who participated in Olympic games. Its organizational purposes are: (1) to improve the health conditions of Korean immigrants by holding various sports contests; (2) to organize and send a team of Korean-American athletes to major sports contests in South Korea; (3) to provide South Korean athletes with up-to-date training opportunities and facilities in the United States. In 1977 the organization was officially promoted into an American branch of the Korean Athletics Association in South Korea. In 1977 the organization and the Korean Amateurs Sports Association in the West jointly sent a team of 48 delegates, 36 being athletes, to the 58th National Athletic Contest in Kwangju, South Korea. The team represented all Korean Americans in the United States. The organization has, since 1976, held annually an "indoor sports contest" for Korean immigrants in New York. Community associations, churches, and big business firms constitute the basic units for competition. A community newspaper and the Korean Consulate General have sponsored the contest (field notes).

The Korean Veterans' Association in the East was founded in 1969 by a group of retired high-ranking officers of the Korean Army. All Korean veterans are eligible for membership. The organization enlisted in 1977 a total of 384 active members. It became an official American branch of the Korean Veterans' Association in South Korea. Although an official aim of the organization lies in mutual assistance, the organization has a deep political commitment to the Park regime. The Korean Veterans' Association in South Korea is Park's political tool to control millions of Korean veterans under his powerful governmental bureaucracy.

The Korean Veterans' Association in the East and the Korean Association of Greater New York, an umbrella organization for Korean immigrants in New York, jointly initiated an anti-North-Korean rally in New York City. The Korean Veterans' Association in the East has held community marathon contests at Flushing Meadows Park. In 1977 the association had 32 members taking part in the parade on Korean Army Day. It conducted a fund-raising campaign to send money and gifts to Korean soldiers in the front lines of the South Korean combat area (field notes).

The following two artists' associations typify the associations in the second cell.

Nineteen Korean painters in New York City, Philadelphia, and Washington D.C. established in 1977 a painters' association named the Korean Painters' Association in the East. Their organizational purposes lie in (1) making a group debut in the arena of American painting; (2) exchanging mutual help and improving the professional skill of its members; (3) disseminating "with a sense of national pride" Korean paintings in the new land; (4) encouraging promising young painters in the Korean community. Since 1977 the association has held two exhibitions, alternately, in Washington D.C. and New York City. The New York exhibition was held at the Korea Center at 460 Park Avenue. The Korean consulate general in New York sponsored the exhibition (field notes).

The Emile Opera Company is one of the Korean musicians' associations in New York City. It is composed of some 60 musicians in the New York metropolitan area. It was formed in 1977 with the following purpose: "In New York City, a world capital of the arts, we Korean musicians have earned an international reputation for artistic creativity. This is a fruit of our tenacious efforts to overcome hardships and difficulties facing us in the new land. At this moment of gaining international recognition of our artistic quality, we have founded the Emile Opera Company in order to enhance our status, pride, and confidence by entering the international arena of music with a more positive self-determination."[6]

In November, 1977, the company put on before an audience of 2,500 Koreans and Americans three performances of a traditional Korean opera, *Chunhyangjeon*, which was adapted from an old Korean novel of the same title. The total operating expense of the show was $40,000, a part of which was collected by the company's holding a "Dinner and Music Night" for established Koreans. The South Korean Ministry of Culture and Information contributed $12,000 and costumes to the opera. More than 100 staff and cast members were involved in the show. The *New York Daily News* covered the show. A community newspaper, the *Hankook Ilbo*, sponsored the performance on the occasion of the tenth anniversary of the establishment of its branch in New York City.

[6] *Hankook Ilbo*, February 11, 1977.

In the spring of 1978, a group of outstanding Korean musicians in New York City, including some members of the Emile Opera Company, were invited to the Korean Arts Festival in Seoul, in which they showed their talents to Korean audiences. The festival was held by the Seoul city government in order to celebrate the opening of the Saejong Hoekwan, Seoul's equivalent of New York's Lincoln Center (field notes).

Korean Associations Focused on Purely Intraethnic Activities. The associations in the third cell are formed on the basis of common experiences in the new land, and their organizational activities are confined to intraethnic affairs. Thus the associations have little or no interaction with the larger society. Unlike the associations in both the first and second cells, the associations in the third cell have no organizational links with corresponding institutions in the homeland. We shall see immediately, however, that the Korean Scientists' and Engineers' Association in America is an exception.

Golfers', tennis players', hunters', and mountaineers' associations or clubs organize, encourage, and conduct recreational activities for some segments of the Korean population in the New York metropolitan area. Their members are predominantly well-established Koreans who have started their hobbies or sports activities in the New Land. These leisure activities have become the basis of their recreational associations.

In contrast, age and sex determine membership in the Korean American Senior Citizens Society, called Sangroghoe, and in the Korean Women's Association. A group of old ministers, many of whom entered the United States before the National Origins Act of 1924, was a leading force in establishing the Korean American Senior Citizens Society in 1976. Koreans who are 55 years old or over are eligible for membership, which increased from 30 in 1976 to 178 in 1977. The association has its headquarters and recreational facilities at the Korean Medical Center in Flushing, where a group of Korean doctors conduct a group practice for Korean immigrants. Community organizations such as the Lions Club, the Korean Women's Association, and the Korean Church Council have frequently entertained the members with Korean food, dancing-shows, and music. The lonely and isolated life confronting the Korean aged, most of whom were forced to immigrate to a new land in order to join sons or daughters, necessitated the formation of the association.

The Korean Women's Association is "high society." It was founded in 1974 by a group of female celebrities, including wives of big businessmen. The association is inclined to preserve the traditional virtues of Korean femininity. It has held seminars on flower arrangement, cooking, hair cutting and dressing, and so forth. It once initiated a "Buy-Korean-Products" campaign, urging Korean housewives to purchase only consumer goods imported from South Korea. It also raised funds to be sent to Korean orphans in the homeland. Both the Korean American Senior Citizens Society and the Korean Women's Association have received some assistance from the Korean Consulate General in New York City.

The Korean Scientists' and Engineers' Association—an Exception. The Korean Scientists' and Engineers' Association in America, Inc., deserves detailed description because it is the most influential and important association illustrated in the third cell.

> The Korean Scientists' and Engineers' Association was created in 1971 by scientists and technical engineers, most of whom entered the United States as students and established successful professional careers in American science and technology. The association has two main goals: (1) to exchange new ideas and news of the accomplishments of its members; (2) to contribute to the technological and scientific development of South Korea. The South Korean government was indirectly involved in the formation of the association partly because South Korea needs Korean-American "brains" in its process of rapid industrialization.
>
> The association has its headquarters in Washington D.C. and 22 branches throughout the United States. In 1978 some 1,500 Korean scientists and engineers were organized in the association. Its major activities include: (1) annual seminars in Seoul, with the participation of South Korean scientists; (2) sending newly produced tools, machine equipment, and new books to South Korea. In 1977 the association made a "Mutual Assistance Treaty" with the Korean Institute of Science and Technology (KIST), which is called the "Korean brain tank." An ex-president of the association was cited by the South Korean government for his devotion to the establishment of the association.
>
> In New York City, a group of Korean scientists and engineers formed a New York branch, which has had regular meetings at Korean restaurants (field notes).

Korean Associations Focused on American Issues. The associations in the fourth cell share the following two attributes: members are recruited on the basis of common interests in the new land, and their activities are directed toward the larger society. As the next chapter will show, the anti-Park organizations, whose memberships were formed by making the Park regime the common enemy, tried to alienate the United States from the Park government. By doing this the organizations attempted to influence the politics of South Korea. The Korean-American Political Association (KAPA), on the other hand, has basically tried to defend the interests of Korean immigrants, but also to influence the South Korean-government by participating in American politics. In addition, small businessmen have formed their own specialized associations. The greengrocers', Korean-food grocerymen's, fish retailers', drycleaners', liquor retailers', garment retailers', garment subcontractors', and cab drivers' associations have emerged independently of the Korean-American Chamber of Commerce, which claims to represent the whole Korean business community in the New York metropolitan area. The Korean Produce Retailers Association has become one of the most influential and powerful community organizations, as we shall see.

"The establishment of mutual friendship and the expansion of common interests" is the main organizational goal of all small businessmen's associations. This mutual friendship is usually strengthened by picnics and parties in which the members' families participate. Thus, Korean small businessmen's associations also assume recreational functions. Because of this double role, Korean businessmen have formed associations in every area of business into which they have entered. For example,

> Twenty Korean dry cleaners [of some 150 Korean drycleaners in New York City] met on last April 15 [1978] at the Woori House Restaurant and officially declared the foundation of the Korean Drycleaners' Association of New York. The association is designed to promote mutual assistance and friendship and to pursue common business interests. After listening to Mr. Yong-bom Lee's lecture on how to handle new clothing materials, they unanimously adopted the charter of the association. The charter is composed of five articles and twelve rules. They elected as the first president of the association Yong-bom Lee, who commands good English and has a close relationship with NCA (Neighborhood Drycleaners' Associations).
> . . .
> Mr. Yong-bom Lee made a brief speech. He said: "About five years ago Americans were reluctant to leave their clothes to Orientals. But now they are glad to receive drycleaning services from Orientals because of Orientals' reputation of doing a good job on drycleaning service. This good credit results from our hard work. . . ."[7]

[7] *Joong Ang Ilbo*, April 17, 1978.

CONCLUSION

In face of the seemingly hostile institutions of the larger society, Korean immigrants have self-consciously and rationally organized sub-community activities directed along almost every line of their differentiated and segmented interests. At the same time, they have attempted to establish a "pseudo-gemeinschaft" feeling, a sense of belonging. This is particularly pronounced with respect to family groups or associations, which constitute the "primitive," molecular units of the Korean community. Some family groups exist within larger secondary associations, but others are autonomous.

The emergence of secondary associations in almost all major spheres of life points to the high level of occupational, business, and professional differentiation of the Korean immigrants' urban community. Associations whose memberships are derived from shared occupational or professional education, training, and work experiences in the homeland maintain systematic ties with the corresponding institutions of the homeland (see table 7.1). But for associations whose memberships are based upon common interests or life chances in the new land, this kind of institutional interlocking with the homeland is almost negligible. A conspicuous exception is the Korean Scientists' and Engineers' Association, however, because the Korean government encouraged Korean-American scientists and engineers to establish the association in order to utilize them in the development of South Korean technology.

Interaction between community associations and the larger society takes place largely in the economic associations and depends upon a certain amount of economic friction between Koreans and agencies of the larger society. The conflict between the Korean Pharmaceutical Association and the larger society occurred over the "licensing problem." Korean pharmacists think it unreasonable that all state governments except New York's restrict the issuance of licenses to immigrant pharmacists, who were supposedly qualified to enter the United States by virtue of their pharmaceutical skill. One of the main purposes of small businessmen in establishing their associations also lies in protecting and expanding their common business interests in relation to the larger society. Similarly, the Korean *taekwondo* instructors' associations in New York have hosted world or American *taekwondo* contests as a means of promoting and popularizing *taekwondo* among Americans.

It must be noted that almost all major community associations, regardless of their membership structure and degree of interaction with the larger society, are associated with the Korean Consulate General in New York City. This does not mean that the Consulate General directs all organizational activities; it means that all major community organizations, except the anti-Park organizations and the churches, have been eager to receive some financial, material, or moral support. The Consulate General has been willing to help community organizations in order to make Korean immigrants loyal to the Park regime. This relationship between the Korean Consulate General and community organizations will be investigated in detail when we deal with community politics, in the next chapter.

We have noted that Korean immigrants, unlike earlier ethnic immigrants to New York, do not live in territorial enclaves. In the absence of residential niches, secondary associations generate major community activities and become the fabric that weaves different segments of Korean populations into an "associational community." As we shall see in the next chapter, no effective, central organization has emerged to coordinate and integrate the diverse community activities produced by these secondary associations. The Korean Association of Greater New York is not sufficiently effective or powerful to do so; instead, the Korean Consulate General works with the major secondary associations, and this, in turn, causes most secondary associations to identify with the Consulate General, a surrogate of the South Korean government.

CHAPTER EIGHT

The Politics of the
Korean Community

W<small>E HAVE</small> seen, so far, some basic patterns in the routine and diffuse community activities generated by churches and by secular secondary associations. Another facade of community life can be examined by focusing upon "core" community organizations such as the Korean Consulate General, the Korean Association of Greater New York, and the ethnic media. "Core" organizations attempt to represent and shape communitywide activities: community elections, politics, leadership, and public opinion in its reaction to both the larger society and the homeland. These activities and opinions have made headlines in the two daily community newspapers.

As we shall see, community politics is centered in "core" community organizations and is deeply connected with the political and economic institutions of the homeland. A small number of community leaders have emerged and have self-consciously organized these community activities. These leaders have tended to have close ties with the home government, and their business success in the United States is largely determined by access to licenses, to the setting of export quotas, and to capital provided by the home government. Some are businessmen who have economic interests in the homeland; some are intellectuals who are deeply committed to the politics of South Korea.

Partly because Korean immigrants have a strong sense of nationalism and therefore identify with the home government, the Korean Consulate General in New York City, a surrogate of the home government, has emerged as the most influential link between the community and the home government. It has determined the basic tone of communitywide politics. But as Korean immigrants have become accustomed to their new society and have begun to learn how to manage their relations with the larger society and how to create autonomous institutions in the new land, community politics has begun to turn toward "American" issues. New ethnic power brokers, who link the community with city, state, and federal government agencies and political officials, have begun to appear. This shift in community politics has been precipitated by such issues in the larger society as "Koreagate," the

227

KCIA, the controversy surrounding the Unification Church, and anti-Koreanism, especially among blacks.

THE SOUTH KOREAN GOVERNMENT AS A COMMUNITY ORGANIZATION

The Korean Consulate General in New York City has been the most influential and powerful organization in New York's Korean community. It has directed, financed, sponsored, or coerced major community activities. The influence of the Consulate General is founded on the reciprocal interaction between the community and the home government: almost all Korean immigrants are still Korean citizens. Even though the immigrants become American citizens, they rarely renounce their Korean citizenship. The South Korean government, in turn, regards overseas Koreans, even those with an immigration visa, as its subjects in need of its constant care and protection as well as its "corrective guidance and education." Partly because of the Korean cultural tradition of confusing power with moral supremacy, the majority of Korean immigrants express a sense of loyalty to the home government and thereby to the consulate, even though the Park regime and its successor has been viewed as dictatorial and "indecent" by the American public.

Korean nationalism is deeply embedded in Korean immigrants. For example, a substantial number of immigrants share the South Korean government's interpretation of "Koreagate," which is to say that they see nothing wrong in the Park Tong Sun affair, because Park Tong Sun tried to pursue the national interest of South Korea. (Park Tong Sun, or Tong-sun Park, a Korean rice dealer, was accused of illicit lobbying for South Korea: he attempted to "buy" American congressmen with campaign contributions, cash gifts, and free trips to South Korea.)

It is no exaggeration to say that the Korean Consulate General is the informal government of New York's Korean community and that the consul general is its "mayor," though appointed by the home government. The following detailed report on a luncheon party that community leaders held in honor of a new consul general shows one facet of this relationship.

A reception party for the newly appointed consul general, Dou-soon Chong, was held last April 14 [1975] at the Korea Center in which a group of sixty community leaders exchanged dialogues with the new consul general. The Korean Association arranged the meeting.
. . .
The first speaker was Dr. Jae-tack Kim, professor at John Jay Col-

lege. Dr. Kim, saying that, unlike the embassy, the consulate exists for the sake of the community, advised the new consul general to exert efforts for the interest of the community. Dr. Kim added that "in a community there is no such division between the Opposition Party and Government Party [of South Korea]. Fellow countrymen only endeavor to make some contributions to Korea. But there has been a rumor that the [Korean] government recently blacklisted some immigrants, subjecting them to a government surveillance." Dr. Kim asked the new consul general whether the rumor is true.

The second speaker was Mr. Kwang-han Moon, an ex-chairman of the membership committee of the Korean Association. With the open statement that he and the new consul general have maintained a brotherlike relationship, Mr. Moon said that "the new consul general is not such a man as to be offended by Dr. Kim's remark."

On the other hand, Mr. Suck-joon Yoon, a grocer in New Jersey, was pleased when his wife received a phone call of invitation from the Korean Consulate General; but when he arrived at the welcoming party, he found that he was an uninvited guest. The Korean Consulate General mistook him for the vice president of the Korean Grocers' Association. But Yoon was given a chance to make a speech: "The guests who are invited here do not have any problems. The fellow countrymen who can't present themselves at this party are troubled by tremendous financial problems. The new consul general should help those people who struggle at the bottom. . . ."

The new consul general responded as follows: "It is heartening that many fellow countrymen have successfully entered business and educational fields. . . . The Korean Consulate General will do its best to help fellow countrymen adjust to the new society."

With respect to the recent communist takeover of South Vietnam, the new consul general remarked: "The home government and people have the strong confidence and will necessary to deter any future North Korean military attacks. Fellow countrymen should not loosen their solidarity with the fatherland. They should help the home government solidify its alliance with the United States."[1]

The Korean Consulate General in New York City has administrative jurisdiction over the immigrant or nonimmigrant Koreans living on the entire eastern seaboard, excluding Virginia and Maryland. It performs administrative, political, economic, and cultural functions for the Koreans under its jurisdiction. In carrying out these functions, the consulate has directly or indirectly applied various policies of the South Korean government to the Korean-American community. Its administrative services range from the issuance or extension of passports or

[1] *Hankook Ilbo*, March 15, 1975.

visas to the validation of English translations of Korean documents and the confirmation of financial affidavits. These services are needed by Korean immigrants who wish to visit the home country or bring their close relatives to the United States under the "relative preferences" of the Immigration Act of 1965. In addition, immigrant couples seeking divorce consult with and report to the Consulate General if they were married in the homeland. The majority of the Koreans in New York are attached to the Consulate General through these types of legal functions. During 1976, for instance, the consulate performed a total of 36,509 civil transactions, most of which involved services provided to the Koreans under its jurisdiction.

The consulate has also taken an economic role as promoter and facilitator of trade between the United States and South Korea, and thereby it has had a direct impact on the economic activities of Korean-American businessmen who sell South Korean products. We have noted in chapter four that, when the Korean wig market in the United States was in chaos, the South Korean government intervened. The home government thinks this kind of economic intervention necessary because, as has been noted in chapter three, the South Korean economy has a vital stake in exports.

Korean diplomats in foreign countries are expected to function as salesmen promoting South Korean products. In New York City, this means that some 190 branches of homeland businesses, 7 bank branches, the Korea Traders Representative Club, the Korea Trade Promotion Center, and the Korea Traders Association are all under the guidance of the Consulate General. The vice-consul for economic affairs specializes in coordinating and directing the activities of such organizations. For instance, the consul general and the vice-consul for economic affairs are consultant members of the Korea Traders Representative Club, whose membership is drawn from representatives of almost all of the South Korean economic organizations in New York City.

The Korea Traders Representative Club and the Korea Trade Promotion Center, the latter a semigovernmental agency designed to promote Korean products throughout the world, have kept close ties with various community business organizations. One of the main functions of these two South Korean organizations is to induce community businessmen to participate in "the export front" of South Korea. The Korea Trade Promotion Center has urged community businessmen, mostly importers of South Korean products, to take part in the annual Korean Fair in Seoul; and the two organizations recently held a seminar entitled "Commercial Laws on American Business Transactions" in order to teach community businessmen how to run a business in the new land. An ethnic newspaper reported,

In keeping pace with the Korean business world, which set a goal of $10 billion in exports for the year of 1977, the Korea Traders Representative Club and the Korea Trade Promotion Center held on September 12, 1977, a seminar on "Commercial Laws on American Business Transactions," designed to make community businessmen familiar with American business. Some 100 community businessmen participated in the seminar, which lasted three hours, at the 6th-floor conference room of the Korea Center.[2]

The seven South Korean bank branches in New York City have also contributed to the economic life of Korean immigrants; for example, they have extended loans by mortgaging properties in the homeland still owned by the immigrants. The total amount of such loans has been small, however, compared with the amount granted to South Korean business firms in New York City. The banks have been hesitant in loaning to Korean immigrants, on the grounds that "their economic foundations are unstable." An ethnic newspaper recently criticized the banks for this "stingy" loan policy, and in a recent meeting with the Consul General Ho-gan Yoon a group of community leaders attached to the Korean Association of Greater New York formally asked the consul general to press the banks to adopt a liberal policy in extending loans to community members. One bank, however, has been an important source of funds. The New York branch of the Korea Exchange Bank, a government bank, loaned as of September 1976 a total of $2.7 million to community members from a $6 million fund set up in 1975 by the South Korean government to help Korean emigrants establish themselves in foreign countries.[3] The government thought the fund

[2] *Joong Ang Ilbo*, September 13, 1977.

[3] The following table shows the types and amounts of loans provided by the Korea Exchange Bank to Korean immigrants in the New York metropolitan area as of September 30, 1976:

	Cases	Millions of Dollars	Percent of Dollars
Business loans			
MORTGAGES:			
Korean properties	108	1.70	63
Local U.S. properties	85	0.76	28
Personal guarantee	9	0.62	6
Resettlement loans			
MORTGAGE:			
Personal guarantee	39	0.08	3
Totals	241	2.70	100

SOURCE: *Korean Guardian*, October 16, 1976.

NOTE: The maximum loan in each case is $20,000; the annual interest rate for business loans (to raise business capital) is 9 percent, while the interest rate for loans for resettlement expenses is 8.5 percent.

necessary for emigrants because, according to South Korean emigration law, they are allowed to take only a small amount of dollars to the receiving countries.

The consulate, in addition to its administration and economic functions, fosters and promotes Korean culture, the Korean language, and nationalism. These are, of course, the cultural backbones necessary for creating one kind of community solidarity in the new land. The consulate has endorsed, occasioned, and often financed almost all major cultural and social activities that have been conducted by ethnic secondary associations of artists, musicians, athletes, veterans (Korean), the elderly, women, scientists, and small businessmen. It has also supplied materials such as books and films to Korean-language schools, to newspapers, and even to some churches. The vice-consul for community affairs undertakes the job of promoting cultural and social activities in the community. Korean immigrants are inclined to give much more weight to group activities sponsored or endorsed by the consulate than to those that are not, and so consulate participation bestows a kind of official recognition on activities that deserve wide community attention.

The consulate is also a morale booster for the community. Whenever a large number of immigrants gather to observe Korean national holidays, or to organize community medical checkups, picnics or parties, or funeral services for robbery victims, the Consulate General sends its representatives. In fact, ethnic newspapers have sometimes criticized the consulate for failing to send its officials to a major community activity.

Consul General Yoon, who took office in 1977, recently visited the Hunts Point Market in the Bronx, where a group of Korean greengrocers had gathered to commemorate the anniversary of the "March 1 Anti-Japanese Movement Day." He made a brief speech and was quoted as saying, "Even though we are far from our fatherland, our patriotic forefathers, who fought for the Independence of our nation, are worthy of our recollection. Fortified with the true spirit of our patriotic forefathers, let us unite to erect a golden tower of our immigration history."[4] Through the Consulate General, the home government has honored community leaders for their dedicated service to community life and has singled out "model immigrants" for their pioneering economic achievements. In 1977 the government chose, with the recommendation of the consulate, a greengrocer as the "model immigrant."

All the aforementioned functions of the consulate supplement its primary function, which is political. The primary mission of both the con-

[4] *Hankook Ilbo*, March 1, 1978.

sulate and the Korean Central Intelligence Agency (KCIA) "station" is to discourage Korean immigrants from joining "unpatriotic," "anti-state," and "antinational" movements in the United States. The home government paid special attention to Korean immigrants during the influence-buying scandals because it viewed the anti-Park movements in the United States, which were led by a small number of Korean ministers and intellectuals, as detrimental, although not a serious threat, to the Park regime and to South Korean diplomatic overtures to the United States. Anti-Park expressions in the United States usually took such forms as mass petitions to the United States Congress and mass demonstrations in front of the United Nations building, the White House, and the Capitol.

THE ROLE OF THE KCIA IN THE COMMUNITY

The political influence of the home government on the Korean community in the United States has been intensified since the defeat of the United States in the Vietnam War. Immediately after the end of the war, President Park consolidated his rule on the grounds that North Korean communists would provoke another Korean War and seek the same kind of communist victory as in Vietnam. More broadly, the Park regime's concern with the Korean community in the United States was a reaction to a proposed shift in United States policy toward South Korean military security, a proposal that called for the gradual withdrawal of United States troops from South Korea. President Park therefore felt a need for consensus among all segments of the South Korean population including Koreans living overseas, especially in the United States. In order to curb the anti-Park movements in America, the first step of the home government was to promote Park's "strong leadership." The anti-Park organizations, on their part, kept a peculiar, ambivalent relationship with the Consulate General. Whenever a group of dissidents in Seoul mounted specific protests against Park's dictatorship that resulted in mass arrests, anti-Park organizations in New York organized and staged mass demonstrations denouncing Park's rule in front of the Korea Center (on Park Avenue in New York City), which houses the Korean consulate. (Anti-Park movements were sustained by various organizations that were split along different personal networks and that advocated conflicting ideologies. Some were branded by a Korean newspaper as "pro-North Korean" organizations.)

The Consulate General is a diplomatic agency that must observe diplomatic norms; it does not have a free hand in carrying out specific South Korean policies toward the United States and toward Korean communities in the United States. It is through the KCIA that the

South Korean government makes direct but covert attempts to control Korean communities as well as to influence American policy toward South Korea. The following report highlights some recent activities of the KCIA in the United States.

> A House subcommittee disclosed today a 1976 plan by the South Korean Central Intelligence Agency to manipulate the Ford Administration, Congress, American news organizations, academicians and the clergy to Seoul's advantage, overtly and covertly. . . .
> Creating American public opinion that favored South Korea with a variety of lures, including inviting "influential" United States journalists to visit Korea to convert them.
> Converting academic critics with invitations to Korea, financing seminars, and publishing materials not identified as coming from the K.C.I.A.
> Encouraging supporters of the Korean Government among Korean residents of the United States and frustrating activities of antigovernment organizations. . . .
> The plan showed that the Seoul Government's objectives were to thwart North Korean efforts to open contacts with the United States, to guarantee the efficacy of the American security commitment to South Korea and to prevent anti-Seoul movements among Korean residents of the United States.[5]

In the United States, most KCIA officials operate under cover of diplomatic status. From its headquarters in the Korean Embassy in Washington D.C., the KCIA operates six "stations" in five major cities where a large number of Korean immigrants have settled. The "stations" are attached to the Korean Observer Mission to United Nations and to the Korean Consulates General in New York City, Los Angeles, San Francisco, Chicago, and Houston. The number of KCIA officials in the United States seems to be small: "A list in the possession of the grand jury [the United States] thus shows that in 1976 there were 23 K.C.I.A. agents in this country under diplomatic cover and an unknown number of operatives using other covers."[6] In spite of their small number of personnel, the KCIA "stations" are powerful in the major Korean communities in the United States. This is so simply because the "stations" are an extension of the homeland KCIA, which has emerged as the most powerful institution in South Korea. As we have noted in chapter three, the KCIA is the basic political tool by which President Park Chung-hee consolidated and legitimized his dictatorial

---

[5] *New York Times*, November 30, 1977.
[6] Tad Szulc, "Inside South Korea's C.I.A.," *New York Times Magazine*, March 6, 1977, p. 50.

regime. The following statement depicts the basic functions of the KCIA in South Korea.

The operations of the agency as of mid-1973 were believed to be organized into eight functional bureaus under two assistant directors, one for external affairs, and one for internal affairs. The second, third and fifth bureaus (there was no fourth bureau because Koreans believe the number unlucky) were concerned with domestic cultural (press control and propaganda) affairs, counterintelligence, and internal security, respectively. The sixth bureau was a special mission, or "dirty tricks," operation; the seventh bureau performed the conventional foreign intelligence-gathering function. The eighth and ninth bureaus dealt entirely with North Korean affairs, the former specializing in psychological warfare operations, whereas the latter was in charge of intelligence gathering and analysis. In addition, there was an unnumbered bureau that handles the political work relating to negotiations with North Korea.

Agency personnel were stationed in branch offices in each provincial capital and city. Control over the seminal activities of government and society was exercised through the assignment of KCIA personnel to ministries, the military, banks and businesses, newspapers, labor organizations, and cultural associations.[7]

As in the homeland, the KCIA "station" in New York City controls all major South Korean organizations in the United States, including the Consulate General, business firms, and banks. The agency uses a vast network of "informal" informers such as South Korean government officials and representatives of South Korean organizations. In addition, as we shall see, many community leaders who want to receive political and economic favors from the home government have become close "associates" of the Consulate General and are subject to "review" by the KCIA "station."

With this kind of power the KCIA "station" in New York City has attempted to dominate the Korean community by conducting many of the same operations among Korean immigrants as the homeland KCIA does among Koreans in South Korea. The mission of the "station" has included: (1) neutralizing North Korean communists' infiltration into the community and supporting anti-North Korean community rallies; (2) setting up "front" community organizations to carry out various South Korean policies toward both the immigrant community and American society; (3) subsidizing major community activities—academic, cultural, and commercial—to enhance the national prestige of

---

[7] Vreeland et al., *Area Handbook*, pp. 335-336.

South Korea and thereby contribute to the legitimacy of the Park regime; (4) regulating and sanctioning the fraudulent commercial behavior of community businessmen whose business activities are connected with South Korea; and (5) thwarting anti-Park movements. This last function seems to have been the most important mission assigned to the "station."

By intimidating Korean immigrants who were active in the anti-Park movements, the "station" attempted to keep Korean immigrants away from the movements and to neutralize them. *The New York Times* reported on the harassment of anti-Park activists.

> The South Korean Intelligence Agency appears to have resumed a campaign of threats against Korean residents of the United States who are critical of President Park Chung Hee's Government. . . .
>
> The government in Seoul evidently fears opposition by Koreans here because it reaches the ears of American leaders who influence the military, political and economic support the United States gives to Korea. Dissent here also filters back to Korea, and the Government fears that it will encourage anti-Government feeling there.
>
> In one case, the publisher of a Korean newspaper here said he had received three threatening telephone calls and a disturbing letter from his father, who lives in Korea. The publisher, Chung Kee Yong, puts out the *Han Min Shin Bo* about twice a month with the news of the Government's opponents and articles criticizing President Park. Mr. Chung said . . . he was certain that the letter from his father had been dictated by Korean Intelligence agents, because it contained political views that he had never heard his father express. . . .
>
> One said he had seen Korean intelligence agents watching his house and noted that his associates in a business venture had suddenly quit. The other said through a friend that he had just received word from Seoul that his father had been dismissed from his job because the son here was engaged in what the agency considered to be anti-Government activity.[8]

In 1967, KCIA agents kidnapped a number of anti-Park activists in West Germany and brought them to their home country; in 1973 they kidnapped Dae-jung Kim, a prominent homeland opposition leader who was in Tokyo at the time. Because of this ubiquitous KCIA activity, the majority of Korean immigrants were extremely reluctant to take part in anti-Park movements even though many of them were angry about the Park regime. They were afraid of KCIA-supervised reprisals for "antigovernment and antistate behavior." This fear is indicated

[8] *New York Times*, May 22, 1977.

in such comments as "Watch your mouth, otherwise you can't visit Korea"; or, "I can't take part in the demonstration, because I left my family in Seoul." In addition, the South Korean government and the official ruling party proposed special legislation to enable the government to confiscate all the property and pensions of overseas Koreans who engage in "antistate" behavior.[9]

Partly because of these various forms of government harassment, threats, and indirect punishment, the anti-Park movement was able to muster only a small number of intellectuals, ministers, and students. But antigovernment organizations have nonetheless claimed to represent the Korean community in opposition to claims by the Korean Association of Greater New York, which has been under the influence of the Consulate General. Whenever New York's Korean community has observed major South Korean national holidays such as August 15 (Independence Day) and March 1 (Anti-Japanese-Movement Day) there have been two separate community meetings: one has been jointly held by the Korean Association of Greater New York and the Consulate General; the other by antigovernment organizations.

To sum up, we have so far discussed the administrative, economic, cultural, and political or ideological influence of the home government on New York's Korean community. In doing this we have described the specific interaction between the community and homeland organizations such as the Consulate General, the KCIA, and South Korean business branches, banks, and other business associations. We have also dealt with some community activities insofar as they have been affected by these South Korean government agencies and private organizations. A group of community leaders has emerged to facilitate this interaction, and the Korean Association of Greater New York is the community organization around which this sort of community politics has evolved.

THE KOREAN ASSOCIATION AS "COMMUNITY GOVERNMENT"

In all the major cities or metropolitan areas with a large Korean population, Korean Associations, called Haninhoc, have been founded. The associations claim to represent all Korean settlers in specific metropolitan areas by automatically enlisting them as members. The president of a Korean Association is selected through a community election. The extent to which an association is actually accountable and responsive to the needs of its members, however, varies from region to region and largely depends upon the leadership structure of the specific commu-

[9] *Joong Ang Ilbo,* December 5, 1977.

nity in question. Many of the Korean Associations are only symbolic representations to the larger society; but the associations in New York City, Philadelphia, Washington D.C., Chicago, and Los Angeles are influential organizations. Furthermore, the home government has influenced Korean communities through the Korean Associations.

Four Korean Associations have emerged in the New York metropolitan area: one in Connecticut, two in New Jersey, and one in New York City. The latter is called the Korean Association of Greater New York. It originally claimed ethnic jurisdiction over the whole tri-state area; but, as the number of Korean immigrants rapidly increased in Connecticut and New Jersey, "local" ethnic leaders appeared. They have set up, since 1975, their own Korean Associations "in response to the specific regional needs of our countrymen." By describing how the Korean Association of Greater New York evolved and how it operates, we can ascertain some of the basic characteristics of intraethnic politics and thus perceive some fundamental aspects of the Korean community structure.

The Korean population in New York began to increase gradually after the end of the Korean War, and in 1965 a group of articulate Koreans reactivated the Korean Association of Greater New York, which had almost died out by becoming a club of aged Korean immigrants who belonged to the original, pre-1965 immigration. This club had been led by a minister. In order to put new breath into the association and give it a new image, seventeen Koreans, most of whom were old-timers, gathered and founded a new Korean Association of Greater New York after dissolving the old one. Koreans thus renewed their sense of identity and solidarity in a city that had a growing Korean population. Until 1967, no heated politics were involved in the presidential election of the association. The position of president usually went to an elder who was a respectable but somewhat active old-timer eager to lead ceremonial community activities, that is, the observances of South Korean national holidays. The majority of Koreans, however (mostly students), were indifferent to the new Korean Association because "they were too busy establishing themselves." Students formed their own association, whose main program was to give an annual New Year's party for Korean students in New York. Through both the Korean Students' Association and the New York Korean Church, students remained committed to the social life of the entire Korean community. Eventually, as they graduated and became established in their occupations, they politicized a number of major community activities and took over the leadership of the Korean Association from the old-timers.

Nineteen sixty-seven was a crucial year for New York's Korean community: it was the year when the United States Immigration Act of 1965 became fully effective. The number of Koreans who entered the United States increased substantially (see table 1.1). In response to this influx, New York's Korean community began to change rapidly. Ethnic organizations started to multiply. Interestingly enough, two economic organizations in South Korea were among the first to respond to the long-range business prospects of the expanding Korean community in New York. In 1967 the Korea Exchange Bank opened its New York office, which was later raised to branch status. In that same year a Korean businessman in New York City began to import from South Korea the *Hankook Ilbo*, a Korean-language daily newspaper, and to circulate photocopies among Korean immigrants. Also in that year word came from the consulate in New York City that "the home government will help New York's Koreans build or purchase a 'Korea Center' [Korean community building]." This was the first time the South Korean government gave a specific content to the community actions of the Korean Association. Consequently, the Korean Association initiated that year its first substantive community program, the annual dancing party called the Korean Night Ball, in order to raise funds for purchasing a community building. The first ball was unexpectedly successful. A huge number of Koreans, including men dressed in tuxedos, showed up at the fund-raising dance. The association made a net profit of $3,800 and opened a savings account to deposit the money. The Korean Consulate General in New York kept two separate savings-account books for the accumulating fund, whose amount increased to some $50,000 by 1976.

The institution of the Korean Night Balls has had some significant implications for New York's Korean community. First, by gathering a large number of immigrants in one place, the balls have aroused a sense of solidarity and communal feeling, especially when top South Korean singers and entertainers have been hired to stir up nostalgia for the homeland. This kind of Korean meeting for entertainment— Korean music, dancing, and food—has become a pervasive element contributing to Korean ethnic solidarity (as we have noted in discussing the secondary associations). Second, the Korean Consulate General has, willingly or unwillingly, been involved with the fund-raising campaign. This is just an example, as we have seen, of how the South Korean government has influenced community activities. Third, a group of community leaders has emerged (and has divided) over the issue of establishing a "Korea Center," which aims to "enhance national pride among Koreans by propagating the Korean cultural heritage and spirit." This, in turn, has intensified organizational activities.

SCHISMS IN THE "COMMUNITY GOVERNMENT"

The Korean Cultural Center. As has been noted, the Korean Association of Greater New York initiated the Korean Night Ball under the encouragement of the consulate. But when Dr. A, an old-timer, finished his term as president of the Korean Association of Greater New York in 1967, he attempted to get the Korean Cultural Center, an ethnic organization he had founded earlier, to take over and continue this fund-raising campaign. For this purpose, Dr. A and his associate members in the Korean Cultural Center succeeded in incorporating their organization; soon after, the Korean Association of Greater New York was deprived of its most important function, that of holding the Korean Night Ball. Even so, until 1972 there was no conflict between the association and the center over who had jurisdiction over the fundraising campaign, because the leadership of the two organizations interlocked. The presidents of the Korean Association of Greater New York were either elected from among the board members of the Korean Cultural Center or were supported by the center. However, in 1972 Mr. F, an outsider to this interlocking network, became president of the Korean Association of Greater New York and attempted to reclaim sponsorship of the Korean Night Ball. Mr. F decided to hold a competing party under almost the same title: The Korean Night. In response, the cultural center threatened to bring suit against the association. The Korean consul general then intervened. He persuaded the association to stop its plan to hold a dance, but with the condition that the cultural center would pay the association $2,500 as compensation for the expenses incurred in preparing The Korean Night. Thus, only through the arbitration of the Korean consul general was the dispute settled.

Partly because of this kind of "issueless" division of community leadership, the movement to establish a "Korea Center" has slowed down since 1972. The movement, it is true, failed to bring forth sufficient participation by the various community organizations, but the fatal blow came from the South Korean government. After large numbers of South Korean business organizations emerged in New York City as a result of the rapid increase of trade between Korea and America, the Korean Trade Association of South Korea, a government agency, bought a building in 1974 at 460 Park Avenue for $15 million. The building, named the Korea Center, not only houses South Korean organizations such as the Korean Consulate General, the Korea Traders Association, Korean Airlines, the Korean National Tourism Corporation, the Korea Traders Representative Club, South Korean banks, and South Korean business branches but also provides space for the community activities of Korean immigrants in New York. The Korean Association also has its headquarters in the building. From 1975 to 1976, some twenty community meetings, ten exhibitions, and fifteen community receptions were held in the building. Thus the annual events of the Korean Night Ball have lost their original purpose of establishing a Korea Center for the autonomous Korean community of New York. The majority of community leaders think that it is useless to continue the fund-raising campaign, since the Korea Center has already been established by the South Korean government. But some community leaders associated with the Korean Cultural Center have insisted on going on with the fund-raising party. The history of the "Korea Center" is an example of how the South Korean government dominates major community activities. A similar episode highlights one of the basic patterns governing New York's Korean community.

The Korean Community Foundation. The community leaders involved in the Korean Cultural Center engaged in internal as well as external feuds over the distribution of power. In 1969, some founding members or board members of the organization resigned and set up their own organization, the Korean Community Foundation, for a similar purpose —to preside over a ball in order to raise funds for cultural activities in the community. The Korean Community Foundation held a couple of parties under the name of the International Friendship Night. In 1976, the president of the Korean Community Foundation claimed to represent New York's Korean community when the mayor's office invited the representatives of some fifty national or ethnic groups to discuss preparations for the American Bicentennial. Mr. O, president of the foundation, participated in the City Hall meeting without the endorsement of other community leaders and without consulting them. At the same time, Mr. O wrote a personal letter to South Korean President Park Chung-hee, asking him for $200,000 as financial support for the foundation's plan to build a Korean-style pavilion in New York City as a gift to the Bicentennial.

These "exceptional" actions taken by Mr. O provoked wild controversy among community leaders. The leaders centered in the Korean Association and the Korean Cultural Center felt that they were "outflanked" by Mr. O. They criticized him for his "extremely individualistic behavior harmful to the unity of the Korean community." Mr. O responded by saying that all the preliminary plans concerning the Bicentennial are officially endorsed by the consulate. Seeing that the Korean Community Foundation, led by Mr. O, was incapable of organizing Korean participation in the Bicentennial in the face of such protest, the Korean consul general directly undertook the project of preparing unique Korean cultural shows for the Bicentennial festival in New York City. At the invitation of the consul general some fifty Korean leaders representing South Korean government agencies, banks, and business firms as well as Korean immigrant organizations gathered on April 26, 1976, at the Korea Center in order to discuss the matter. There they formed an ad hoc committee entrusted with organizing a group of Korean cultural delegates to participate in the festival. The consul general was elected chairman of the committee, and Mr. Han, the Korean ambassador to the United Nations, became honorary chairman. In the meeting the consul general revealed his plan to invite the Korean Folk Artists' Mission from South Korea, a group of some fifty folk musicians and dancers. The folk artists came to New York City at the expense of the South Korean government and put on their shows for American audiences. Thus, owing once again to the intervention and support of the Korean Consulate General, another dispute was resolved. New York's Korean community had an excellent group from the homeland to represent the local community at the Bicentennial festival in New York.

These two episodes reveal some basic patterns in the leadership structure of the Korean community in New York—leadership in the sense that it involves community representation. The Korean Consulate General, as an agency of the home government, has organized groups of leaders and has willingly or unwillingly played the role of arbitrator whenever conflicts arose among them. In assuming this role, the Consulate General has become an informal government for Korean immigrants in the New York metropolitan area. Moreover, one of the main functions of the indigenous community leadership lies in acting as a liaison between the ethnic community and the consulate. As we shall see, many community leaders have become virtual functionaries of the consulate and have competed among themselves in currying favor with it. Partly because of this subordination of community leaders to the consulate, no autonomous community leadership has emerged.

The Korean Association of Greater New York as an Umbrella Organization

These patterns of community leadership are clearly embedded in the leadership structure of the Korean Association, which originally sought an independent role in representing the Korean community to the larger society. As has been noted, the presidency of the Korean Association is a nonpaid, elected job. The association is theoretically financed by membership dues from Korean residents in the New York metropolitan area. All Koreans in the area are automatically enlisted as members, but the majority of Koreans are indifferent to the association. Instead, they are loyal to the Korean Consulate General. Only a negligible number of Korean residents have paid their membership dues to the Korean Association, and for this reason the association has become technically insolvent. The expenditures incurred by the association have been largely covered by contributions from its presidents and board members. Mainly because of this fragile financial structure, the association has not been able to initiate and execute the kinds of programs that might help new immigrants adjust to the larger society. This fact, in turn, has alienated Korean immigrants from the association.

Except for organizing and sponsoring ethnic picnics and ceremonies on South Korean national holidays, the activities of the association have been called forth by sporadic external events. Whenever natural disasters producing a large number of victims have hit South Korea, the association has led community relief campaigns "to extend our brotherly love to the hopeless people of our fatherland." Whenever North Koreans have provoked hostilities against South Koreans or American soldiers, as in the slaying of two American officers at Panmunjom in 1976, the association has organized or sponsored rallies or demonstrations denouncing North Korean aggressiveness and atrocities. All these community activities have been coordinated with corresponding actions taken by organizations in South Korea.

With these kinds of activities, the association seeks to attain a broad community consensus and participation—on the basis of unfortunate events in the homeland. This has contributed to some sense of community solidarity among New York's Koreans. Thus the Korean Association has its own reason for existence even though it lacks a substantive program of community activities and services. Furthermore, the Korean Association stands for all Koreans as a group in its dealings with large-scale organizations of the larger society. Thus the Korean Association is the umbrella organization under which all other ethnic organizations cluster and through which Koreans pursue and defend their interests in relation to the larger society.

Because of the Korean Association's role as community representative, high status has accrued to its presidency. Since 1967, when the Korean immigration to the United States began, a group of businessmen and American-educated professionals has politicized the presidential election of the association. In the old Korean community of the 1950s and early 1960s, the presidency was a symbolic job that automatically went to honorable and respectable elders. After the new influx of Koreans into New York, however, community politicians could increase the range and number of community activities, and so the elections became real contests. Here is a typical example.

Mr. A is a retired colonel of the South Korean Army who runs an antique shop in New York City. When he ran for the presidency of the Korean Association in 1967 he provoked a sensation, and concern over the election, by transporting a large number of his people to the voting place. An old timer ridiculed Mr. A's zealousness over the election: "He used Cadillacs to get his people to the voting place."

Mr. A was the first to seek the election of the presidency of the Korean Association actively. He is believed to be an informal functionary of the South Korean government. He became the 8th president of the Korean Association. After leaving the presidency, he organized a "one-man organization" called the Overseas Pan-Korean Association, which claims to represent all Korean organizations in Japan, Latin America, North America, and Europe. The goal of the association is "to fend off the North Korean communists' intrusion among our overseas Koreans." He recently emerged as a "freedom fighter" against communism when his organization and the Korean Association jointly organized a big "Anti-Kim-Ilsung, Freedom-Preservation Rally" in 1976 in front of the office building of the North Korean observers to the United Nations. The rally came as part of a community commemoration of the 26th anniversary of the outbreak of the Korean War. Mr. A became chairman of the rally by enlisting major community organizations, South Korean business associations and firms, and the Korean Associations in other areas as sponsoring organizations.

But the Korean Church Council, whose name was printed as a sponsoring organization in the ads for the rally in ethnic newspapers, protested that Mr. A used its name without previous permission. A spokesman for the organization said: "The title of our organization cannot be misused for a political purpose." This implies that the rally was inspired by a South Korean government agency.

Mr. A has been an active supporter of the controversial Unification Church, which does not appeal to Korean immigrants. He has helped the Unification Church to induce Korean immigrants to participate in the entertainment meetings offered by the church. He once defended his involvement in the Unification Church by saying that "I am not a member of the Unification Church. But I have helped Mr. Moon Sun Myung because he is a Korean, and, with the Korean flag in his hand, he has led anticommunist movements" (field notes).

Five businessmen, one lawyer, and one political scientist have been elected president of the Korean Association since 1967. Five of them had entered the United States under student status and had received their higher education in the United States. The small number of community leaders who have won the presidency of the Korean Association have reaped personal, political, economic, and honorific rewards. All these gains have been made possible by the broad interaction between the Korean community and the homeland or the home government.

HOMELAND POLITICS AND COMMUNITY LEADERSHIP

In 1972 South Korean President Park Chung-hee gained absolute power after proposing a new constitution, the Yusin Heonbeob (Constitution for Revitalizing Reforms), which was approved in a plebiscite held under martial law. The Yusin Heonbeob empowered President Park, among other things, to appoint one-third of the 219-member National Assembly. The 73 assemblymen who were handpicked by President Park did not belong to any political parties but instead formed another progovernment party in the National Assembly. This group of assemblymen, called the Yujeonghoe, was loyal only to President Park, who in turn used this appointment system as a means of co-opting intellectuals. A couple of seats in the Yujeonghoe were given to overseas Koreans who led emigrant Korean communities along lines consistent with South Korean government policies. One ex-president of the Korean Association of Washington D.C., for instance, was appointed by President Park as a member of the Yujeonghoe for his outstanding progovernment activities in trying to gain the support of Korean residents in the Washington area for the new Korean constitution. He had issued, under the name of the Washington D.C. Korean Association, a declaration in support of the referendum for the new constitution, and this declaration had been widely disseminated by the major South Korean newspapers. As a result of such maneuvers, the presidential elections of the Korean Associations in major Korean-American communities have been hotly contested since 1972; and the introduction of the homeland political issues has contributed to the creation of new Korean Associations by homeland-oriented, politically minded Koreans in cities where Korean immigrants have recently begun to concentrate. For example, two new Korean Associations have recently emerged in Jersey City and Trenton, New Jersey, respectively. In discussing the 1978 presidential election of the Korean Association of New York, a Korean ethnic newspaper editorialized about the con-

nection between Korean community politics in America and homeland politics.

It is a pity that community leaders have revived the traditonal Korean political pattern of factional strife even in this democratic
country, the United States. The fact that community politics is an
extension of homeland politics derives from the interest of community leaders in homeland politics. Community leaders vaguely expect
that if they take the leadership position of the Korean Association in
New York or in the Washington D.C. area, they will earn membership in the Yujeonghoe assembly. In fact, they have been encouraged
to become involved in community politics by the fact that Mr. Jin-
hwan No, an ex-president of the Korean Association in the Washington D.C. area, is now active in the National Assembly as a member
of the Yujeonghoe. . . . Someone might think that in the new land
the presidency or board membership of the Korean Association is a
ridiculous status. But whenever they visit the homeland, they are
treated well. If they are lucky, they even meet such powerful men
as the president and prime minister or ministers.[10]

Mr. Y is a perfect example of how an ambitious Korean claims community leadership in America as a step toward self-advancement in
the peculiar political structure of South Korea. Mr. Y, a student-turned-
lawyer and a political scientist, received a doctoral degree in international politics from a prestigious private university. He was little
known to the Korean community until 1974, when he suddenly turned
up in community politics by running for president of the Korean Association of Greater New York. Since community politics had been
dominated by businessmen, the sudden appearance of this nonbusi-
nessman was an unusual phenomenon. By skillfully bargaining behind
the scenes, Mr. Y eliminated all other aspirants to the presidency. Thus
he was elected unopposed. During 1974 he was looked upon as an
active president, but in 1975 he unexpectedly resigned after he made
a brief visit to South Korea. His visit "coincided" with an important
political interval during which President Park screened potential new
members of the Yujeonghoe. Mr. Y was not on the list of the newly appointed national assemblymen.

This kind of close political interacting between the immigrant community leadership and the home government is one of the major characteristics of community politics in the new land. In addition, community businessmen have used the status of the presidency of Korean
Associations to expand their business operations. For example, community businessmen who import or wholesale South Korean products

[10] *Joong Ang Ilbo*, March 13, 1978.

have sought the presidency in order to receive special favors or protection from the home government in return for taking on the role of organizing support for it. The title of president has, in addition, become the basis for receiving loans from South Korean and American banks. This interlocking of business and politics in the new land is derived from the economic structure of the old land.

We have noted, in chapter three, that the major economic activities of South Korea have been controlled by a powerful government bureaucracy. We have also noted that South Korean businessmen have bribed high-ranking governmental officials for special favors that provide access to economic opportunities. As the trade between the United States and South Korea has become steadily more vital for the South Korean economy and as Koreans in the United States have played a larger role in facilitating that trade, the interlocking connections between business and politics in South Korea have been extended to Korean communities in the United States. Korean businessmen can gain special favors or protection from the home government when they take the role of organizing support in the United States for the South Korean government. A typical example is Tong-sun Park, who participated in the Korean government's influence buying in the United States Congress in return for exclusive rights to arrange rice exports from the United States to South Korea. Park "testified under oath in Seoul that his only reason for cultivating the friendship of three consecutive directors of the KCIA was to fend off his business enemies and keep a lucrative rice agent's assignment."[11] Tong-sun Park was exceptionally successful, but he is paradigmatic of many Korean businessmen whose interests lie in the trade between the two countries.

The businessmen who have pursued the presidency of the Korean Associations have not been motivated purely by economics. In some cases, businessmen expect the direct political rewards that we have discussed above. Yet it is more accurate to say that community businessmen strive for a combination of economic and political rewards from the home government. The expectation of economic benefits, however, is the basic factor underlying the business domination of Korean community politics. As we shall see, pervasive but hitherto opaque economic motivations were made transparent when two rival groups of community businessmen exchanged attacks and counterattacks during the 1976 presidential election of the Korean Association of Greater New York. An analysis of this election casts more light on how businessmen have initiated and expanded community activities in pursuit of their economic goals.

[11] *New York Times*, March 1, 1978.

CONFLICT AND CLEAVAGE IN THE KOREAN ASSOCIATION

In the 1976 presidential election, two groups of businessmen competed for control of the Korean Association of Greater New York. One group was led by Mr. B, who represented the established leadership of the association. Mr. B was the director of the Board of the Korean Association when he decided to run for president. He was supported by almost all the ex-presidents, board members, and the staff of the association. The solidarity of Mr. B's group was largely derived from the fact that they came from Jeola province, the southwestern part of South Korea. Anticipating a powerful opposition, Mr. B's group changed the electoral law by adding new qualifications and requirements for presidential candidates, including a mandatory five-year residence in New York. This partly prevented the announced opposition candidate from entering the election; Mr. B was elected without opposition. His profile follows.

Mr. B was a student-turned-businessman. He was an importer of South Korean products. Mr. B had been actively involved in major community activities long before he became president of the Korean Association; he was at one time president of the Korean Cultural Center. Mr. B and Mr. A are close associates, both being from Jeola province. They have organized anti-North Korean rallies.

Mr. B is also a founding member of the Korean-American Chamber of Commerce and Industry, which claims to represent Korean-American businessmen. He is now president of that organization. An opponent of Mr. B charged that "the KACCI is a one-man organization without membership and financial resources. It has its office at B's business office."

Under the name of the KACCI, Mr. B organized and led, during 1975 to 1976, group visits of Korean-American businessmen to South Korea. The visits were made at the invitation of the Korean Trade Association in South Korea. Its aim was "to strengthen mutual solidarity and common interests between Korean-Americans and homeland businesmen and thereby open the way for Korean-American businessmen to contribute to an increase in Korean exports to the United States, and to the economic development of fatherland. . . ." The itinerary included visits to the prime minister, foreign minister, and minister of commerce and industry as well as to historical sites, industrial complexes, and the demilitarized zone.

In 1975, on the occasion of August 15, Korean Independence Day, Mr. B, as one of the Korean-American delegates to the Korean National Unification Council (a "people's congress" where the South Korean president is elected), met President Park and recommended that the government (1) set up a special fund designed to help Korean immigrants establish themselves in the United States; (2) adopt a more positive policy toward the education of a second generation of Korean immigrants; (3) adopt a more liberal eligibility policy toward emigration; (4) extend support and cooperation to the Korean Associations in the United States (field notes).

In response to the irregular election of 1976, the opposition group of businessmen founded another type of Korean Association, the Korean Community Federation. It elected as its new president an ethnic lawyer who had once operated an emigration company that went bankrupt mainly because of new restrictions by the United States (starting in 1975) on the influx of skilled immigrants. The vice-presidency of the Korean Community Federation went to a wig importer and wholesaler who was once president of the Korean Wig Union. This new group of community leaders was partly financed and supported by a famous businessman, Mr. D, who became a millionaire as a result of his wig business. A brief profile of Mr. D follows.

Mr. D came to the United States as an employee of the Korea Trade Promotion Center (KOTRA), a semigovernmental agency whose function is to promote South Korean exports throughout the world market. Mr. D quit the agency in 1962 and entered the wig business by setting up a small wig factory in Seoul. His wig business prospered, and he entered garment manufacturing, shipping, and real estate. In the early 1970s, when he switched from the wig to the garment business, he established a retail-clothing chain store by importing men's clothes produced in his factories in South Korea. In setting up a chain of retail clothing stores, he encroached upon the territory of small garment retailers, many of whom had bought their retail products from him. He opened his chain stores near established Korean retail-clothing stores in New York. Thus, a group of Korean garment retailers publicly accused him of "immoral commercial behavior." One Korean retailer called the Korean Consulate General and denounced his "shameful" action. In response, Mr. D filed a $1 million libel suit against the Korean Association of Garment Retailers.

Mr. N, a close associate of Mr. B, was president of the Korean Association of Garment Retailers when Mr. D filed suit. Mr. N had been deeply involved in the operation of the Korean Association represented by Mr. B. With the intervention of the Korean Consulate General in the dispute, Mr. D later dropped the libel suit.

Mr. D has twice been cited by the South Korean government for his contribution to the exports of South Korean products to the

United States market. In 1968 he became president of the Korean Association of Greater New York after he entertained a large number of Koreans at Korean restaurants. An ethnic newspaper reported that during his term he spent about $8,000 of his own money to cover the expenses of the association. But somehow, he had become alienated from the establishment of the Korean Association, led by Mr. B and his associates, though he had actively been involved in establishing and maintaining other community organizations. With a largess of $30,000, he helped a group of ministers found the Korean Community Activity Center, which was to become the most active service organization in responding to the needs of new Korean immigrants. The center recently received a U.S. grant in support of its activities. Mr. D was also one of the founding members of the Korean Cultural Center, the Korean Radio Broadcasting Corporation, and a Korean language school.

Meanwhile, he has acquired a good deal of credit from Korean and American banks. A South Korean journalist reported that he once borrowed some $2 million from American banks. A Korean businessman in talking about him said: "He has never used his own money in running his business." Mr. D's business was in trouble before the community election took place; he sold his building near Koreatown (field notes).

After the emergence of the Korean Community Federation (which, like the Korean Association, claimed to represent New York's Korean community), the Korean Association, represented by its newly elected president, Mr. B, began to engage in personal attacks on the central figures of the Korean Community Federation: its president, vice-president, and their supporter, Mr. D. The Korean Association issued the following declaration, which was advertised in a Korean ethnic newspaper.

According to a fellow countryman, businessmen who owe a large debt to American banks have tried to set up another Korean Association in an attempt to defer their debts under the pretext of being officials in the Korean Association. We hope that this is not true. A fellow countryman said that some businessmen have frequently visited Korea, displaying their business cards on which titles of presidents of all kinds of organizations are printed. They have used their business cards to make deals in the homeland. A fellow countryman further indicated that those kinds of businessmen have chosen Mr. X as their pawn in their conspiracy to establish a bogus Korean Association, named the Korean Community Federation. We must say that the Park Young-bok affair[12]—as the biggest bank scandal in Korea—should not occur again. . . . As we all know, Mr. X was a controversial figure, well publicized in Korean newspapers, when he declared his emigration business bankrupt. It is a great disappointment to us that such a man is now running for president of a second Korean Association.[13]

This attack was a response to the following declaration, which the Korean Community Federation advertised in a Korean ethnic newspaper in order to denounce Mr. B and his associates in the Korean Association.

Mr. B's side attempted to create circumstances of unprecedented terror, fear, and violence when a man disguised as an agent of an intelligence agency [the KCIA] made threatening phone calls to ex-board members of the Korean Association.[14]

The consul general became a mediator in this conflict. Insisting that there should be only one Korean Association in New York City, Consul General Dou-soon Chong presided over several negotiating meetings between representatives of the rival groups. But, as we shall see in the next chapter, Mr. B later revealed that the consul general and his personnel sided with the opposition group of businessmen and attempted to destroy Mr. B's leadership. The meetings produced no agreement for the merger of the two associations. Thus, from 1976 to 1977, the Korean Association and the Korean Community Federation both claimed to be the genuine community representative. During the competition, the two organizations initiated various new community activities.

In pursuing personal interests by seeking leadership positions in the Korean Association, a small number of businessmen and intellectuals have made community politics hotly contested affairs even though most Korean immigrants have been apathetic toward community politics. In the presidential elections of the Korean Association an average of 200 or 300 Koreans have turned out. Most of them have been and still are friends, relatives, or schoolmates of the community leaders concerned. Despite the general apathy, a small number of community leaders have "reached out" to generate a number of community activities, most of which are beneficial to the community as a whole.

[12] Young-bok Park, a penniless crook, was able to receive some $15 million in loans from major South Korean banks owing to the backing of a senior official of the KCIA.

[13] *Hankook Ilbo*, December 1, 1976.   [14] *Hankook Ilbo*, October 18, 1976.

THE EFFECT OF THE "KOREAGATE" SCANDAL
AND OF REV. MOON ON NEW YORK'S KOREANS

A deep change in community politics has begun to take place since 1976, for Korean immigrants have become increasingly aware of their collective socioeconomic position in relation to the larger society. Korean immigrants are also becoming more conscious of their ethnic identity. The articulation of a collective consciousness and of common interests has facilitated by external events: the Korean influence-buying scandal in Congress, the controversial Unification Church, and anti-Korean campaigns among some segments of the black population. A Korean ethnic newspaper reflected this new way that Koreans perceive their collective position in contemporary American society as follows.

Because of their progressive economic spirit and dynamic life force, Koreans in the United States have acquired a special nickname characterizing their unique traits. They have gained the nickname of "Asian Jew," which may have good or bad connotations. Regardless of the racial definition of Jew, the name "Jew" has a universal application as the description of industrious, diligent, thrifty or stingy personalities. This Jewish idiosyncrasy has become a secondary national characteristic for Koreans in the United States.

Recently, an ethnic community in the Philadelphia area publicly criticized Koreans there, saying that "Koreans are not cooperative but only know money." This anti-Korean campaign has shocked not only Koreans in the Philadelphia area but also all other Koreans who are aware of it. Koreans are surprised and distressed not only because the campaign is unfair but also because it has turned Koreans to self-reflection and a self-evaluation of their life in American society.

The Park Tong-sun scandal, the KCIA, and the Unification Church have provided names that symbolize Koreans in the United States. Koreans have suffered from an American public identification of Koreans with these big events. Koreans, who have so far lived without friction in American society, have begun to ask themselves an agonizing question: "How can we live in American society?"[15]

The Korean reaction to "Koreagate" was a mixture of shame and amusement. In the face of tenacious attacks by the American mass media on an indecent but normal Korean political maneuver, many Korean intellectuals felt shame: "We are now branded as that kind of people." But privately the majority of Koreans were also amused by

[15] *Hankook Ilbo*, September 23, 1977.

their own caricature of American congressmen: "Koreans bribed poor American congressmen in order to help them make a living." However, this kind of private amusement or self-defense was replaced by a public seriousness when Koreans were taunted over the scandal. The following report describes the effects of the bribery scandal on the Korean community in the Washington D.C. area.

Just before Christmas last year, several Korean children living here made little gifts for their school teachers, in the custom of their homeland. But the teachers, so the story goes, politely refused the gifts because they feared the taint of accepting anything from a Korean.

Koreans here recite that tale with a touch of humor and some bitterness. They laugh at the comic twists in their lives that the Korean bribery scandal has caused, but they consider many of its consequences less than funny.

Some Koreans say they have been the butt of teasing and jokes since last fall, when newspapers began publishing allegations of South Korean bribes to American Congressmen and covert attempts to manipulate public opinion. . . .

Some are quick to disassociate themselves from the Koreans alleged to be involved in the scandal. "We are different from Park Tong Sun and Moon Sun Myung," says a shopowner, referring to the wealthy businessman and the controversial preacher who are alleged to have been operatives for the South Korean government.

"I am not interested in Park Tong Sun and Reverend Moon," he says. "I have my way, they have their way."

Others say the scandal has caused them to lose face. "At first, we were angry about Park Chung Hee," says one Korean, speaking of the President of Korea. "He ruined our country's face. . . ."

Some of the Koreans say that they have been hurt because perhaps half of their neighbors refuse their invitations or just do not show up. A few have seen vulgar anti-Korean signs on the streets.

Korean businessmen say business has dropped off a bit. A storekeeper selling wigs says he has fewer customers. An auto mechanic reports that he is not getting as much work as before. Workers find it harder to get jobs.[16]

New York's Korean community also suffered from adverse publicity. The Korean-American Cultural Federation was established in 1976 by some well-established Koreans in order to disseminate traditional Korean culture, arts, and music among the American public. It recruited

[16] *New York Times*, April 13, 1977.

as members some notable American business executives or business-men who had "cultural" (or business) interests in South Korea, but it was forced to dissolve because American business executives wanted to "avoid the image of Korea itself." When two Korean churches in New York were audited by the IRS because of "the controversy surrounding the Unification Church," some community church leaders angrily said, "It is quite exceptional that religious organizations like churches are audited." In Westchester County, where the Unification Church possesses vast real estate holdings, Koreans have met some resistance from county residents when trying to buy houses. The residents tend to confuse Koreans with "Moonies," followers of Reverend Moon. Some segments of the Westchester population are afraid that the Korean properties will be transferred to his Unification Church, whose properties are exempt from taxation. They are afraid of the possible increase in their own property taxes.

Mainly owing to the bribery scandal, there has been a growing communitywide feeling that community leaders should not be involved in homeland politics. "Don't look to the politics of the homeland" has been a commonly used phrase when community opinionmakers such as ministers, journalists, and intellectuals have discussed community affairs. The scandal has forced community leaders to reconsider their "blind" loyalty to the home government. The Korean Association of Greater New York, for example, attempted to hold a public hearing on the scandal. The hearing, entitled "The Impact of the Park Tong Sun Affair on the Korean Community," was scheduled to be held on December 4, 1977, with the participation of representatives of the home government, the Korean consul general in New York, and the Korean Ambassador to Washington D.C., as well as representatives of anti-Park organizations in New York. This bold initiative from the Korean Association, which had never before taken a political position independent of the home government, was a surprise to the community. Some Koreans argued that the hearing was a political tactic for gaining votes in the forthcoming 1978 presidential election of the association. However, a spokesman of the association said, "We feel that a public hearing is overdue. We must have the meeting because so many of our fellow countrymen have inquired of us about the scandal. We think it necessary to distinguish between what is right and what is wrong."[17] It was reported that the association was forced to cancel the public hearing because the Korean consul general refused to take part.[18] In addition, the Korean Community Federation (the second Korean Association) strained its relationship with the Consulate General because its president presented himself before the House Ethics Com-

[17] *Hankook Ilbo*, November 17, 1977.   [18] *Hankook Ilbo*, December 1, 1977.

mittee as a lawyer for Hyong-wuck Kim, an ex-director of the KCIA, when Kim told the committee what he knew about the Korean bribery operations.

THE RISE OF INDIGENOUS POLITICS

A new community consensus is clearly indicated by the 1978 presidential election of the Korean Association of Greater New York. When the Korean Produce Retailers Association entered community politics by proposing one of its members as a candidate, it confronted the established leadership of the Korean Association, which had chosen one of its board members, a wig importer and wholesaler, to run for president. The two groups engaged in a bitter struggle for hegemony, and the greengrocers won. Their victory was largely due to the fraternal solidarity of greengrocers and to their association's vast financial resources. Greengrocers were determined to unify the community leadership by crushing the established leadership of the Korean Association. In the campaign, the Korean Community Federation supported the greengrocers and suggested that it would dissolve itself if the greengrocers would take over the Korean Association. After the election, the Korean Community Federation was voluntarily dissolved. The Korean American Senior Citizens Society, which is highly esteemed because of a cultural respect for old people, also supported the greengrocers. With the entry of greengrocers into community politics, as a news headline showed, the community was "Swept by Heated Political Winds." More than 2,000 Koreans registered to vote, and some 1,400 turned out in the 1978 election. The Korean Produce Retailers Association made good use of its well-organized internal network in getting its members and their families and supporters to the voting place.

The greengrocer's debut in community politics marks a radical departure from established political patterns in two respects. First, community politics has begun to take shape along the lines of organizational groups rather than around specific individuals. As has been noted, community elections had been dominated by businessmen who had commercial or political interests in the homeland; the fruit and vegetable business, however, has no connection with the homeland and its economy. Second, this new development in community politics is a response to a prevailing mood in the community that says, Let us not get involved in homeland politics, but tackle American politics. In this respect, the new politics of the Korean community is to pursue autonomy from the homeland. If the movement persists and succeeds, it could establish a genuine politics based on indigenous leadership, issues, and interest. Accordingly, one of the main platforms of the Korean Produce Retailers Association was to "defend and pursue the common interests of our fellow countrymen in the new land." The association has promised that it will set up a special bureau to be a liaison with city, state, and federal organizations. In this context, some community leaders have recommended that Koreans, like blacks, should shift toward service-oriented community programs and away from overt ideological or political movements. The Korean community wants a piece of the welfare state—access to state and federal money.

KAPA and Korean Participation in Domestic Politics. A group of American-educated Korean intellectuals has already started to develop such an ethnic politics. The Korean-American Political Association (KAPA), which was founded in 1971 and became a nationwide organization with headquarters in San Francisco, has focused on Korean politics in relation to the larger society. This organization participated in American politics for the first time in the history of Korean-Americans when it contributed some $3,000 in campaign funds to the election of Jerry Brown (Edmund Brown Jr.) as California's governor in 1974. When Brown won, he appointed a Korean as a judge. (In the presidential election of 1976, the organization supported Gerald R. Ford rather than Jimmy Carter because the South Korean government opposed Carter's campaign promise to withdraw American military forces from South Korea.) KAPA has a branch in New York City that has held conferences to which the United States immigration officials were invited to explain various immigration and naturalization problems facing Koreans in the New York metropolitan area. The organizer in charge of KAPA's New York branch said, "If we could unite naturalized Korean-Americans and cast a single ethnic bloc vote, we could make substantial political and economic gains" (field notes).

One college professor who belongs to KAPA, Mr. Z, has actively engaged in linking the New York Korean community with the politics of the larger society. Since 1976 he has been a Korean representative in the Asian-American Coalition of Greater New York. When the green-grocers took over the Korean Association, in the spring of 1978, its new president, Mr. P, appointed Mr. Z as director of the board. Mr. Z has emerged as a most effective community leader since his participation in the Korean Association. He has systematically contacted, on behalf of New York's Korean community, City Hall, its Police Department, and several Asian-American interest groups. He has also participated in an Asian-American campaign to organize New York's Asians for the reelection of Governor Hugh Carey. Thus, the participation of Mr. Z in the Korean Association has generated an organizational or leadership interlock between KAPA and the Korean Association of Greater New York.

The Korean Response to Black Anti-Koreanism. The growing awareness among Korean-Americans of their collective fate in the new land has partly been caused, as we have noted, by anti-Korean campaigns launched by some segments of the black population. Anti-Korean incidents have taken the form of murder, picketing, and press attacks against Korean merchants who run businesses in black ghettos. Racial conflicts between blacks and Korean shopkeepers have occurred sporadically in Philadelphia, Baltimore, and Washington D.C. In New York City there have been no major overt incidents between the two groups, although "numerous" Korean businessmen have been robbed by both blacks and Hispanics. Three Korean merchants in New York's ghetto were killed in separate holdups between 1975 and 1978, and one Korean owner of a supermarket in a black neighborhood was shot to death by two black youths for reasons other than robbery.

Because of this kind of racial conflict between Korean merchants and black ghetto residents or businessmen, Koreans in New York were disturbed when they first learned that some Philadelphia black leaders had overtly criticized Korean merchants in that city. The attack started with anti-Korean articles in a biweekly black newspaper, the *Tribune* (July 12 and July 16, 1977). The articles were immediately followed by an open letter (July 26, 1977) denouncing Korean merchants, which was sent by an influential black leader to the United States congressman representing West Philadelphia. A Korean ethnic newspaper summarized the contents of the two articles and the open letter.

(1) Koreans find it easier than blacks to receive loans from the Small Business Administration. This should be investigated to ascertain whether irregularities are involved in the handling of business loans by the Small Business Administration. The sources of capital for Koreans should be traced.

(2) Koreans are not thankful to the blacks who participated in the Korean War and helped Koreans fight against the communist invasion. Instead they despise blacks. They invade and exploit the black community.

(3) Koreans do business in black neighborhoods, but they do not employ blacks.

(4) Koreans are not cooperative in community affairs. They do not enlist themselves in community business associations. They never pay their membership dues. They never contribute money to the

operation of community affairs such as street decoration during the Christmas season.

(5) Koreans have a superiority complex over blacks despite the fact that they are yellow.[19]

In addition, *Good News*, a black daily newspaper published in Baltimore, argued (February 8, 1978) that the business enterprises of Korean ghetto-merchants are a conspiracy of foreigners. It implied that, as in the Korean influence-buying scandal, the South Korean government encourages and finances Korean businesses in black ghettos.

The above charges against Koreans illuminate the peculiar racial and ethnic relationship between ghetto blacks and Korean ghetto-merchants. Black grievances against Korean merchants focus on the "parasitic" commercial behavior of Korean small businessmen. Black complaints might be summarized in one sentence: "Koreans milk cows without feeding them." This protest, however, simply restates in negative form the economic situation facing marginal Korean immigrants. Koreans are a typical example of the so-called middleman minority. As has been indicated in chapter four, the inability of Korean immigrants to enter the mainstream of the American economy and politics has caused a high proportion of Korean immigrants to seek economic advancement through ghetto business enterprises. In addition, Korean immigrants are economically aggressive and thus dare to enter ghetto businesses that involve high risks of robbery, fire, looting, and burglary. The following report describes a typical hardship facing Korean ghetto businessmen.

> Mr. Na opened on July 15, 1975—a grocery store at 2116 Coronaga Avenue [in Queens]. During the last year and a half, Mr. Na met four pistol robberies, two burglaries, and one window smashing by black youths. Mr. Na keeps his store open from 9 A.M. to late midnight. Whenever Mr. Na's wife took care of the business, they underwent these misfortunes.[20]

Partly because of these kinds of security problems, Korean ghetto-merchants do not intend to remain in their ghetto businesses permanently. By catering to low-class blacks and Hispanics they want to earn enough to start other businesses. Thus they do not have a sense of belonging to the areas in which they do business. Objectively and subjectively, they are strangers to the ghetto. They are marginal traders who go home every night to predominantly white lower-middle-class neighborhoods.

[19] *Hankook Ilbo*, August 5, 1977.   [20] *Hankook Ilbo*, November 23, 1976.

The anti-Korean campaigns among blacks have thus stimulated sensitive Koreans to think about their own marginal status as immigrants. This, in turn, has contributed to attempts to create a deeper and greater ethnic solidarity. Community leaders and businessmen in New York City, Philadelphia, Baltimore, and Washington D.C. have held a series of meetings, conferences, and seminars in order to discuss how to cope with black attacks on the Korean community. In Philadelphia's Korean community, a record number of small businessmen, who had been indifferent to community affairs, took part in the meetings and engaged in serious discussions of the issue. They formed an ad hoc committee to negotiate with black leaders. An ethnic newspaper reports that "Philadelphia community leaders indicated that the incidents occurred when the Korean community in the United States confronted a difficult and embarrassing situation due to the bribery scandal in Congress and other events. They have urged fellow countrymen to show community cooperation and solidarity."[21] In the 1978 presidential election of the Korean Association of Greater Philadelphia, "how to cope with blacks" was a major issue. In New York City, community businessmen gathered and discussed measures they might take to prevent a racial conflict similar to that in Philadelphia. They formed a new business association called the Beonyeonghoe (the Prosperity Association), whose major aim is to protect Korean businesses as a whole from other racial groups.

CONCLUSION

Community politics were at first characterized almost exclusively by an involvement in homeland politics and an acceptance of home government policies. A small number of community leaders organized and led communitywide activities along paths that reflected the policies of the home government toward both New York's Korean community and toward the United States government. However, the majority of community members were apathetic to these efforts to promote vast communitywide activities. Korean immigrants, as we have seen, prefer to participate in much smaller-scale activities and associations.

The Consulate General, an agency of the home government, has directed, influenced, and intervened in almost all communitywide activities. In addition, the Korean Central Intelligence Agency located its "station" in the Korean Consulate General. The KCIA "station" has exerted a ubiquitous influence on major community organizations through its informal, extralegal, illegal, and clandestine activities. However, the assassination of President Park in October of 1979 by

[21] *Hankook Ilbo*, August 5, 1977.

the head of the KCIA, Jae-kyu Kim (who was later executed), upset KCIA routines in both the homeland and its overseas "stations," including New York City. Overseas KCIA agents were deeply concerned about their future. At the time of writing, Lieutenant-General Too-hwan Chon, who heads the Defense Security Command, a military intelligence organ, has emerged as a strongman in the South Korean army. General Chon has taken over the KCIA and has purged about 300 KCIA senior officials in order to consolidate his command over the agency. General Chon and other military leaders have set up a semi-military junta called the National Security Measures Committee, a device to control the civilian government. Thus it is assumed that the KCIA "stations" in the United States, under the new leadership, have resumed their operations against those Korean-Americans who lead a political movement against the military-dominated South Korean government.

Regardless of the recent turmoil in the homeland, Korean immigrants have acquired a new perspective on their relation to the larger society. They have developed social and economic institutions, such as the Korean Produce Retailers Association and KAPA, that are increasingly independent of the homeland and its government. A new pattern of community politics has emerged: influential new community groups are turning away from the homeland and developing an ethnic politics within the larger society. This maturity in pursuing the common interests of Korean immigrants in relation to the larger society has also been fostered by social events that are external to the immediate affairs of the ethnic community but that nonetheless affect all Koreans. "Korea-gate" and conflicts over the Unification Church, for example, have brought all Koreans into disrepute and have suggested that Korean immigrants must try as a group to dissociate themselves from such scandals.

All these events, internal and external, precipitated basic changes in the pattern of community organization. Community leaders have become more concerned with American society than with the homeland, and community politics has begun to shape itself along the lines of indigenous associations, whereas earlier it remained the personal affair of a small number of self-selected leaders whose political activities in the community reflected their economic or political ambitions in the homeland.

Finally, the marginal economic role that Korean immigrants have played near the lower depths of society has put them in conflict with blacks in urban ghettos. This conflict has further stimulated Korean immigrants to assess their collective fate and identity in the new land, and consequently it also has caused the community to search for some collective mechanisms whereby ethnic solidarity could be marshaled to deal with the larger society. As Korean immigrants have thus increasingly turned their political energies toward indigenous issues in relation to the larger society, ethnic media have emerged as a most powerful means for enhancing the new ethnic solidarity, as we shall see in the next chapter.

CHAPTER NINE

Ethnic Media as a Mechanism of Community Integration

As HAS been noted, in the absence of "natural" ethnic population centers for face-to-face interaction, churches and restaurants are the focal points for major community activities. Korean restaurants are not just places where meals are served, and Korean churches are not just places for delivering religious services. Similarly, the Korean ethnic media go beyond delivering news. By informing geographically dispersed immigrants of community meetings and events, the media are a most powerful means of integrating and sustaining the community. They also maintain and to some extent reinforce Korean nationalism among Korean immigrants, whose ethnic solidarity largely depends upon a strong identification with the homeland. This sense of a common identity, in turn, helps hold together the community. In fact, without the ethnic media, the nonterritorial community could not exist.[1]

The Korean ethnic media in the New York metropolitan area are made up of two daily newspapers, two radio programs, one television program, and one semimonthly newspaper. As carriers of advertising for ethnic business enterprises, commodity sales, housing rentals, jobs, and so forth, the community media facilitate the expansion of economic activities. They also publicize many of the special activities conducted by secondary associations and thus arouse communitywide interest in activities that otherwise would go unnoticed. As we shall see, the ethnic media also assume the role of a "moral entrepreneur" in attempting to judge the moral quality of community activities. By thus taking a partisan position in community affairs, they politicize community life. And yet, in creating or focusing on community issues, they rarely violate one taboo. Like the major community organizations, the ethnic media wish to avoid offending the home government, for they are subject to all the indirect and direct pressures of that government.

---

[1] This issue was first raised by Morris Janowitz. By focusing upon the community press, he was able to identify metropolitan subcommunities, or communities within the metropolis. See Morris Janowitz, *The Community Press in An Urban Setting: The Social Elements of Urbanism*, Chicago, The University of Chicago Press, 1967, pp. 1-7.

THE ETHNIC MEDIA

A Korean businessman set up the Korean Television Corporation (KTC) in 1975 to organize and broadcast a regular weekly program. During its first year of broadcasting, the KTC was twice forced to stop airing its program because of a financial pinch. In 1977, the KTC conducted a fund-raising campaign in the community. In making its appeal, the KTC felt that it had to announce that it was receiving no financial support from the home government; the assumption that it had such support made immigrants reluctant to contribute. Another basic reason for the corporation's financial problem was that community business enterprises were not large or strong enough to invest a sufficient amount of money in television advertising. Contributions and advertising were needed to offset the major cost in running the community television program, which is incurred in renting broadcasting facilities from American television stations. (The KTC pays some $3,000 for a one-hour rental.) Until 1977, the major portion of the program was filled with rebroadcast videotapes imported from the Korean Broadcasting Station, a government agency. But the KTC recently changed its format and some of its programs; it has added local news with Korean ex-radio-announcers and one television announcer. Every Saturday morning, when the Korean television program appears on channels 60 and 68, an audience of Korean television-watchers forms throughout the tri-state area. Many Koreans give up the opportunity to sleep late on Saturday mornings to be able to view the program, which lasts an hour and a half. As a consequence, community businessmen, especially those catering to Korean customers, are now willing to buy commercial time.

By similarly renting time and equipment from American radio stations, two big Korean churches run two separate radio programs. One is produced by the Korean Methodist Church in Queens, the other by the Sunbogeum Gyohoe, the Pure Gospel Church. The former program came into being in 1977 after the Korean Methodists took over the financially troubled Korean Radio Broadcasting Company, which was set up in 1972 by a Korean (who was a former radio announcer) with the support of some community businessmen. As we have noted in chapter six, the two churches broadcast these radio programs as one way of claiming ethnic leadership in interchurch representation. Sermons are an essential part of the programs, but Korean secular songs are also transmitted to a general Korean audience. Like the television program, each of the two radio programs is beamed for several hours a week. This time limitation prevents the television and radio programs from becoming as powerful a means of ethnic communication as are the ethnic newspapers.

THE TWO DAILY NEWSPAPERS

Two daily newspapers, the *Hankook Ilbo* and the *Joong Ang Ilbo*, provide the primary mass-communication, information, and advertisement services to Korean immigrants in the New York metropolitan area. They are the public channels for community issues and opinion as well as for announcements of major community cultural events. The newspapers are not sold on newsstands but are sent directly to each Korean subscriber by second-class mail. Each newspaper, published by its "headquarters" in Seoul, is airmailed daily from the Kimpo International Airport to Kennedy Airport. The New York branch of each newspaper then reproduces each issue by photocopying on an electronic copier, which reproduces 12,000 papers per hour. Before the paper is finished, each New York branch adds local news to the original edition. This influx of the homeland newspapers, which compete with one another for the largest share of readers, has forced two small, locally produced newspapers (a bimonthly and a weekly) out of business.

Subscribers to the two daily newspapers are spread over the entire eastern seaboard, with a heavy concentration in the New York metropolitan area. The two newspapers reach, as of 1978, about 14,000 subscribers: the *Hankook Ilbo* has some 9,000 subscribers; the *Joong Ang Ilbo*, about 5,000. In the New York metropolitan area alone the *Hankook Ilbo* serves some 7,000 subscribers; the *Joong Ang Ilbo*, 3,500. The *Joong Ang Ilbo*, which began publishing in New York City later than did its competitor, has focused upon the Korean communities in Philadelphia, Baltimore, Washington D.C., and Atlanta. Many Koreans, especially businessmen, are subscribers to both newspapers; more than 50 percent of the Korean householders in the New York metropolitan area subscribe to at least one of the newspapers.[2] Most readers are established community members; perhaps new arrivals cannot afford the monthly rate of six dollars. For Koreans who have difficulty reading English-language newspapers, the two Korean dailies are a major source of steady information about the larger society as well as the homeland. Because of this, almost a third of the "local news section" under the masthead of "New York Hankook" or "Eastern American Edition" is made up of the articles translated from English-language newspapers and magazines.

The *Joong Ang Ilbo*, with a total circulation of 930,000, is a subsidiary of the Samsung *jaebeol*, a South Korean conglomerate corporation. The *Hankook Ilbo* was founded and run by Gi-young Chang, who

---

[2] According to a recent sample survey conducted in 1977 by Choon-goon Kim, 81 percent of Korean householders in southern California subscribed to at least one Korean-language newspaper, *Hankook Shinmoon*, October 22, 1977.

once served the Park regime as a vice-premier. When he died in 1977, his son took over the newspaper, which has a total circulation of 350,000. Both newspapers have branches in New York City, Los Angeles, and Chicago. And both newspapers took a progovernment stance long before the South Korean government restricted the freedom of the press in the early seventies. In fact, it is because of their long-term service in defending the Park regime that the South Korean government authorized them to set up their branches in the United States. Thus the two newspapers have monopolized the mass media serving Korean communities throughout the United States. According to a well-informed source, the *Dong-A Ilbo*, a South Korean newspaper that was the sole voice of media opposition to the South Korean government until it yielded in 1975 to government harassment (the KCIA informally banned all commercial advertisement in the newspaper), could not establish its branches in the United States, because of its antigovernment stance. At present, however, a New York businessman is preparing to set up a New York branch of the *Dong-A Ilbo*, but it is no longer an opposition paper.

In addition to the two daily newspapers, an indigenous bimonthly newspaper called the *Hae Oe Han Min Bo*, the *Overseas Korean Journal*, has existed since 1973. It has represented the political views of the anti-Park overseas movements and in so doing has expounded three political goals: (1) "This newspaper rejects the dictatorship [of Park] that exploits and oppresses the Korean people"; (2) "This newspaper proposes a peaceful unification of the fatherland"; and (3) "This newspaper arouses national consciousness among overseas Koreans." The newspaper has appealed only to a small number of Korean immigrants, for the most part articulate Koreans sympathetic to the anti-Park cause. The newspaper pays little attention to ordinary community affairs. It focuses on the activities of dissidents in South Korea as well as on the anti-Korean-government movements of Korean nationals in the United States, Canada, Japan, and West Germany. It agrees with the North Korean communist regime on such a controversial issue as the withdrawal of the United States forces from South Korea, a policy that almost all South Koreans, including the major opposition leaders, oppose. The tone of the paper is inflammatory, as one headline clearly indicates: "The Flame of the Resistance Movement Burns up Again at Seoul Campus." (The headline refers to continual but intermittent demonstrations by a group of college students in Seoul.) An official of the consulate has labeled the *Hae Oe Han Min Bo* a *bulon* paper. (The term *bulon* roughly means a "break," a South Korean government euphemism for communism or radicalism.)

Ordinary Korean immigrants greet the "*bulon*" paper with a sense of confusion, at best, because in the homeland they accepted the official anticommunist ideology. That acceptance was partly based upon North Korea's totalitarianism and its military aggressiveness against South Korea, but it was also reinforced by South Korean propaganda. Thus readers are irritated when they encounter such phrases as "labor exploitaiton," "workers' solidarity," "the alliance between intellectuals, students, and workers," "union movement," and "monopolistic capitalism." They think that these are communistic slogans, and some immigrants react with, "This is a red paper!" Mainly because of this ideological gap, the newspaper has little impact on the formation of "ordinary" community issues and opinion. This is so despite the fact that the *Hae Oe Han Min Bo* is a powerful organ for expressing and disseminating the political views of a small segment of antigovernment intellectuals.

The Roles of the Two Daily Newspapers

Social Integration. By propagating Korean culture and values, the two daily newspapers play a primary role in building a value consensus among Korean immigrants. Through a vicarious daily encounter with one another via the ethnic newspapers, Korean immigrants, who are scattered over the tri-state area, maintain a communal feeling. Typical headlines are "Korean Musicians [in New York] Enhance the Pride of National Culture," "August 15, Korean Day: the Korean Association Recommended to the City Hall," and "Two Graduates *Summa Cum Laude*: Illuminating the Superiority of the Second Generation." The stories behind the headlines are designed to raise a sense of "Koreanness" among Korean immigrants. At the same time, the Korean dailies reflect the common and continuing concern of immigrants with the problems facing South Korea. In the early summer of 1978, headlines announced "The Worst Drought in Thirty Years," "The Worst Inflation Since 1970: Prices Jump Daily." By focusing on these and similar problems, and on Korean culture and the homeland, the community newspapers reinvoke the common origins of all Korean immigrants.

In addition to this general buttressing of "ethnicity" in relation to the larger society, the community newspapers coordinate the disparate life patterns of Korean immigrants in specific ways. First of all, the papers often announce community events conducted by secondary ethnic associations. Community organizations also buy ads in the papers in order to draw communitywide attention to their activities. (As we have noted, when churches conduct special programs and religious meetings, they claim interchurch leadership by advertising them in the community newspapers.) By publicizing their activities through ads or announcements, secondary associations attempt to raise their organization's status and prestige in comparison with similar organizations. In other words, community leaders attempt to have their leadership roles "legitimized" in the community as a whole by having their activities advertised or, better yet, reported in the papers. Thus, at the end of "uncommon" activities and meetings, media-conscious leaders usually raise the question of how to make their activities public: "Let us summarize our activities and send the summary to each newspaper"; "I know Mr. X works for the *Hankook Ilbo*, I'll call him immediately."

For communitywide events such as the presidential election of the Korean Association or an annual community festival or picnic, the community newspapers send their reporters to the scene. In informing their readers, the newspapers frequently pass judgment on the content of an event and thus play the role of "moral entrepreneur" for the community. The following report, for example, attacks an internal leadership conflict of the Korean Church Council.

> The fourth general assembly meeting of the Korean Church Council was held on June 29 [1978] at the Korean Church of New Jersey.
> The internal feud over leadership hegemony in the council, which has existed since the foundation of the organization, revealed itself again in the meeting. The feud took the form of a conflict between the big churches and small churches over the election of staff members. Shouting and disorderly conduct characterized the meeting, which continued until midnight. The secular manners of the ministers, who take a major community leadership role in the name of God, have caused a serious disappointment to our community.[3]

As we shall see, this kind of moral judgment sometimes evokes wild controversy itself.

Newspaper coverage provides an additional benefit to the community leaders concerned. When community service organizations apply for grants from federal, state, city, and philanthropic organizations, they use news articles on their activities as evidence of their "accomplishments" for the community. Furthermore, community leaders use newspaper articles dealing with basic community problems in order to highlight those problems for the larger society's institutions, especially when the leaders are asking for financial support. This was the case when a community leader, who teaches education at a college in New York City, helped a high school in Queens to set up a bilingual program for Korean immigrant students. When the high school applied for a grant to the United States Department of Health, Education, and Welfare, the community leader translated into English some newspaper articles discussing the language problem facing Korean students.

[3] *Hankook Ilbo*, June 30, 1978.

The newspapers provide advertising services to individuals as well as to organizations. The daily advertisements of job offers, store sales, commodity sales, and rental and housing sales provide vital information to new arrivals. Marriages can be arranged through such an advertisement as "A 29-year-old man, a born-again Christian, seeks a born-again female Christian as a life-long marriage partner." A husband carried an advertisement in an effort to persuade his wife, who had left home, to return: "Sookhee's mommy! Please come back home. I forgive you for everything. Let us start again. Children wait for you."

In addition to these roles, the newspapers themselves initiate and operate various cultural and recreational programs for the community. For instance, the New York branch of the *Hankook Ilbo* presides annually over the Miss New York Beauty Contest (whereby three Korean girls in New York are selected and sent to the Miss Korea Contest in Seoul), the community painters' exhibition, the community soccer contest, the community children's drawing contest, the community musical show by "homeland" entertainers, and other events. The New York branch of the *Joong Ang Ilbo* hosts similar programs, but fewer. In order to compensate for this inferiority, it runs a unique program called the "24-Hour Telephone Service to Readers," in which its personnel attempt to answer all questions posed by community members. These concentrate on such problems as jobs, "green cards," education, and marriage. In launching many of these programs the newspapers seek support from the Consulate General (with the implications discussed in chapter eight). This is one reason why the papers do not upset the Consulate General when they report news critical of the home government.

Issue Definition. The *Hankook Ilbo* carried on March 21, 1975, the following headline in its "New York Hankook": "Rice Powdered by Talc Causes Cancer: An Alarm to Koreans Using Rice as a Staple." Talc is a chemical that American rice-producers use as a preservative to keep rice free from vermin and moisture. The community newspaper "scoop" was that talc is also a cancer-causing agent—a long-established theory among medical professionals. The newspaper report provoked a sensational reaction in the community. In response, the newspaper carried a follow-up item by interviewing an American expert. Community leaders representing every secondary association spontaneously reached an agreement to open a public hearing on the matter, and the *Hankook Ilbo* reported as follows.

The public hearing on rice powdered by talc was held on April 16 [1975] at the Hankook Hoekwan restaurant by the Korean Association. Mr. Jung-won Kim, president of the Korean Association, presided over the hearing. After listening to various opinions by community leaders representing business, education, and consumer groups, the participants agreed upon the formation of an ad hoc committee designed to deal with the matter.

Before the decision about the establishment of the committee, there were heated exchanges of various views. Mr. Yong-duck Lee, who represented the owners of Korean-food stores, expressed his view: "Talc has not yet been responsible for a single Korean death in the United States. The FDA [the Food and Drug Administration] has not yet confirmed whether or not talc causes cancer. In spite of this, the newspaper has reported subjectively about the matter and has created a panic among our consumers. This biased report is a blow to our business; it is an intrusion into public interest. . . ."

Mrs. Jin-ho Yom, president of the Korean Women's Association, presented her view: "What benefit does talc give to us if we must wash it away before cooking? On this occasion we should unite and decisively tackle the problem. By doing this we contribute to the development of our community. . . ."[4]

Because of this community uproar, American rice-growers, especially the Japanese in California (who virtually monopolize the supply of rice to Korean immigrants), were forced to stop applying talc to their products. This was the first genuine, grass-roots campaign that the community newspapers touched off. It involved spontaneous participation (direct or indirect) by all segments of the Korean population because talc was said to affect the health of all "rice-eating" Koreans.

Since then, the community newspapers have not generated another campaign involving such broad grass-roots participation, although they have raised minor issues. The *Joong Ang Ilbo*, for instance, raised the issue of tax evasion by some Korean small businessmen when it reported on the frequent auditing of Korean small businessmen by the IRS: "Let us Not Evade Tax: A Campaign to Build A Pleasant Community." The report pointed out that some Korean greengrocers do not "sufficiently" pay their taxes and cited a specific case in which a greengrocer was forced to close his store for not reporting income taxes. This report might have generated another public hearing, one to educate Korean small businessmen on the technical procedures of tax reporting; for many of them became "victims" of the IRS because they did not know how to keep books. Instead, the article evoked a wild protest from the Korean Produce Retailers Association, which insisted that "no member belonging to our association has ever been audited by the IRS." The association demanded that the *Joong Ang Ilbo* apolo-

[4] *Hankook Ilbo*, April 21, 1975.

gize and write a correction. Some greengrocers, armed with knives, visited the office of the newspaper and shouted this demand. The newspaper did not submit to the demand and replied that the report was factual. In response, the association wrote a declaration denouncing the "irresponsible" and "false" report and submitted it as an advertisement to the *Hankook Ilbo*, the main competitor of the *Joong Ang Ilbo*. The *Hankook Ilbo* did not accept this advertisement, however, on the grounds that it had to abide by an unwritten ethical code of the press. As a last resort, the greengrocers boycotted the *Joong Ang Ilbo*. But the report had some impact on Korean small businessmen: a large number of them contacted their ethnic accountants to get their books in order and to solve their tax-payment problems.

These two episodes are examples of how the community newspapers generate communitywide or group actions by raising specific issues. Except for the protest against the use of talc in packaging rice, however, the issues have activated only limited segments of the Korean population. This was the case with the issue of tax evasion, and this group specificity can also be found in another instance. When the *Joong Ang Ilbo* reported on the Bronx High School of Science—its academic tradition and quality, its admission standards, and the "excellent" performance of the Korean students there—a group of well-established Koreans with school-age children telephoned the *Joong Ang Ilbo* in order to acquire detailed information about the school.

The community newspapers suffer one serious limitation in raising issues: they cannot report on issues related to the South Korean government that reflect negatively on that government. Forbidden subjects include the political operations of South Korean agents in the United States such as in the influence-peddling scandal. This failure to report on major events and issues central to the interests and experience of Koreans in both the homeland and the United States is mainly due to the indirect intervention of the home government in the affairs of community newspapers.

Relationship to the Home Government. Although the two daily newspapers claim to be "branches" of homeland newspapers, they are not branches in the strict sense. The New York Korean papers are financially independent of their "headquarters" in Seoul. In this respect, they are different from their counterparts in Los Angeles, which are directly run and managed by the Seoul headquarters. In Los Angeles, the *Hankook Ilbo* is run by its publisher's brother; the *Joong Ang Ilbo*, by the business branch of the Samsung *jaebeol*, the conglomerate.

The *Hankook Ilbo* began circulation in the United States in 1967, when a student-turned-importer in New York started to distribute copies of the paper to 125 Korean immigrants. The head office of the *Hankook Ilbo* in Seoul had wanted at that time to expand its circulation into the United States. As the business of distributing photocopied newspapers turned out to be profitable because of the rapid increase of Korean immigrants in New York after 1967, the "headquarters" in Seoul resorted to all kinds of means to take over the photocopying business from the importer. The New York businessman did not succumb to these pressures. In 1971 he began adding local news to the original edition. With the influx of Korean immigrants to New York and the growth of their business enterprises, circulation increased and advertising thrived. By 1978, the New York publisher employed some thirty full-time workers, five of whom were reporters. This New York *Hankook Ilbo*, a pseudobranch, monopolized mass communications in the community until the *Joong Ang Ilbo* reappeared in New York City in 1976. The latter was originally run by a student-turned-businessman who once served as president of the Korean Association of Greater New York and who has engaged since the late 1960s in the emigration and employment business. In the early 1970s he set up the New York *Joong Ang Ilbo*, but he abandoned the business because the head office in Seoul demanded key money. In addition, the population and incomes of Korean immigrants were too limited to support two daily newspapers. In 1976 a student-turned-wig-wholesaler tried to revive the New York *Joong Ang Ilbo*. He invested all the money he earned from the wig-wholesaling business. In the first year he operated his new business at a loss, but, largely owing to the continuous influx of new arrivals and the increasing demand by community businessmen for ethnic advertisements, his business ran in the black in 1977. By 1978 the New York *Joong Ang Ilbo* employed twelve full-time workers, three of whom were reporters.

The peculiar status of the pseudobranches brought direct intervention from the Korean Consulate General and the KCIA "station" in New York. The two newspaper "branches," because they maintain financial independence from Seoul, claim autonomy in reporting local community events. Many community events, however, such as anti-Park rallies and the "Park Tong Sun Affair," are viewed as detrimental to the South Korean government. Furthermore, such community events eventually reach the ears of United States government policymakers, for major community news is translated into English by Korean employees at some federal departments and agencies. From the point of view of the Consulate General and the KCIA, the two community newspapers, run by Americanized businesmen, need the "corrective guidance" of the home government, which has taken the form of ex post facto censorship. A community member who once worked for one of the newspapers described this censorship.

> If we carried news unfavorable to the home government, we immediately received phone calls from them [the governmental agencies]. Sometimes, he [the branch publisher] was subject to indirect pressure from headquarters in Seoul. Headquarters, pressured by the KCIA, threatened to stop sending him its master newspaper if he continued to show a poor performance in self-censorship. This caused him, when he received some delicate news reports, to call the Consulate General in order to ascertain whether the news could be printed. The government side [the Consulate General and the KCIA "station"] even prohibited him from printing translated articles from the New York Times on the Korean bribery affair in Congress by saying that "it is unnecessary to inform the community members, who are unable to read English, of the scandal."

Regardless of this direct and indirect pressure from the home government, the community newspapers try to avoid upsetting the Consulate General simply because the latter is a vital source of news, news that the Consulate General generates in dealing with community affairs. In addition, the community newspapers need moral and material support from the Consulate General when they host major cultural activities for the general community. Consequently, Korean immigrants in the New York metropolitan area receive community and homeland news that is directly or indirectly censored. Through this censorship, the home government attempts to manipulate Korean immigrants in order to isolate and defeat its opponents. This is one of the mechanisms by which Korean immigrants achieve ethnic solidarity.

This South Korean policy of "implanting in overseas Koreans a positive outlook on the fatherland" does not always work. This is so partly because the publishers of the newspapers cannot control the professional ideology of their reporters. Seven of the eight reporters (excluding photographers) employed by the two newspapers are first-rate professional journalists who have long working experience with major daily newspapers in Seoul. The majority of them came to the United States in order to study at American universities. Partly because of their higher education and partly because of their rearing in the antigovernment tradition of South Korean reporters (this tradition is still manifest in a recent declaration for the autonomy of the press by a group of reporters of the Joong Ang Ilbo in Seoul), they have an objective eye in dealing with news. There are, of course, conspicuous exceptions. In general, however, professional ideology and pride frequently dictate that the reporters write "unexpected" articles or essays that are critical of the home government.[5] In one case, two reporters engaged in a serious dispute with their publisher over coverage of an important anti-Park meeting. They insisted on covering it, but their boss would not let them go. The two reporters did not cover the meeting.

Involvement in Community Politics. By supporting different groups of community leaders, the two community newspapers have had a great impact upon community politics. In this area, their most important role has been to raise issues and mold opinions.

As we have noted, the politics of the New York Korean community has centered in the leadership of the Korean Association of Greater New York. In the 1976 presidential election of that association, two groups of businessmen, both of whom were loyal to the home government, clashed. One group, led by Mr. B, represented the established leadership; the other group, faced with the first group's change in the electoral law, was unable to list its candidate, Mr. Z (a college professor), on the ballot. The latter group, which was partly financed by Mr. D, a big businessman, then formed a rival association named the Korean Community Federation and elected a lawyer as its president. In 1978, a greengrocer, Mr. P, who was supported by the Korean Produce Retailers Association, won the presidency of the Korean Association of Greater New York and ousted the establishment represented by Mr. B. The community newspapers were deeply involved in all these elections.

In 1976 the *Hankook Ilbo* sided with the antiestablishment group in the Korean Association. During the electoral campaign, the *Hankook Ilbo* almost daily attacked the way in which Mr. B's group ran the Korean Association and handled the election. The newspaper even engaged in a personal attack by quoting an accusation made against Mr. B by a businessman belonging to Mr. D's group: "You [Mr. B] said [to the South Korean prime minister] that some Koreans [in New York] should be abducted [from the United States to South Korea for their antigovernment activities] when you were in Seoul."

The reason why the *Hankook Ilbo*, the sole community newspaper at that time, undertook a press campaign against the establishment of the Korean Association of Greater New York is complex. First of all, Mr. B's group, whose solidarity was based on regional ties from Jeola province in Korea, was "clannish" and "manipulative" in handling some community activities. For example, the change in the electoral law was regarded as underhanded. Thus Mr. B's group was resented

[5] As we have seen in the discussion of community politics (chapter eight), these "unexpected" articles or essays were important sources for this study.

by the community in general. Second, Mr. K, the editor-in-chief of the *Hankook Ilbo*, was a friend of the college professor, Mr. Z, who withdrew his candidacy. Both graduated from a prestigious university in Seoul. Third, the consul general directly intervened in the election in favor of the new group of businessmen. A businessman associated with the antiestablishment group said, "The top persons [the Korean ambassador to the United Nations and the Korean consul general] think that they [Mr. B's group] are not capable of dealing with this growing Korean community. They [Mr. B's group] don't know how to connect the community with American society." This intervention was revealed in a long declaration that Mr. B wrote two years later, which was printed in a special issue of the Korean Association's newspaper and which, as we shall see, was published under special circumstances.

> At that time, when the election campaign was in full swing, the consul general mobilized, under the direction of ambassador H, all his personnel in order to force me to give up the presidency. At first, they attempted to persuade me with all kinds of sweet and beautiful words. But I did not bow to their pressure. At last, they resorted to a press campaign aimed at calling a public hearing, which would then ostracize me. The ambassador, a big businessman, and Mr. K [the editor-in-chief] campaigned together to elect Mr. Z [the college professor] president of the Korean Association of Greater New York. . . .[6]

When the *Joong Ang Ilbo* reemerged in New York City in the spring of 1976, the Korean Association, led by Mr. B, allied itself with that newspaper. The alliance was based upon mutual necessity. The *Joong Ang Ilbo* needed the Korean Association and its influence to expand its circulation, and the Korean Association needed a mouthpiece to defend and advertise the community activities it conducted. In addition, Mr. B and the publisher of the newspaper were close friends. The position of the Korean Association, whose image had been badly tainted among Koreans by a barrage of press attacks in the *Hankook Ilbo*, was strengthened and enhanced by the favorable coverage the *Joong Ang Ilbo* gave to its activities. Staff members of the Korean Association and reporters of the *Joong Ang Ilbo* frequently drank together at Korean restaurants and bars.

In the 1978 election the *Hankook Ilbo* again criticized the Korean Association for the way in which it handled the electoral procedures. (We might recall that the Korean Association chose one of its board members, a wig importer-wholesaler, to run for the presidency.) At

[6] *New York Hanin Wolbo*, April 24, 1978.

the same time, the *Hankook Ilbo* systematically promoted and defended the views and positions taken by the Korean Produce Retailers
Association. On the other hand, the *Joong Ang Ilbo* interpreted elec-
tion-related events in favor of the established leadership of the Korean
Association. In 1978, no evidence could be found to show that the consul general directly intervened in the election. But this time personal
patronage and loyalty were responsible for the deep involvement of
the two community newspapers. Mr. P, the candidate representing the
Korean greengrocers, was a friend of Mr. K, the editor-in-chief of the
Hankook Ilbo; Mr. K, Mr. P, and Mr. Z all earned bachelor's degrees
in political science from the same private university in Seoul. This
"alumni" connection constituted one of the reasons why Mr. K engaged
in the press campaign in favor of each of his alumni brothers and
against the establishment of the Korean Association during the two
elections. But also, in the election of 1978 Mr. K received a favor from
Mr. P: Mr. P extended his personal endorsement of Mr. K's notes when
the latter applied for a loan of $20,000 from the New York branch of
the Korea Exchange Bank. This "secret" exchange of favors was made
public in a violent incident in a Korean bar.

On the night of April 15, 1978, some of the *Hankook Ilbo* staff, including reporters, the publisher, Mr. K, and other personnel, went to a
Korean bar and accidentally encountered there Mr. B and some of his
friends, who were *taekwondo* instructors. Seeing Mr. K, his staunch
enemy, Mr. B, somewhat intoxicated, seemed to "lose his reason."
Mr. B approached the table occupied by the *Hankook Ilbo* men and
began to scuffle with Mr. K, shouting that "you are selling [the support
of] the *Hankook Ilbo*. I got information that you have received a favor
from Mr. P." Physical violence erupted between the *Hankook Ilbo* men
and Mr. B's group, and policemen were called in.

On the next day the *Hankook Ilbo* reported the incident, bitterly denouncing the "unreasonable" and "immoral" action of Mr. B. Mr. B was
also criticized on television. The *Joong Ang Ilbo*, however, reported
the event in a neutral tone. Personal charge and countercharge followed. The *Hankook Ilbo* reported an "open secret" among Korean
businessmen that Mr. B was once interrogated by the home government
on the charge of fraudulent commercial deals when he visited Seoul.
In response, Mr. B's group revealed through the *Joong Ang Ilbo* that
Mr. P, the candidate supported by the *Hankook Ilbo* and the greengrocers, was charged with "smuggling diamonds" [from the United
States into South Korea] when he made a brief trip to Seoul.

With public opinion overwhelmingly against him, Mr. B had to find
a way by which he could defend himself and the Korean Association
he represented. This time he could not issue a declaration in the form

of a newspaper advertisement, which is a conventional means for community leaders to express and disseminate their views. Mr. B had to do something more to improve his public image and that of "his" Korean Association because the incident took place only two weeks before the election, in which one of his close associates was a candidate. Moreover, the *Joong Ang Ilbo* would not carry Mr. B's declaration because of an unwritten ethical code of the press, the violation of which would antagonize the *Hankook Ilbo*. In fact, the *Hankook Ilbo* men telephoned their colleagues at the *Joong Ang Ilbo* and urged them not to carry a declaration by Mr. B's group. Consequently, in order to disseminate Mr. B's version of the incident as well as to publicize the achievements of the Korean Association, Mr. B and his associates decided to publish a special issue of the *Hanin Wolbo*, the organ of the Korean Association, which had been intermittently published for a limited audience. The *Joong Ang Ilbo* helped Mr. B's group to publish the issue; the editor-in-chief wrote and edited "almost all the articles and essays" intended to advertise the achievements of the Korean Association. One of the essays, entitled "This Is True," with Mr. B as its writer, denounced Mr. K personally. The essay documented all the "unfair and irresponsible articles" written anonymously by Mr. K. This special issue of the *Hanin Wolbo* was mailed to all the Korean householders in the New York metropolitan area, whose addresses were available to the Korean Association. As noted earlier, Mr. P, representing the greengrocers, won the election.

CONCLUSION

The community media, especially the press, are a major mechanism for sustaining and to some extent reinforcing Korean nationalism and culture. By upholding common Korean values and sentiments, the media integrate the segmented and differentiated life patterns of the Korean community. Since Korean immigrants have not yet established natural residential enclaves, the various noteworthy community activities run by organizations or individuals are publicized by the mass media; the community also responds through the media. Like the churches, the ethnic media are thus extremely effective in continuing and cementing together a community without a territorial base.

Within this general media role, we have identified and described some of the specific relationships between the press and secondary associations, the home government, and community politics. First, the community press is the place where secondary associations advertise their activities and thus compete in claiming prestige and status that will be recognized by the community as a whole. With such paid advertisements and with local reporting, secondary associations gain a general audience and recruit a selective membership. In addition, the community press itself is an organizer of major cultural activities. Second, we have noted that the community press raises some issues and sometimes provokes controversies that invite participation and reaction from various segments of the community. The community press thus expands community activities. But, in raising issues, the press finds it difficult to cross one particular boundary: it cannot question the legitimacy of the authoritarian rule of the home government or criticize its policies with regard to the United States government or the Korean-American communities; nor can it expose the corruption and crimes of agents of the home government. This is so because the community press, like most community organizations and like a free press generally, is subject to strong pressures and even coercion from the home government. Finally, the community press, by taking partisan positions, politicizes community elections and thus stimulates the interest of community members in community politics. Since community leaders must deliver their message to the community as a whole, personal animosity or alliance between a newspaper and a particular group of leaders has been a fundamental element in community politics.

PART IV

The Basis of the New York Korean Community in the Historical Development of Korea

CHAPTER TEN

The Origin of the Character Structure
of Korean Immigrants

W<small>E HAVE</small> seen how deeply Korean immigrants are committed to so-cioeconomic mobility both in their business enterprises and in their community activities. Korean immigrants have ventured into almost every kind of retail business. In the process, they have invaded black ghettos and touched off racial conflict. Korean immigrants are willing not only to enter the ghettos but also to toil unceasingly, as their record in taking over fruit and vegetable businesses from Jewish or Italian proprietors indicates. But partly because of a strong tendency to migrate to the suburbs after achieving economic success in the inner city, Korean immigrants have not created an inner-city ghetto like Chinatown.

It is remarkable that Koreans have made economic gains even when the United States economy has been troubled by structural obstacles and when the urban economy, in the case of New York City, has seemed no longer able to support an influx of new immigrants. Moreover, as we have indicated, Korean immigrants have entered and succeeded in small businesses even though a high degree of centralization and bureaucratization has typified the dominant business structure. The economic aggressiveness of Korean immigrants has to some extent offset this structural limitation. No other immigrant group that has entered the United States since the Immigration Act of 1965 has achieved such rapid economic mobility as have Koreans. In New York City, for instance, Filipino immigrants have been negligibly active in small business although they have entered this nation at the same time as Koreans and are, like Koreans, carefully selected by the United States immigration law, which puts a heavy emphasis on medical professionals.[1] And Chinese immigrants to New York are largely concentrated in Chinatown, where they have not yet significantly expanded their business enterprises beyond such traditional businesses as hand laundries and restaurants.[2]

---

[1] Illsoo Kim and Tania Azores, *A Preliminary Report on Asian Americans in New York*, submitted to the Asian American Mental Health Research Center, 1975.

[2] Ibid.

This disparity in the socioeconomic adjustment of new immigrant groups leads us to raise the following questions: (1) How do the cultural and motivational traits, or social character, that immigrants internalized in their homeland support or impede their socioeconomic success in the new land? (2) How are homeland experiences in urbanization, economic mobility, and educational achievement related to socioeconomic mobility, psychological adjustment, and the formation of communities in the new land? These two questions are interdependent. The first focuses on the long-term historical and cultural processes that mold a national character. With respect to the second, we have already discussed the rapid urbanization and economic development of South Korea; recent Korean immigrants underwent these changes before their arrival in the new land. We have also pointed out that this rapid economic development has effectively removed traditional barriers to migration. South Koreans who have already migrated from rural areas to cities are psychologically ready for emigration from the homeland to other nations, especially to the United States. The rapid economic development has also caused a revolution of rising expectations that has in turn spurred economic, geographic, and social mobility. In this context, we have noted that highly professional, well-educated, and sophisticated urban middle-class Koreans, most of whom could not "make it" within the new economic structure of South Korea, have shown a strong propensity to emigrate to the United States. In sum, Korean immigrants have experienced a "Great Transformation" within South Korea, a rapid industrialization and modernization whose pace is much faster than it was in most Western nations. This experience has contributed to their economic shrewdness and aggressiveness and to their unrivaled commitment to work and mobility in the new land.

But this is only a partial explanation of why Korean immigrants are so committed to upward mobility. In this chapter we shall view Korean immigrants' motivational structure in a broader cultural and historical context, as it has evolved from a preexisting national character.[3] We cannot attempt to provide a definitive answer to the question of why one immigrant group "takes off" while others lag or seem to be overcome by the very process of immigration. Instead, we can make some suggestions for further investigation in the form of hypotheses derived

---

[3] The use of this cultural and institutional perspective in explaining the interconnection between ethnicity and economic structure can be traced back to Max Weber and Werner Sombart, both of whom addressed the problem of how purely cultural and religious behavior and attitudes are transferred to economic behavior. See Max Weber, *The Protestant Ethic and the Spirit of Capitalism*, New York, Charles Scribner's, 1958; Werner Sombart, *The Quintessence of Capitalism*, London, T. F. Unwin, 1915.

from an analysis of the Korean immigration since the Immigration Act of 1965.

THE EXTERNAL FACTORS OF KOREAN HISTORY

Korea, which occupies a small peninsula between the Sea of Japan and the Yellow Sea, is overshadowed by the vast Asian continent. The historical fate of Korea has been interlocked with the rise and fall of military powers on mainland China and in Manchuria, Mongolia, and Japan. Korea was subject to two great Chinese invasions in the sixth century A.D., Mongolian conquerors in the thirteenth century, Japanese piratical raids during the thirteenth and fourteenth centuries, the two great Japanese invasions of 1592 and 1597, and the Manchu invasions of 1627 and 1638. These are only some major examples of many humiliating and devastating invasions by neighboring powers. Whenever Korea was subjugated by a foreign power, it underwent deep social, cultural, and political changes. The Chinese empires were especially influential. Korean kings were never called emperor, because Korea was a vassal state of Chinese empires since approximately A.D. 676; but Korea had been importing cultural and political institutions from China since 108 B.C., when Emperor Wu Ti of the Chinese Han dynasty established four colonies in the northern part of the Korean peninsula. In this context, Japanese and Korean historians have constructed a theory of "geopolitical determinism," which looks to the geopolitical influences of foreign powers in explaining the historical processes of Korea. That theory implies that Korea has no internal dynamic of its own. Japanese colonialists misused the theory to legitimize their rule over Korea. According to Gi-back Lee, a Korean historian,

> Some Japanese scholars have vigorously expounded this concept [geopolitical determinism]. According to them, because of the peripheral geographic position of the Korean peninsula, Korea has been marked by a long but stagnant history with little contribution to the construction of a glorious world history. Korea has always suffered from oppressions by her neighboring powers such as Japan, China, Mongolia, and Manchuria because of the characteristic of the Korean peninsula—its multiple adjacency to those powers. . . .
> According to Japanese scholars, Korea could overcome this historical fatalism attributed to the Korean peninsula owing to a humanistic Japanese rule [over Korea].[4]

Proponents of the geopolitical theory neglected the unique and creative response of Koreans to the challenges of their peculiar location.

[4] Gi-back Lee, *Hangugsa sinron*, p. 1.

The continual foreign threats, invasions, and interventions have helped Korea achieve a special kind of national unity and solidarity. This has been expressed in an extreme form of political, bureaucratic, economic, and cultural centralism. Given the small size of the country, Korean centralism is unique in its intensity and duration. Its impact on the formation of Korean social structure is multidimensional: cultural and racial homogeneity, a lack of both regional and private civic institutions, and a class structure emphasizing mobility, especially during the later period of the Yi dynasty (1392-1910), are among the social elements that have directly or indirectly resulted from an intense form of Korean centralism.

The Korean State Bureaucracy. The Silla kingdom (ca. A.D. 300-935) first unified the Korean peninsula in 676 by attacking and conquering the two other Korean kingdoms: Koguryo in the north, which included a substantial portion of southern Manchuria, and Paekche in the southeastern portion of the peninsula. The bureaucracy of the Silla dynasty became pervasive and ubiquitous. For instance, a government document from 755, which was revised every three years for the purposes of taxation and corvée, listed the population of four villages by sex and age, grade of houses, cows and horses owned, amount of land cultivated, and even by ownership of taxable trees.[5] The village, or *chon*, was the smallest administrative unit in Silla society. It was settled by an average of ten consanguineous families and was governed by a village chief appointed by the central government. When the authority of the central bureaucracy began to decline in the mid-eighth century, the Silla dynasty attempted to introduce a rudimentary form of the Chinese civil-service examination system. But the system was not fully accepted. Its operation was imperfect due to the opposition of hereditary nobles, whose status was embodied in a rigid hereditary system of hierarchical classifications called the "bone ranks system." However, the Silla dynasty collapsed mainly because local lords emerged and cut state revenues by destroying the tax base.

Centralism reemerged during the Koryo dynasty (A.D. 935-1392), which was established by Wang Geon, a general and local lord who rose to power during the last days of the Silla dynasty. Under the Koryo dynasty the state continued to own all the land. In order to destroy local military lords and the aristocratic families, many of whom were "meritorious subjects" who helped to found the new dynasty, King Kwang-jong adopted the civil service examination system from China in 958 and recruited Confucian literati as bureaucrats. Furthermore, the new government bureaucrats, the *yangban*, were divided into two groups, military and civil; each group was dependent upon

[5] Ibid., pp. 98-99.

the king. The power basis of the literati officials was not solid, because the Koryo dynasty accepted Buddhism as both the state religion and as a magic force to help repel foreign aggression, especially that of Mongolian invaders. Thus Buddhist monks and aristocratic families began to form a formidable upper class, and after 982 they frequently revolted against the king. In addition, the king's recruitment of Confucian literati through the use of civil service examinations led to an unbearable discrimination against the older military families. The grievances of military officials deepened and led to a military coup in 1170. The coup was followed by nine decades of military rule in which the king was a puppet. Even during the consecutive dictatorships of several military families, centralized rule continued; no independent and rivalrous local elites emerged, as happened in feudal Japan. During this period (1170-1258), the Koryo dynasty engaged in a series of wars with Mongolians and thus created the national solidarity they needed.

It was during the Yi dynasty (A.D. 1392-1910) that the central state bureaucracy again became formal and rigid. General Yi Song-gye, who ascended to the throne by a palace coup during the golden age of Neo-Confucianism, looked to Korean Neo-Confucianists, followers of the Chinese scholar Chu Hsi (1130-1200), for the principles of his government. He consolidated his new dynasty by adopting Neo-Confucianism as a state creed and by undertaking land reforms that favored a group of Neo-Confucianists who in turn gave ideological support to the new dynasty and thereby legitimized rule by the Confucian creed. These changes brought forth two important social consequences. First, Confucian political, social, and ethical ideals formed the dominant value system defining social relationships in Yi society and thus became firmly embedded in the structure of the Korean national character. Second, a ruling stratum of Confucian literati emerged on the basis of prebendal offices and became the class whose idealized character was the model for the rest of the population. Competitive civil service examinations became the basic avenue for achieving upward social mobility.

Class and Status in Yi Society. Yi society was stratified into four social classes or status groups. The *yangban*, a ruling class, occupied the top rung of the social ladder by monopolizing virtually all government positions. In principle, the rulers obtained their *yangban* status by passing examinations. In return for their service to the government, they acquired a prebendal right to the yield of state lands or to other public income. In addition, they were exempt from taxation, the corvée, and military service. Since they were Confucian literary generalists, they (like Chinese Mandarins) had little technical knowledge and could not perform such specific administrative functions as collecting taxes or building and repairing waterways and irrigation systems. The *jung-in* class (ideographically, middlemen) consisted of technical professionals such as medical doctors, translators, weathermen, accountants, legal experts, copiers, painters, geographers, and policemen. They were hired to do the specialized administrative work of the government. A large number of the *jung-in* were sons of the *yangbans'* concubines, who were officially deprived of the right to take the civil service examinations. Since they claimed but were denied *yangban* status, the boundary between *yangban* and *jung-in* was often obscure. The *sangmin* class (commoners) constituted the majority of the population. Peasants, merchants, artisans, and fishermen, they were the citizens burdened with the duties necessary to sustain the administrative regime, the *yangban*, the *jung-in*, and the court. They paid heavy taxes, manned the corvée, and were subject to military service. Since the economic ideology of the government favored agriculture and despised trade, the status of peasants was higher than that of merchants, artisans, or craftsmen. At the bottom of Yi society was the *cheonmin* class, the lowborn, composed of serfs, slaves, butchers, actors, shamans, *gisaeng* (female entertainers), acrobats, and clowns. *Cheonmin* status was theoretically hereditary.

This division of the Yi population into four classes is a social fiction —an ideal-typical blueprint constructed by the *yangban*. If we consider the mobility patterns of the non-*yangban* classes, we will see that the class structure of Yi society was highly volatile. It could not maintain strict and rigid boundaries among the four classes. An analysis of the dynamics of Yi social classes will provide us with insight into the national character of contemporary Koreans.

Mobility Patterns of the Yi Classes. Mainly for the purposes of taxation and corvée, the central government conducted a comprehensive census every three years. Every household in Korea had to update its *hojeog*, a brief history of its family. Utilizing such *hojeog* materials from the Taegu area, located in the southeastern part of Korea, Shikata Hiroshi, a Japanese political economist, pioneered in the study of the class structure of Yi society. The following is a brief summary of Shikata's findings.[6] (1) The total population of the area was relatively

[6] The following table indicates the long-range upward class mobility among the population in the Taegu area, as percentage of households by social classes:

Year	Yangban	Sangmin	Cheonmin	Total	(N)
1690	9.2	53.7	37.1	100.0	(3,156)
1783-89	37.5	57.5	5.0	100.1	(3,092)
1858	70.3	28.2	1.5	100.0	(2,985)

SOURCE: Hiroshi Shikata, *Ijoingue gwanhan sinbun gyegub-byeoljeog gwanchal* [A

stable during the period from 1670 to 1858. (2) During the same period, the percentage of *yangban* households increased from 9.2 to 70.3 percent; *cheonmin* (lowborn) households decreased from 37.1 to 1.5, and *sangmin* (commoners') households dropped from 53.7 to 28.2 percent. In percentage of population during the same period the *yangban* increased from 7.4 to 48.6 percent, and the commoners fell from 49.5 to 20.1 percent. And, during the period from 1690 to 1789 (roughly), serfs fell from 43.1 percent of the population to 15.9 percent. (3) This shift in the population of each class was not due to a differential natural rate of increase within each class but to a long process of social mobility. That is to say, a large number of commoners moved up into the *yangban* class, while the overwhelming majority of serfs achieved the status of commoners and subsequently jumped up into the *yangban* class.

This massive upward mobility was not confined to the area of Taegu. Similar studies of other areas show almost identical results.[7] Yi society did not adhere to the status boundaries formally recognized by the central government: the *yangban* class failed to monopolize status because of a "*yangbanization* of the entire population." There are basic underlying factors explaining this mobile class structure. Shikata, for instance, identified some patterns of formal or informal upward mobility. The patterns include raising one's status by faking birth records, by marriage, or by acquiring higher status from the government in return for the contribution of grain and money. Keeping in mind the findings of Shikata and other Korean scholars, we can identify and describe other structural factors accounting for this mobility that existed even in the preindustrial and traditional society.

---

study of the population of the Yi dynasty by social classes], trans. from Japanese to Korean by the Sociology Department of Yihwa University, Seoul, Yihwa University Press, 1962, p. 25.

NOTE: For a technical reason, the *jung-in* class (or professionals) and the nonserf *cheonmin* class (or the low-born) were included in the category of the *sangmin* class (or commoners). Thus the category of the *cheonmin* class was entirely made up of serfs who, unlike household slaves, maintained separate residences from masters.

[7] Some Korean scholars have recently added qualitative expansions to Shikata's study, which was originally published in 1939. Among the recent studies on the class structure of Yi society are: Yong-sop Kim, "Joseon hugie iseoseo eui sinbunje dong-yo wa nongji jeomyu" [Ownership and change in the status system in the later period of the Yi dynasty], *Sahag Yeongu*, no. 15, 1963; Sok-jong Chong, "Joseon hugie sinbunje bungoe" [The breakdown of the status system in the later period of the Yi dynasty], *Daedong Munhwa Yeongu*, no. 9, 1972; Yong-hi Choi, "Imjin waenan eui saehoe dong-yo" [The Imjin Japanese invasion and social unrest], *Hangug Yeongu*, 1975. A comprehensive analysis of the class structure of Yi society can be found in Jong-mock Son, *Joseon sidae dosi sahoe yeongu* [A study of the urban society of the Yi dynasty], Seoul, Il Ji Sa, 1977, pp. 112-200.

First of all, this class mobility was partly due to the way in which the civil service examination was operated. The Korean examination system can be appreciated as an enlightened form of recruiting civil servants, for the Yi dynasty did not legally discriminate against commoners in setting eligibility requirements for the examination.[8] For instance, a recent study indicates that

> . . . the civil examination system during the early part of the Yi dynasty was not closed to all who were not members of the *yangban* class. It was open to commoners who qualified by devoting their energies to Confucian scholarship. While it cannot be denied that one's *yangban* lineage background and membership in a certain influential clan offered clear advantage in the civil examinations, there was at the same time no restriction against men of commoner origin taking part in this important state recruitment system. . . .
>
> As a consequence, the social stratification of early Yi Korea was probably not as rigid as has been once believed and the class barrier between commoners and *yangban* was less insurmountable.[9]

In addition, since the examination was the only outlet for upward social mobility, persons at the bottom of the society who were ineligible to take the examination resorted to every possible technique to qualify. In 1538 a court historian commented on this type of covert upward mobility.

> The recruitment examination is of major importance to the state, and candidates are allowed to participate only after their four ancestors (father, paternal grandfather, paternal great grandfather, and maternal grandfather) have been screened. This [screening] is aimed at differentiating the lineage background [of candidates] so that the channel of recruitment may remain untainted. Recently, however,

---

[8] There was a controversy over this issue. For instance, Sang-baek Yi, an expert on the social stratification of the Yi dynasty, noted: "There was an important restriction based on one's social status, and, in principle, no one but a *yangban* was qualified for the civil service examination." Sang-baek Yi, *Hangugsa: Geunse jeongi pyeon* [Korean history: early modern times], Seoul, Jindan Haghoe, 1962, pp. 278-279. But Yong-ho Choe, in his recent study of the civil-service examination system of the Yi dynasty, argued that the central government placed no legal restrictions on participation by commoners. He specifically quoted the Great Codes of the Yi dynasty, which stipulated eligibility for the examination: "The Great Codes stipulate that a person in any of the following categories is to be barred: (1) one who, having been convicted of a crime, is permanently excluded from government service; (2) sons of corrupt officials; (3) sons and grandsons of remarried widows and of immoral women; and (4) descendants of concubines." Yong-ho Choe, "Commoners in Early Yi Dynasty Civil Examinations: An Aspect of Korean Social Structure, 1392-1600," *Journal of Asian Studies* 33 (1974): 612-614.

[9] Choe, "Commoners in Early Yi Dynasty," p. 637.

public morality has deteriorated, and men born of concubines, descendants of merchants and artisans, and men of low birth, completely disregarding their positions, illegally take part in the examinations, either by fabricating their family registries or by falsely including a governmental official among the four ancestors, or, in the cases of men born of immoral women, forging names of their sponsors.[10]

Furthermore, the timing of the civil service examination, which was officially triennial, was subject to the whims of the king. Whenever some good fortune fell from heaven, "irregular examinations" took place as part of a national festival.[11]

All these peculiarities of the examination system resulted in an oversupply of *yangban* in relation to the limited number of jobs available in the state bureaucracy, for Yi society was based on a primitive agrarian economy with a limited need for government functionaries. At the top level of the central bureaucracy, this oversupply mainly contributed to factional striving among individual patronage networks, which were not based on hereditary classes or parties. Court bureaucrats fought one another over such issues as the proper period of mourning for a deceased queen, criticism of the writings of a court historian on the subject of a court event, and the designation of an heir apparent. Court battles over the limited job opportunities constituted the most fundamental aspect of politics during the Yi dynasty. The great purges of the literati that occurred in 1498, 1504, and 1545 were examples of this intense court politics.[12] After such purges, degraded *yangban* families that were excluded from the power circles in Seoul settled predominantly in rural areas. They became the *hyangban*, or rural *yangban*.

These processes were the specific means of *"yangbanizing"* the lowborn rural population. Gregory Henderson, a Koreanologist, has written about the degradation of *yangban* families into *hyangban*.

Those who thought themselves eligible steadily increased, but the number of jobs that were the formal justification for status apparently remained, until the coming of foreign influence, not much over 1,000, hopelessly few in proportion to the demand. As generations passed, most *yangban* found themselves ever more distant from their ancestor's position and from their own possibility of renewing it. The result on the one hand tended to sanction almost any scheme—in-

[10] Quoted in ibid., p. 615.   [11] Lee, *Hangugsa sinron*, pp. 211-212.
[12] For a study in English of these factional strifes, see E. Willett Wagner, *The Literati Purges: Political Conflict in Early Yi Korea*, Cambridge, East Asian Research Center, Harvard University, 1974.

fluence peddling, corruption, or even crime, however base—in order to get a government position. On the other, it contributed to the creation of an enormous "in-between" class of shadowy or pretender *yangban*. Many of these had "fallen from the capital" and are often called by Koreans *hyangban* or *t'oban*, "local squires. . . ."

Gradually, capital connections wore thin; the elite function of influencing or moderating local officials through central connections eroded. Strict marriage custom, avoidance of both work and money, the paraphernalia and food requirements of Confucian ceremony became harder and harder to maintain. Marriage with daughters of other local families, then commoners, finally even slaves, was contracted. Lands were divided or forfeited to the more powerful. Heavy debt brought sale or exchange of status.[13]

This forced migration of *yangban* families to rural areas and their contribution to the "*yangbanization*" of local people partly caused a higher proportion of *yangban* in the rural population than in the urban. For instance, according to Shikata, the *yangban* population in the urban part of Taegu increased from 9.7 percent in 1708 to 15.1 percent of the total population in 1858, while the *yangban* in the rural area of Taegu jumped from 8.2 percent to 61.3 percent during the same period of time.[14]

The greater increase of the *yangban* population in rural areas than in cities needs further explanation. Cities were not a proper place for the downwardly mobile *yangban* to make a livelihood. Because of Confucian status norms, the *yangban* who lost their government jobs could not engage in trade or crafts, which, as we shall see, began to rise in the private sectors of the urban economy after the eighteenth century. On the other hand, the poverty-stricken commoners and the serfs or slaves in rural areas, who could not raise their status, migrated or escaped to cities.[15] In order to prevent peasants and serfs from leaving the land and to maintain the corvée and taxation system, the Yi central government used a nationwide identification system called the Hopae-beob.

This gradual collapse of the Korean class and status system continued for almost five hundred years. Given the general internal process of "*yangbanization*," which was linked to the bureaucratic monopolization of scarce economic rewards and status symbols, several external events hastened the loss of a status monopoly by the original *yangban* class. The Japanese invasions of 1592 and 1597, which shook the whole

[13] Gregory Henderson, *Korea: The Politics of the Vortex*, Cambridge, Harvard University Press, 1968, pp. 41-43.

[14] Son, *Joseon sidae*, p. 176.   [15] Ibid., pp. 179-181.

East Asian continent, including China, caused a tremendous change in Yi society. Yi Korea underwent a massive displacement of population, starvation, and a breakdown of its system of taxation. The war also caused a breakdown of the class and status system. Slaves or serfs burned almost all government records concerning the registration of slaves. In addition, the central government sold titles to commoners and to serfs in return for grain contributions as a supplement to tax revenues, which had dwindled owing to the war's devastation. During times of war, the government adopted the Myeoncheon system, liberation from legally defined lowborn status, as an incentive for recruiting members of the previously despised lowborn classes into the army: slaves, Buddhist monks, and sons of concubines. In order to increase and reward the resistance and heroism of guerrilla warriors, the government created a special reward system: a higher status or government positions were granted to commoners and serfs who presented Japanese heads as evidence of their bravery. Frequently, however, they beheaded starving Koreans. The Japanese invasions thus added momentum to the lower classes' drive to liberate themselves from the shackles of the estate system of the traditional society.

The Primitive Capitalism of Yi Society. Nevertheless, the emergence of a primitive capitalism in Yi society during the middle of the eighteenth century is perhaps the most crucial factor responsible for the gradual but continuous increase in status mobility. Although no systematic study has as yet been conducted on the relationship between the development of a money economy and the breakdown of the traditional class structure, Korean scholars have pointed out that the emergence of trade was followed by a rapid increase in economic mobility, as Shikata indicated, after the late eighteenth century.[16]

In China the powerful state bureaucracy, plus a peculiar Confucian ethos, was a formidable traditional barrier to the development of Western-type capitalism.[17] In spite of some major differences, this statement is roughly applicable to Yi Korea. In Yi society individual economic status was determined by political position. The highest economic position was a prebendal office, but lower economic institutions such as craft and merchant guilds and markets were also controlled by the central bureaucracy. No legal concept of the inviolability of private property emerged. In the Confucian ethos, technical experts and traders were despised; Confucian scholar-generalists were extolled; and acquired wealth was not reinvested but spent as a secular means to

[16] For instance, see Lee, *Hangugsa sinron*, pp. 280-281.
[17] Max Weber, *The Religion of China*, trans. and ed. by Hans H. Gerth, New York, The Free Press, 1951, pp. 226-249.

good health, the accumulation of concubines, or the bureaucratic success of descendants. But Yi Korea was different from China in many respects.[18] Partly because of the small size of the country (Korea is smaller than most medium-sized Chinese provinces), the Korean central bureaucracy was much more direct and pervasive in its effect on the underlying population than was the Chinese. Yi Korea did not suffer as much as China did from regional or provincial particularism, especially financial particularism; and Yi Korea, unlike China, could easily carry out centralized and unified economic policies or reforms, which, as we shall see, could change the course of economic life.

In spite of the central bureaucracy, the recent consensus of Korean scholars is that Yi Korea developed some elements of modern capitalism.[19] For instance, Jo Gi-june, an expert on the Korean political economy, wrote in 1969: "It cannot be denied that, since the late eighteenth century, many elements conducive to modernization began to spring up from the internal structure of the Korean economy. The emergence of agrobusinessmen among feudal landlords, the growth of independent farmers among feudal tenant-farmers, the increase of currency and a money economy, the decline of government-run handicraft factories, and the predominance of independent, self-employed artisans—all these phenomena can be interpreted as signs of approaching modernization."[20]

The crucial factor underlying the emergence of a primitive capitalism lies in the government's shift of its taxation policy and its adoption of metal money as a universal means of exchange. After the Japanese invasions of 1592 and 1597, the taxation system was in disarray. Destruction of land registers during the war enabled prebendal officials to transfer taxable state land to their private possession. In order to increase revenues, the central government adopted the Daedongbeob, a tribute system in which rice replaced local products as a means of paying the state tax. This taxation policy, which began in 1608, aimed at eradicating the various irregularities produced by local officials who were brokers between taxpayers and the government.

Under the new taxation policy, local products no longer flowed di-

[18] Weber's brief description of traditional Korean society, in which he saw Korea in the context of China, is unreliable because of a number of erroneous statements based on false history. See Max Weber, *Religion of India*, trans. and ed. by Hans H. Gerth and Don Martindale, New York, The Free Press, 1967, pp. 269-270.

[19] This issue was an implicit and explicit reaction of Korean scholars to the so-called Japanese colonialists' perspective on Korean history, whereby many Japanese scholars argued that Korea did not generate the dynamics of capitalism until it was forced to open its door to Japan in the late nineteenth century.

[20] Gi-june Jo, *Hanguk gyeongje baldalsa* [The historical development of the Korean economy], Seoul, Bom Moon Sa, 1969, p. 3.

rectly to the Seoul government. Consequently, the government had to purchase the various goods necessary to run its vast bureaucratic organizations, including the military. A group of government contractors called the *gong-in* emerged to fill the government's orders. This government demand facilitated the expansion of private economic organizations such as handicraft factories and merchant and craft guilds. At the same time, government-run handicraft factories declined, and government-indentured artisans escaped to private sectors of the economy. Government-controlled markets and the monopoly rights of licensed traders over certain commercial items declined in favor of private markets, which were established throughout the countryside.[21] These new economic developments occurred almost simultaneously with the emergence of the money economy. The latter began in 1651, when coins replaced rice and textiles as a means of exchange.

This emergence of trade had a tremendous impact on the class and status system of Yi society. Capitalists largely came out of the *gong-in*, the government's contractors; but displaced peasants also became merchants, mainly peddlers—the so-called *bobusang*. In the late nineteenth century, these peddlers numbered about 2 million or 200,000, depending upon one's sources.[22] Despite frequent government warnings, the downwardly mobile *yangban* surreptitiously began to engage in trade, while non-*yangban* merchants purchased lands and government titles. Thus, by the late nineteenth century, social and economic status did not necessarily flow from political status: there was a strong tendency for commoners to become landlords or rich farmers and for the *yangban* to degrade themselves to tenants or poor farmers.[23] Taking advan-

---

[21] Since the early 1960s Korean historians and political economists have conducted detailed studies on these processes leading to the development of capitalism in Yi society. For a systematic and theoretical presentation of the development, see Kwan-woo Chon, *Hangugsa eui jaebalgyeon* [Rediscovery of Korean history], Seoul, Il Jo Gak, 1974, pp. 274-280.

[22] Son, *Joseon sidae*, p. 93. The *bobusang* formed a peddlers' guild, which emerged in the late nineteenth century as a most powerful civic organization controlling private markets throughout the country. But they did not develop themselves into a coherent merchant class. They did not demand their own trading terms against the various commercial restrictions and barriers imposed on them by the central government. Instead, they were co-opted by the central government: at the turn of the century they provided the government with postal, fire-fighting, body-guard, and intelligence-agency services; they frequently emerged as a terrorist group employed by the government against Christian-led democratic demonstrations.

Peddling, as an easy and quick way of making money beginning with only a little capital, had been a widespread phenomenon among Koreans until the recent rapid economic development. Korean immigrants' peddling activities in the United States inner cities might be derived from this old, lowest technique of commerce in their homeland.

[23] Kim, "Joseon hugie," p. 29.

tage of their professional and technical knowledge and their marginal status, members of the *jung-in* class (that is, the traditional professional and administrative classes) ascended economically. During the Japanese occupation from 1910 to 1945, a majority of the biggest landlords and merchants came from this class. Yet they lacked their own class identity, solidarity, and ideology. Many of them were collaborators with the Japanese as well as claimants of *yangban* status.

THE IMPACT OF THE STATE BUREAUCRACY ON THE FORMATION OF THE KOREAN CHARACTER

The Koreans of Yi society experienced both an upward social mobility and a circulation of elites, which is akin to the mobility attributed to modern mass society. In addition, the central bureaucracy was so ubiquitous that Yi society did not develop regional powers, local particularism, autonomous guilds, private armies, or civic guilds, all of which were associated with the development of feudalism and feudal traditionalism. The Yi dynasty is a classic example of what Karl A. Wittfogel called "Oriental Despotism." Traditional Korea never experienced the Western-type feudalism that conditioned the emergence of autonomous civic organizations and thereby of coherent, rigidly divided social classes. In addition, the powerful central bureaucracy conditioned a remarkable degree of ethnic and cultural homogeneity.[24] This plus the smallness of the country contributed to the formation of a highly atomized class structure in which social classes or groups were not able to define and enforce rigid boundaries, interests, and ideologies—that is, in which individuals were highly mobile. The central state bureaucracy provided a single but limited magnet by absorbing all purely social aspirations and by monopolizing the dominant status levels, symbols, ideologies, and bureaucratic reward systems. In addition, since provincial particularism was weak, the state bureaucracy could execute unified economic policies that contributed to the reshaping of the class structure by generating some capitalistic economic opportunities. Traditional Korean classes emerged but never stabilized into permanent castes or estates.[25]

[24] This cultural and ethnic homogeneity is best indicated by the heavy concentration of Korean family names. Three family names—Kim, Lee (Yi), and Park (Pak)—designated in the traditional society a bulk of the royal and the *yangban* clans. In 1975 there were a total of only 249 family names in South Korea; persons with these three names comprised 45 percent of the total population: Kim represented 22 percent, Lee 15 percent, and Park 8 percent. This concentration results largely from a covert upward mobility by families belonging to lower classes; people born to a low status clandestinely adopted the three names associated with a higher social status. For a statistical distribution of the South Korean population by family names, see the *Hankook Ilbo*, February 22, 1978.

[25] The pattern of Korean class and status mobility stands in contrast to that of

In the absence of class-bound or organization-bound norms or bonds, individual initiative largely determined economic success even in the traditional society. In traditional Korea the seeds of a social character with an elective affinity for survival in modern mass society were already sown. That is to say, if modern industrial society favors individuals who strive for rapid social mobility, Koreans have already prepared themselves historically and culturally. Largely due to the cultural and social legacy of centralism, Koreans are prepared to accept and emulate any new social and economic system once they view it as offering economic opportunities and as being powerful and ascendant. Long before the recent Korean immigration to America, this social character was already developed and had already adjusted to tremendous social and economic changes: the Japanese-imposed colonialism in 1910, independence, the Korean involvement with the United States since the end of World War I, and the Korean War. An emphasis on economic motivation and mobility has contributed to acculturation in the new land because it was already a deep part of contemporary Korean culture and values.[26]

For Koreans, education itself has become a national ideology because, in their Confucian past, the civil service examination provided the only official outlet for upward social mobility. Among Korean literati who were edged out of power positions in the central bureaucracy, an indigenous and original school of Confucianism, the Sil-hag school (a pragmatic school), began to emerge in the late sixteenth century. The Sil-hag school opposed the abstract, formalistic, void philosophy or ideology of the Neo-Confucianism that was embedded in the state bureaucracy: "they [the Sil-hag literati] sharply criticized Chu Hsi philosophy [Neo-Confucianism] on the basis of a rather systematic brand of textual criticism. From this beginning, the school came to

India, which is expressed in the concept of the "Sanskritization," whereby Indian subcaste groups move upward as groups by claiming a ritually higher status than has been recognized by local opinion.

[26] Richard Halloran, who once stayed in South Korea as a correspondent for the *New York Times*, observed one aspect of the Korean character:

Let me confess an unabashed admiration and affection for Korea and the Koreans. This is a rugged and sometimes harsh land and it breeds a tough and sometimes brutal people. But they work hard to make the best of the meager resources that nature has allotted them.

They are perhaps the most independent and individualistic people in Asia, loyal to their friends and fierce with their enemies.

The men are handsome, lay warranted claim to being hard drinkers and consider themselves the world's greatest lovers.

The women are beautiful. Koreans are romantic and stubborn, disconcertingly direct and warmly humorous. They are a feisty lot, not unlike my ancestors in Ireland—which may explain my feelings for them. (*New York Times*, October 3, 1976).

stand for the inductive method of research which led to application of this method to the fields of history, phonetics, and etymology. As a rebellion against the primarily deductive, literary, and abstruse methods of thought, this school was somewhat closer to Western and scientific viewpoints than were the Neo-Confucian schools; its advocates were also more open to Western influence and methodology."[27]

This Sil-hag school was later adopted and expanded by the *nam-in*, a factional group of Confucian literati, who were ousted from the central bureaucracy during the eighteenth century. It was also popular among such marginal social groups as the sons of concubines of the *yangban* and among the *jung-in* professional and administrative classes. When Korea began to accept Western culture in the late sixteenth century, largely via China, Sil-hag literati became agents introducing it. A large number of Sil-hag literati belonging to the *nam-in* faction converted to Roman Catholicism and were subjected to frequent persecutions by the central government. Although the Sil-hag school was never accepted by the central bureaucracy, many Korean scholars today argue that the school has, since the late nineteenth century, offered a powerful national ideology for modernizing Korean society.[28]

In the late nineteenth century American missionaries began to proselytize Koreans. North Koreans, especially in the northwestern provinces, accepted American Protestantism enthusiastically, especially Presbyterianism. They were often literati who were alienated from the central bureaucracy largely because of discrimination against North Koreans in access to government positons. (The theory behind this discrimination was that North Koreans, heavily intermixed with Manchurians or "northern barbarians," were ambitious, aggressive, and rebellious and that they were directly or indirectly influenced by the unorthodox Sil-hag school.) These Christianized North Korean literati "Koreanized" the American Protestant ethic. By emphasizing technical education and by building "national" factories, markets, and corporations, they created an indigenous capitalism, as opposed to that created by the invasion of Japanese capitalism after the late nineteenth century.[29]

This peculiar North Korean acceptance of American Protestantism has had an impact on the Korean immigration to the United States. As has been noted in chapter one, the older Korean immigrants to the

[27] Key P. Yang and Gregory Henderson, "An Outline of Korean Confucianism (Part 2): The Schools of Yi Confucianism," *The Journal of Asian Studies* 18 (1959): 268.

[28] Chon, *Hangugsa*, pp. 107-139.

[29] Kyong-bae Min, *Hangug minjog gyohoe hyeonseong saron* [The historical formation of Korean nationalistic churches], Seoul, Yonsei University Press, 1974, pp. 182-256.

United States were predominantly North Korean Christians; American Protestant missionaries in Korea persuaded them to emigrate to the Hawaiian Islands. The post-1965 Korean immigration, as we have noted, has also been heavily composed of former North Koreans who, with the advent of the North Korean communist regime, were forced to take refuge in South Korea. They are mostly Christians. We have also noted, in chapter six, that Korean ministers, most of whom were born and educated in North Korea, have immigrated to the United States and have assumed crucial leadership roles in the Korean community in the New York metropolitan area. These ministers have promoted a disciplined, Protestant moral life in the Korean community as a whole.

For Koreans, the high value placed on education has, since the late nineteenth century, made education an effective tool in accepting and adjusting to Western culture and technology. Koreans enthusiastically accepted American missionary schools as well as Japanese schools. In addition, they built their own schools: during the decade from 1910 to 1920, for instance, Koreans founded some 3,000 high schools and colleges.[30] The cultural emphasis on education helped Koreans prepare for emigration when, as we have noted, education such as medical training was required as a condition for entry into the United States. In addition, as we have seen in chapter three, the desire for "education for their children" constitutes one of the main pull factors for Korean migration to Seoul and to the United States.

The distinctive character of contemporary Koreans has evolved from the social structure that we have discussed. Koreans are both individualistic and marginal. They are pragmatic, concerned with "fruits" rather than "roots." They are culturally flexible in discarding cherished norms or vested ideals that might block their upward mobility. And they do not let traditional aversions of lack of experience interfere with their thirst for mobility. As we have seen, although they despised the idea of adornment via wigs, they embraced the wig business because it provided the only avenue for making money. They embraced the fruit and vegetable business not because they had an affinity with that business but because it was the one business that allowed an individual with a small amount of capital to succeed in competition with a highly capitalized chain store—by virtue of hard, continuous work, family exploitation, and devotion to business. The same motility enabled educated Koreans to embrace small business as an economic pursuit even after they failed to find acceptance as educated professionals in large-scale American corporations. In fact, given the exigencies of their economic position in the United States, the central values in the Korean

---

[30] Lee, *Hangugsa sinron*, p. 268.

personality appear to be a devotion to do whatever work is necessary for mobility and a complete motility in discovering economic opportunity. However, Koreans so far have not been attracted to organized crime.

Since the long tradition of centralism, which still exists in contemporary Korean society, deprived Korea of the strong intermediary social organizations that channel social mobility, individual success has been dependent upon individualistic means such as education, patronage, family loyalty, and chance. Mainly because of the lack of group or class norms, ideals, and notions of status honor, shady and dubious techniques are culturally permissible in pursuing economic goals. This commitment to success is identical with the success ideology of nineteenth-century American society, in which means were justified by economic ends.

Mainly because of long experience with a central state bureaucracy, Koreans are submissive to power in whatever form it takes. They quickly switch to what is viewed as an ascendant idea, fashion, or system. This power-conscious personality is well expressed in the Korean concept of *sadaesasang*, the ideology of worshiping bigness. Korean scholars use this concept to denote an historical Korean propensity to bow to the social systems, ideas, and culture of invading big powers. Again, the rise of the *sadaesasang* ideology is mainly due to the fact that Korea could not sustain, in the face of external invasions, a coherent and aristocratic upper class that would assume nationalistic leadership in political, economic, and cultural domains. Nor could the Korean upper class that did exist stabilize and rigidify a traditional cultural system to such an extent that Koreans would resist modernization, industrialization, and economic and cultural penetration by the Japanese and by Western societies. On the contrary, Koreans embraced the new whenever the new was powerful and promised economic opportunities and social mobility.

CONFUCIANISM AS A SOURCE OF THE KOREAN CHARACTER

The character structure manifested in contemporary Koreans originates from other sources than the traditional class and status structure. Given the single magnet of the central state bureaucracy, Confucianism has played an important role in motivating Koreans to strive toward prevalent economic rewards and status symbols.

As Max Weber noted in his essays on China, Confucianism was an ideological bulwark of traditionalism. Politically and socially, Confucianism functioned to pacify the masses by defining and maintaining "the Great Five Relationships"—father and son, husband and wife, ruler and subject, elder and younger, and friend and friend. Each of these relationships was governed by sanctified norms and ethics; rebelliousness against the established patterns constituted a cardinal sin. Economically, Confucianism hampered the development of rational, bourgeois capitalism because of its peculiar rationalization of the world. Confucianism offered no metaphysical foundation for manipulating or transforming society. It precluded radical change in economic, political, and social systems because it related them to a cosmic and harmonious order to which man should adjust.

In addition to these features of Confucianism, which tend to preclude modern, rational economic action, Weber provides us with two essential points that are central to our concern with Korean character formation. First, like the Puritans, Confucianists were sober men: they methodically controlled their impulses for immediate gratification. Second, Confucianism bred a practical rationality.[31] It was not concerned with a supermundane sense of "sin," as is the Judeo-Christian ethic, but with "shame" caused by improper social behavior. Since Confucianists lacked the inner constraint of the transcendental Western God and His eternal code of ethics, their behavior was flexible. Confucianists could modify their behavior in accordance with almost every situation, provided that the norms in that situation were either clearcut or sufficiently ambiguous to disallow loss of face. Thus Confucianists were traditionally "other-directed" men. These two Confucian qualities have become powerful dynamics when such capitalistic developing countries as South Korea, Taiwan, Hong Kong, and Singapore began to abandon traditionalism and launch economic development programs by accepting Western technology and capital. These four Confucian nations are front-runners among the latecomers to industrialization.

As far as the socioeconomic adjustment of Korean immigrants is concerned, there is a value congruence between Confucianism and the Protestant ethic in the sense that both of them are directed toward self-control and self-abnegation, even though they are derived from different sources and point to different rationalizations of the world.

---

[31] Weber noted, on the Confucian practical rationality: "A true prophecy creates and systematically orients conduct toward one internal measure of value. In the face of this the 'world' is viewed as material to be fashioned ethically according to the norm. Confucianism in contrast meant adjustment to the outside, to the conditions of the 'world.' A well-adjusted man, rationalizing his conduct only to the degree requisite for adjustment, does not constitute a systematic unity but rather a complex of useful and particular traits. . . . Such a way of life could not allow man an inward aspiration toward a 'unified personality,' a striving which we associate with the idea of personality. Life remained a series of occurrences. It did not become a whole placed methodically under a transcendental goal" (*The Religion of China*, p. 235).

We are not concerned here with the face-value differences between the two systems but with their manifest common consequences for the long-term internalization of values compatible with success in the modern world. That is to say, Confucianism is no longer a vital, manifest religion among contemporary Koreans; in the same way, original, theological Protestantism is no longer vital among white middle-class Americans. But contemporary Koreans still maintain Confucian values such as a concern for propriety, the control of impulses and emotions, respect for age, deference to authority, and industriousness. These Confucian values correspond to white middle-class Protestant values such as an emphasis on work, politeness, family authority, diligence, cleanliness, and neatness.[32]

Furthermore, a high proportion of Korean immigrants are in fact Protestants who have been closely affiliated with American Protestantism. For instance, the New York *Sunday News*, which largely reflects the values of the white lower-middle class entrenched in the inner city, deliberately emphasized this aspect of the Korean character.

> The Rev. Han told a story of an elderly immigrant that depicts the fiber of the Korean people.
> "The old man had little money and was in dire need of an operation," he said. "We took him to Kings County Hospital where he was operated on and released after full recovery. He was embarrassed because he had no money to pay. This bothered him even after we told him there were medical programs for the needy. The old man scrimped and saved and eventually paid the hospital bill in full, even though he didn't have to."[33]

The Confucian habit of saving face constitutes a core value among contemporary Koreans. For another example, a Korean community leader inflated some positive aspects of Korean community life in his address to the New York State Advisory Committee to the United States Commission on Civil Rights.

> Koreans are an extremely ambitious, industrious, law-abiding and diligent people. They have a great deal to contribute to the growth

[32] For instance, some studies conducted on the Japanese-American personality in a similar context argued that the high economic achievement of the Nisei, the second generation of Japanese Americans, was largely due to the compatibility of the values found among the American white middle class with the traditional Japanese values found among Japanese Americans. See William Caudill and George De Vos, "Achievement, Culture and Personality: The Case of the Japanese Americans," *American Anthropologist* 58 (1956): 1103-1126; Setsuko M. Nishi, "Japanese American Achievement in Chicago: A Cultural Response to Degradation," Ph.D. diss., University of Chicago, 1963, chapter xi.

[33] *New York Sunday News*, November 4, 1973.

and development of the United States. In Korea, the literacy rate is over 90 percent, one of the biggest in the world, and a remarkable fact for a country which is classed as underdeveloped. . . .

Koreans do not make demands on the American system. We don't draw welfare checks or unemployment benefits. As recent immigrants, there are not even very many of us who draw Social Security benefits. We don't want public housing or bilingual education or special social services. We don't want a free ride anywhere, anytime. Today, most Americans have grown up in a climate of affluence, and many people seem to feel that America owes them a living. We Koreans believe that it is we who are indebted to America.[34]

Confucian values and norms also imposed an indelible stamp on the institution of the Korean family, for they governed both intra- and interfamily relationships.

Within the family household an individual's status depended on his generation, relative age, and sex. Generation was the primary factor, and grandparents and parents of either sex had to be treated with considerable respect by their descendants. Within a generation, however, sex and age were the determinants; a wife was inferior to her husband, a sister to her brother, and a younger brother to his older brother. Within a larger societal context, an individual's status was in part related to his age but was also greatly related to the status of his family in society, whether noble or common, a family of scholars or of peasants. Family status also depended on the number of generations of ancestors whose memorial tablets were kept and honored.[35]

Largely from the influence of this Confucian past, Koreans still closely attach themselves to the family. Its preservation and propagation still constitutes a paramount social norm, and loyalties and obligations toward the family supersede all others. In order to ensure the continuation of the past in the present through the family, traditional Koreans systematically worshiped their ancestors. This ancestral worship still continues among contemporary urban Koreans: in the 1978 Chuseog (a national holiday for the memory of ancestors), more than a million Seoul citizens went to their rural villages in order to pay tribute to their deceased ancestors.[36] Furthermore, an individual is still defined and evaluated as a part of the family. One's success is con-

[34] "Equal Opportunity for Asian Americans in the New York Metropolitan Area," unpublished report by the New York State Advisory Committee, U.S. Commission on Civil Rights, 1974, pp. 136-138.

[35] Vreeland et al., *Area Handbook*, p. 85.

[36] *Joong Ang Ilbo*, September 18, 1978.

strued as a success for the family; one's failure is counted as a family failure. Koreans still scold their own family members by saying that "you are a shame to our family," or "you are a cause of disgrace to our family."

Nonetheless, the Korean family has undergone tremendous change in the rapid urbanization, industrialization, and modernization of South Korea. The nuclear family has begun to replace the three-generation extended family, the ideal traditional Confucian family form. Large-scale social institutions have begun to take over the original functions of the Korean family. Centers for the elderly and nursing homes have come into being, and gerontology has recently been accepted as a field of social science. And parental authority has declined in favor of the authority embedded in such large-scale social organizations, as the *New York Times* reported in the following story.

The challenge, however, can be disturbing within one's own family. Mr. Kang obeyed his father, who even chose his son's bride. But Mr. Kang's son has announced that he will pick his own wife, and the father agreed—provided he can still offer advice.

To assure continuity with tradition and the past, Mr. Kang insists on weekend family dinners and occasional trips to ancestral graves. And while Mr. Kang generally accepts the social changes washing over his country, he sometimes has glimmers of doubt.

"My roots were in the land," he says. "I can fall back on the farm, the large family we had, my father's memories. But my children's roots seem much weaker. These young people are better off. They are more assertive. And they have the right now to complain. But I don't know if that's enough."[37]

In spite of these recent changes, the institution of the family is still a primordial social force in South Korean society. According to a recent survey, 41.1 percent of Korean householders spend the largest portion of their income on the education of their children.[38] In the new land, this family-centered success ethic has greatly facilitated upward mobility. As has been noted, Korean success in labor-intensive small businesses presupposes the willingness of all family members to devote themselves to their family business. As a result, many Korean small businessmen in New York City are able to send their children to Ivy League schools. A Korean greengrocer said, with pride, "My son comes here every weekend from Princeton to help me." And of course Korean parents with school-age children worry about inner-city schools, saying

[37] *New York Times*, June 20, 1978.   [38] *Joong Ang Ilbo*, October 4, 1977.

that "we have to move to the suburbs for the education of our children."

CONCLUSION

The character structure of contemporary Koreans has evolved from the fluid class and status structure of Yi society as well as from Confucianism and Protestant Christianity. The central state bureaucracy, which derived its ideological support from Korean Confucianism, has indelibly marked the Korean character. An atomized class and status structure, cultural and ethnic homogeneity, and a lack of regionalism are derivatives of the long history of centralism. In this sense, it would not be an exaggeration to say that preindustrial Korean society was similar to modern mass society in the way that central political, bureaucratic, and economic institutions determined the biography of an individual.

Korean centralism has fostered distinctive traits that still exist among contemporary Koreans. Koreans are both marginal and individualistic. When they arrive in the affluent new land, where economic competition is not as great as in the homeland, they are quick to grasp every possible economic opportunity. In addition, their heritage of Korean Confucianism reinforces their economic acumen and family-centered success ethic. Sober-minded, industrious Korean immigrants have swiftly adjusted to marginal sectors of the United States economy that provide the merest toeholds for upward mobility. Korean immigrants are armed with a double-bladed cultural sword—Korean Confucianism on the one hand and their historical training by the central bureaucracy on the other. They dare to do sweatshop work in ghetto businesses and in the crime-ridden inner city. This kind of character gives Korean immigrants an elective affinity with marginal economic opportunities that American natives, who have more opportunities in the mainstream occupations, have shied away from. As we have witnessed, Koreans have conspicuously entered such labor-intensive businesses as the fruit-and-vegetable, fish, dry-cleaning, and garment-subcontracting businesses.

The character structure of Korean immigrants is reflected not only in their economic activities but also in their way of organizing basic community activities. As we have noted, the South Korean government has influenced major community activities by extending its power to its "subjects" in the new land. In this process, community leaders have emerged and attempted to advance themselves by carrying out South Korean policies toward the United States and the Korean community. They have expanded or politicized community affairs for the sake of establishing a patronage connection with the South Korean government. Such patronage has its historical roots in traditional society. Lately, under the rule of President Park, this mobility pattern effectively governed individual success in the business, intellectual, and political world. And in turn, partly because Koreans have lived for a long time under a central bureaucracy, the majority of Korean immigrants identify themselves with the Korean Consulate General, a surrogate of the South Korean government. This fact, plus the Confucian taboo against political rebellion, contributes to a remarkable degree to the Korean immigrants' passivity toward irregular, indecent, and inept behavior on the part of the home government.

The variety of secondary-group associations also manifests fundamental patterns of the Korean character structure. Membership in these associations is based on achieved rather than ascribed status. The members' previous upward mobility in education, urbanization, and professional occupations are responsible for this pattern of ethnic solidarity. No kinship or regional associations based on homeland provinces have emerged in New York's Korean community, because regionalism and kinship or clans are not a strong factor in determining social relationships among contemporary Koreans, though they have not entirely disappeared.

But the diverse secondary associations have not yet united toward establishing an ethnic solidarity. Like an individualistic Korean, each association has its own interest and ideology. Each conducts its own organizational activities by directly contacting the home government or the corresponding institutions in the new land. Korean immigrants cannot make the Korean Association powerful enough to coordinate, direct, and channel the various community activities. Like the Korean class structure in the homeland, the Korean community in New York is highly atomized and individualized. Moreover, the Korean propensity to "concretize" loyalties—that is, to avoid the abstractions of large numbers, in Confucian style—has caused them to seek group activities involving relatively few persons. Koreans personalize social relations within larger associations such as churches, alumni associations, and business associations by forming subdivisions, clublike cells, or pseudo extended-families. Such an affinity with concrete personal relations could, of course, limit the effectiveness of attempts to organize an abstract, ideological community.

Conclusion: The Future of the Korean Community in the New York Metropolitan Area

THE question of whether Korean immigrants have actually created a community is the problem of this study. In the classic sense, a community is based on a deep commitment to shared values, a unique culture, and autonomous institutions, within which the members of a purported community can live most of their lives. In this sense, a Korean community in the New York metropolitan area is only in the process of being created. Whether or not such a classic community will ultimately emerge or whether, in the modern world, the realization of such a community is even possible is problematic. Until now, we have been concerned with the process, regardless of the final and as yet unknowable outcome. We shall conclude, however, with a tentative answer to this question.

We have analyzed the initial stages of the creation of a community that is a special modern type of community—a community that has only begun to emerge in the past fifteen years. Yet it is different in many ways from the classic notion of community as defined in sociology, in which the gemeinschaft or the folk society, based on mechanical solidarity among its members, is the ideal type of social organization, one that sociologists accept as a generic form. The process of studying the community involves the study of how it is held together, how it functions, and how it responds to changes, especially changes brought about by large-scale urbanism, industrialism, capitalism, and mass society; but the Korean community in the New York metropolitan area is a community that will emerge, if it does at all, within a world already metropolitan, industrial, and capitalistic. It is emerging not out of an integrated folk community but as a result of the immigration of many people from a wide variety of places. It is not emerging, like most American ethnic communities, from the immigration of peasants to a new urban world, but rather from the immigration of a people who have recently undergone the process of urbanization in the homeland. In this respect, Korean immigrants may be similar to older immigrants such as the original English settlers in the American colonies, the German forty-eighters, and the Russian Jews. (Some of the newer immigrants to the United States from Latin America have also been urbanized, but, by and large, these urbanites were peasants who had not completely adjusted to urban life before they entered the United States.)

The study of the emergence of a Korean community in the New York metropolitan area at so late a date in the worldwide history of modernization allows us to ask questions that have generally not been asked with respect to earlier immigrants to the United States. We are able to ask what are the sources of the push from the recently industrialized homeland and the pull attractions of the large-scale urban society. Immediately after World War II the United States was the dominant industrial power of the world. Its policies and opportunities may have affected the course of immigration in ways that did not affect emigration and immigration in any other period of American history. We are thus able to ask questions as to how the policies and the image of the host country determine even the individual decision to emigrate. We are also able to raise questions as to how the sending country responds to the pull of the receiving country by formulating policies designed to facilitate or impede emigration.

In the initial and simple (perhaps even simple-minded) attempt to answer these questions, we have studied the United States Immigration Act of 1965, which resulted in the great influx of immigrants that began in 1967. Koreans have studied the United States immigration laws in fine detail, noting the rulings of the Department of Labor and the fluctuations of the labor market in order to pinpoint areas of labor shortage and areas where the possession of special skills and education facilitates entry into the United States and then economic success, once entry is achieved. They have pursued this sort of education or training in the homeland, and this drive for self-advancement through education accounts for the large number of doctors, nurses, and pharmacists among Korean immigrants. Yet the underlying economic processes that have shaped the service-oriented economy of the United States have largely determined the characteristics of Korean immigrants.

Korean immigrants have entered American society after its basic industrial development, based on a primary capital accumulation, was over. They entered when the primary economic opportunities that were available to earlier immigrants, in unskilled work or in agriculture, no longer existed. White-collar employment after higher education is now the area of growth for those who seek economic mobility. But Koreans are penalized because of their difficulties in mastering the English language and because of a diffuse racism that has limited their access to the mainline economic opportunities. Despite these handicaps, Korean immigrants have done a remarkable job of achieving economic success. But they have done this largely by entering marginal sectors of the occupational structure, areas that have been abandoned by older ethnic groups. They have used these opportunities to make perhaps the most dramatic advances that have ever been achieved in such a short time by any immigrant group in American history. Part of this study has focused upon explaining this remarkable mobility. Korean immigrants have entered ghetto businesses in large numbers, for example, catering to racial minorities at the bottom of American society. They have done so because they have not been able to gain white-collar employment and advancement commensurate with their level of education, fields of expertise, and work experience in the homeland. Korean medical professionals are an exception to this trend, but even they have had to enter the marginal sectors of the medical industry, those which are either unpopular among American-born doctors or which the latter abandoned in their flight to suburban medical centers.

Thus, given the tendency for Koreans to enter any marginal, low-status business occupation that provides economic opportunity, Korean immigrants play the role of the "middleman" between the less-favored ethnic groups and classes and the dominant society. As a result of the Koreans' marginal minority-group status, on the one hand, and their exceptional motivation, on the other, their social, economic, and political situation has become sandwiched between dominant and subordinate groups.[1] Since the "middleman" status presupposes a high degree of economic motivation, the Korean role of "middleman" in the new land is derived from a unique cultural and historical experience in the homeland.

KOREA effectively entered the modern world in 1910. Until that time, the Korean peninsula had been under the suzerainty of China and had been isolated from Western influences except for some primarily American missionary efforts. In 1910, when Japan annexed Korea, the Japanese overlords did not try to industrialize Korea to a very great degree. The Japanese preferred to exploit their colony as a source of labor and to limit the competition of Korean capitalists with their Japanese counterparts. The first trickle of Korean immigration came to the United States as a result of the opposition by Korean intellectuals, primarily Christian, to Japanese domination. These intellectuals left their home-

[1] See Hubert Blalock, *Toward A Theory of Minority Group Relations*, New York, John Wiley & Sons, 1967; Lewis Coser, "The Alien as a Servant of Power: Court Jews and Christian Renegade," *American Sociological Review* 37 (1972): 574-581. Harry H. L. Kitano, "Japanese Americans: The Development of a Middleman Minority," *Pacific Historical Review* 43 (1974): 500-519.

land either as refugees, organizers of opposition, or as religious students and leaders who found their native land inhospitable.

Only with the end of World War II and with partition did Korea come under the dominant influence of the United States, and American influence became intense only after the Korean War in 1950-1953. American military expansion in South Korea provided a local economic base for modernization and introduced the consumption ideals of an advanced industrial society, which were transmitted to Koreans through the behavior of troops, officers, and suppliers to South Koreans. Although the American presence undermined whatever traditionalism existed in South Korea, we have pointed out that Koreans, having experienced continual foreign conquests, invasions, and domination throughout their long history, never developed the great worship of tradition that often appears in underdeveloped countries and that is assumed in gemeinschaft-gesellschaft models of urbanization and industrialization.

The division of Korea after World War II also caused a vast internal migration from North to South Korea. A high proportion of the internal migrants had already been alienated, by their conversion to Christianity, from the traditional Korean Confucian culture. Moreover, their affinity to Christianity undoubtedly reflected their marginal status with respect to the Korean version of a Chinese mandarin bureaucracy. That is, the early Korean Christians were displaced members of a Korean bureaucratic class who were driven out of office and out of Seoul as a result of the normal but high turnover rates in the corrupt political bureaucracy. They had been forced to degrade themselves by becoming merchants and professionals, and, thus alienated, they found it easy to become Christians. Many Christian families with this historical background took refuge in South Korea after the communist takeover of the northern part of the peninsula. These North Koreans in the South felt a great fear of being overwhelmed by the communist "menace." They were political, religious, and economic enemies of the communists and felt that they would be specially treated as traitors in the event of a North Korean triumph over the South. They were traditionally marginal. They were marginal as North Koreans living in South Korea, as small businessmen in a society that valued land ownership and bureaucratic officeholding, and as Christians in a Confucian-Buddhist nation.

Because of their marginality in their homeland, North Koreans with Christian backgrounds became primary candidates for emigration when such opportunities became available. Marginality in the homeland also accounted for the first trickle of Korean immigration to the United States, which took place at the turn of the century. Many of these older immigrants were also Christians from what is now called North Korea. A small number of them settled in New York City and clustered around the New York Korean Church near Columbia University. They were highly educated, and, although their settlement is not the basis of the Korean community as it now exists, in many ways it was a magnet for succeeding migrations and a moral base for the emerging Korean community. Moreover, as we have seen, their tradition of a church-centered community life is still particularly important in helping new arrivals to adjust to the immediate problems of settlement in a new society. Moreover, church-centered social life provides a framework for public or private associations that can knit together a Korean life that is otherwise dispersed due to the lack of territorial centers. The Korean immigrants who came to the United States were thus not typical homeland Koreans. They were primarily Christians who were well educated, middle class, and highly motivated toward economic mobility. But these characteristics recapitulate the whole history of marginality within Korean society. In the twentieth century Korean marginality became the basis of migration, and the creation of new communities in new forms continues.

The impact of American economic and political policies on South Korean society has been far greater and more direct than the influences described so far in this chapter. After the Korean War American grain was dumped into the Korean economy under the guise of foreign aid. That policy was pursued in order to solve the problem of surplus grain production in the United States. But the impact of massive imports of subsidized, low-price grain contributed to a vast migration of Korean farmers into urban areas, primarily Seoul. Korean farmers were driven off the land because they could not produce rice at prices competitive with American grain. This urbanization would not have resulted in the recent emigration to the United States, however, had it not been for a peculiar Korean ability to adapt to adversity.

South Korea is not a land of great natural resources. Given the population explosion and overurbanization, the chief export item of South Korea must be its labor force. In order to alleviate population pressures, the South Korean government in the early 1960s encouraged Koreans to emigrate or migrate as contract workers to the United States, West Germany, Canada, and Latin American nations. A substantial number of these emigrants and migrant workers receive job training in South Korea in order to prepare themselves for the kinds of jobs that would be available in the receiving countries and that would qualify them for immigration visas. In particular, given the earlier development of Korean medical institutions by American missionaries at the turn of the century and given the shortage of medical professionals in the United States, some 13,000 Korean physicians, nurses, and pharmacists have entered the United States; they are now the second-largest group of immigrant medical workers. A large proportion of them have settled in the New York metropolitan area and have constituted an important economic and social base for the emerging Korean community. For example, many Korean nurses, as we have seen, provide the necessary capital for their husbands' small businesses. Yet in addition to internal conditions in Korea, Korean medical professionals owe their international mobility to the development of a service-oriented economy in the United States, and this is why medical services constitute one of the major economic entry points for Korean immigrants.

Due to a peculiar change in American fashion, the wig industry emerged in South Korea and provided vast economic opportunities to Korean immigrants. In the mid-1960s wigs became an item of high fashion, especially in the United States. American and Japanese wig-makers, again reflecting the influence of the outside industrial world on the home economy, began to purchase the hair of Korean women in order to manufacture wigs. At this time, Koreans began themselves to manufacture wigs in Korean sweatshops for export to the United States. Koreans, whose Confucian cultural background made wigs repugnant to them, nevertheless found the profit from the sale of wigs to Japanese and American exporters great enough to overcome their repugnance to manufacturing useless items of personal adornment. Thus the first step in the development of a South Korean export-oriented economy was the development of wig manufacturing and exporting. When Japanese technology refined synthetic fibers as a replacement for human hair, Koreans took over the process and began to dominate worldwide wig markets. Koreans were able to do so because, in light of the new urban poverty caused by massive rural-to-urban migration, they were willing to exploit themselves and one another in labor-intensive sweatshops. The wig industry provided a great deal of the foreign exchange necessary to underwrite the industrialization of South Korea. In saying this, of course, we should not underestimate the effects of American military and foreign aid as well as of the American and Japanese commercial bank loans given to South Korea, which also underwrite its industrialization.

The wig business was a typical vehicle for Korean immigration to the United States in general and the New York metropolitan area in particular. It established, to a large degree (medical professionals excepted), a basic characteristic of the Korean community in the United States. This type of initial economic penetration is not at all exceptional. Almost every immigrant group to the United States has found

a unique path of entry into the economic structure of American society. The entry point is determined by the character of the immigrants
and the stage of economic expansion in the United States at the moment of entry, that is, by those industries that can provide economic
opportunity to an immigrant group and that are compatible with
the characteristics of that group. Italians arrived when work in the construction industry began to expand as urban America was developing
its municipal transportation and public works programs. Jews used the
garment industry, which was just entering mass commercial marketing
at the time of their arrival. Then eastern-European Jews entered that
industry after German Jews had developed it for some fifteen years
before, because a small number of the eastern Jewry had worked in
the garment trade in Kraków and Warsaw before they entered the
new land. And Slavs arrived when steel manufacturing and coal min-
ing were beginning to expand.

But the wig business was more than an economic opportunity for
individual Korean immigrants. It was a major means for the South Korean wig-manufacturers and the government to acquire foreign exchange and to finance further economic development of the homeland.
As a result, the South Korean government was deeply involved in the
American wig-business. When the mad scramble for economic opportunities in the United States occurred and when peddlers, retailers,
wholesalers, and manufacturers were often competing for the same
market, the South Korean government was called in to organize the
market and regulate competition, especially after the wig market in
the United States began to contract. It is perhaps ironical that the
Korean Wig Union, a front organization of the home government, was
organized in violation of American antitrust laws. More important is
the Korean government's interference in domestic retailing and wholesaling, which perhaps established a precedent for other home governments.

As has been noted, Korean immigrants had no special affinity with
the wig business or with other industries of personal adornment. The
wig business presented itself only as an historically accidental entry
point. Having once arrived and established a characteristic presence
in urban America, Korean immigrants, prompted by the decline of the
wig business in the early 1970s, began to look for other economic opportunities. As alternatives to the wig business, they entered garment,
handbag, false-eyelash, and other miscellaneous businesses selling
items from the homeland that could be produced by low-paid homeland labor. But the quest for economic opportunities did not stop
there. The intense desire for economic mobility led Koreans especially
into retail and service organizations, which do not depend upon flu-

ency in English and work experience in American large-scale bureaucratic industries. Korean immigrants have followed native Americans and older immigrant groups into labor-intensive small businesses for example. Korean small businessmen exploit themselves, their family members, and even more recent arrivals in order to keep their shops open for long hours. They exploit greenhorns until the latter find alternatives to being exploited by their ethnic compatriots, which alternatives, of course, include opening their own exploitative businesses.

All Korean-run retail businesses are characterized by labor-intensive work. The success of the businesses depends upon intensive care for one's inventory and concern for one's customers. Thus Korean immigrants found an ideal small enterprise in the fruit and vegetable business. Once the discovery was made, they began to flood into that business, which is also ideal for aggressive Korean immigrants because it requires little capital. Thus the fruit and vegetable business became a secondary economic entry point for Korean immigrants. To a lesser extent, so have retail fishmarkets, taxi driving, drycleaning, liquor stores, and garment-industry subcontracting. These secondary businesses do not import their merchandise from the homeland, nor are their products related to ethnicity. Their existence is based upon the fact that Korean immigrants are willing and able to perform the required work and services within a totally American commercial and service economy. This economic autonomy has had profound consequences for the Korean community in the New York metropolitan area because the businessmen of these enterprises are in no way dependent upon the homeland government for export or import licenses, nor on any economic or political connection with the homeland and its government.

THE economic and occupational niches that Koreans have occupied in the United States constitute the foundation of their attempt to construct a community. The ministers, students, and political refugees who entered the United States prior to the Immigration Act of 1965 have provided the basic leadership. The ministerial class in particular has provided moral and intellectual guidance and social services to the would-be Korean community. The professional class, primarily medical, has provided the structure for a prestige community and has filled many lay leadership positions in the churches. The business class, especially that class oriented toward the homeland by importing and exporting, has provided a forum for the public presentation of the homeland and its culture to the outside American society and has attempted in turn to control and coordinate the Korean community. It has done so with the cooperation of, and at times under the direction and control of, the Korean Consulate General in New York, an agency of the home government. Small businessmen, especially those not attached in any way to the homeland economy, were initially excluded from leadership partly because of their long hours of work and their commitment to individual and family mobility. But we have noted that, because of their independence from the homeland government, they have become a second source of leadership in competition with the government-oriented businessmen.

In addition, Korean immigrants in every specific industry and profession have tended to organize themselves into merchant, professional, occupational, or alumni associations. These secondary associations cut across the total life of the would-be Korean community, breaking it into segments. The associations in most respects are not a classic "community"; they tend more to resemble a classic MacIver-like conception of associations.[2] They are "societal" rather than communal organizations in that they are not necessarily bound together by deep-seated feelings of belonging. And yet because of the experience of being immigrants in the alien society, Koreans feel forced to band together in ways that go beyond the narrow interests of associationalism.

These group activities based on secondary associations provide a point of departure for community studies. In American community studies,[3] "class" has been a paramount conceptual element both in describing community life and in defining community structure. But "class," if this term indicates a collectivity of individuals who display and pursue common economic interests or life styles, has not yet emerged as a factor governing social relationships among Korean immigrants. This is partly because Koreans, as new immigrants, have not yet had enough time to establish socially recognized class distinctions among themselves. All Korean immigrants are struggling for economic gains on roughly equal terms. In this sense, their social and economic life is to a large extent divided by occupation and by occupational groups rather than by class. The significant occupational categories are various: medical professionals, businessmen, ministers, blue-collar workers, and nonmedical professionals, for example. This lack of clear class distinctions also originates in the "class structure" of the homeland. As has been noted in chapter one, Korean immigrants were largely drawn from a relatively homogeneous, urban, white-collar mid-

[2] Robert M. MacIver, *The Web of Government*, New York, The Macmillan Company, 1947.

[3] For instance, Lynd and Lynd, *Middle Town in Transition*; W. Lloyd Warner and Paul S. Lunt, *The Social Life of a Modern Community*, New Haven, Yale University Press, 1941; Vidich and Bensman, *Small Town in Mass Society*.

dle class. Moreover, as has been noted in chapter ten, the Korean class structure has long been fluid and atomized because of special historical factors that have shaped Korean culture and the social structure.

What is especially interesting, perhaps unique, in Korean group activities is the rise of "pseudo extended-families." Traditionally, Koreans were strongly attached to a kinship system based on Confucian ideals of kinship piety. As we have noted, this extended kinship system was weakened in the homeland itself during the process of urbanization and population displacement, especially during the Korean War. Furthermore, all large-scale transcontinental migrations tend to weaken the traditional extended family in part because initial migration is usually undertaken by a single male. Later the spouse and children, and sometimes individual brothers and sisters and other family members, follow the original migrant. But the extended family usually does not emigrate as a unit. Thus the nuclear family is the family of immigration and urbanization, if and when the family is involved in such processes.

Koreans have faced special problems in immigrating to the United States because they arrived relatively late, came in relatively small numbers, and were linguistically and racially distinct from the host population. They have felt a sense of isolation and alienation from the dominant society and have attempted to do something about it. As a result, they have created pseudo extended-families. As we have indicated, the pseudo extended-family is the voluntaristic formation of a group of nuclear families that act as an extended family in the provision of social support, mutual aid, recreation, and companionship. The immediate origin of such an arrangement is unknown, but it may have devolved from the *gye* association. Once learned, the principle of the pseudo extended-family was adopted with a degree of self-conscious rationality that is truly remarkable. Pseudo extended-families exist as an organized institution within Korean churches and clubs, and within alumni, professional, and business associations. Korean immigrants apparently need to experience a sense of community in relatively small-scale, personal, face-to-face relationships. Large-scale associations, which they have also organized at almost the drop of a hat, are apparently not sufficient to meet the personal needs of Korean immigrants. Perhaps a need for the particularism of the extended family, which had already been lost partly in homeland urbanization and partly in the experience of being strangers in a new land, caused them to organize pseudo extended-families.

A reliance on relatively small groups as the basis for social life outside of work, and the form these small groups take, may tend to atomize Korean life to the point that large-scale organizations become ineffective. On the other hand, the Korean immigrants' commitment to a personal mobility that includes the nuclear family may limit the power and scope of the pseudo extended-families. A differential rate of mobility and success among the heads of the various nuclear families that make up a pseudo extended-family may weaken that family structure. If this is the case, the Korean pseudo extended-family may be a temporary expedient similar to the eastern-European Jews' *Landsmanshaft Verein* (mutual aid and benefit society) and the credit and sports associations among other older immigrant groups.

Yet the basic patterns of the Korean community in the New York metropolitan area are quite different from those of immigrant communities at the turn of the century. First of all, the economic entry and adjustment of Koreans is based on a vastly different development of the economic institutions of both sending and host countries. That is to say, the selective interactions of international trade and labor markets provide new and different channels for emigration and economic advancement. In the processes of these interactions, various government policies are involved. We have particularly emphasized how Korean immigrants have self-consciously and rationally responded to specific policies of the United States. The most important aspect of this response is that a high proportion of Korean immigrants have prepared themselves with some means of economic adjustment, and these means have been more specific and advanced than those brought by earlier peasant immigrants from southern and eastern Europe. In addition, because of prior urban experience in the homeland, Koreans have not been as troubled with anomie, crime, social disorganization, and lack of access to institutional resources as were the older immigrants. In fact, Korean immigration to the United States resembles an internal migration from city to city. In this sense, the old "folk to urban" paradigm, which has been used for the analysis of older immigrant communities, is not applicable to the Korean experience in the United States.

Korean immigrants are also unique in having settled in the New York metropolitan area without having established an ethnic territorial enclave. This is in part due to the fact that many of them have entered the United States as professionals, especially as medical professionals, skilled workers, and businessmen. They have initially settled in widely dispersed areas close to the sources of their livelihood. Furthermore, they have arrived on the scene when antidiscrimination statutes and policies in employment and housing were beginning to be enforced. This has prevented them from being segregated involuntarily. They have settled wherever they wanted to live, within their financial resources. In addition, their number, being governed by the immigration quota system, is small, approximately 80,000 to date. Even if they had wanted to form a residential territory, with such small numbers they could not have dislocated the residents of urban ghettos who now occupy these traditional sites of initial immigrant enclaves.

The new Korean immigrants have nonetheless formed a special type of "community"—a community that does not have a territorial base but is centered in segmented organizational and institutional activities. On the basis of such activities, scattered Koreans, as we have noted, share a sense of belonging, an "ethnicity" or "Korean-ness" through which they attempt to pursue common interests in relation to the larger society. Thus Koreans constitute a new kind of community: they live in multiethnic local communities, but their population is dispersed throughout the larger metropolis. It is becoming increasingly clear that this type of nonterritorial community is a distinctive feature of many new immigrant groups and that it can be found as well among native white populations. If this is the case, the theory of "natural areas" and its implications for unilineal succession, adaptation, and assimilation is not appropriate to the phenomenon of the nonterritorial community.

Koreans suffer some disadvantages in not forming a territorially based residential community. They do not constitute an electoral majority in any one electoral district, for example, and thus the new community lacks electoral clout in dealing with city, state, and federal agencies. This is most particularly felt now that ethnic minority communities are increasingly self-conscious and policy-oriented, focusing on such issues as federal and state budgets, work and educational programs, and on their desire for a share of other government benefits. Furthermore, lacking a territorial base, Koreans cannot effectively mobilize their own ethnic vote in competition with other ethnic minorities in a given area. Whether a Korean community leadership will emerge that is capable of overcoming these problems is an open question.

Is there a community in the process of being constructed? In one sense, the answer is no. The Korean community as it exists and as it is represented by the Korean Association of Greater New York cannot be considered a community, even if it has some attributes of a community, to the extent that it is a creation of the home government. We have noted that community politics, especially the leadership conflicts centered in the Korean Association of Greater New York, were greatly influenced by the home government. A group of local leaders emerged and attempted to seek personal gain through access to a patronage connection with the home government. Community leaders conducting export-import businesses involving homeland products were eager to receive favors and protection from the home government. And community businessmen and intellectuals sought government positions in the homeland as rewards for their leadership in the New York community. In this sense, the leadership of the Korean community was a product of the home government. Through control of the homeland media and through social pressures and public opinion, agents of the home government can even influence the definition of public issues in Korean communities in the United States. They can determine the flow of information in the ethnic media and organize a community consensus. This was particularly true when the home government felt it necessary to organize an American response to the Korean influence-peddling scandal in the United States Congress.

The South Korean government's intervention in the New York Korean community reflects its desire to continue receiving American military and economic aid. However, the South Korean government cannot be accused of totally dominating the leadership of the Korean community. Because Korean immigrants hold deep-seated Confucian values, they want to respect their established political leadership in the homeland. For Koreans, the home government, whatever form it takes, represents the Korean nation—its interests and culture—to the American public. Furthermore, the home government, via the Korean Consulate General, supports the activities of immigrants in the new land. When the actions of the home government did not at first produce a scandal among the general American public, Koreans in the United States remained silent about many of the corrupt and repugnant practices that they knew were going on. They remained silent as long as Americans did not know of these actions or of their magnitude.

To be sure, not all movements to construct a great Korean association of all the little associations are the exclusive product of the home government. In many instances, Korean leaders, especially import-oriented businessmen, have appealed of their own free will to the consul general to solve leadership conflicts within their associations. Thus the consul general became a most influential leader of the Korean-American community by being a symbol of authority without always manipulating the community. But if a Korean community is to emerge, it must emerge indigenously from its own resources. So long as community leaders are puppets of the home government, some groups within the Korean population are automatically excluded or exclude themselves from the community. This includes intellectuals who are opposed to the home government on political grounds and religious leaders who attack it on moral grounds.

The attempts of the home government to control the Korean community produced their own dialectics of authenticity and opposition.

The Korean influence-peddling scandal fostered a deep sense of shame among Korean immigrants because of the negative publicity that the scandal created in the American mass media. This, together with the development of autonomous economic institutions that are now in no way dependent upon export and import licensing and government-sponsored credit, has allowed some Koreans to express themselves independently. In this sense, an autonomous public opinion is beginning to emerge, and so is a Korean community; for only when an autonomous public opinion emerges can one say that a genuine community exists. Otherwise, the community is a public-relations front for an external government and a source of opportunities for those who would curry favor with that government.

However, there are structural limitations to the degree to which the Korean community can become independent of the home government. Given the government "control" over the community newspapers and given the ideological and financial dependence of the community on the home government, community leaders are not likely to antagonize it. And yet, as Koreans become increasingly aware of their collective fate in the new land, they may overthrow government "control" of their community. The victory of Korean greengrocers in the 1978 presidential election of the Korean Association of Greater New York is a step in that direction.

Another factor that tends to make a Korean community possible is the response that their presence elicits from other ethnic groups. At present, it is the response of blacks that is relevant. We have noted that Koreans have concentrated much of their retail activities in black ghettos. In doing so, the pursuit of the American dream by Koreans conflicts with the aspiration of blacks to gain control of their ghettos. The aggressive activities of Koreans in ghetto businesses may be viewed as an insult to the aspirations of blacks. In only a few years Koreans have acquired, with little capital or resources, an impressive number of retail stores in the ghettos. Blacks have aspired to such business ownership but have not had dramatic success in similar ventures. Consequently, Korean shopkeepers have been accused of being sharp traders, price gougers, and exploiters. In this respect Koreans, who are taking over many retail ghetto businesses being abandoned by Jews and other nonblack ethnic groups, have inherited negative images attributed to these ethnic groups. This rise of anti-Koreanism has forced Koreans to organize on political and ethnic grounds to counteract such quasi-public sentiment. As with all ethnic communities, such antiethnic attitudes ultimately strengthen the aspiration of Koreans toward their ethnic organization, delaying the process of acculturation and assimilation.

The racial characteristics of Koreans set them visibly apart in the

United States and are also likely to help Koreans develop and maintain a community. Like blacks, the Japanese, and the Chinese, Koreans will find it difficult to assimilate, and for at least a generation or two they may be driven into themselves by their racial differences from the white majority. Until they completely master the American language, education, and culture, Koreans will be forced to rely on one another. Furthermore, the first-generation Korean immigrants have a strong desire to maintain part of their own culture even though, in terms of their economic motivation—small business capitalism—they seem to be more American than contemporary Americans.

But a fundamental cultural characteristic tends to mitigate these isolating forces. Korean immigrants to the United States have combined the pragmatism of a Confucian economic ethic with the driving mobility and aspiration of the Protestant ethic. Thus they have pursued opportunities wherever these existed, and they have exploited themselves in whatever way necessary to achieve success, especially in primary capital accumulation. They appear to have all the original virtues of the Protestant ethic—prudence, devotion to business and to work, and avoidance of self-indulgence and sloth. They also have a remarkable ability to shift from one industry or business to another as new opportunities arise, or seem to arise. But above all, Koreans are historically committed to education and to individualistic and bureaucratic success. The first-generation Korean immigrants have been handicapped, apart from the medical profession, from employing all of the administrative and bureaucratic skills they learned in the homeland. If Koreans maintain their "Protestant" character and master American education, however, especially professional education, they will be able to enter the white-collar, managerial ranks of business and government and to proceed along mainstream mobility paths that are now denied them; and they will have new opportunities for economic and professional assimilation. In so doing they may be submerged by American mass culture with all that implies, good or bad, from the standpoint of traditional Korean values, however weak the latter may be. If and when this occurs, they will be pulled out of the cultural and linguistic enclaves that the first generation of immigrants have been forced into.

Certainly, differential access to opportunities may partially test the boundaries, that is, the unity and loyalty, of the emerging Korean community. In the next two generations, Koreans will have an opportunity to create a voluntary community based on their own aspirations and culture. They may find that their emerging Americanization will overcome their sense of identity with an already withered traditional culture, and thus overcome their sense of community. And yet this process of assimilation is likely to take at least a generation or two. In the meantime, an autonomous Korean community is likely to emerge. Whether it will ultimately disappear or be submerged in other types of communities—based on class, religion, wider ethnic ties, or race—is an open question.

In the future as in the past, the Korean community will be shaped by American immigration policy. The present Korean community has emerged because the United States Immigration Act of 1965 abolished national origins quotas. (It did not specifically address Koreans.) The 1976 Amendment to the Immigration Act of 1965 has altered the character of this Korean immigration by making it more difficult for professionals and skilled workers to enter. Yet the amendment still allows for the continuous influx of Koreans (some 35,000 annually) largely to effect "family reunions." As compared with the older immigrant groups, the total influx of Koreans is small; and their small number could conceivably fall below the critical mass of population within which the Korean culture can be maintained. If Koreans continue to enter the United States, the Korean community will be sustained by contact with the homeland culture that new immigrants will bring with them. And yet one must note that, since South Korea is being rapidly urbanized and Americanized, Korean assimilation to American society begins in the homeland and is completed in the United States. In the long run, economic success, and social and political integration, will be the main *obstacle* to the emergence of a segregated Korean community in the United States; but racism, and exclusion from mainstream economic activities, will create a ghetto community.

Selective Bibliography

An, Lim. *Hagug gyeongjeron* [Theory of the Korean economy]. Seoul, Korea: Bom Moon Sa, 1961.

Bensman, Joseph, and Vidich, Arthur J. *The New American Society: The Revolution of the Middle Class.* Chicago: Quadrangle Books, 1971.

Bensman, Joseph, and Vidich, Arthur J., eds. *Metropolitan Communities: New Forms of Urban Sub-Communities.* New York: The New York Times Company, 1975.

Blalock, Hubert. *Toward A Theory of Minority Group Relations.* New York: John Wiley & Sons, 1967.

Caudill, William, and De Vos, George. "Achievement, Culture and Personality: The Case of the Japanese Americans." *American Anthropologist* 58 (1956): 1103-1125.

Choi, Ho-jin. *Geundae hangug gyeongjesa* [The recent history of the Korean economy]. Seoul, Korea: Dan Moon Moon Go, 1973.

Chon, Kwan-woo. *Hangugsa eui jaebalgyeon* [Rediscovery of Korean history]. Seoul, Korea: Il Jo Gak, 1974.

Coser, Lewis. "The Alien as a Servant of Power: Court Jews and Christian Renegade." *American Sociological Review* 37 (1972): 574-581.

Drake, St. Clair, and Cayton, Horace R. *Black Metropolis.* New York: Harcourt, Brace & World, 1945.

Faris, Robert, and Dunham, H. Warren. *Mental Disorders in Urban Areas.* Chicago: The University of Chicago Press, 1936.

Fisher, Maxine P. "Ethnic Identities: Asian Indians in the New York Area." Ph.D. Dissertation, The City University of New York, 1978.

Frazier, E. Franklin. *Black Bourgeoisie.* New York: Free Press, 1957.

Gans, Herbert J. *The Urban Villagers: Group and Class in the Life of Italian Americans.* New York: Free Press, 1962.

Glazer, Nathan, and Moynihan, Daniel P. *Beyond the Melting Pot: The Negroes, Puerto Ricans, Jews, Italians, and Irish of New York City.* Cambridge: the MIT Press, 1970.

Gordon, Milton. *Assimilation in American Life: The Role of Race, Religion, and National Origins.* Oxford: Oxford University Press, 1964.

Gordon, Monica H. "Identification and Adaptation: A Study of Two Groups of Jamaican Immigrants in New York City." Ph.D. Dissertation, The City University of New York, 1979.

Handlin, Oscar. *The Uprooted.* New York: Grosset & Dunlap, 1951.

Houchins, Lee, and Houchins, Chang-su. "The Korean Experience in America, 1903-1924." *Pacific Historical Review* 43 (1974): 548-575.

Howe, Irving. *World of Our Fathers.* New York: Harcourt Brace Jovanovich, 1976.

Huizinga, Johan. *Homo Ludens: A Study of the Play Element in Culture.* Boston: Beacon Press, 1955.

Janowitz, Morris. *The Community Press in an Urban Setting: The Social Elements of Urbanism.* Chicago: The University of Chicago Press, 1967.

Kim, Chi-ha. *Cry of the People and Other Poems.* Hayama, Japan: Autumn Press, 1974.

Kim, Yong-tae. *Komerican eui naj gwa bam* [Day and night of Komericans]. Seoul, Korea: Han Jin Sa, 1976.

Kitano, Harry H. L. "Japanese Americans: The Development of a Middleman Minority." *Pacific Historical Review* 43 (1974): 500-519.

Ko, Sung-je. *Hangug iminsa yeongu* [A study of the history of Korean emigration]. Seoul, Korea: Jang Moon Gak, 1973.

Kornblum, William. *Blue Collar Community.* Chicago: The University of Chicago Press, 1974.

Krickus, Richard. *Pursuing the American Dream: White Ethnics and the New Populism.* New York: Doubleday & Company, Anchor Books, 1976.

Kwon, Tai-hwan; Lee, Hae-young; Chang, Yun-hik; and Yu, Eui-young. *The Population of Korea.* Seoul, Korea: The Population and Development Studies Center, Seoul National University, 1975.

Lee, Gi-back. *Hangugsa sinron.* [A new approach to Korean history]. Seoul, Korea: Il Jo Gak, 1967.

Light, Ivan H. *Ethnic Enterprises in America: Business and Welfare among Chinese, Japanese, and Blacks.* Berkeley and Los Angeles: The University of California Press, 1972.

Lyman, Stanford M. *The Asian in the West.* Western Studies Center, University of Nevada System, 1970.

Lynd, Robert S., and Lynd, Helen M. *Middle Town in Transition: A Study in Cultural Conflict.* New York: Harcourt, Brace & World, 1937.

MacIver, Robert. *Society.* New York: Holt, Rinehart & Winston, 1937.

———. *The Web of Government.* New York: Macmillan, 1947.

Mills, C. Wright. *White Collar: The American Middle Classes.* New York: Oxford University Press, 1951.

Nishi, Setsuko M. "Japanese American Achievement in Chicago: A Cultural Response to Degradation." Ph.D. Dissertation, University of Chicago, 1963.

Novak, Michael. *The Rise of the Unmeltable Ethnics: Politics and Culture in the Seventies.* New York: Macmillan, 1971.

Park, Robert E. *Race and Culture.* London: The Free Press, 1950.

Park, Robert E., and Burgess, Ernest W. *The City.* Chicago: The University of Chicago Press, 1925.

Pirenne, Henri. *Medieval Cities: Their Origins and the Revival of Trade.* Trans. by Frank D. Halsey. Princeton: Princeton University Press, 1971.

Shaw, Clifford R. *Delinquency Areas: A Study of the Geographic Distribution of School Truants, Juvenile Delinquents, and Adult Offenders in Chicago.* Chicago: The University of Chicago Press, 1929.

Sombart, Werner. *The Quintessence of Capitalism: A Study of the History and Psychology of the Modern Business Man.* London: T. F. Unwin, 1915.

Son, Jong-mock. *Joseon sidae dosi sahoe yeongu* [A study of the urban society of the Yi dynasty]. Seoul, Korea: Il Ji Sa, 1977.

Stein, Maurice R. *The Eclipse of Community: An Interpretation of American Studies.* Princeton: Princeton University Press, 1960.

Suttles, Gerald D. *The Social Construction of Communities.* Chicago: The University of Chicago Press, 1972.

————. *The Social Order of the Slum: Ethnicity and Territory in the Inner City.* Chicago: The University of Chicago Press, 1968.

Thomas, William I. *Old World Traits Transplanted.* Montclair, New Jersey: Patterson Smith, 1971.

Thomas, William I., and Znaniecki, Florian. *The Polish Peasant in Europe and America.* New York: Octagon Books, 1971.

Thrasher, Frederic M. *The Gang: A Study of One Thousand Three Hundred Thirteen Gangs in Chicago.* Chicago: The University of Chicago Press, 1929.

Vidich, Arthur J., and Bensan, Joseph. *Small Town in Mass Society: Class, Power and Religion in a Rural Community.* Rev. ed. Princeton: Princeton University Press, 1968.

Vreeland, Nena; Just, Peter; Martindale, Kenneth W.; Moeller, Philip W.; Shinn, Rinn-sup. *Area Handbook for South Korea.* Washington, D.C.: United States Government Printing Office, 1975.

Ware, Caroline C. *Greenwich Village.* New York: Houghton Mifflin, 1935.

Warner, W. Lloyd, and Low, J. O. *The Social System of the Modern Factory.* New Haven: Yale University Press, 1947.

Weber, Max. *The City.* Trans. and ed. by Don Martindale and Gertrud Neuwirth. New York: Free Press, 1958.

————. *From Max Weber: Essays in Sociology.* Trans. and ed. by Hans H. Gerth and C. Wright Mills. New York: Oxford University Press, 1946.

————. *The Protestant Ethic and the Spirit of Capitalism.* Trans. by Talcott Parsons. New York: Charles Scribner's Sons, 1930.

————. *The Religion of China.* Trans. and ed. by Hans H. Gerth. New York: The Free Press, 1951.

Whyte, William F. *Street Corner Society.* Chicago: The University of Chicago Press, 1961.

Wittfogel, Karl A. *Oriental Despotism: A Comparative Study of Total Power.* New Haven: Yale University Press, 1957.

Zorbaugh, Harvey W. *The Gold Coast and the Slum.* Chicago: The University of Chicago Press, 1929.

adoptions of Korean children, 42
Allen, Horace Newton, 160
Americanization, 10, 44, 320
American life styles, emulation of, 33
American Medical Association,
  supply of physicians and, 151-152
anomie, older immigrants and, 4
antidiscrimination policies, effect on
  residential patterns, 315
anti-Japanese movement: of Americans,
  21n, 22; of overseas Koreans, 22-23
anti-Koreanism. *See* conflicts; "Koreagate"
anti-Oriental movements: in California, 21-22; effect on Korean
  community, 17, 23-24
antitrust law, violation of, and wig
  business, 135. *See also* Sherman
  Antitrust Act
"Asian Jew," as a description of
  Korean character, 252
assimilation, acculturation and, 4-5,
  181, 318-319

baby boom, post-Korean War, 51, 69
black life styles: artificiality of, 121-
  122, 145; use of wigs as an
  expression of, 139-142. *See also*
  life styles
black nationalism, impact of, on wig
  fashion, 121
"brain drain," medical, 164-165
Buddhism, 190, 285

censorship of community press, 265,
  271-272. *See also* Korean Central
  Intelligence Agency
centralism: effect on Korean character
  structure, 295, 303; effect on overurbanization, 76-77, 97; effect on
  status mobility, 290, 294; historical
  background of, 284
centralization: of the economy, and
  the shift to small businesses, 144;
  of the health-care system, and the
  influx of immigrant physicians,
  149-150

character, national: affected by state
  bureaucracy, 294-295; community
  structure and, 303-304; small
  business enterprises and, 303
Chicago school of sociologists, 4
Chinese empires, influence on Korean
  history, 283
Chinese immigrants, 21-23, 44
Chon, Too-hwan, 260
Chu Hsi, 295. *See also* Neo-Confucianism
cities, primary, 76-77
civil rights movement: effect on wig
  fashions among blacks, 121;
  passage of Immigration Act of
  1965 and, 17, 27
civil service examinations, status
  mobility and, 285-286, 288-289
"class," concept of, and community
  study, 313
"command industrialization," 81
community: concept of, 6-7; nonterritorial bases of, 6, 184-187,
  208, 226, 262, 276, 313, 315-316
community politics, issues of: Anti-
  Kim-Ilsung Rally, 244; fund-raising
  campaign for Korea Center, 239-
  241; preparation for the Bicentennial, 241-242; response to "Koreagate," 252-254; talc as a cancer-
  causing rice powder, 268-269;
  "tax evasion" of greengrocers, 269-
  270
competition for church membership,
  198-199, 202
conflicts, interethnic: between blacks
  and Koreans, 143, 257-261, 281,
  299, 318; in fruit and vegetable
  business, 118-119; in wig business, 133-134
conflicts, intraethnic: in churches,
  204-205; in fruit and vegetable
  business, 116-118; in wig business,
  132-137
Confucianism, practical rationality
  of, 299. *See also* Neo-Confucianism; value-congruity

Confucian nations, 299
consumption, conspicuous, 95-96.
    See also upper class
consumption culture, 114
consumption ideals, 308
continuum, as a theoretical model
    for older immigrants: between
    folk and urban societies, 4, 315;
    between gemeinschaft and gesell-
    schaft, 3. See also paradigms
craftsmanship, as an ideology, 128-
    129
culture, youth-oriented, effect on wig
    fashions, 122
"cultural revolution," American,
    effect on wig fashions, 122, 144

defense, psychological: as a role of
    the churches, 191, 207; of wig-
    men, 138-139
demographic transition, 50
dependency, economic, of South
    Korea, 83-86
discrimination, racial, 21, 28, 103-
    104, 320
disorganization, older immigrants
    and, 4
dollar smuggling: channels of, 66-68;
    and investment in the United
    States, 64, 110; as a source of
    "investment" immigration, 36-37
dumping practices with wig products,
    128, 132-134

ecological models of Chicago school,
    6
economic autonomy, new community
    politics and, 312
ecumenicalism, 197
education: as a causal factor for
    migration and emigration, 77-79,
    297; as an ideology, 79, 295
elderly persons, church life and,
    195
emigration frauds, 62-63
emigration policy, 52, 62, 69
ethnic customers, 106
ethnic market, 110
ethnic press, relationships: to the
    Consulate General and KCIA, 271-
    272; to the Korean Produce Retailers
    Association, 269-270, 275; to
    secondary associations, 267-268
ethnic succession: in the fruit and
    vegetable business, 120, 145; in
    small businesses, 110-111, 144

ethnic tastes, 104
ethnocentrism, 18
Exchange-Visitor Program, 161, 171,
    174, 183
exploitation of labor: in the homeland,
    86-88; in the new land, 114-115.
    See also self-exploitation

family: change in, 302; effect of
    immigration law on, 44-46; structure
    of, 301
family groups, as a pseudo extended-
    family: in churches, 191, 199-201,
    207; as a result of migration,
    314-315; in secondary associations,
    210-212. See also rotating credit
    associations
family labor, small businesses and,
    112, 114-115, 120
folk society, 3, 4, 305

gemeinschaft, 3, 7, 305
gemeinschaft and gesellschaft: as a
    model of immigration, 3; as a
    model of urbanization and
    industrialization, 308. See also
    continuum; paradigm
"geopolitical determinism" of Korean
    history, 283
"Great Transformation," 282
green card: "investment" immigra-
    tion and, 36, 142; as a source of
    status anxiety, 31

Handlin, Oscar, 4

ideology: education as, 79, 295;
    of modernization, 81; occupational,
    128-129; professional, 272-273;
    ruling, 80, 189; of sadaesasang, 298
immigration, kinship-centered, 46, 70
immigration policy, 28-30, 165
interaction between Korean com-
    munity in America and the home
    government, 246
interlocking of business and politics,
    246-247
"invidious comparison": as a motive
    for industrialization, 81; as a
    source of status anxiety, 95.
    See also status anxiety

Japanese colonialism, 90, 160-161,
    177, 294-295, 307; effect on
    Korean diaspora, 19-21

Japanese corporations, 84-85. *See also zaibatsu*
Japanese immigrants, relationship to Korean immigrants, 20-23
Japanese invasion, effect on status mobility, 290-291
Japanese technology, borrowing of, 84-85
Johnson, Lyndon B., Immigration Act of 1965 and, 28

Kennedy, Edward M., Immigration Act of 1965 and, 27
"key money," 116-118, 270-271
Kim, Chi-ha, 93
Kim, Hancho C., 90
Kim, Hyong-wuk, 255
Kim, Il-sung, 22, 244
Kim, Jae-kyu, 260
"Koreagate," 227-228, 252-253, 260
Korean Association of Greater New York, 198, 202, 227; community politics and, 237-245. *See also* community politics
Korean Central Intelligence Agency (KCIA): censorship by, 265, 271-272; involvement in the community, 233-237; as a means of repression, 80; Park Tong-sun and, 247
Korean Consulate General in New York, 185, 187, 227; functions of, 228-232; involvement in Korean Association of Greater New York, 237-245; relationship to ethnic media, 271-272; relationship to secondary associations, 209, 223, 225. *See also* community politics
Korean immigrants, older: characteristics of, 22-23; economic ventures of, 21-22
"Korean-ness," 181, 266
Korean Produce Retailers Association: conflict with an ethnic press, 269-270; functions of, 117-118; involvement in community politics, 255-256; rotating credit associations in, 212
Korean students: change of status, 37; class background, 38; as a source of community leadership, 183-184
Korean War, fear of another, as a "push" factor of emigration, 33-36, 95, 96

Korean War brides, 33, 41, 53, 212
Korean Wig Union: functions of, 134-136; relationship to the home government, 134-136; in violation of antitrust law, 136, 311
"Koreatown," 108-109

land reform, 73-74
Landsmanshaft Verein, 314
land speculation, 75
Latin American nations, immigration to, 54-55, 69
licensing system: and blue-collar workers, 57; and emigration companies, 63-64; and nurses, 61, 174-176; and physicians, 169-173; as a source of community activities, 216-217
life styles, artificial: effect on wig fashions, 121-122, 144-145. *See also* black life styles
loans of Korean government to immigrants, 231-232

MacIver, Robert M., 313
maldistribution, geographic: of physicians in America, 151-152, 176; of physicians in South Korea, 163-165
marginal character of Koreans, 297
marginality of Korean history, 309
marginal minority group, Koreans as, 307
marginal opportunities in the medical industry, 147
marginal sectors in the medical industry, 158-159, 177
marginal status, 259, 308
marriage, interracial, 23-24
marriage market, female surplus in, 44
marriage ventures, 46
mass consumption: among ethnic minorities, 107, 144; of medical services, 147, 150-151
medical professionals, church leadership of, 193-194, 203
medical technology, preventive, 48-49, 69, 86
middle class: classification of, 88-89; mobility consciousness of, and emigration, 96-97
"middleman" minority, Koreans as, 258, 307
military institutions, penetration of, into political institutions, 80-82
military involvement of United

military involvement (*cont.*)
States in Korea, effect on
emigration, 33
military service, compulsory: as a
barrier to emigration, 42; effect
on life chances of physicians,
174
ministers: classification of, 198;
meaning of existence of, 198-199
Moon Sun Myung, 118, 244,
253-254. *See also* Unification
Church
motivational structure, 282
multinational corporations, effect
on industrialization, 83, 85

National Origins Act, 21, 71, 182,
192, 222; relationship to Immigration Act of 1965, 26-28
"natural areas," 4-5, 316
negritude, 121
Neo-Confucianism, 285, 295, 296.
See also Chu Hsi
North Korean refugees: in fruit
and vegetable business, 113;
as a leading force of Protestantism
in South Korea, 189; marginal
status of, 308; selective immigration of, 35; as a source of
ministerial leadership, 190

occupational groups, occupation and,
as a basic stratification system in
the community, 313-314
organized labor, 86
"Oriental Despotism," 294
overurbanization, 71-72, 94, 309

paradigms: folk to urban, 5, 315;
of new immigration, 3
pariahs, international, Koreans as,
17, 22, 35, 47, 189
Park, Chung-hee, 90, 91, 245, 253,
259; ruling ideology of, 79-81
Park, Tong-sun, 247, 253-254
pathology, 4
"picture marriage," 24, 44
"population explosion," 48
population policy, 50-52
prebendal rights, 285
Presbyterianism, 203, 296
pronatalist stance of South Korean
government, 50
Protestant ethic, 206, 319. *See
also* value-congruity
Protestantism in North Korea,
296-297

Protestant missionaries, influence
of: on democracy, 190; on
emigration, 23; on medicine, 160,
194
push and pull factors, concept of,
9-11

restaurants: in "Koreatown," 108-
109; as a place for community
activities, 106
revolution of rising expectations,
51-52, 282
rotating credit associations, 208,
210-212, 314

"Sanscritization," 294n
self-exploitation, 120. *See also*
exploitation of labor
serendipitous opportunities in small
business, 145
serendipitous phenomena in immigration, 17, 47
service-oriented economy, medical
service and, 150-151
Sherman Antitrust Act, 135
Shil-hag school, 295-296
small business capitalism, 319
social distance, 138-139
specialization of medicine, effect
on the influx of foreign
physicians, 149-150
standardization of wig products,
126
state capitalism, industrialization
and, 85
status, monopoly of, caused by
state bureaucracy, 287-290, 294
status anxiety: effect on the emigration of middle-class Koreans,
96; as a source of church
leadership, 204
status mobility, caused by primitive
capitalism, 291-294
suburbanization: effect on shortage
of physicians in inner cities, 153,
176-177; effect on small business
opportunities in inner cities,
110-111, 144; and Korean immigrants, 184-185
surplus grain products, United
States: effect on population increase, 49-50; effect on urbanization, 74-75

taekwondo, 184, 195, 275; commercialization of, 109-110

transitional areas, 110, 137, 142-143

Unification Church, 118, 196, 244, 252, 254
upper class, industrial: conspicuous consumption by, 95-96; "dollar flight" and, 68-69; formation of, 89-94
urbanization: models of, 308; rate of, 308
urban mentality, and personality, 5, 98
urban-to-urban migration, 4, 209
"usury capitalism," 19

value-congruity between Confucianism and Protestantism, 209, 300. *See also* Protestant ethic; Confucianism

Weber, Max, 298-299
West Germany, Korean migration to, 53-54, 70, 77
Wittfogel, Karl A., 294

Yujeonghoe, 245-246
Yusin Honbeob, 79, 245

zaibatsu, 84-85

Library of Congress Cataloging in Publication Data

Kim, Illsoo, 1944-
  New urban immigrants.

  Bibliography: p.
  Includes index.
  1. Korean Americans—New York (N.Y.)   2. New
York (N.Y.)—Social conditions.   3. United States—
Emigration and immigration.   4. Korea (South)—
Emigration and immigration.   I. Title.
II. Title: Korean community in New York.
F128.K6K55   305.8'957'0747   80-8556
ISBN 0-691-09355-5   AACR2

*Illsoo Kim is Assistant Professor of Sociology at Drew
University.*